CLASSIC
MONSTERS UNMADE

The Lost Films of Dracula, Frankenstein, the Mummy and Other Monsters

By John LeMay

BICEP BOOKS
Roswell, New Mexico, U.S.A.

BICEP BOOKS
Roswell, New Mexico, U.S.A.

For Christopher Martinez.

THIS BOOK HAS BEEN DISCARDED BY JONATHAN HARKER
FROM THE LIBRARY OF CASTLE DRACULA

TABLE OF CONTENTS

Acknowledgments...5
Introduction...6

1. *Frankenstein and the Monster* (1956)...11
2. *Horror of Dracula* Uncut (1958)...21
3. *Tales of Frankenstein* "The Face in the Tombstone Mirror" (1958)...43
4. *King Kong vs. Frankenstein* (1958)...53
5. *Three Faces of Dr. Jekyll* (1958)...61
6. *Disciple of Dracula*: Before *Brides of Dracula* (1960)...65
7. *Frankenstein vs. the Human Vapor* (1963)...83
8. *Curse of the* (Giant) *Mummy's Tomb* (1964)...90
9. *Godzilla vs. Frankenstein* (1964)...94
10. *Batman Fights Dracula* (1967)...103
11. *Nights of the Werewolf*: Paul Naschy's Lost Werewolf Movie (1968)...113
12. *Dracula's Feast of Blood* (1969)...115
13. *Taste the Blood of Dracula* Without the Count! (1969)...118
14. *Scars of Dracula* starring John Forbes-Robertson (1970)...123
15. *Vampire Virgins*...129
16. *Blood from the* (Unmade) *Mummy's Tomb* (1971)...135
17. *The Unquenchable Thirst of Dracula* (1970-1977)...143
18. *Victim of his Imagination* (1972)...155
19. Richard Matheson's *Dracula* (1973)...169
20. *The Seven Brothers* (Don't) *Meet Dracula* (1974)...173
21. *Black the Ripper* (1975)...181
22. *Dracula and the Curse of Kali* (1974-1977)...185
23. *Invisible Man vs. the Human Torch* (1975)...200
24. *Dracula: The Beginning* (1974)...209
25. Ken Russell's *Dracula* (1978)...214
26. Remake from the Black Lagoon Part I (1983)...235
27. *Legendary Beast Wolfman vs. Godzilla* (1983)...245
28. *Vlad the Impaler* (1992)...248
29. Clive Barker's *Mummy* (1992)...251

30. Remake from the Black Lagoon Part II (1992)...255
31. Joe Dante's *Mummy* (1993)...268
32. George Romero's *Mummy* (1994)...274
33. Remake from the Black Lagoon Part III (1997)...279
34. *Sherlock Holmes and the Vengeance of Dracula*
    (1999)...286
35. *Bride of Frankenstein* (2000)...312

Special Sections:
The Mummy Uncut, too?...38
Hammer on TV...106

Appendix I:
Complete Project Listing...326
Appendix II:
Alternate Cuts & Deleted Scenes...367

Bibliography...369
Index...372
About the Author...377

Acknowledgments

As usual, I couldn't have done this without my usual crew of Kyle Byrd, Justin Mullis, Ted Johnson, and Jolyon Yates (who also did the cover for the color edition), who fed me plenty of information on these lost films, plus Jay Ford, who gave me several scripts I didn't even know existed, like *Bride of Frankenstein* (2000,) among others!

INTRODUCTION:
UNSEEN HORRORS PART II

Hello, and may I bid you welcome to Volume II of *Classic Monsters Unmade*. These lost films, what sweet music they make... or would have made if they had gotten past the script phase. Okay, okay, that was corny. I'm sorry, but I wasn't exactly sure how to kick off the introduction to this second volume since many of you, I assume, already have Volume I. If that's the case, I apologize, because some of this will be a bit redundant for you. But, on the other end of the spectrum, for those that don't have the first volume, I do feel there's a need to explain the parameters of this book. So, with that in mind, I'll do my best to be brief when explaining the difference between this book and the first.

My initial plan was to do only one book as I did with *Kong Unmade* and *Jaws Unmade*. But, when it came to *Classic Monsters Unmade*, there was simply too much material for one volume, so I decided to split it into two. And when I use the term "classic monsters," I predominantly mean the famous gothic horrors of Dracula, Frankenstein, and the various werewolves and mummies made famous by Universal Pictures and Hammer. As such, this book isn't about horror or monster movies in general so much as it's specifically devoted to lost films (like *Batman vs. Dracula*) and unproduced screenplays (like *Dracula and the Curse of Kali*) featuring Dracula, Frankenstein, and their undead kin.[1] And whereas the last book focused quite a bit on Universal, this book, due to the era, leans more heavily on the horrors of Hammer, a studio that had a bevy of unfilmed projects.

But this book is not devoted exclusively to Hammer. It just so happens that there were more unmade Hammer projects during this time period than any other. And, if any studio came in second to Hammer in this regard during this period, it is oddly enough Toho in Japan. That studio occasionally strayed from Godzilla into human-sized monster movies, like *Invisible Avenger* (1954) and their Bloodthirsty Trilogy of Hammer-inspired vampire films from 1971-1974. Some of their heretofore unknown lost projects will no doubt shock you, for in addition to *Frankenstein vs. Godzilla,* there was also *Frankenstein vs. the Human Vapor*, a proposed sequel to their 1960 film *The Human Vapor*, and *Invisible Man vs. the Human*

CHRISTOPHER LEE · PETER CUSHING

LA MASCHERA DI FRANKENSTEIN

HAZEL COURT · ROBERT URQUHART .....TERENCE FISHER · TECHNICOLOR ·.........GOLD FILM

Torch. In that regard, this second volume is a bit more diverse than the first.

This second volume was also a bit more fun to research because it was more difficult. Film historians Philip Riley and Tom Weaver made it way too easy when it came to the unmade horrors of Universal in their various books on the subject. By comparison, the unmade history of Hammer and Toho can be a bit more nebulous. In looking into the lost projects of Hammer I had to scour issues of *Little Shoppe of Horrors*, audio commentaries,[2] and various Hammer-related books. In terms of Toho, Japanese sources had to be roughly translated into English to get to the bottom of their lost Frankenstein and Invisible Man features.

And, on the note of research and researchers, in the last volume I also put forth a little warning that better books on the subject of lost horror films already existed. I was referring, of course, to the indefatigable Philip J. Riley along with others like Tom Weaver, who had thoroughly examined unmade Universal horror movies and wildly different proto-versions of completed films in their books. But, in this case, I shall warn you of the opposite; that being that better books than this will likely exist in the future. If I'm not mistaken, I believe I saw that Wayne Kinsey is working on a book about unmade Hammer. Likewise, Kieran Foster's thesis on Hammer's lost works is a book in of itself, and I hope/assume that one day it will be used as the basis for a truly authoritative volume on the subject. (Then, of course, there's the special edition magazine from *Little Shoppe of Horrors* called *Last Bus to Bray* which listed all of Hammer's unmade projects, not just horror, which is also a treasure trove of information.) Last but not least, a new book looms on the horizon and will probably be out by the time that you read this: *Untold Horror*. I don't know exactly what it contains yet, but I do know that it includes interviews with the likes of George A. Romero, John Landis, and Joe Dante on their unmade monster movies.

But, until those wonderful books come to fruition, you'll have to make due with this one, and I hope you enjoy this journey into an alternate world of 'what if' scenarios: What if Van Helsing had fought Dracula in India? What if Peter Cushing had starred in *Blood from the Mummy's Tomb* rather than Andrew Kier? What if King Kong had fought a giant Frankenstein monster, or, if not Kong, Godzilla? What if Hammer's shelved Frankenstein TV series had made it beyond one failed pilot episode? For this and so much more, dive into the pages ahead, if you dare...

John LeMay
Summer 2021

Section Notes

---

[1] As such, I won't be covering things like Hammer's unmade Dennis Wheatley adaptations or random vampire films that didn't go before cameras. (*Vampire Virgins* is tied into *Carmilla*, so therefore it gets a pass.)

[2] Constantine Nasir was particularly helpful because, like me, he seems to have an affinity for comparing early scripts to the finished films.

PART I:
THE HAMMER ERA

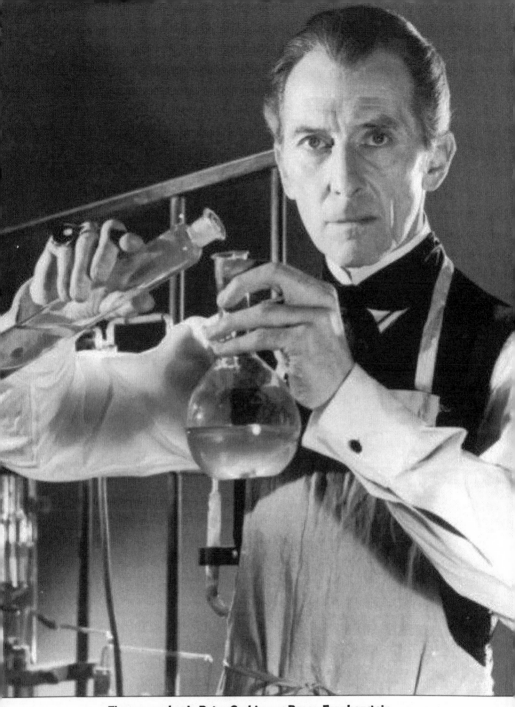

The one and only Peter Cushing as Baron Frankenstein.

1.
FRANKENSTEIN AND THE MONSTER

Developed: 1956

Screenplay by: Max J. Rosenberg & Milton Subotsky **Proposed Cast/Characters:** Victor Frankenstein, the Monster, Paul Krempe [Victor's mentor], Elizabeth [Victor's fiancé], Dr. Waldman [Victor's professor], Henri Clerval [Victor's best friend]

PLOT A young Dr. Frankenstein creates a monster...

COMMENTARY By the 1950s, the "Classic Monsters" established by Universal Pictures were basically finished as far as new productions went.[1] The old Gothic Monsters were out and had been supplanted by aliens and mutants, not unlike Universal's own Gillman from *The Creature from the Black Lagoon* (1954). Furthermore, the last time Universal had utilized its classic monsters was only to serve as fodder for *Abbott and Costello Meet Frankenstein* (1948). But then, in 1957, came Hammer Films with *The Curse of Frankenstein*. Shot in Technicolor with bosoms and blood, it was a far cry from the 1930s and 40s Universal horror films. And audiences loved it.

However, as is the case with many films, *Curse of Frankenstein's* early iterations weren't anything like the final product. The project began in America in 1956 when Max J. Rosenberg and Milton Subotsky reached out to Elliot Hyman of Associated Artists. Together they proposed an update of *Frankenstein* in color.[2] Hyman recalled Hammer's recent success with *The Quatermass Experiment* and suggested the duo pitch their script to them. They did so by May of that year, meeting with Hammer head James Carreras. According to some, the script brought to Carreras wasn't exactly impressive, and if filmed, would barely make up even an hour's running time.[3] Carreras told the duo to expand upon the script but to set the new scenes in the same locations (if the two ran wild, that would mean building more sets than Hammer could handle).

ALLIED ARTISTS presents

BORIS KARLOFF in "FRANKENSTEIN-1970"

Co-Starring TOM DUGGAN • JANA LUND • DONALD BARRY • CHARLOTTE AUSTIN

Produced by AUBREY SCHENCK   Directed by HOWARD W. KOCH   Filmed in CINEMASCOPE

58/262

BORIS KARLOFF AS THE BARON? Various sources state that at one point Boris Karloff was envisioned as playing Victor Frankenstein. One source even claimed it was Milton and Subotsky that hoped for this, but this is in direct opposition to their screenplay which presented Victor Frankenstein as a young man! Perhaps someone had ideas of Karloff playing another character like Krempe, or Victor's father, and it became misconstrued to be Victor? In any case, in 1958 Karloff played the doctor in *Frankenstein 1970*.

12

And what is the script like? Keiran Foster sums it up best in his thesis on unmade Hammer, observing that the Subotsky script emphasized the monster over the Baron, similar to Universal's *Frankenstein* sequels. In fact, the script's many similarities to the Universal films is what eventually led to it getting canned by Hammer. For instance, Subotsky's written description of the monster features the electrodes distinctive of the Jack Pierce makeup. But, there are far more similarities than just that in the script, which was at first simply called *Frankenstein* and later *Frankenstein and the Monster*.

Like *Bride of Frankenstein*, Subotsky's script began with a historical prologue set in the summer of 1816 on the night that Mary Shelley began writing her famous story. (So, perhaps in Subotsky's mind this was a remake of sorts of the Universal films?) Like *Bride*, the flashback included several other historical characters, including Jane Clairmont (Shelley's half-sister), Percy Shelley, Lord Byron, and John Polidori. However, no dialogue is spoken by the characters, and instead, a narrator would have told us what we were witnessing. As the narrator reveals that the group has made a pact to create a horror story, the title "Frankenstein" would appear onscreen. The screen would then dissolve into a heavy rain, and the credits would display over that.

After this, as in *Curse of Frankenstein*, we would meet Victor Frankenstein in a prison cell of sorts (specifically, in this case, he's confined to an asylum). Also, as in *Curse*, Paul Krempe comes to visit him, but sans Elizabeth. As the imprisoned Baron begins to rant and rave, we would then flash back to the real narrative in earnest. (In a way, this is a bit convoluted, going from an 1816 historical prologue, then to a flashforward in the jail cell, then flashing back to tell the real story.)

Unlike *Curse*, which flashed back to a much younger Victor from the cell, Subotsky's script kept him the same age, that of a collegiate, through the entire narrative. The first scene has Victor bidding his friends and family goodbye before he sets off to go to a university. Among his well-wishers are his father (still alive in this script), Elizabeth, his fiancé, and a best friend named Henri Clerval. (In the rewrite by Jimmy Sangster, Paul Krempe and Henri Clerval would essentially be combined into a single character.) Notably, on his way to the University, Victor would spot a dead body hanging from a noose. At the University, Victor meets Paul Krempe, a friend of his father's who will serve as his mentor there. Rather than being taken by Victor's brilliance as in the finished film, this version of Krempe is disturbed by Victor's talk of wanting to probe into the unknown.

Eventually, Victor's family begins to worry about him when letters from him cease to arrive back home. Henri reveals to Victor's father and Elizabeth that in one letter, Victor had expressed a desire to bring the dead back to life. Victor's father decides to reach out to Krempe about the matter. However, one of Victor's professors, Waldman, has already done so. Waldman tells Krempe that Victor hasn't shown up to any of his classes as of late. Krempe then goes up to Victor's attic laboratory (yes, that really is where his lab is kept) to visit him. He's shocked to see that Victor has begun constructing a new body from corpses. He doesn't order Victor to stop though, and just voices some skepticism as to whether or not he can reanimate the dead! Victor informs him that all he needs is an intelligent brain to finish his creation. Cut to Professor Waldman's funeral, and Victor has his answer. (Did he kill Waldman, or did he just get lucky? The script doesn't say.)

As soon as he's planted in the ground, that night, Victor comes and robs the dead Waldman of his brain and places it in a glass jar. Something startles Victor on his way out of the cemetery, and he accidentally drops the jar, contaminating the brain with glass shards. (In *Curse*, it's a scuffle between Victor and Krempe that causes this.) As such, Victor digs up another fresh corpse to harvest a brain from. However, the corpse came from an insane asylum...

When Victor successfully reanimates his creation in the lab, he is incredibly startled by what he's done—so startled that he accidentally gives the monster an electric shock which enrages it. Terrified, Victor runs from the room and locks the door. He goes to fetch Krempe to show him what he's done, but the monster is gone when both men arrive at the lab. (This is significant, because not only did Krempe not help create the monster as he would in *Curse*, he never even sees it in this draft.)

Similar to the James Whale Frankenstein films, the monster sets out to explore the world. As the monster walks past a lake, he spots a girl struggling in its waters, about to drown. He goes in to save her, but the child is terrified by his appearance and screams, attracting her father and a group of villagers who misunderstand what they are witnessing. They attack the monster who flees into the woods. Like in the book and *Bride* both, the monster finds solace with an old blind man who takes him in. However, when the blind man's family returns home, they turn out to be the family of the girl. This time, when the father attacks him, the monster kills the man in self-defense.

In the next scene, Krempe bursts into Victor's room to inform him that one of the villagers has been killed, and that a party is being organized to hunt down the murderer. Outside, a mob chases the monster through the woods, where it finds refuge in a cave. But a hunting dog trails him there and attacks him. Though the monster kills the dog, he is still apprehended by the villagers, who subdue him and tie him to a pole à la *Bride of Frankenstein*. The monster is paraded through the streets—which Victor sees through his bedroom window—and then thrown into a dungeon. However, it escapes soon after by killing its guards.

Later, as Victor and Henri go fishing at a nearby lake, they are accosted by the monster, who injures Henri but does not kill him. The monster delivers Victor an ultimatum to make him a mate or he'll kill his loved ones. Victor complies, working tirelessly on the monster's bride even as his own wedding to Elizabeth rapidly approaches. However, Victor comes to his senses and destroys the female creature before it can be "born." This enrages the monster, and a fight ensues between it and Victor, though it eventually leaves the lab with Victor still alive.

The climax of the script takes place after Elizabeth and Victor's wedding when the monster pops up to kidnap the newlywed bride. He carries her across the moors with Victor in hot pursuit. Victor corners the monster on a cliff bluff and shoots him in the head, but it doesn't kill him. Enraged, the monster pushes Elizabeth off the cliff and then charges Victor. From there, the script fades into Victor's jail cell, where he's telling Krempe how he ran away from the monster, which is still out there, somewhere. (What exactly did Victor get arrested for in this script? I don't know, but presumably, Elizabeth's death had something to do with it.)

The final two pages of the script were reproduced in Marcus Hearn's wonderful *Hammer Vault*. The ending was very melodramatic compared to Hammer's more elegant ending of the Baron walking towards the guillotine. In *Frankenstein and the Monster*, Frankenstein rants on that,

> Heaven help me, I should have let him kill me, but I turned and ran. As for his wound... I am sure it healed quickly enough... for you see.. I had made him... indestructible. And so he will go on living... and go on killing... for he has a hatred for all mankind.[4]

Curse of Frankenstein's most notorious deleted scene had the Baron disposing of a severed head in a vat of acid. The first cut of the film actually included a very brief shot of the prop head being dissolved in the acid. The BBC insisted that it be cut, and it was replaced by a quick shot of Frankenstein's face with the bubbling sound effects. © 1957 Hammer Film Productions Ltd.

Frankenstein turns to Krempe and begs him to warn the world. But Krempe claims that he "saw nothing" and that the whole thing is in the Baron's mind. (Again, in this version, Krempe never saw the monster, so he's not lying, unlike Krempe in *Curse,* who is lying when he denies the existence of the monster. So, if ever you wondered why Krempe denied existence of the monster in *Curse,* it was a carryover from this script.) Like Peter Cushing's Baron, this one too was scripted to grab Kempe by the shirt collar and shake him violently before he's led away by a doctor and an attendant. Finally, Victor would turn to the camera to look at the audience, screaming, "He'll live forever... killing... killing... KILLING..." Finally, Victor would say to we, the prospective audience while looking into the camera, that, "He'll.. get... you..."[5] We would then cut to a

LONG SHOT. A SHADOW comes out of the night... toward the CAMERA. It is the CREATURE.

He is in a rage. He comes closer, closer, closer... reaching out... for YOU....

FADE OUT[6]

Though not as effective as Hammer's ending where the Baron is marched to the guillotine, there's a certain charm to that final shot—gimmicky though it may be. This is just my conjecture, but I halfway wonder if this final shot would have been set in the 1950s? I say this because more than one source claimed this script took place in the modern era. Perhaps that falsehood emerged from the final scene, which could have taken place in the present as a way of spooking the audience?

When Hammer announced the project in the trades, the first entity they heard from was Universal, which made it clear that their version of the story had better not resemble theirs too closely. This gave Hammer an excuse to do something they had wanted to do anyway: throw Rosenberg and Subotsky's script out the window. In Hammer producer Anthony Hinds's opinion, the duo's script was just a watered-down version of the Universal films anyways. In addition to being a bit amateurish (it lacked proper direction details—not even specifying if a scene took place during day or night), it was also a bit too ambitious for Hammer's money men.

One of the few similarities between *Frankenstein and the Monster* and *Curse of Frankenstein* is that they are both bookended by scenes of the Baron incarcerated. © 1957 Hammer Film Productions Ltd.

So, on the basis that not only was the script not very good, Hammer threw it out for fear of litigation by Universal. They had also by this time discovered that *Frankenstein* was in the public domain, so they didn't even need a deal with the two Americans. The duo was given a $5,000 severance fee, and off they went.[7] Hinds then offered the project to their *X the Unknown* writer Jimmy Sangster.

As we all know, Hammer's version of Frankenstein was a huge success that ignited a renaissance of the Classic Monsters that would last into the late 1960s.

Chapter Notes

[1] They did still play in re-releases and eventually on television, where they were quite popular.

[2] Several sources also attest that this version would be set in modern times, but the script features a horse and carriage at one point so I don't think this is correct.

[3] Philip Nutman, who read the script and wrote about it in *Little Shoppe of Horrors* #21, says that he'd estimate it to run at around 77 minutes.

[4] Hearn, *Hammer Vault*, p.14.

[5] Ibid.

[6] Ibid.

[7] Rosenberg and Subotsky would eventually get their revenge by way of establishing Hammer's main rival in the realm of horror: Amicus Productions. Rosenberg would also one day distribute Hammer's *Legend of the 7 Golden Vampires* in America as the badly butchered *Seven Brothers Meet Dracula*.

2.
HORROR OF DRACULA
UNCUT

Release Date: June 16, 1958

Directed by: Terence Fisher **Screenplay by:** Jimmy Sangster
Special Effects by: Sydney Pearson, Les Bowie and Phil Leakey
Music by: James Bernard **Cast:** Peter Cushing (Van Helsing),
Christopher Lee (Dracula), Michael Gough (Arthur Holmwood),
Melissa Stribling (Mina Holmwood), Carol Marsh (Lucy
Holmwood), John Van Eyssn (Jonathon Harker)

1.66 : 1, Technicolor, 82 Minutes/83 Minutes (uncut version)

PLOT Vampire hunter Jonathon Harker arrives at the castle of
Count Dracula under the auspices of being his new librarian.
Harker kills Dracula's bride but fails to kill the Count. Dracula
then gets his revenge by vampirizing Harker's fiancé, Lucy
Holmwood. When a stake is driven through Lucy's heart by
vampire hunter Van Helsing and Lucy's brother, Arthur, Dracula
turns his attention to Arthur's wife, Mina...

COMMENTARY Having found success with Frankenstein,
Hammer naturally turned their attention to Bram Stoker's
Dracula. There was one problem, however: *Dracula* was not yet in
the public domain. As Bram Stoker had died in 1912, and being
that it took 50 years for a work to fall into the public domain,
Dracula would not be up for a copyright-free remake until 1962.
Therefore, Hammer struck a deal with Universal to adapt the film,
with Universal getting to distribute the picture as an added bonus
(eventually, Universal would agree to let Hammer remake their
classic library of monster movies, including *The Mummy*).
  Jimmy Sangster, the writer for *The Curse of Frankenstein*, was
instructed to adapt Stoker's novel and not Universal's 1931
Dracula. Whether this was because the film was a rather boring
stageplay adaptation or because Hammer was not allowed to
specifically emulate Universal's version is up for debate. In any
case, Sangster was instructed to keep it cheap. This eliminated

21

some of the grander bits, such as Dracula traveling by ship to England, etc., and the action became more centralized. As to the elimination of characters like Renfield, that was simply done because there was no room in the story's runtime. (Remember, back then, movies often played as double features, meaning studios wanted each film to clock in at under 90 minutes).[1]

Fundamentally, Sangster's first draft is the same as the finished film[2] aside from altered dialogue and a few deleted scenes, one of which occurs right after the credits roll.

For starters, Sangster's version takes place in 1899, not 1885. Sangster's envisioned credit sequence says nothing of the castle backdrop in the opening shot, just dark clouds blocking out the sun so that the shot would only be colored in grey black and black grey. Otherwise, he does get in the bit about displaying the title over the coffin.

Sangster's first scene was either deleted after filming or not shot in the first place, though the former is the more likely of the two options. As Sangster describes a carriage coming along a bend in the road, with a driver and a companion at the helm (a shot present in the film), we were then to cut to the inside of the carriage. There he reveals five passengers: Jonathon Harker and a priest on one side, and on the other, a middle-aged husband and wife, and a "fat worried looking" merchant.[3]

Sangster makes it clear that this has been an uncomfortable ride for the passengers, who seem taught with the tension of an argument recently ended. Through the dialogue, it soon becomes apparent that the passengers are well aware of Harker's destination and have been doing their best to dissuade him from going to Castle Dracula.

The woman makes an appeal to Harker that if he has any loved ones then he dare not go for their sake, while her husband chides Harker as an "obstinate fool."

The priest then takes a turn. "I am a man of God my son. The words that I speak are words that I feel in my humble way, God might speak."

"If dissuasion is what you wish to speak then those will not be the words of God," Jonathon replies.

Greatly incensed, the male passenger exclaims, "Blasphemous too...mad and blasphemous."

Of course, the occupants have no idea that Jonathon is on a secret mission to destroy Dracula, in essence, God's work. Nor would we, the audience, at this point know this either had the footage been included.

Just as the carriage rolls to a stop, the priest indicates that the castle is the gate to Hell itself. The companion of the driver then pokes his head down through the window to ask Harker if he still wants to get off.

Harker affirms that he does, stands to thank the woman for her concern, and is then rudely pulled out of the carriage by the driver's companion. The fat merchant shouts for them to get away from the place as Harker's luggage is thrown at his feet. The carriage drives off as he looks on.

The film, as we all know, opens with a voice-over from Harker, and the first shot is of his diary. Harker explains recent events and that he is on his way to Castle Dracula, in essence speeding up the action. Even Sangster felt the V.O. was an improvement over the scene he had written. But once again, we must ask the question, was the carriage scene filmed at all?

Director Terence Fisher was asked about this "deleted scene" by Gary R. Parfitt, and Fisher claimed that it was never filmed.[4] There is evidence to the contrary, however. The actors to play the parts were listed in both the British publicity folder for the film as well as Universal International's press sheet. They were as follows: Guy Mills (Coach Driver), Dick Morgan (Driver's Companion), Stedwell Fulcher (Man in Coach), Judith Nelmes (His Wife), Humphrey Kent (Fat Merchant in Coach), and William Sherwood (Priest in Coach).[5]

Sangster, on the other hand, speculated that the carriage scene was cut for budgetary reasons. In *Inside Hammer,* he writes, "I wasn't around at the time, but I imagine this change was made for budgetary reasons. A coach, possibly with back projection, five actors, half a day to shoot it...lotsa money. I see from an original cast line that all these parts were cast, so it was possibly the schedule that forced them to cut it."[6]

In the finished film, we do see one exterior shot of the carriage as it goes by. Two drivers sit at the helm, while four passengers are visible inside. If the exterior was filmed with multiple people seen in the carriage, then perhaps the interior scenes were shot too?

Some film historians have also speculated that because the Universal *Dracula* had scenes of Harker within a carriage, that this would make the two films too similar. Remember, Hammer was not remaking Universal's *Dracula* as they would later do with *The Mummy.* In this case, Universal only sold them the rights to adapt Stoker's novel.

In any case, in the film, Harker also seems to give an embittered look over his shoulder as he walks through the woods. Though the narration tells us that his coach driver wouldn't take him all the way, it's possible that actor John Van Eyssen was reacting to the previous scene, looking back at his sour companions from the carriage with distaste. This is actually also in Sangster's script, though he imagined Harker looking back at the coach with "no resentment in his face." Obviously, either Terence Fisher or Van Eyssen disagreed.

Heeding the words of producer Anthony Hinds to keep it cheap, Sangster describes the castle as "a cross between a house and a castle." In the film, Harker merely opens the door to the castle and walks inside, but Sangster planned on something a bit more foreboding. In his version, Harker must use a large knocker to pound on the door. When he does, a bat flutters past him for a good scare. From this point forward, until the entrance of the vampire bride, what plays out in the script and on the screen is the same. The dialogue between Harker and the bride is extended in the script. In the film, the bride's first words to Harker are, "You will help me, won't you?" In the text, her first lines are, "Will you tell him that you've seen me?"

"Who?" Harker responds.

"You mustn't tell him...promise me?" the woman pleads, still not naming Dracula.

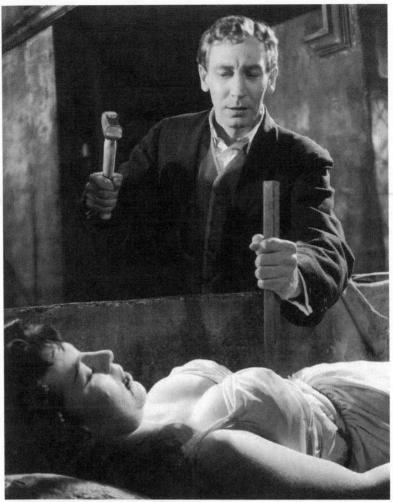

Harker (John Van Eyssn) prepares to stake the vampire bride (Valerie Gaunt). © 1958 Hammer Film Productions Ltd.

Harker quizzically speaks his name, she nods, and he assures her that he won't. Then the dialogue that we see in the film begins.

Christopher Lee himself decided to change Sangster's version of Dracula's entrance ever so slightly. After the girl runs off, we hear Dracula off-screen call out to Harker. Lee suggested that we see Dracula standing atop the staircase before he comes down and speaks. This is evidenced by the fact that Lee wrote on his copy of the script the following note: "Isn't it more effective to have presence bring J. round...no voice."[7]

Sangster's description of Dracula is also slightly different, as he has him wearing a cloak with a "high pointed collar" and also has him carrying a black hat. Sangster also suggested briefly showing Dracula's canines, though Fisher wisely saved that for later.

As to other differences, Sangster's version of Dracula is slightly more loquacious. But, the gist of the conversation is the same, with Harker stating his enthusiasm to begin work and Dracula acting as though he's happy to have him there. Notably, in Sangster's script, Dracula says, "...it is most unfortunate that I have to go again immediately. Your impressions of me as a host must be abysmal..."

Also, in the script, on the way to Harker's room, Harker takes note of a door in the hallway slowly closing shut, implying that the woman has been watching him again. No such scene or hint of it occurs in the film.

The dialogue between Harker and Dracula is somewhat rearranged from the script in the movie. On film, Dracula informs Harker that he must go out on business and won't be back until sundown tomorrow. He leaves the room, and Harker takes out a photo of Lucy Holmwood and places it on his desk. Dracula then walks back into the room to give Harker a key to the library and notices the photograph. In the script, a nosy Dracula spots the picture within Harker's suitcase and asks if he may take it out and look at it! After having examined the photo, he leaves the room and doesn't return.

Fisher again improves upon the structure of Sangster's script when Harker goes to write in his diary. In the script, Harker observes Dracula leaving the castle, "his billowing cloak [creating] the impression of a giant bat flying..." After observing this, Harker goes to write in his diary, and we were to fade out on an image of the diary page. Fisher's transition is more dynamic, as Harker goes to write in his diary first, and we cut to Dracula (accompanied by his wonderful theme) walking into the night for the end of the scene.

Having seen the film many times, I can safely say that Sangster's version of the following scene gives me a different perspective on the sequence between Harker and the bride. For starters, it had always been my assumption that this scene took place shortly before dawn on the cusp of the sunrise. Sangster makes it very clear that he wanted the scene to take place at night, describing Harker entering a room bathed in moonlight. (I get no such impression from the film.) The exchange between Harker and the woman is basically the same, but with an added section of dialogue where the bride asks Harker, "You're not...not one of..."

Her sentence trails off, leaving me to wonder, is she asking Harker if he's a fellow vampire, or is she actually suspecting the truth that he is a vampire hunter? In either case, Sangster's version of the scene gave me the impression that the bride is genuinely wanting to escape and is begging for help. She only gives in to her base desires when she comes into close contact with Harker in his embrace. The film, on the other hand, gives me the notion that she is manipulating Harker into a false state of compassion. But that's just me.

Sangster's version of the scuffle with Dracula is slightly more violent. The only notable detail worth repeating is that Sangster envisioned Dracula with bloodstained clothes from his wild night out. Either the makeup men didn't want to go to the trouble to add this detail, or perhaps Hammer simply knew this might be too much for the censors. So too did Sangster envision Harker finding the bride in her sarcophagus with blood dripping all the way down to her breasts (this was probably objected to by the censors). Fisher also chose not to show the staking itself (it's represented in shadow) so as to save it for Lucy's staking later.

Most film historians, like Ronald V. Borst, agree that Fisher's handling of Dracula's entrance into the scene is rather silly. As it is, Dracula leaves his coffin, goes outside, and comes back inside from the top of the staircase for dramatic effect. And it is dramatic for the audience, but within the world of the film it's a bit silly when one stops to think about it. Jimmy Sangster said that "...the cut should have been to Dracula at the top of the steps just closing the door. In other words, he gone up the steps to close the door before coming back down."[8]

Sangster's idea, as written, was to have Dracula awaken. We would then get a POV shot of Dracula looking at Harker, who has his back turned, as the sun goes down. Dracula would then disappear and not be seen again. We were to simply hear the door atop the mausoleum close, followed by Harker's scream.

After the implied death of Harker, Van Helsing's introduction at the inn isn't terribly different in the script apart from a few details. The script has Van Helsing already in the inn, angrily questioning several men as to Harker's whereabouts to no avail, while Fisher chose to show Van Helsing enter the inn. Furthermore, the script sets up a subplot of sorts where the locals try their best at every turn to entice Van Helsing to leave. Though there are a few lines that imply this in the film, overall, the subplot is watered down.

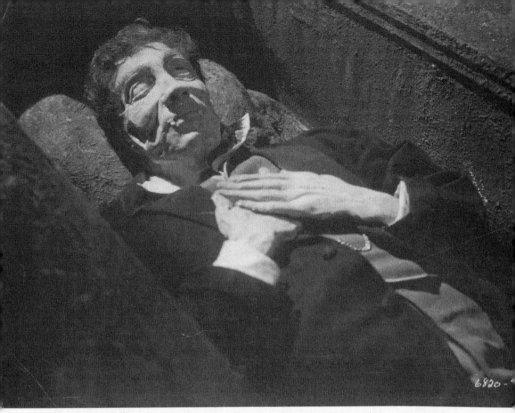

Unused dummy of actor John Van Eyssn meant to portray the vampirized Harker. © 1958 Hammer Film Productions Ltd.

As we all know, Van Helsing eventually sets out for Dracula's castle to seek out Harker (unaware he is now a vampire). In the film, we see Harker, as played by Van Eyssen, sleeping in Dracula's old sarcophagus with vampire fangs. Not so in Sangster's script, where he describes Harker as looking like he has been drained of all blood and is a "living skeleton" with a malevolent smile. To film Sangster's version of the scene, a dummy was created. Photographs were taken of it, but it's unknown if any scenes were shot with it. Fisher apparently felt it more effective to simply have Van Eyssen for the shot. Furthermore, as Van Helsing prepares to stake Harker, Sangster imagined looping in a V.O. from Harker's diary: "I can only pray that whoever discovers my body will have the knowledge to do what is necessary to release my soul."

Moving onto the script's second act, Sangster's version of Arthur Holmwood is a bit of a hothead, and many of his angrier lines were deleted by the time of shooting. For instance, when Van Helsing informs Arthur that Harker was cremated on his authority, Arthur

28

exclaims, "You're out of your mind...you're insane." Furthermore, after Van Helsing leaves (he is not escorted out by Gerda in the script), Arthur says, "I shall report his actions to the police."

The Holmwoods visit with Lucy also has some enlightening dialogue cut from the film that reveals that Arthur and Mina are themselves newlyweds. Lucy says to them, "Now why don't the two of you go into the parlour and turn down the lights...or has the novelty worn off after only a month of wedded bliss."

Sangster's version and Fisher's version of the scene where Lucy prepares for Dracula's arrival are similar, but Sangster envisioned showing the bite marks on Lucy's neck as soon as the Holmwoods left her room. Fisher wisely let this be the scene's final big reveal before cutting to Van Helsing.

What Van Helsing's Dictaphone reads back to him in the following scene was changed from the script. In the text, it reads like a P.I.'s monologue discussing a murder case, as Van Helsing ruminates over past events regarding Harker's death. But, in the film, it enlightens we, the audience, as to "seven facts" regarding vampirism. The purpose of the inn worker who comes into his room also differs. In the film, he comes because Van Helsing has called him to fetch a letter. In the script, the worker is pressuring Van Helsing about leaving—carrying over the theme of the townspeople wanting Van Helsing to leave.

Also, in the script, Van Helsing's final line spoken into his Dictaphone is a muse, wondering what Dracula wanted with the photo of Lucy. The film ends the scene with him stating that the vampire king must be destroyed, at which point we cut to Dracula standing outside Lucy's open window in both versions.

The following scene has Mina walking out of Lucy's room with a doctor who has just examined her. As it turns out, this is Dr. Seward, one of the main characters in Stoker's novel, relegated to a cameo in this iteration. Sangster says that three of his scenes (numbers 48-50 to be exact) involving Dr. Seward examining Lucy were cut. Sangster speculated that they were probably taken out for the sake of the run time, and wrote that, "...I doubt [they were shot], because in subsequent scenes, the doctor is just a rather ineffectual character and no longer the pompous arsehole as I wrote him."[9]

As to what he means by Seward being a "pompous arsehole," this is likely due to the belittling attitude he has towards Gerda. When Mina tells him how worried Gerda is, Seward says that a "domestics place is in the kitchen." He's also a tad patronizing to Mina as he examines Lucy. Speaking of the examination scene, it was probably cut because it was too similar to the scene of Van Helsing later examining Lucy when she dies.

The meeting scene where Mina goes to see Van Helsing is also softened a bit. In the script, it is he who demands to see Lucy when he learns she is sick. He exclaims, "This time your husband will not stop me." In the film, it is Mina who invites Van Helsing to examine Lucy as a second opinion.

Our next deleted scene has Mina placing the garlic flowers in Lucy's room. When Lucy remarks upon the terrible smell, Mina says, "That's probably why [Van Helsing] suggested them. You've been bitten by something...the garlic is to keep it out of the room." If only she knew. Before Mina leaves, we also learn she and Arthur are going out on a business dinner. Also deleted, or left un-shot, was a scene of Gerda bidding the Holmwoods goodbye as they leave for the evening.

The scene where Lucy is found dead the next morning is tenser, with Van Helsing being confronted by Seward and Arthur when he appears. It's also interesting to note that Seward mentions how he's heard of Van Helsing before and knows that he's an "important man" as he puts it. The script's version of this scene ends with Van Helsing angrily informing everyone there that had they followed his instructions Lucy would still be alive. The film ends with Van Helsing giving Arthur the diary of Jonathon to read for himself.

As it turns out, Fisher more or less combined the scene in the film with a deleted scene from the script (which was most certainly not shot). The following scene in the script is Lucy's funeral, likely cut as an expense. (Since the tomb set was already built, as it appears later in the film, the added expense would have been in the form of the actors needed to play the priest and selected mourners.) The scene has a procession led into the family tomb, and afterward, Van Helsing approaches Arthur to give him Jonathan's diary.

The following sequence, where a policeman brings Tanya (Gerda's little girl) home to the Holmwoods, is also extended in Sangster's script. Here, Tanya is named Vera, and after Tanya/Vera's reveal that she saw Lucy, the policeman tries to question Holmwood about her. In the film, we fade into the graveyard shortly after Lucy's name has been dropped. In the script, the policeman would seem to imply that Lucy was trying to entice Vera into a "nasty business." When he insists on questioning Lucy, Arthur informs him that she died three days ago, and we fade to the cemetery.

Dracula (Christopher Lee) puts the bite on Mina (Melissa Stribling) in
Horror of Dracula.© 1958 Hammer Film Productions Ltd.

Van Helsing (Peter Cushing) and Arthur Holmwood (Michael Gough) make plans to defeat Dracula. © 1958 Hammer Film Productions Ltd.

This is followed by another trivial deleted scene that would have shown Gerda sleeping. Next to her is an empty cot meant to imply Vera's absence. We would then cut to Vera out wandering in the night. After she regroups with Lucy and the duo walk to the crypt, there is a very telling line that was cut. Vera says, "Aunt Lucy, my neck is sore." Lucy then offers to kiss it again to make it better. Clearly, in Sangster's script, the child has already been bitten, but no implication is made in the film that she was. To hit the point home, Sangster wanted blood to be visible on Lucy's chin.

While many of Sangster's scenes are long on dialogue, his scene for the staking of Lucy is incredibly short. Van Helsing says nothing to Arthur as he approaches Lucy's tomb with a hammer and a stake. Arthur says, "I will do it...It is my responsibility...and it is my fault that it happened." This is the only dialogue in the scene before he goes to stake her.

In the film, Van Helsing explains what must be done. Furthermore, Van Helsing suggests they use Lucy to lead them to Dracula, which Arthur refuses. In the film, Arthur leaves the tomb to take Tanya home and return at sunrise, while in the script,

Arthur stakes his sister then and there. In the film, Van Helsing does the deed (though, in the script, Arthur begins the process but can't seem to finish it, so Van Helsing does).

The next scene takes place in Van Helsing's room at the inn with Arthur. Sangster's version has a slightly different tone, with Van Helsing still lamenting the loss of Lucy as his only lead to Dracula. As Van Helsing attempts to teach Arthur all the ways to defeat a vampire, Arthur asks why they couldn't have simply exposed Lucy to sunlight instead of traumatically driving a stake through her heart. It is here that Sangster reveals yet another twist on the mythos. Van Helsing claims that only a stake through the heart releases the soul back to purity, while death by sunlight will not! Since Dracula was to perish by sunlight, perhaps Sangster wanted us to know that his soul would regain no sense of purity.

More differences follow. When Van Helsing goes to see the customs official about the whereabouts of the hearse and the coffin, in the film, this is intercut with Mina's scene. In the script, Mina's scene comes first and isn't intercut with the customs office. Furthermore, Van Helsing gets the information he seeks by yelling at the man in the script, but the movie gets a laugh when Arthur simply bribes him—the movie's version is better.

The scene of Arthur and Van Helsing trying their best to track Dracula's missing coffin, set in the Holmwood parlor where Mina sits knitting, is greatly condensed in the film. The script is wrought with exposition, such as Van Helsing mentioning a honeycomb of tunnels that Dracula can hide within beneath his castle. A seemingly skeptical Mina (by now bitten by Dracula) questions the men on their superstitions. Van Helsing shares with her a story about a cursed village in Transylvania that would allow within it no holy symbols of the church. Van Helsing relates how the villagers searched him and took from him a small crucifix. He takes it from his pocket and then tosses it to Mina. When she catches it, it burns her hand.

In the film, this is all simplified by having Arthur ask Mina to carry the cross for protection. Things play out similarly in both versions for a bit, though Sangster envisioned more blood on Mina in the aftermath of Dracula's attack. The discovery of Dracula's coffin in the cellar is handled differently in terms of the dialogue leading up to it (Gerda asks about a strange box in the cellar rather than refusing to go down there), but otherwise is like the film's version. Sangster also gives the frantic Gerda an extra line about how Dracula looked like a giant bat due to his fluttering cape.

Though the movie doesn't bother to tell us how Dracula acquired his getaway coach, the script does. In the scene, a coach driver whistles to himself along a lonely road when he spots a woman lying unconscious in his way. It is Mina. He dismounts the carriage to check on her. The scene would have ended with the coach driver looking behind him to see Dracula standing over him. From there, we would have dissolved into the following scene, where Van Helsing finds the dead man's body. This scene is in the film too, but in the script, Van Helsing states that the man's throat has been cut (if this is to imply that Dracula bit his throat or to suggest that he literally "cut his throat" is unknown).

Usually, Sangster's cut dialogue was no loss, but the script has some exposition between Van Helsing and Arthur that I found illuminating. As a kid, I had always wondered why on earth Dracula was burying Mina in the ground. In fact, I found the scene almost comical (probably because, in my mind, I can't imagine Dracula using a shovel). Sangster offers an explanation via Van Helsing, though.

The good doctor informs Arthur that Dracula will bury Mina in the ground. "If she dies while enclosed in Dracula's native soil, she will rise again when he chooses to call." Actually, the rules of vampirism aren't terribly well explained in the film, but several times in the script Sangster makes it clear that a woman bitten by Dracula must actually die before she becomes a vampire herself. Therefore, it's a bit clearer that by killing Dracula, Mina will never become a vampire.

In the film, we will also remember a humorous scene where Dracula's coach crashes through a border checkpoint, and upon being repaired, Van Helsing bursts through it next. In the script, Van Helsing actually stops to speak to the official. The official informs him that he must fill out the proper paperwork first. As he walks inside, he hears another crash and Van Helsing does what Dracula did earlier. Once again, the film's version is better. Following this, there was also supposed to be another humorous scene where the villagers watch Dracula's coach race by followed by Van Helsing's that was never shot.

As all Hammer aficionados will already know, the original climax was a bit less exciting. As soon as Dracula slams shut the trap door, Van Helsing busts out his crucifix and forces Dracula into the sunlight. That's basically it. To his credit, though, Sangster's disintegration scene as written is close to what occurred in the film's uncut version—we'll get to that in a moment.

34

Excellent still of the disintegration scene which was censored in all territories but Japan. © 1958 Hammer Film Productions Ltd.

As it was, Peter Cushing felt Van Helsing's finishing move on Dracula lacked excitement. In *Flesh and Blood: The Hammer Heritage of Horror,* he joked that he had brandished so many crosses already throughout the film that he felt a bit like a crucifix traveling salesman! He felt that to whip out another was too easy and so suggested that Van Helsing make one out of candlesticks. Allegedly, this idea came from the 1933 film *Berkeley Square,* starring Leslie Howard. It was also Cushing's idea to run across the table and tear down the curtains.

Though Cushing and Fisher changed his ending, Sangster maintains that it's actually his favorite scene in the film! "Shows I'm very amendable. My choice as best scene, and I didn't even write it."[10]

To finish discussing Sangster's script, he envisioned the final shot taking place outside as Van Helsing reunites with Mina and Arthur. Birds were to begin singing, tying into the opening where Harker remarks that no birds were singing outside the castle. It's unknown if this scene was shot, and the film rolls the credits over Dracula's signet ring.

Now, onto the disintegration scene. For years fans talked about a "lost" Japanese cut of the film, which included an even more grotesque, extended version of the scene. Though men like Michael Carreras had more or less confirmed in interviews that extra footage was shown in Japan (where censors were less strict), said footage could never be found.[11]

Then, in 2010, a writer/cartoonist named Simon Rowson who lived in Japan got to digging. A friend, Stuart Hall, had suggested that Rowson look for the lost footage via a post in the British Horror Forum. Rowson's wife Michiko suggested that he look for it in the archive of the National Film Center outside Tokyo. At first, things looked bleak. As it turned out, the Center's print of *Dracula* had been partially destroyed in a 1984 fire. Luckily, this comprised of the first five reels, which had no additional footage anyways. Fortunately, reels 6, 7, 8, and 9 survived the fire.

Eventually Rowson was able to view the footage and confirmed that it was indeed an extended cut. And it wasn't just relative to the ending. The first extended scene concerned Dracula's assault on Mina in her home. It's a bit more suggestive and shows Dracula push her onto the bed. Actually, it's not just an extended scene, but it also utilized a different camera angle that shows Dracula's gaping mouth as he moves in to bite Mina.

The disintegration scene had extended shots of Dracula's legs and arms beginning to turn to dust. In the normal version, we see his leg begin to deflate, so to speak, but in the extended version, his pant leg begins to roll up exposing his charred flesh. The same is true of the shot of his hand. The real gem of the bunch shows Christopher Lee in grotesque makeup, clawing the skin off of his face as he utters a terrible groan! There's also a short shot Van Helsing reacting to this in disgust.[12]

Rowson was ecstatic to report his find to the BFI, but before he could, a horrible earthquake struck Japan only two days later. Once again, the film reels were in danger of becoming lost. But, just as they survived the fire, they also survived the earthquake. In 2012 began a process on the part of the BFI to restore the film to its full, uncut version, which is thankfully now available on Blu-Ray..

Chapter Notes

[1] Sangster specifically created a Renfield-like character for *Dracula - Prince of Darkness* (1965) because of this, though.

[2] I will say that Sangster misspells Van Helsing as "Van Hesling" throughout the entire script, but I will not repeat that spelling error in the main text.

[3] Coincidence or not, a fat worried merchant in a stage coach figures heavily into the opening scenes of *Taste the Blood of Dracula* (1970).

[4] Borst, "Production Background", *The Horror of Dracula*, p.17.

[5] Fellner, *Encyclopedia of Hammer*, p.112.

[6] Sangster, *Inside Hammer*, pp.46.

[7] Borst, "Production Background", *The Horror of Dracula*, pp.18.

[8] Ibid, p.21.

[9] Ibid, p. 47.

[10] Ibid, p.49.

[11] They began this trend on *Curse of Frankenstein*.

[12] In the 1970s, the famed Toho Studios of Japan, which created Godzilla, did their own take on Hammer's vampire films with *Lake of Dracula* (1971). That film's ending is an homage to both *Dracula Has Risen from the Grave* (1968) and *Horror of Dracula*. In fact, the vampire's end disintegration is a near shot for shot remake of the uncut Japanese version of *Horror of Dracula*.

THE MUMMY UNCUT, TOO?

Additional gruesome footage included in the Japanese releases of Hammer horror films was a tradition started with *Curse of Frankenstein*. It continued into *Horror of Dracula*, and although no one can find the footage, it may have carried over into 1959's *The Mummy*. And it wasn't just gore this time, but nudity as well.

But don't take it from me; here it is straight from the proverbial horse's mouth. Michael Carreras described the extra footage as "a trend that we had picked up" in *Little Shoppe of Horrors* #24. Carreras elaborated,

> I think we did do a nude version of *The Mummy*. They were all colored ladies, I remember. But it couldn't have been done without Fisher, because the only way to do it was "Take 1/Take 2"; it would have cost a fortune to do the whole thing, then send Terry to the pub and do the whole thing again while he was having a pint! But knowing Terry's attitude – Terry wouldn't do anything like that – in the case of the procession, I have a feeling that I came on the set and we stayed an hour. I think Terry did what he was supposed to do and we stayed another hour. They couldn't have been terribly exciting, because I remember the girls! But we shot what we shot and we weren't allowed to show what we weren't allowed to show. It was never: "We will shoot a 'foreign' version." We shot it like that but we took a "protective" with the clothes on, instead of the other way round. We didn't do one for England and then say, "Okay, let's see the tickets for the foreign one." Because at that time, we might well have got away with it – although we obviously didn't.[1]

Back in the late 1970s, Carreras made similar comments in his own magazine, *Hammer House of Horror*. He had just been asked if it was true that he had made different versions of his films for different markets. Carreras responded:

We've never made different versions of the same film. We make the film as we think it should be made, which is, if you like, the master version, but you never expect that to be the whole version. What happens to it then is dictated by one's own ideas of what is acceptable we self-censor it until we're happy it tells the story the way it should be told and then we release it. But obviously different things are acceptable in different countries and so some of the prints will be cut further and that's how the different versions evolve. I don't remember ever going back on the floor of the studio for any picture and shooting extra material with more nipple or more blood for any territory in the world. We've never done that.[2]

Despite Carreras's claims that no special consideration was given for overseas versions, several other members of the Hammer family begged to differ. Harry Oakes, a member of *The Mummy* crew, also corroborated this statement in *Dark Terrors* #8, when he told interviewer Mike Murphy that a version where the maidens were topless was shot "for some overseas markets" but that they "had tops on for the British version."

Len Harris was also asked about the nude procession in *Little Shoppe of Horrors* #14.

LSOH: On *The Mummy*, was the procession reshot nude?
LH: Yes, topless. Pretty much the whole procession. This was for overseas release. It involved a lot of women. I think there were others. Other studios did it, too. Those were policy decisions. It would take extra time to shoot things twice.[3]

Furthermore, Marcus Hearn and Alan Barnes wrote in *The Hammer Story* that the topless scenes were shot without Fisher's knowledge. According to the authors, "Michael Carreras reshot the actresses playing the Egyptian handmaidens topless." Another deleted scene was to show Kharis, pre-mummification, getting his tongue cut out. *The Hammer Story* reports, "A courier version of Christopher Lee's tongue removal also existed, but shots of the detached tongue and a stream of blood from Lee's mouth were cut before the film was submitted for certification."[4]

And on this same note, in *Inside Hammer*, Jimmy Sangster wrote that, "In the original version, the cutting out of the High Priest's

tongue was shown in gory detail. But even Hammer got cold feet about this and they took the scene out before submitting the movie for censor approval."[5]

"I think things like the tongue-cutting – all our films, for that matter – really suffered from overcautious censorship," Carreras said in yet another interview. "Because we knew the censors too well, we were penalized more than anybody else. Often we had material cut that would appear later, which was interpreted as additional material shot."[6]

Richard Klemensen asked makeup man Roy Ashton about the Japanese versions in *Little Shoppe of Horrors* #14 as well.

LSOH: Do you recollect having worked on so-called Japanese versions of certain Hammer films?

RA: I was given to understand that the Japanese were more fond of blood and gore than the English or the continental people. Thus, in two or three additional takes, we piled on cuts, broken legs, etc. a little more. They would say it was for the Japanese market: whether or not this was true, or mentioned to me as a joke, I couldn't tell. It was difficult anyway to know exactly what was shown, and where. Besides, I can't recall for which film that was, thought it might have been in *The Mummy* or *The Curse of the Mummy's Tomb* that they included these cruel sequences of Egyptian ceremonies.[7]

Section Notes

[1] Meikle, "Remembering 1959: Michael Carreras in Conversation with Dennis Meikle", *Little Shoppe of Horrors* #24, p.25.
[2] *House of Hammer* #17, 1977.
[3] Meikle and Lynch, "Len Harris: A Tribute…" *Little Shoppe of Horrors* #14, p.70.
[4] Hallenbeck, "The Making of the Hammer Classic *Blood from the Mummy's Tomb*," *Little Shoppe of Horrors* #24, p. 44.
[5] Sangster, *Inside Hammer*, p.59.
[6] Meikle, "Remembering 1959: Michael Carreras in Conversation with Dennis Meikle", *Little Shoppe of Horrors* #24, p.26.
[7] Klemensen, "Roy's Nightmares: The Life of Hammer's Makeup Master Roy Ashton (1909-1995)", *Little Shoppe of Horrors* #14, p.66.

© S.G.I. 4234-5

Publicity still of Anton Diffring as Baron Frankenstein and Don Megowan as the monster in *Tales of Frankenstein*.

3.
TALES OF FRANKENSTEIN
THE FACE IN THE TOMBSTONE MIRROR

Produced: 1958

Directed by: Curt Siodmak **Teleplay by:** Catherine and Henry Kuttner (based a story by Curt Siodmak) **Music by:** Stock library themes **Cast/Characters:** Anton Diffring (Baron Frankenstein), Helen Westcott (Christine Halpert), Don Megowan (The Monster), Richard Bull (Paul Halpert)

Academy Ratio, Black & White, 28 minutes

PLOT At the same time that Baron Frankenstein has just created a monster, a terminally ill man and his wife arrive in town seeking help from the Baron. Frankenstein lets the man die and then harvests his brain to put into his monster. The man's wife finds out and goes to confront the Baron...

COMMENTARY Naturally, after the success of *Curse of Frankenstein*, Hammer planned a sequel. However, unlike the Universal films, where the monster was the focus, Hammer's focus would be Baron Frankenstein as made popular by Peter Cushing.

Hammer hadn't quite painted themselves into a corner where sequels were concerned. *Curse of Frankenstein* had ended with the Baron being marched to a guillotine which we never see drop. In spite of that, either serious or joking, when the *Sunday Express* asked James Carreras how he planned to revive the Baron, he said, "Oh, we sew his head back on again!" Joke or not, in the eventual sequel, Frankenstein is killed at the very end. His pupil, Hans, then transplants Frankenstein's brain into a perfect duplicate body that Frankenstein had created as a contingency plan in case of his death. Coincidentally, this idea was quite similar to one being bandied about for a potential Frankenstein TV series...

During the writing of *Revenge of Frankenstein*, to be released by Columbia whom Hammer had struck a deal with, Columbia brought up the idea of a Frankenstein TV series. Michael Carreras

43

then asked Jimmy Sangster to come up with a television script for a potential series in addition to the burgeoning *Curse of Frankenstein* sequel. Sangster swiftly wrote Carreras a letter detailing all the different avenues that they could take the Baron down. Potential ideas included voodoo, black magic, and even zombies. One idea that was almost in the vein of the modern *Saw* franchise was that the Baron would experiment on an individual to see just how much pain one human being could bear!

Here is Sangster's full letter to Carreras:

Dear Mike, as for the further adventures of Frankenstein:

One. He starts to travel, visiting various new cities and countries. There he is feted as an important man by the medical councils, and he does nasties to some of their patients.

Two. He has a set-to with Zombies, on the assumption that he has worked for years putting life into dead bodies, while here there are dead bodies that move around without any life whatsoever. This to him is fascinating.

Three. He dabbles in some voodoo and gets himself a big Black assistant for a while.

Four. He becomes interested in Black Magic and the power of the Devil? He considers the Devil and he have a certain affinity.

Five. He works on mutations and retrogressions whereby his dabblings in time factors turn people into primeval slime.

Six. He works on the preservation of living tissue whereby he freezes bodies in blocks of ice for long periods of time.

Seven. He works on the property of the vacuum, where if you put a human being in one, its blood boils.

Eight. He works on the theory of pain. How much pain can a human stand. To do this he extracts by surgery the main nerve centers. Imagine having a tooth drilled where the drill touches a nerve as thick as your finger.

Love, Jim the Nasty P.S. The above are all copyright (as from now)[1]

In addition to this "monster of the week" format, Jimmy Sangster also outlined a more serialized version of the series. The first episode would begin with a man trying to blackmail the baron, but in the end, the Baron takes the man's brain and uses it for a monster. (The episode was titled "The Single Minded Blackmailer".) The next three episodes would focus on

Frankenstein prepping his monster, which would finally come to life at the end of the third episode. The next four episodes would show the monster and the Baron interacting, and by the thirteenth episode, the monster would die. Sangster also wrote outlines for a second and third season, though we don't know what his ideas were.

One article on the fledgling series claimed that Boris Karloff would 'host and occasionally star' in it. However, by October 23, 1957, *Variety* reported that Karloff was off the project. So, as you can see, plans for the series were constantly changing. For instance, Carreras next asked Sangster if he could write only six, thirty-minute-long stories for the series (with the rest of the episodes being done by other writers). At one point, the plan was to film 39 episodes, twenty shot and produced in the U.S. under Bryan Foy, with the remaining 19 under James Carreras in the U.K. By February 28, 1958, a long-term plan for the series was mapped out. What is today known as a series Bible, it outlined the various sets that would be available, plus profiles for reoccurring characters. This document had reduced the series to only 26 episodes. And the oddest detail of all, only eight of the episodes would include the good doctor himself!

Though the future of the series seemed to be in a constant state of flux, eventually a half hour pilot was settled on, then titled *Baron Frankenstein*, to be co-produced with Screen Gems (a subsidiary of Columbia). Under Screen Gems, Hammer would even be allowed to use the famous Jack Pierce Frankenstein makeup, once forbidden by Universal. (This was because Screen Gems had TV rights to Universal's classic library.) Actually, it wasn't Hammer that wanted to use the Jack Pierce makeup; it was Screen Gems.[2]

Ultimately, it would seem that Screen Gems wanted Hammer's name on the series and nothing else. Anthony Hinds said that Michael Carreras flew to Hollywood to help produce the pilot. Hinds told Mike Murphy in *Dark Terrors* that, "[Carreras] took with him story ideas, set drawings, casting ideas, all of which were thrown out by Screen Gems, who gave him a contract writer and a director to whom they owed a film and told him he would have to use some sets left standing from another show." The director Hinds spoke of was none other than Curt Siodmak, who had written *The Wolfman* (1941). Sangster's pilot was thrown out, and Screen Gems commissioned husband and wife writing team Henry and Catherine Kuttner to write their pilot.[3]

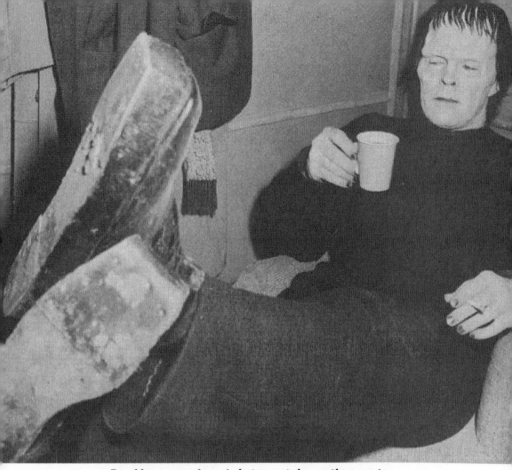

Don Megowan relaxes in between takes as the monster.

The wheels of production turned so slowly that it was delayed to the point that Carreras had to go back to England to work on one of the films! Hinds said, "I was sent to Hollywood and quickly realized that I was redundant; the script was written and, particularly with screenplays for TV, not one word could be altered because the sponsor had given his okay. The director (with whom I got on famously, happily) and I cast the thing, and we shot it. It never saw the light of day."[4]

The pilot he spoke of was shot in early January of 1958 under the title of "The Lives of Frankenstein". However, upon completion, it was retitled *Tales of Frankenstein,* and the pilot episode was titled "The Face in the Tombstone Mirror." As stated before, because Screen Gems had rights to air Universal's horror films on television, this also enabled them to use the classic makeup denied Hammer for *Curse of Frankenstein.* More than that, they

46

could also use footage from said films! Various clips from *Dracula* (1931) and Universal's *Inner Sanctum* (1943-1945) series were used in the pilot episode as *Tales of Frankenstein* begins with a series of typical but still fun horror images such as a wolf howling at the moon and a stagecoach traveling at night. A narrator (a head in a crystal ball) explains how Frankenstein's name has become synonymous with all things shocking and horrific:

> From the beginning of time, many men have sought the unknown, delving into dark regions where lie those truths which are destined to destroy us. Of all these eerie adventurers into darkness, none was more driven by insatiable curiosity than the unforgettable Baron Frankenstein. So infamous were his exploits that his name stands forever as a symbol of all that is shocking, unspeakable, forbidden! Thus, in our day, any story which chills the soul and freezes the blood is truly a 'Tale of Frankenstein.' Now—join us in the mystery, the excitement, and the stimulation that comes when we tell a story so weird, so dark, so harrowing that it deserves to be called one of the many 'Tales of Frankenstein'!

Despite American meddling, there are still a few subtle ways in which the TV pilot is similar to *Curse of Frankenstein*. Both begin with a group of people exiting the Baron's castle, only here it is his servants (not allowed to stay there after the dark) rather than funeral-goers. Coincidentally, the other male lead is even named Paul. However, there's no student-teacher relationship here, nor is there a love triangle. Paul and his wife, Christine, are here to see Frankenstein in hopes that he can cure Paul's condition. But, like the Cushing Frankenstein, the Baron is a jerk, for lack of a better word, and lets Paul die so that he can harvest his brain for his monster.

The monster, as usual, has a damaged violent brain that Frankenstein is obsessed with replacing, another similarity to *Curse*. Frankenstein also gives the monster Paul's hands as Paul was an artist. (If you're a fan of *Curse*, you'll remember that the Baron gives his monster the hands of an artist.) Upon being resurrected, the monster is chained to the wall, also comparable to *Curse*. The ending is similar to a degree, too. The monster gets loose in the house, chases the female lead, and Frankenstein gets a gun to shoot him with.

The chase goes all the way back to the cemetery. Just as Paul/the monster is about to kill the Baron, Christine appeals to his remaining humanity, urging him not to kill. Paul lets Frankenstein go, and then oddly seems to just drop dead, falling into his grave. Frankenstein doesn't waste a second and begins shoveling dirt onto the monster! The police then arrive to arrest him, again, quasi similar to *Curse*.

And what of this watered-down TV version of Hammer's Frankenstein? The sets aren't bad for TV, but it doesn't feel like a Hammer production at all (visually at least) due to being in black and white. Anton Diffring's Baron Frankenstein has a slight German accent from time to time, something the character actor was famous for. However, Diffring naturally isn't as appealing as Cushing, and it would be hard to imagine TV viewers ever becoming attached to him as the doctor. Even when he was vile, Cushing's Frankenstein had a certain amount of likeability to him.

A test screening of the pilot was held for executives of the ABC network, and it was received positively. Five more episode treatments from Hammer followed and were written during March and April of 1958. They have no titles and are simply called "Story Number 1" and so on. The first story was written by A.R. Rawlinson and was actually the future basis for *Frankenstein Created Woman* (1966). It involved a man named Peter wandering outside Frankenstein's castle. He meets a mysterious and beautiful woman named Lisa before the Baron runs him off. Worried that Lisa might be a prisoner, Peter returns to the castle in an attempt to rescue her. But he is caught again by the Baron, who offers a challenge to him: if Peter can get the girl to show actual emotion (something she is devoid of as the Baron's creation), he will let Peter take her away. Instead, Lisa comes at Peter with a knife when he declares his love for her. She stabs him in the shoulder, and so Peter and the Baron ward Lisa off, and she falls down a flight of stairs and is killed. The Baron explains to Peter how she'd slowly become evil over time and lost her humanity. Peter leaves and the Baron returns to his laboratory. Anthony Hinds liked the story up to the point that Lisa died and stipulated that the character should live on to become a semi-regular character that could pop up when needed.

Story No. 2 was written by Hugh Woodhouse and sounded like it was inspired by

Various screengrabs from *Tales of Frankenstein.*

the ending of *Revenge of Frankenstein* (which was for certain scripted by then). In the story, the Baron creates an exact physical double of himself. But, like Lisa, it has no soul. Unable to reign in its subconscious desires, which are identical to the Baron's, the clone goes on a murder spree that takes the lives of a writer and a priest.

These publicity stills from *Frankenstein Created Woman* (1967) have
become beloved yet notorious in fan circles because there is nothing in the
actual film resembling them! As you can see here, the genesis for that film's
story came from *Tales of Frankenstein*. © 1967 Hammer Film Productions Ltd.

Story No.3, by Cyril Kersh, again seemed preoccupied with the soul, and also probably influenced *Frankenstein Created Woman*. In the story, the Baron and an unnamed assistant conduct experiments on life after death (in other words, where does the soul go?). Specifically, the Baron kidnaps and kills a doctor, who he revives, but the man has no memory of what happened.

Story No. 4, by Edward Dryhurst, continued the *Created Woman* streak of future story elements. In this one, the Baron takes in two travelers from the cold and then experiments on freezing them to prolong life (remember, the Baron uses freezing in his first experiment in *Created Woman*).

Story No.5, a five-page treatment dated May 8, 1958, was submitted by Peter Bryan and concerned a hypnotist from the Orient called Kotan. The mystic was said to be a direct descendant of a priest who had once guarded the "Temple of Man" and was also a keeper of the "Hidden Secrets of the East." Like in *Evil of Frankenstein* (1964), the Baron just happens to catch Kotan performing in a traveling circus. When Kotan uses his skills in hypnosis to hypnotize a man, the Baron gets an idea: could Kotan revive his dormant monster? When the Baron approaches Kotan, he of course does not tell him the truth. He tells him that he wants him to use his skills on a "patient" who has no will of his own after undergoing an extreme mental shock.

Just as the Baron wasn't entirely truthful, neither was Kotan. Though he does possess hypnotic powers, he is really from Austria and he made up the Asian aspect to appear more mysterious. Furthermore, his last patient was his wife, and when he put her under extreme hypnosis, she never woke up again and died. A girl named Kaarina, a knife thrower in the circus, is also his daughter (though she doesn't know this).

Kotan does his best to reanimate the brain of the monster (if this was the monster seen in the very first episode is unknown). The monster comes to life, gets angry, and kills Kotan! However, in his final moments, Kotan psychically transfers his mind or spirit into the monster. Naturally, Kotan doesn't want to stay in the hideous body and disguises himself. Going out into the village, he would look for a man to project his consciousness into. And, it's not just that his new body is grotesque, but the monster's bad habits are beginning to take over. The episode would end with him erasing Kaarina's memory of him before the monster takes over. Then, in his last act, Kotan manages to commit suicide.

Screen Gems/Columbia disliked all of these pitches and threw them out. They wanted the whole thing to be an American production with Hammer's name on it. Screen Gems brought in American writers to pitch new stories. Notably, Screen Gems ordered a second script from American sci-fi writer Jerome Bixby entitled "Frankenstein Meets Dr. Varno." There were intentions to film this second episode, but the series was canned before that could happen. And it's probably for the best. Had the series been filmed, then it's possible that classics like *Frankenstein Created Woman* would have never gone before cameras, as their subject matter would have already been used on the inferior series.

Today, "The Face in the Tombstone Mirror" is easily accessible online and appears as a special feature on the Blu-Ray for *Evil of Frankenstein* from SCREAM Factory.

Chapter Notes

[1] Newsom, "The Series That Never Was: *Tales of Frankenstein*," *Little Shoppe of Horrors* #21, p.78.

[2] Hammer had their own designs for the monster. When Carreras saw the production's design, he didn't feel that it went far enough and that it should have more burns and scars along the face, which they ignored.

[3] Henry and Catherine Kuttner often wrote under the pen names of "Lewis Padgett" and "Lawrence O'Donnell". Sadly, Henry would pass away the next year in 1958.

[4] Murphy, "Anthony Hinds," *Dark Terrors* #16, p.9.

Concept paintings by Willis O'Brien for *King Kong vs. the Gingko.*

4.
KING KONG VS.
FRANKENSTEIN

Developed: 1958-1961

Producer: John Beck **Screenplay by:** Willis O'Brien (drafts 1-2), George Worthington Yates (draft 3) **Proposed Special Effects Director:** Willis O'Brien **Proposed Cast/Characters:** Carl Denham (first two drafts only) **Proposed Creatures:** King Kong, the Gingko/Prometheus

PLOT King Kong is retrieved from Skull Island and put on display in San Francisco alongside a giant version of the Frankenstein monster. The two beasts escape and do battle...

FRANKENSTEIN'S CREATION.

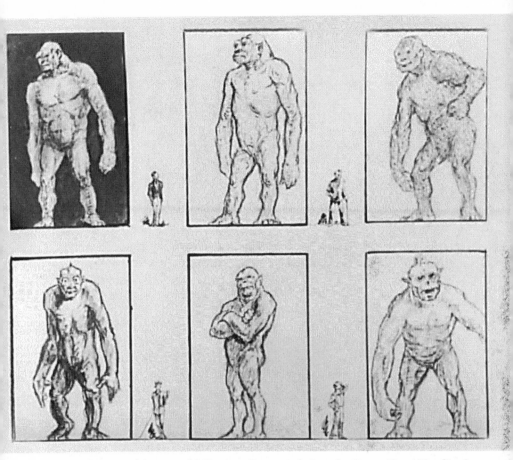

This page, previous, and following: Concept designs for Prometheus/the Gingko by Willis O'Brien.

COMMENTARY In addition to King Kong, stopmotion animator Willis O'Brien also had an affinity for Frankenstein, which earlier in his career he had attempted to make a stopmotion version of. Perhaps then it's no surprise that as his career was winding down in the late 1950s that O'Brien came up with "King Kong vs. Frankenstein." Actually, for fear of legal backlash from Universal, O'Brien never called his proposed story that; he called it *King Kong vs. the Gingko.*[1] Ironically enough, O'Brien needn't have worried about Frankenstein, which was in the public domain. It was his own creation, Kong, that he didn't have the rights to! But, I'm getting ahead of the narrative. Before O'Brien discovered the difficulties surrounding his old creation, he wrote a story treatment. In it, it's revealed that Kong didn't actually die when he

55

fell from the Empire State Building. Instead, his comatose body was smuggled back to Skull Island by Carl Denham. Nearly 30 years later, Denham, for some reason, returns to Skull Island and recaptures Kong. (Never mind that Skull Island sank in *Son of Kong*!) At the same time in Africa, Dr. Frankenstein's grandson stitches together a gigantic new lifeform from dead matter. (Supposedly in this first draft, the giant body was made of human corpses rather than animals.) Both giant creatures are put on display in San Francisco, escape, and do battle in the streets.

The next draft fleshed out the first and changed the Frankenstein monster into one created from various animal parts instead of humans. (Supposedly, the monster would be comprised of African animals such as rhinos and elephants.) It is Denham who gets the idea to stage a prizefight between the two monsters in San Francisco (O'Brien had a vested interest in boxing) when the Frankenstein monster kills its creator and escapes from the lab in Africa. The monster is captured and brought to San Francisco for the match with Kong, himself brought over from Skull Island. Actually, there is no boxing match depicted in any of the concept art, just a joint display of the two beasts. Trouble occurs when Denham has a girl walking a tightrope over the Gingko, holding the rope in his outstretched arms. When her rope breaks and the Gingko catches her, Kong thinks he is attacking the girl and becomes enraged, breaking out of his cage. The two battle through San Francisco until they both climb the Golden Gate Bridge. The battle concludes with both monsters falling into the waters below.

O'Brien took the script to Daniel O'Shea, then president of RKO, who informed him that even though he animated Kong, he didn't have legal rights to the character and would have to pay over $200,000 to use Kong! O'Shea connected O'Brien to producer John Beck, who would look for a studio to finance the project. Beck, in turn, hired George Worthington Yates to do a third draft of O'Brien's script. Yates changed the title to *King Kong vs. Prometheus*, which was a nod to the subtitle of *Frankenstein, or a Modern Prometheus*. Fundamentally the script was the same, only here a new layer is added to the Frankenstein monster. In this version, the doctor, Kurt, who creates Prometheus, isn't revealed to be a descendant of Frankenstein until later in the script in a surprise reveal. He also has the ability to remote control the monster—or so he thinks. The intelligent creature only pretends to follow the doctor's remote control commands in Candlestick Park in San Francisco. He soon kills Kurt, goes on a rampage, and King Kong (also on display in Candlestick Park) then plays the hero in defeating the monster with the same climax from draft #2. Other noteworthy changes included the deletion of the Carl Denham character, or so one source says. As for other details, Kurt Frankenstein has designs on creating a whole army of monster workers to do his bidding.

As always, there are still more alternating reports as to what the different story drafts contained. For instance, in 1970, Kevin Brownlow interviewed Darlyne O'Brien, who gave him this very interesting information:

This picture ended in San Francisco, and [O'Brien] was gonna have King Kong riding a cable car, but he didn't get the illustration finished, and he had marvelous action in it. There were wonderful ideas for action...They were supposed to meet on this island, and have this big battle. People would come all over the world to see this big fight.[2]

Her last comment is somewhat confusing, considering most sources place the final battle in San Francisco, but perhaps she was just remembering the details wrong. Kong riding the cable car would have certainly been something to see though! She also confirmed that the Frankenstein monster's design would not resemble the Jack Pierce makeup:

57

FRANKENSTEIN'S MONSTER		KING KONG
20'4"	HEIGHT	19'8"
34 TONS	WEIGHT	38 TONS
28 FT.	REACH	27 FT.
14 FT.	CHEST	17 FT.
11 FT.	WAIST	11 FT.
8 FT.	NECK	9 FT.

The Gingko and Kong on display in San Francisco in Willis O'Brien's wonderful concept art.

O'Brien: That first version [she's speaking about Universal's Boris Karloff Frankenstein] he decided against that one...
Brownlow: There was no thought to make it like Boris Karloff?
O'Brien: No, not intentionally, I don't believe.[3]

As to more differing reports as to what the drafts contained, the magazine *Cinefex* wrote:

The film (would) pit Kong and the Frankenstein monster against each other. A descendent of the original Victor Frankenstein creates a new monster, nearly twenty feet tall, in his hidden laboratory deep within the African jungles. The monster escapes, however, killing the doctor and destroying his lab. Reports of its rampage, along with scattered photographs, drift back to civilization, and a group of San Francisco promoters set out to capture the creature and bring it back for public display. At more or less the same time, another group sets sail for Skull Island to capture Kong. They decide to display Kong in San Francisco and the city becomes the center of worldwide attention as preparations are made to exhibit the two beasts side by side in a large stadium. For the film's climax, the monsters were to break loose from their cages and have a thundering fight to the death in the streets of the city.

As one can see, though essentially the same as other descriptions, there are slight variations. And why can't we provide a concrete synopsis of what occurs in the two treatments and the screenplay? Though O'Brien's treatment does indeed still exist today, it is in the hands of a private collector who bought it on eBay in April of 2001.[4]

As to why King Kong vs. Frankenstein was never made...in a strange way, it kind of was. After the project was passed up by nearly every U.S. studio, Beck took the idea overseas to Italy, but they weren't interested either. Eventually, Beck connected with Toho in Japan, no doubt aware of their own giant monster movies. The studio readily agreed to the production—their only caveat was that Frankenstein would be thrown out in favor of their own creation: Godzilla! This Beck did not tell O'Brien, though, and more or less stole the project from him when he learned RKO—not O'Brien—was the sole legal rights holder for King Kong. Reportedly, O'Brien called Beck for developments often, so it seems as though Beck deliberately didn't tell him about bringing the project to Toho—whom he had even convinced to foot the bill for the rights to King Kong! O'Brien would only learn about Beck and King Kong vs. Godzilla when he read about it in the newspaper. As he was off the project, this meant he would not handle the stop motion effects as hoped. Instead, to his horror, Kong would be brought to life by suitmation instead. Merian C. Cooper was also enraged, suing RKO for using what he thought was his creation. In her interview with Kevin Brownlow, Darlyne O'Brien also had something interesting to say about the Toho situation, stating that many of O'Brien's drawings were taken to Japan and never returned to him! Donald E. Hughes, O'Brien's nephew, also commented on the situation, stating, "I think there was a lawsuit pending, [but] it was dropped and nothing came of it. I don't recall how [Obie] found out, but he did, and that's when they instigated the lawsuit."[5] As for O'Brien, he died on November 8, 1962, not long after King Kong vs. Godzilla was released in Japan.[6]

Though some crazy concepts like this are best left unmade, I think it's a shame that King Kong and Frankenstein, both of whom had hugely successful films in the early 1930s, never fought it out on the big screen.

Chapter Notes

[1] The name uses all the letters of King Kong but reshuffled.

[2] O'Brien interview with Kevin Brownlow as quoted in *Willis O'Brien: Special Effects Genius* on p.80.

[3] Ibid, p.83.

[4] Specifically it was apparently O'Brien's second draft entitled *King Kong vs. the Ginko*. It consisted of a nine-page treatment with two pages of introduction.

[5] Hughes's interview with Steve Archer and Stephen Pickard as quoted in *Willis O'Brien: Special Effects Genius* on p.83.

[6] Ironically, O'Brien's aborted concept ended up reviving the Godzilla series since *King Kong vs. Godzilla* went on to become the highest grossing Godzilla movie of all time, and still holds that title today if adjusted for inflation. Also, the idea of a giant Frankenstein stuck in Toho's mind, for eventually they produced *Frankenstein Conquers the World* in 1965. In that film the still beating heart of the Frankenstein monster is transported to Japan from Nazi Germany shortly before the bomb is dropped on Hiroshima. The heart then mutates into a gigantic version of the monster which battles a reptilian menace similar to Godzilla. Likewise, Don Glut claims that Toho themselves pondered filming *King Kong vs. Frankenstein* and the March 1965 *Monster World* #7 announced that project was in development at Toho along with "Dogora, the Space Monster" and "Godzilla vs. the Giant Devilfish"! Furthermore, Toho did at one time have a film in development called *Frankenstein vs. the Giant Devilfish*, and *Dogora the Space Monster* was released in 1964.

5.
THE THREE FACES
OF DR. JEKYLL

Developed: 1959

Screenplay by: Wolf Mankowitz **Proposed Cast/Characters:** Dr. Henry Jekyll (Laurence Harvey), Mr. Hyde [Jekyll's later ego], Kitty Jekyll [Jekyll's wife], Paul Allen [friend of Henry and Kitty], Litauer [friend of Jekyll]

PLOT Dr. Henry Jekyll uses a potion to unleash his darkest desires as the young, good-looking Mr. Hyde.

COMMENTARY In 1959, Hammer turned their attention to Robert Louis Stevenson's classic novella, *The Strange Case of Dr. Jekyll and Mr. Hyde.* While one might've thought perhaps Hammer would cast Peter Cushing as Jekyll and Christopher Lee as Hyde, Hammer, or rather screenwriter Wolf Mankowitz, decided to take a different approach to the tale. In a publicity release for Columbia, the film's distributor, Mankowitz said, "Evil is attractive to all men. Therefore it is not illogical that the face of evil should be attractive."[1] As such, Mankowitz made Dr. Jekyll an older,

61

AFTER *TWO FACES OF DR. JEKYLL*, HAMMER HAD IDEAS OF ADAPTING *THE PICTURE OF DORIAN GRAY*, OSCAR WILDE'S BOOK PUBLISHED IN 1891 (AFTER BEING SERIALIZED IN 1890). A SIMILAR STORY TO *DR. JEKYLL AND MR. HYDE* ABOUT MORAL DUALITY, IT'S NOT SURPRISING THAT IT WAS ON HAMMER'S TO-DO LIST AT THE TIME. THE STORY CONCERNED A WICKED, GOOD-LOOKING MAN, DORIAN GRAY, WHO WISHES TO NEVER GROW OLD. INSTEAD, HE WISHES A PORTRAIT OF HIMSELF TO AGE FOR HIM. HIS WISH IS GRANTED. BUT, NOT ONLY DOES IT AGE, BUT WITH EVERY SIN THAT GRAY COMMITS THE MAN IN THE PORTRAIT COMES TO LOOK MORE AND MORE MONSTROUS. CONSIDERING THAT THE FILM WAS IN DEVELOPMENT IN LATE 1959 AND EARLY 1960, THE SAME TIME AS *CURSE OF THE WEREWOLF,* IT IS THOUGHT THAT OLIVER REED WOULD HAVE BEEN THE PRIME CANDIDATE TO PLAY GRAY. BY THE SAME TOKEN, SINCE CHRISTOPHER LEE HAD JUST PLAYED A MORALLY BANKRUPT LADIES' MAN IN *TWO FACES OF DR. JEKYLL*, IT'S THOUGHT HE WOULD HAVE LEAPT AT THE CHANCE TO PLAY LORD HENRY WOLTON, WHO AIDES GRAY ALONG AS HE SINKS DEEPER AND DEEPER INTO DEBAUCHERY. FURTHERMORE, IT'S THOUGHT THAT SINCE JIMMY SANGSTER WAS TAKING A BREAK FROM GOTHIC HORROR AFTER *BRIDES OF DRACULA*, THAT ANTHONY HINDS WOULD HAVE TO HAVE BEEN THE ONE TO WRITE THE *GRAY* SCREENPLAY. APPARENTLY A SCRIPT OR TREATMENT WAS WRITTEN AND SUBMITTED TO THE BRITISH BOARD OF CENSORS, WHO REPORTEDLY ABHORRED IT AND ADVISED AGAINST PRODUCING IT. HAMMER WOULD RETURN TO THE IDEA AGAIN IN THE EARLY 1970S, IRONICALLY AGAIN AROUND THE TIME THEY WERE PRODUCING ANOTHER ITERATION OF JEKYLL AND HYDE.

bearded man who, upon taking his potion, would become the younger, more attractive, clean-shaven Hyde.

There were no redeeming qualities to any of the characters at all. In Mankowitz's original version, Jekyll is fully aware of the hypocrisy of society and creates Hyde as an alternate identity and a means of reveling in sin. These sins would have included cockfighting, sleeping with underage prostitutes, drugs, and even occult ceremonies!

The original title was *The Three Faces of Dr. Jekyll* (though I'm not sure what that was supposed to allude to other than perhaps *The Three Faces of Eve*?). Mankowitz wrote the film to star actor Laurence Harvey (eventual star of *The Manchurian Candidate*) as

Jekyll/Hyde. But, Harvey turned down the role (supposedly he wanted to take the part, but his agent felt it was a bad move). Christopher Lee was interested in the Jekyll/Hyde part as well but was turned down! (Lee said, "I'll admit I was really put off at not playing Jekyll/Hyde. I thought I deserved the opportunity, although Paul Massie was certainly good. My supporting role, however, was one of my favourites - and still is."[2]) And lastly, Terence Fisher wanted Louis Jourdan for the role. In any case, writer Wolf Mankowitz was given free rein by Hammer on the script. When Mankowitz's script proved too depraved for Fisher, who said he couldn't find any sympathetic characters within the whole thing, he altered quite a few scenes to make it to his liking, which naturally disappointed Mankowitz.

The original ending was much more ambitious. In the film, the character of Litauer realizes that the dying Jekyll and Hyde are the same being. The script was more ambitious and had Hyde captured and about to be hung from the gallows in front of a crowd of onlookers. As Hyde begs them not to do it, he reverts to Jekyll in front of Litauer and the others (a woman screams in shock). "Jekyll! May God help you!" Litauer gasps as he sees a now aged Jekyll with white hair. "I have destroyed him," rasps Jekyll in reference to Hyde. "And yourself, my poor friend, Litauer responds. Let's go to the script for the rest:

As the POLICE close in on JEKYLL we come in close to his eyes.

JEKYLL (overlaid)
Only I could destroy him.

We go through the eyes.

JEKYLL (Hyde's voice)
Only I could destroy him.

In the far distance, looking as though it were through JEKYLL's eyes, we see a double image of a man on the gallows the moment before the trap falls.

We move in very fast till we are close to the face of JEKYLL, the images moving into one as we approach.

Lobby card for the U.S. version entitled *Jekyll's Inferno.*

Unseen by us (for we remain in close-up), the trap swings away, the body jerks as the rope tautens.

There is a violent movement of JEKYLL's head and we watch for the first and only time JEKYLL changes back to HYDE...

THE END [3]

Considering the abysmal failure that *Two Faces of Dr. Jekyll* was at the box office, perhaps Hammer might as well have tried their hand at *Three Faces* instead.

Chapter Notes

[1] Hearn, *Hammer Vault*, p.39.
[2] Johnson, "Christopher Lee: He May Not Have Been Who You Might Have Thought He Was," *Little Shoppe of Horrors* #35, p.170 (Kindle Edition).
[3] Hearn, *Hammer Vault*, p.39.

The most evil **DRACULA** of all!

BRIDES OF DRACULA

TECHNICOLOR®

Starring PETER CUSHING · FREDA JACKSON · MARTITA HUNT · YVONNE MONLAUR
Screenplay by JIMMY SANGSTER, PETER BRYAN and EDWARD PERCY · Directed by TERENCE FISHER · Produced by ANTHONY HINDS
Executive Producer MICHAEL CARRERAS · A Hammer Film Production Released by Universal-International through Rank Film Distributors Ltd.

This poster for *Brides of Dracula* appears to feature the Count and Baron Meinster both.

6.
DISCIPLE OF DRACULA
BEFORE BRIDES OF DRACULA

Developed: March 1959-January 1960
Release Date: July 7, 1960

Screenplay by: Jimmy Sangster (First Draft; *Disciple of Dracula*), Peter Bryan (Second Draft; *Brides of Dracula*), Edward Percy (Third Draft, *Brides of Dracula*), Anthony Hinds (Uncredited Fourth Draft, *Dracula II*) **Proposed Characters (*Disciple of Dracula*):** Latour [vampire hunter], Maggy [English teacher], Baron Meinster [vampire], Pauline [schoolgirl], Baroness Meinster [vampire's mother], Dracula (Christopher Lee) **Cast (*Brides of Dracula*):** Peter Cushing (Prof. Van Helsing), David Peel (Baron Meinster), Yvonne Monlaur (Marianne), Martita Hunt (Baroness Meinster), Freda Jackson (Greta)

PLOT When the vampire Baron Meinster is set free from his chateau by a naïve traveler, he runs afoul of a local village and an all-girls finishing school. And, to defeat the Baron, a local vampire hunter will need the help of none other than Dracula's ghost...

COMMENTARY Legend has it that the 1958 release of *Horror of Dracula* was so successful that it saved Universal from bankruptcy. This wouldn't have been the first time either, since the successful release of the Bela Lugosi *Dracula* in 1931 did the same thing. That's neither here nor there though, we're here to talk *Horror of Dracula* sequels—and Universal most certainly wanted one. As a matter of fact, according to *Last Bus to Bray Vol. 1*, the follow-up was being planned as *Horror of Dracula* premiered in American cinemas! It was titled *Dracula the Damned* and written by Jimmy Sangster. Plot details aren't known outside of having Lee and Cushing reprise their roles. Contrary to that, Sangster himself remembers the first sequel pitch being called *The Revenge of Dracula* (perhaps to match 1958's *The Revenge of Frankenstein?*). Supposedly the proposed story had Dracula revived by a band of gypsies, and the Count goes out to get—what else—revenge upon the locals. As Dracula terrorizes village after village, the sister of one of his victims sets out for revenge. For the climax, Dracula is killed by the spire of an old church that topples off and impales him. (The plot points I just mentioned come from online chatter; Sangster never mentioned any of these things, so take them with a grain of salt!)

Sangster mentioned the project in *Inside Hammer* as a precursor to *Dracula – Prince of Darkness* (1965):

> After the first *Dracula* movie, Hammer asked me to do a screenplay for a sequel. This I did, calling it *The Revenge of Dracula*. The mixture pretty much as before, with Chris Lee and Peter Cushing reprising their original roles. Then, for reasons unknown to me at the time, they decided to go with *Brides* instead. [1]

While *Brides of Dracula* featured Van Helsing as the hero, seen here played by Peter Cushing, *Disciple of Dracula* featured a different vampire hunter named Latour. © 1960 Hammer Film Productions Ltd.

Allegedly, *Revenge of Dracula/Dracula the Damned* didn't happen because Christopher Lee was afraid of being typecast and did not wish to return to the role. Other sources say he was simply too busy making movies elsewhere...which doesn't make sense considering Lee found the time to do both *The Mummy* and *The Hound of the Baskervilles* for Hammer in 1959. Others say Hammer simply didn't care to have him reprise the role...

British film historian Jonathon Sothcott believes that at the time, Lee simply wasn't considered a name draw compared to Cushing. Case in point, Lee was still listed below Cushing and other Hammer players in many films—including *Horror of Dracula,* where he was listed last! Lee wouldn't receive significant billing until *The Devil-Ship Pirates* in 1964. Richard Harland Smith of

Turner Classic Movies concurs that Hammer simply didn't see Lee's value yet. He wrote in his piece on *Brides of Dracula* that:

> Other voices argue that Lee's absence was by fiat of Hammer itself, who considered his costar Peter Cushing their capital asset. Lending weight to this theory is the fact that the studio routinely slotted Lee into character roles (*The Man Who Could Cheat Death* [1959], *The Two Faces of Dr. Jekyll* [1960]) rather than starring ones during this time. Even when paired with Cushing for *The Hound of the Baskervilles* (1959), Cushing's Sherlock Holmes was clearly the star of the show.[2]

The theory that Hammer simply didn't place much worth in Lee would seem to make the most sense. Case in point, why write a cameo for Lee in the next "Dracula film" if he refused to be in it? Because that's precisely what Hammer did. Anthony Hinds had asked Jimmy Sangster to write a script titled *Disciple of Dracula* in which the Count had only a minimal presence. In his biography, *Do You Want It Good or Tuesday?*, Sangster remembers that Hinds told him to "not go overboard with Chris Lee." Sangster elaborated that, "Tony felt [Lee] was playing hard to get...So, on Tony's instructions, I wrote the 'Christopher Lee' part down and made the character of Baron Meinster the principal vampire."[3]

As to why Hinds did this, in his own words in *Little Shoppe of Horrors*:

> I think (although I am not sure) that *Brides* started from a desperate plea from Brian Lawrence to make a Dracula without Christopher Lee (Brian had developed a hatred for Chris' agent, John Redway—probably because John wanted to increase his client's earnings—naturally). I told Brian we couldn't make a Dracula without Dracula (and obviously nobody else could play the Count) but that one could make one with *Dracula* in the title without him.[4]

Sangster's storyline for *Disciple of Dracula* is fundamentally similar to *Brides of Dracula* but without the character of Van Helsing. We open this story with a different vampire hunter, a man named Latour, who is posing as a gravedigger...

Sangster was kind enough to publish excerpts of the original script within *Inside Hammer*.

KISS OF THE VAMPIRE

COLOR

starring
CLIFFORD EVANS
NOEL WILLMAN
EDWARD DE SOUZA
JENNIFER DANIEL
BARRY WARREN
Screenplay by JOHN ELDER
Directed by DON SHARP
Produced by ANTHONY HINDS
A Hammer Film Production

Universal
Release

Lobby Card for *Kiss of the Vampire* showing a scene taken from *Disciple of Dracula*. Kiss of the Vampire © 1963 Hammer Film Productions Ltd.

EXT. CHURCHYARD. DAY.
The year is 1895. The place, somewhere in Europe.
We are shooting through the triangle formed by a shovel stuck in a mound of earth, the ground and the lower half of a man leaning on the shovel.
What we can see of the man puts him down as a gravedigger, his clothes are those worn by a labourer. [5]

This, as we will soon learn in a shocking reveal, is the vampire hunter Latour, whose dead lover is in the casket. The scene continues with the man observing a priest delivering the closing remarks of a funeral. Standing before him is an elderly couple, the mother and father of the recently deceased. The funeral service over, the trio walks away, and the gravedigger walks towards the burial plot.

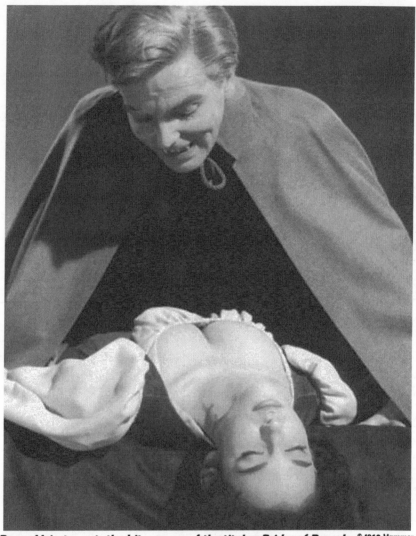

Baron Meinster puts the bite on one of the titular *Brides of Dracula*. © 1960 Hammer Film Productions Ltd.

Sangster envisioned the camera focusing on the grieving parents and the priest. They hear a crash, followed by a bloodcurdling scream. They turn to look. The gravedigger is disappearing into the bushes! They run to the grave, where they discover that he has plunged his shovel into the chest of the deceased woman—it was she who uttered the scream. Blood oozes from the hole in the casket made by the shovel, and Sangster envisioned that the musical score would begin here, followed by the title *Disciple of Dracula.*

Sangster's main protagonists in this script, aside from the mysterious vampire hunter we just met, would also include two British travelers: Margaret (or "Maggy") Leicester and Pauline Carruthers. (In the finished film, they would be consolidated into one character, the French Marianne.) On the way to Badstein, they meet Latour (the man from the pre-title scene) in a coach.[6] During their exchange, we learn that Maggy is 22 years old and "dark and attractive in a slightly sulky manner" while Pauline is only 17 and "fair and pretty."[7] Maggy is only Pauline's companion on the journey to Badstein, as it turns out, and not a fellow teacher. As for Latour, not much is revealed of him in the passage that Sangster shares, but his lines are written so eloquently one has to wonder why the character wasn't simply Van Helsing.

In any case, they part ways with Latour, and Maggy takes a job at the Chateau Meinster as the Baroness Meinster's companion, while Pauline goes on to the finishing school in Badstein.

In the finished film, Marianne remains blissfully unaware of Baron Meinster's "condition" until the picture's climax at the windmill. Not so here. Even Baroness Meinster is implied to be a vampire. (Sangster describes her as a "tainted, monstrous matriarch.") Over dinner, she has two cryptic lines of note, the first being, "I'm not hungry...yet." The second line has her say, "I have found I sleep better by day than by night."

Upon freeing Baron Meinster, apparently Maggy either witnesses him biting his mother, or she sees the aftermath of the act. Whatever the case, Maggy flees the Chateau in terror. She hears a coach approaching, and thinking it to be her salvation, runs to it.

"Please...you must help me," Maggy pleads as the coach comes to a stop. "I've got to—

Her words cut off at the sight of the driver. It is the Baron, with blood dripping from his very noticeable fangs. "Yes, my dear," he says with a wicked smile.

Maggy runs away into the night. The next morning, she stumbles into a nearby town. Just as she is about to enter the local inn, a commotion catches her attention. A parade of villagers is marching down the road carrying a deceased girl (similar in description to the opening scene in *Dracula – Prince of Darkness*).

Maggy is planning to walk closer, but a hand grabs her and draws her into the seclusion of a nearby porch. It is Latour, the man she met in the coach earlier on her journey. He cautions Maggy to remain quiet as the grieving villagers pass. When she says she must tell them that it was the Baron Meinster who did it, he informs her that the villagers live in such fear of Meinster that they would sooner turn her in to the Meinsters rather than try to fight them.

To escape suspicion as a stranger, Maggy invents a story that she was in town to rendezvous with her fiancé. However, he didn't show, and so she is now on her way to the finishing school to meet up with Pauline. In this version, Maggy even rides to the school with the Langs, who run the school and are traveling back that way. On the journey, the Langs offer her a job teaching English.

Meinster eventually shows up at the school, gets the Langs to invite him in, and then bites Maggy on the neck when he catches her alone. Maggy then becomes his accomplice as she is now under his spell and procures girls for his voracious appetite. Latour arrives at the school too, now convinced that Meinster is a vampire.

In the final act, Maggy convinces Pauline to come with her to an old windmill to meet her "fiancé" (aka the Baron). Latour, meanwhile, has decided to summon Dracula's spirit to deal with Meinster, who has broken the Code of the Undead.

Though some think it a bit silly, the scenes of Dracula's ghost, or whatever you'd like to call it, don't seem half bad.[8] Initially, Latour thinks that he has failed in his attempt to summon the King of the Vampires. Latour leafs through an old book to see what he's done wrong, and Sangster envisioned the camera panning back to reveal the tall figure of Dracula standing behind him in the background.

"I am here," says the Count.

The camera was then to use a low angle to show off Dracula's impressive height. (A similar shot, perhaps inspired by this very scene, is used for the Count's reveal in *Dracula A.D. 1972.*)

Latour tells Dracula that he has summoned him to deal with one of the "spawn of your vile breed" who has "violated the fundamental laws infamous creed laid down by yourself."[9] Latour continues that he has been unable to vanquish the vampire on his own, and so he has called upon the original vampire himself. When Latour seems to go on for too long, Dracula humorously interrupts him and says, "I am here...say what you have to."

Upon mentioning the name of Meinster, we would have cut back to the Baron talking to Pauline under the guise of being Maggy's fiancé still. After some chit-chat, he says to Maggy, "I am sure Pauline and I know each other well enough for you to leave us now, my dear..."

This poster for *Horror of Dracula* shows a rather spectral version of the title character that would have been befitting of *Disciple of Dracula* had it gone before cameras. © 1958 Hammer Film Productions Ltd.

This lobby card for *Brides of Dracula* highlights the character of Gina as played by Andree Melly. © 1960 Hammer Film Productions Ltd.

Maggy backs away tepidly, right into the form of Count Dracula (who is apparently corporeal and not a ghost entirely). Thunder sounds at that moment and Dracula asks Meinster if he knows who he is.

"You are the father," the Baron says.

Dracula replies, "I am the father."

There is another thunder burst and then a gust of wind rocks the windmill. The Count then brings forth the following charges against the Baron:

DRACULA

You have broken my laws...you have done that which you should not have done...and you have left unfinished things that you should have completed...you have eaten of the blood of your mother...you have allowed this girl [*indicating to Maggy*] to remain alive even though she was in your power. You have thought more of your own personal desires than of spreading my cult throughout the world. You cannot remain among the undead. I have come out of the darkness to destroy you.[10]

IN *LITTLE SHOPPE OF HORRORS* #10, IN OSCAR MARTINEZ'S ARTICLE "THE VAMPIRE WOMAN AND THE HUNCHBACK — AN INTERVIEW WITH ANDREE MELLY AND OSCAR QUITAK," HE ASKS ABOUT A SCENE FROM THE 1959 VERSION OF THE SCRIPT WHERE GINA WALKS TOWARDS THE OLD MILL WHILE GRETA WAITS FOR HER AT THE DOOR, "CROONING ENDEARMENTS." MARTINEZ SAID TO MELLY, "THIS SCENE IS NOT INCLUDED IN THE 1960 SCRIPT. DO YOU KNOW IF IT WAS SHOT?" MELLY ANSWERED, "I HONESTLY CAN'T REMEMBER I'M AFRAID, SO VERY LONG AGO, WHETHER THE SCENE OF... 'WALKING TOWARDS THE MILL' OR RATHER 'GINA' WALKING TOWARDS THE MILL WHILE I WAITED AT THE DOOR: I DON'T THINK THAT SCENE WAS EVER SHOT. IT DOESN'T RING A BELL, BUT I COULDN'T SWEAR TO IT."

Meinster then begins to back away as he says, "No...I didn't mean—

"Die now Baron Meinster!" Dracula commands. "Leave the world of the shadows...you are sentenced and executed...die now."[11]

The Baron begins to writhe in pain as he looks at the backs of his hands which are beginning to secrete blood. Next, blood begins to drip from his face—the Baron is hemorrhaging to death! The two girls watch in horror as the Baron backs towards an open door, through which we can see lightning as the storm increases in intensity.

The Baron falls to his knees in a puddle of blood, takes one last "anguished look" at Dracula, and then enters his final death throes. Maggy places a hand to her throat and then turns to look in the direction of Dracula, but he has vanished. There's another flash of lightning, and a timber falls across Meinster's dead, drained body.

Pauline pulls Maggy from the windmill. Moments later, the windmill is literally split in half by a lightning strike, and the structure collapses into rubble. And with that, the movie was to end.

Though this author, like many others, is a fan of the ending of *Brides of Dracula*, Sangster's envisioned ending certainly has its merits. Dracula acting as a hero of sorts is intriguing, but Meinster's death would have been difficult to get past censors of the time, something Sangster acknowledges in *Inside Hammer*. He also notes that the effects crew would have had quite a time in trying to bring the scene to life.

Now for the million-dollar question: Why didn't Hammer move forward with this version of the script? According to Sangster, Lee did indeed turn the picture down and that's why *Disciple of Dracula* never came to be. "But like all good vampire legends, it was destined to be reborn," Sangster added in reference to the eventual production. Actually, that's what Sangster says in *Do You Want It Good or Tuesday?* In *Inside Hammer*, on page 60, Sangster writes that "Chris Lee has gone on record to say he was never asked to appear [in *Disciple of Dracula*]."

For whatever reason, Peter Bryan, writer of *Hound of the Baskervilles*, was brought on to revise Sangster's script, which Bryan retitled *Brides of Dracula*,[12] in September of 1959. Due to the circumstances outlined by Sangster in the previous paragraph, Bryan was instructed by Anthony Hinds to remove Dracula altogether.

Now lacking the Count, Bryan thought it best to at least bring back Van Helsing. Thusly, Van Helsing replaced Latour and the two travelers were consolidated into Marianne. However, this still isn't the end of the story, nor the only difference.

Bryan's version retains Sangster's notion that the female lead should learn of Meinster's true nature early on. In Bryan's version, Greta (the crazy Meinster nanny) proclaims to Marianne, "You've set free a vampire!" After seeing the Baroness's dead body, Marianne flees Chateau Meinster into the woods.[13] There she spots a mob of angry villagers carrying torches. The reason for their ire is a dead village girl (Meinster apparently works fast). The villagers, upon sighting Marianne, shout, "She's one...catch her!" Marianne flees from the villagers only to run into Meinster, blood dripping down his pronounced fangs. The villagers are terrified by the sight. They drop the dead girl and run while Meinster leans in to bite Marianne. She is saved by the rising sun, heralded by the cock's crow, and so Meinster runs away.

As in the finished film, Marianne is found unconscious in the woods by Van Helsing. He takes her to town in his carriage but leaves her in it as he enters the village tavern. A funeral is being held for the dead girl, and one of the villagers recognizes Marianne from the forest. The villagers, still thinking she is a vampire, chase her away. Van Helsing then comes to her rescue in his carriage, and they ride away to the Lang Academy.

From here, things play out similar to the finished film. Whereas usually gore was trimmed from the script, this film actually added more as it turns out. The sequence where we see Van Helsing stake the Baroness was not to be shown, only the aftermath. For

FANS REMEMBERING SCENES THAT SEEM TO NO LONGER EXIST FROM CERTAIN FILMS ARE NOT UNCOMMON. THE LOST "SPIDER PIT" SEQUENCE FROM *KING KONG* IS PROBABLY THE BEST-KNOWN, AND RAY BRADBURY HIMSELF CLAIMED TO HAVE SEEN IT AT A SCREENING. SIMILARLY, IN *LITTLE SHOPPE OF HORRORS* #14, TED DI PAOLO REMEMBERED A MISSING SCENE FROM *BRIDES OF DRACULA* THAT HE CLAIMED TO HAVE SEEN. DI PAOLO WROTE A LETTER STATING THAT HE REMEMBERED A SCENE OF BARON MEINSTER ATTACKING MARIE DEVEREAUX (THE FIRST VILLAGE GIRL) AND ALSO A SCENE OF THE BARON CONFRONTING THE VILLAGERS AT NIGHT.[LITTLE SHOPPE OF HORRORS #14, PP.8]

whatever reason, they went ahead and filmed it. Actually, they may have filmed it only with the intention of the Japanese version and then left part of it in.

According to Andree Melly, who played Gina, extra footage was shot for the Japanese version. In *Little Shoppe of Horrors* #14, she says,

> On *The Brides of Dracula*, we were often used to shoot two versions of particular parts of scenes, or particular close-ups—one was as per script, and the other was what [Terence Fisher] used to say was for 'the Japanese version,' which indeed I believe it was. At that time, the Japanese liked their horror pictures far more gruesome than the British, and so they used to do a second version.[14]

Melly recalls the Baroness's staking scene as being one of the ones to be extended. "...for the Japanese version, I know they had a far more gory, pumping heart that sort of burst open, or whatever happened to it."[15]

As we all remember, in the film there is a scene where Meinster goes to the Lang Academy to see Marianne. Just as he is about to bite her, Heir Lang interrupts them. Not so in Bryan's script. Here Meinster does bite her, making Marianne similar to Mina Holmwood from *Horror of Dracula*, not a vampire, but something in between. This, of course, is also in following with Sangster's *Disciple of Dracula* script.

Marianne offers to take Meinster to one of her pupils, Gina (a fellow teacher in the film). Meinster attacks Gina and drains her until she's dead. There is no sequence where the vampirized body is guarded in its coffin. The body is merely locked up and placed in the stables. Marianne sneaks in during the night to open the coffin, crooning to the undead Gina that she'll soon have her free to return to their mutual master.

But Marianne is caught in the act by Van Helsing, who appeals to her humanity. He urges her to realize that Meinster is only using her. He then flips open the coffin lid, asking her if she wants to be like Gina. Marianne sobs in Van Helsing's arms and thanks God for sending him to her.

Marianne does her best to resist Meinster when he later shows up outside her window, beckoning her to let him enter. (Like the myths of old, Meinster can't come in unless invited.) Marianne shuts her curtains, and so Meinster appeals to the Langs to let him in. They do, and he kidnaps Marianne, taking her to the windmill where Van Helsing also awaits (yes, he's bitten in this version too).

The original ending is similar to the first draft, with evil destroying evil. This time, Van Helsing performs a ceremony to destroy Meinster and his brides. In essence, the good doctor more or less inherits Dracula's function from Sangster's script, even charging the Baron with the same crimes. Though Dracula caused Meinster to hemorrhage to death in the *Disciple* script, here a golden mist enshrouds Van Helsing as he conjures a swarm of bats from the underworld to kill the vampires![16]

In November, Cushing was sent the script and he disliked it enough to reject it. His main point of contention was the ending. He balked at the idea, saying Van Helsing would not combat evil with evil. "I just thought it made no sense, that Van Helsing is brandishing crucifixes and holy water all through the film, and then, at the climax, he summons the forces of evil...to destroy the vampire," he told Bill Kelley.[17] Much as he had done on the ending of *Horror of Dracula*, Cushing came up with his own choreography for the climax: Van Helsing turning the windmill into a giant crucifix.

As originally scripted, the bats proceed to tear Meinster apart. Meinster was merely to rush out of the windmill—it's not on fire, by the way—into the night. Suddenly, the clouds part and moonbeams illuminate the windmill, casting the shadow of the cross upon Meinster, who perishes in its holy image. The bats fly away, and Marianne reverts to her normal self.[18] Cushing added in the idea that Van Helsing jumps upon the sails and draws them down into the shape of the cross. "I suggested [the idea] to dear Terry Fisher, and he agreed," Cushing told Bill Kelley.[19]

Publicity photo of Yvonne Monlaur as Marianne in *Brides of Dracula*.
© 1960 Hammer Film Productions Ltd.

However, revising the ending alone wasn't enough. Cushing wanted the whole script rewritten! Carreras countered by getting a writer that Cushing admired, playwright Edward Percy, to give the screenplay a minor facelift. Actually, Hinds said that during a meeting between he and Percy, that Percy gave him his new ideas for the script. "I told him they [the ideas] were excellent (they were quite awful) and to get on with [writing] as quickly as possible as we had a studio date."[20]

THE BRIDES OF DRACULA NOVELIZATION BY DEAN OWEN WAS BASED UPON THE EARLIER SHOOTING SCRIPT WRITTEN BY PETER BRYAN. AS SUCH, YOU CAN READ OWEN'S VERSION OF THE ORIGINAL CLIMAX BY WAY OF OWEN. THAT'S NOT ALL. IN OWEN'S VERSION, MARIANNE AND VAN HELSING FALL IN LOVE (AND IN A VERY UN-VAN HELSING-LIKE MOVE, THE TWO HAVE PREMARITAL SEX!). THE BOOK WAS ONE OF SEVERAL SEXED-UP TITLES FROM MONARCH BOOKS WHO ALSO ADDED STEAMY SCENES TO THEIR NOVELIZATIONS OF *REPTILICUS, KONGA* AND *GORGO!*

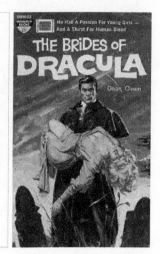

Upon receiving Percy's rewrite, Hinds apparently threw out the new ideas and just kept the bits of dialogue that he knew Cushing would relish. "I left enough of his theatrical bits in to convince Peter it was a rewrite and that's what we used." Among these pieces of dialogue were lines like "[vampirism was] a survival of one of the ancient pagan religions, in their struggle against Christianity." Though Hinds seems to think he pulled one over on Cushing, an interview between Bill Kelley and Cushing shows that Cushing was by no means clueless:

Kelley: What did [Percy] do on *Brides of Dracula*?
Cushing: Not too much in the way of plot, as I recall. He came up with all those great little historical, or atmospheric touches, in the dialogue."[21]

Anyhow, Hinds did one last revision on the script, and seeming to dislike the title of *Brides of Dracula*, retitled it *Dracula II*. Hind's version was completed in January. As Hinds was notorious for doing, he ripped a few pages out of the script. This time it wasn't due to budget or shooting schedules, but for the sake of simplifying the plot. Originally, the idea that Marianne must forget the events of the woods was rather convoluted. By eliminating the woods sequence where Marrianne encounters Meinster as a vampire, Hinds not only made the story easier to follow, but also shortened the shooting schedule and the budget as he liked to do.

The film was a smashing success upon release in July of 1960, and by that Christmas, Universal had already ordered "Dracula 3" from Hammer. The discarded ideas from "Dracula 2", or *Brides of Dracula*, were utilized in 1963's *Kiss of the Vampire*. (announced as "Dracula 3" itself). These two scenes, of course, were the driving of the shovel into the casket and the summoning of the vampire bats to destroy the vampires.

Though *Kiss of the Vampire* is a fine film, it's a shame that there were no more spin-off movies for Cushing as Van Helsing like *Brides of Dracula*.

Chapter Notes

[1] Sangster, *Inside Hammer*, p.111.

[2] http://www.tcm.com/thismonth/article/339818%7C339824/The-Brides-of-Dracula.html

[3] As quoted in "The Making of *Brides of Dracula*," *Little Shoppe of Horrors* #14, p.81.

[4] "Anthony Hinds on The *Brides of Dracula*, *Little Shoppe of Horrors* #14, p.88.

[5] Sangster, *Inside Hammer*, p.62.

[6] In one version of the scene, the driver stops the coach because he sees a dead body in the road. When he finally gets down to remove it, the body is gone! It was a man playing dead to stop the coach, and while the coach driver was dismounting he ran and jumped onto the back of the coach. Something very similar happens in the film, except for the dead body is replaced with a log, though a man still boards the back of the coach. In Brides of Dracula, the character is named Latour, who has gone from the hero to a minor villain that works for the Baroness Meinster.

[7] Sangster, *Inside Hammer*, p.66.

[8] Though I will agree that, like Peter Cushing often argued, that Sangster's dialogue needed some polishing.

[9] Sangster, *Inside Hammer*, p.68.

[10] Ibid, p.69.

[11] Ibid, p.70.

[12] Hammer, it would seem, didn't like this title as they denoted it as a working title only. Furthermore, the shooting script is called "Dracula II."

[13] Though Chateau Meinster is bright and vibrant in the film, Bryan envisioned it as dark and musty, with decaying furniture and the like.

[14] Martinez, "Andree Melly Interview", *Little Shoppe of Horrors* #14, p.89.

[15] Ibid.

[16] Even *Famous Monsters of Filmland* claimed that this was how the picture ended.

[17] Kelley, "Peter Cushing on *The Brides of Dracula*", *Little Shoppe of Horrors* #14, p.85.

[18] The story ends with Marianne reverting to her former self. As to the other two undead brides in the windmill—which didn't catch fire in this version—who knows? Presumably they ceased to exist as vampires upon the death of Meinster.

[19] Kelley, "Peter Cushing on *The Brides of Dracula*", *Little Shoppe of Horrors* #14, p.85.

[20] Ibid.

[21] Ibid, p.86.

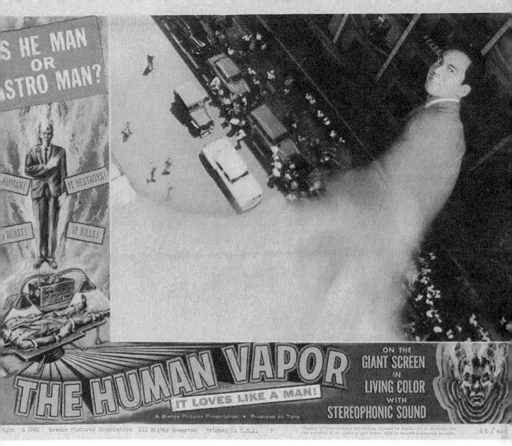

7.
FRANKENSTEIN VS.
THE HUMAN VAPOR

Intended Release Date: 1963
First Draft Date: February 20, 1963

Screenplay by: Shinichi Sekizawa **Proposed Cast/Characters:** Mizuno, the Vapor Man (Yoshio Tsuchiya), Goro Maki [reporter], Fujichiyo [Mizuno's dead lover], Mayumi [Fujichiyo's sister], Michi [Goro's editor], Dr. Gildor [mad scientist], the Frankenstein Monster

PLOT Mizuno, the Gas Human, tracks down a disciple* of Dr. Frankenstein in hopes that he can resurrect his dead love, Fujichiyo...

COMMENTARY To understand this strange little title, some background history is necessary. Shortly after the success of *Godzilla* in November of 1954, Toho studios very quickly greenlit another effects picture called *Invisible Avenger*. It was essentially a Japanese version of *The Invisible Man*, which launched a subgenre of Toho monster movies called the "Transforming Human Series." The next to follow was *The H-Man* in 1958, about people that could transform their bodies into a liquid due to atomic mutation. Next came *The Secret of the Telegian* in 1960, which had a man that could transmit his body electrically. Finally came *The Human Vapor*, also 1960, which had a man who could transform his body into a gaseous state.

This "human vapor" was a meek librarian named Mizuno, who underwent a typical mad scientist procedure to transform himself into a superhuman. Using his new abilities to turn into a gas (which also enables him to fly), Mizuno begins robbing banks. His goals aren't entirely selfish, though. Mizuno is in love with a dancer named Fujichiyo, and the money he's stealing will enable her to give a truly grandiose performance when Mizuno uses the money to rent a theater for her. The police catch onto the relationship between the two and get Fujichiyo in on a plan to rid the world of the Human Vapor. To do so, they will flood the theater with gas and ignite it once everyone but Mizuno is evacuated. In the end, Fujichiyo chooses not to evacuate, and it is she who ignites the gas, destroying herself and Mizuno in a double suicide. The lovers perish as the theater burns down in a tragic but engaging ending... in the Japanese version, at least. Edward Alperson's Brenco Pictures, the U.S. distributor, decided to re-edit the ending so that Mizuno would live! And why would they ruin such a perfect ending? As it turned out, Brenco enjoyed the film so much that they proposed a sequel to Toho.

Supposedly, Alperson approached John Meredith Lucas, a future writer for TV's original *Star Trek*, about writing the sequel. In the tradition of *Frankenstein Meets the Wolf Man*, Lucas's idea was to pit the Human Vapor against the Frankenstein Monster! The idea was given to Toho, who had Shinichi Sekizawa flesh out a full shooting script which was completed in February of 1963. Unfortunately, it's unknown which ideas came from Lucas and which from Sekizawa, but the script is a truly wild ride, especially where the monster is concerned. Far removed from the old Universal films, this script serves up a very different interpretation of the Frankenstein Monster. In a fresh twist, this Frankenstein is fairly well-spoken—for the Monster at least—and has numerous lines of full dialogue. He also partakes in a few action scenes that might take you by surprise.

The script begins late at night in the Frankenstein family cemetery in the United Kingdom. (Yes, yes, we all know that Frankenstein was from Germany, but apparently Sekizawa wasn't aware of this. It's quite possible that he was associating the Frankenstein legend with Great Britain because of Hammer's recent success with the series.) A group of men break into the Frankenstein family mausoleum, and inside they find a mysterious tomb inscribed, "Here lies the Frankenstein Monster sealed here in the name of God." The men open the tomb…

Elsewhere, in a jet airliner that has just landed in Hong Kong, the stewardess is shocked to see a set of empty clothes sitting where a man had sat during the flight. (When Mizuno would turn into his gaseous form in *The Human Vapor*, his clothes would be left behind.) In the case of viewers who had actually seen *The Human Vapor*, this would clue them in to the fact that Mizuno the Vapor Man is in Hong Kong. Meanwhile, Japanese journalist Goro Maki is in Hong Kong on assignment with a co-worker. As the two pull over to the side of the road to remove a piece of wood blocking their way, a strange fog seeps into their red sedan. Moments later, the car takes off—Mizuno has stolen it. Goro walks into the Hong Kong police station at the same time that the stewardess is reporting a missing passenger who disappeared in a cloud of smoke. Another person is at the station to report that her daughter's dead body was stolen…

Inside a laboratory, the dead woman is revealed as the newest experiment of Dr. Gildor, a disciple of Dr. Frankenstein. Dr. Gildor is described as having the traditional mad scientist look with unkempt white hair and a bony face. The Frankenstein Monster is revealed, partially at least, in this same scene. At first, he merely appears to be an overly large man whose feet we glimpse, but never his face. We are clued in to this being the Monster when the camera is directed to emphasize the stitches on his hands. Soon after, the Monster gets a full-body reveal, and apparently Sekizawa envisioned the classic Universal look for the monster, complete with electrodes coming from his neck.

A delivery van with equipment arrives at Gildor's secluded home and is followed by Mizuno in the stolen red sedan. Gildor sends the Monster out to see who the car belongs to. He finds it empty and kicks it over a cliff, which the medicine delivery staff notices from afar. Once back inside, the Monster and Gildor continue their experiment and are successful in reviving the girl... but only for a moment and then she dies again. Soon after, a mysterious figure walks into the laboratory and introduces himself as Mizuno from Japan. Dr. Gildor says that no one may see his lab and live and sends the Monster to kill him. Frankenstein's Monster picks Mizuno up by the neck but Mizuno just laughs and dissolves into his gaseous form.

At the police station, Goro is trying to get in on the investigation of the disappearing man from the plane when employees of the medicine delivery company come in to report seeing a red sedan being demolished. Stating that is his stolen car, Goro and the police are off to Dr. Gildor's house. At Gildor's lab, Mizuno reveals that he wants the doctor's help in resurrecting his dead love, Fujichiyo. Mizuno says he will fund the doctor's experiments if he will. Gildor says he is willing to try but even if he revives her body, her soul is not guaranteed to return. Just as Gildor agrees to accompany Mizuno back to Japan, the police arrive at the house to question Gildor, who refuses to let them enter. Goro, who is riding with the British Hong Kong police, asks about the doctor and the policeman informs him he has heard that Dr. Gildor is obsessed with researching the real-life Dr. Frankenstein.

Later, on his flight back to Japan, Goro unknowingly runs into Mizuno on the plane. Dr. Gildor is also there and below in the baggage hull in a crate is the Monster. Fearing that they may be arrested upon arrival, Mizuno goes below to free the Monster before they land as they fly over Suruga Bay. (What happens next is the script's wildest scene and might come across as either incredibly cool or campy depending upon one's tastes.) Mizuno breaks into the baggage hull to tell the Monster it is time to break free of his crate, which he does. Mizuno then begins to take on his gas form to hide the Monster, which makes some passengers think a tear gas attack is occurring. The Monster then appears in the main passenger cabin and rips off the escape hatch in midair! One of the captains begins shooting at the Monster but hits Dr. Gildor instead, mortally wounding him. Mizuno and the Monster then jump out of the plane wearing parachutes! (A parachuting Frankenstein Monster—an image one either loves or hates.[1]) At the moment that Mizuno and Frankenstein's Monster parachute out the plane, Goro not only snaps a photo, but also catches a photo of Fujichiyo that Mizuno dropped on his way out the door.

Once back in Tokyo, Goro takes the photos to his editor and begins an investigation into who the woman in the photograph is.

One of Mizuno and the Monster's first exchanges occurs in another bizarre scene that has the duo riding together in a station wagon. Mizuno asks the Monster if he can help him bring Fujichiyo back to life even though the Monster is no Dr. Frankenstein. The Monster agrees to try, and off the unlikely duo goes (bizarre as it is, it's an interesting twist on the Frankenstein mythology to even imply that the Monster is smart enough to help recreate his creator's experiments). The true extent of the Monster's intelligence becomes clear when he and Mizuno dig up Fujichiyo's body in the cemetery, and the Monster expresses concerns about how badly burned the body might be. Mizuno then informs him that he used a special preservation chemical on her body when she was buried.

At the same time that Goro figures out the identity of the woman in the photo, Mizuno purchases an observatory to conduct his experiment in. Inside, the Monster stares out the window at an old dead tree that he says reminds him of his resting place. Mizuno looks over Fujichiyo's body and tells her he will see her again soon. The first step in the operation is to repair Fujichiyo's burned face, which the Monster does his best at. However, Mizuno is outraged when he sees the Monster's work on her face and attacks him. While being strangled by Mizuno, the Monster manages to state that the skin grafts may heal later but it will take time, so Mizuno lets up. This scene is rather important, as it makes the Monster the one we are supposed to be rooting for. As it is, Mizuno is nothing but manipulative and abusive towards him. In fact, Mizuno is so one-track-minded and predictable in this script he loses any charm he managed to build up in the previous picture. (In the last film, though misguided, Mizuno was still able to muster a little audience sympathy. In this script, the minute the Monster does something to disappoint him, Mizuno immediately attacks him on several occasions.)

Meanwhile, the police have been contacted by Fujichiyo's younger sister, Mayumi, who says that Fujichiyo's grave has been vandalized recently. Goro, also at the station, shows her the photo he found. The two begin to suspect that Mizuno the Vapor Man may be behind the incident at the grave.

On a lonely road, Mizuno attacks the transport of a blood bank to steal the blood needed for Fujichiyo. The police see this and pursue Mizuno in his jeep. To shake the police, Mizuno grabs the blood in his gas form and floats from the jeep which crashes into a train and explodes. When Mizuno returns to the lab, Fujichiyo's face has been returned to its former beauty through some form of regenerative process known only to the Monster.

Soon after, the script naturally features the perennial Frankenstein lab scene where a lightning storm brings to life a corpse—in this case Fujichiyo. The police, along with Goro, soon arrive at Mizuno's lab just as Fujichiyo is coming back to life. In a bit of a cheat, just as she begins to breathe, Fujichiyo's breathing stops and she immediately dies again. Mizuno shoots the Monster in the chest in his rage, and it drips with black blood. The Monster informs Mizuno that only God can kill him. Then, another freak lightning bolt revives Fujichiyo, who is too overwhelmed with flip-flopping between life and death to recognize Mizuno. As gunfire from the police erupts, Mizuno and the Monster, carrying Fujichiyo, escape out the back door. In a surprise move, the crafty Monster grabs a syringe on his way out and stabs Mizuno in the neck with it. (The chemical compound within it will not allow Mizuno to transform into his gas form.) The Monster picks up Fujichiyo and walks out into the lightning storm, and at one point the lightning strikes the electrodes protruding from his neck in what would have made a fantastic visual. (This was possibly inspired by the opening of Universal's *The Ghost of Frankenstein*.) The Monster eventually sets Fujichiyo down as the police shout at him and he walks off a cliff. The screen would have faded out and the next few scenes would have built to the real conclusion.

The next day, the captured Mizuno is kept sedated in jail while a doctor examines Fujichiyo. Mizuno escapes from his jail cell and makes his way to Fujichiyo. Eventually, while listening to the radio, Fujichiyo gets up and begins to dance, finally beginning to remember her old life. The Monster then unexpectedly breaks into her room and absconds with her. (As it is, the Monster sees her as a kindred spirit having been revived from the dead like him. Presumably, he believes that she wants to return to an eternal slumber with him under the old, dead tree in the swamp that infatuates the Monster throughout the script.) Goro and the police follow the Monster's footprints to the swamp. As the Monster heads for the tree, Goro confronts him, asking the Monster to let him take Fujichiyo away from there. The Monster refuses and then Mizuno shows up. He shoots the monster several times in the chest and then runs up to Fujichiyo, who still does not recognize him. The Monster revives and begins battling Mizuno, dragging him into the swamp. Finally, Fujichiyo recognizes Mizuno and runs after him getting trapped in the swamp's quicksand. In true

Universal Pictures fashion, all three sink into the swamp as Goro looks on, unable to do anything to help. Finally, in their last moments, Mizuno and Fujichiyo join hands as they sink into the quicksand to their doom.

The film was announced by Toho in May of 1963 and then never materialized. Overall, it's better this script wasn't adapted for several reasons. It undermines the ending of *The Human Vapor*, for one, and also demolishes the character of Mizuno. Furthermore, Mizuno spends a great deal of time trying to revive Fujichiyo, who only regains her consciousness moments before she dies along with Mizuno and the picture ends—basically an inferior repeat of the last film. The other reason fans are fortunate that this wasn't made is that if it was, Toho might never have produced *Frankenstein Conquers the World* in 1965, which infamously featured a giant version of the Frankenstein Monster.

Chapter Notes

---

[1] Since Mizuno can effectively fly, it may have been less silly to have him do so while the monster simply jumps into the water rather than both wearing parachutes.

8.
CURSE OF THE
(MONSTER) MUMMY'S TOMB

Developed: 1964

Treatment by: Michael Carreras (as Henry Younger)

PLOT A giant mummy is unearthed and goes on a rampage through Cairo...

COMMENTARY Hammer, like Universal, eventually got around to making several Mummy films. Actually, Universal themselves requested that Hammer remake their Mummy movies. As the original *Mummy* from 1932 was light on actual Mummy action, the sequels, beginning with 1940's *The Mummy's Tomb,* were used as the story basis for Hammer's 1959 *Mummy* movie.

Unlike Universal, however, Hammer did not carry over the character of Kharis into subsequent mummy sequels, instead choosing to focus on a new mummy every time.[1] And indeed, the first new mummy would be very different!

Hammer's first Mummy sequel, *Curse of the Mummy's Tomb,* was shopped to Universal in mid-1963. Universal passed, and one has to wonder if it's because of the story's initial plot. Apparently, the mummy was to be of the giant variety!

According to *Famous Monsters of Filmland,* the plot was as follows:

> A group of archaeologists on a routine expedition into the Sahara desert... Discover an ancient tomb containing the mummy of a pharaoh. Dabbling in things they don't understand, they bring to life a monstrous twenty-foot giant that goes on a murder rampage in Cairo. When the gigantic Creature escapes into the desert, aircraft and parachute troops go in pursuit. All hell breaks loose in a shattering climax.

A pre-production poster even existed for the film—a common practice at Hammer—which showed the gigantic mummy with the girl in hand.

90

5,000 YEAR-OLD MONSTER ON THE RAMPAGE!

COLUMBIA PICTURES presents A HAMMER FILMS Production

THE CURSE OF THE MUMMY'S TOMB

TERENCE MORGAN
FRED CLARK
RONALD HOWARD
JEANNE ROLAND

HENRY YOUNGER · BILL WILL · MICHAEL CARRERAS
TECHNISCOPE and TECHNICOLOR

Michael Carreras liked the concept poster of the giant mummy so much that he used it for the final release! Curse of the Mummy's Tomb © 1964 Hammer Film Productions Ltd.

And for anyone still thinking this may have been a rumor based upon the poster or false reporting on the part of *Famous Monsters*, this isn't the case. James Carreras himself told the press, "There's no holding Hammer!... One of Hammer's most successful horrific's a few years ago was *The Mummy*. A sequel was almost inevitable. Now it is coming in *The Curse of the Mummy's Tomb*, the terrifying story of a gigantic mummy, 3000 years old, which comes to life and terrorizes the Nile Valley."

When it came down to it, the mummy was downscaled back to human size, and Columbia ended up being the film's producer. Actually, Columbia was to blame for the downsize. As they considered Terrence Fisher's production of *The Gorgon* to be the top-billed feature of the proposed double bill, *Curse of the Mummy's Tomb* would be the supporting feature. As such, the latter film's budget was cut significantly. When that was decided, there was no longer enough money to do on-location shooting in Cairo, Egypt—not to mention build the needed miniature model of Cairo for the Mummy to stomp. Writing under the name of Henry Younger (an in-joke referring to Anthony Hinds' pen name of John Elder), Michael Carreras himself quickly rewrote the film along with Alvin Rakoff, a television and film director. In the end,

91

The scene of the Mummy being captured in a giant net might have been a remnant from the original treatment. Curse of the Mummy's Tomb © 1964 Hammer Film Productions Ltd.

Carreras ended up directing the film as well, which was budgeted at 103,000 pounds. Shooting took place at ABPC Elstree Studios starting on February 24, 1964, and it's unknown how much of the original story remained in the finished film. The showman character of Alexander King is rather like *King Kong's* Carl Denham, so one has to wonder if King was in the treatment with the 20-foot mummy? In watching the completed *Curse of the Mummy's Tomb*, it would seem a few vestiges of the giant mummy idea remained. For instance, the Denham-like King was introduced to the audience playing with a monkey, which, if descended from the original treatment, might have been a nod to *King Kong*. Furthermore, King is an American rather than a Brit.

Later in the film, King hosts a special premier to unveil the mummy that is also quite similar to Denham's reveal of Kong. King gives a brief showman's speech about finding the mummy and also makes sure to spotlight the expedition's "beauty," Annette. There's also a very notable shot in the film where the hero observes the mummy's hand quietly emerging from behind a curtain, which very much calls to mind Kong's hand reaching into Ann's apartment in *King Kong*. (Perhaps Carreras still had Kong on the brain during the directing?) Another scene that seems like it might have been adapted from the treatment has the heroes trying to capture the mummy in a large net. The biggest carryover from the treatment was likely the mummy's breathing, which does indeed sound like it belongs to a giant (it sounds like a subway vent).

Had Hammer gone along with their original plan, it's tough to say whether or not the film would've been a huge hit. But one thing's for certain, if it had been made, we'd all still be talking about Hammer's giant mummy to this day!

Chapter Notes

---

[1] Another reason for this is because, technically, Universal owned the rights to Kharis, the mummy, as he was a Universal creation. As such, Hammer had to give their mummies new names as their *Mummy* sequels all had different distributers.

9.
GODZILLA VS. FRANKENSTEIN

Developmental Period: 1963-1964
Draft Date: July 3, 1964

Treatment by: Jerry Sohl **Screenplay by:** Kaoru Mabuchi **Proposed Cast/Characters:** Dr. James Bowen [scientist], Suehiko/Sueko [Bowen's assistant], Kawaii [ship commander], Kawaji [scientist] **Proposed Monsters:** Godzilla, Frankenstein

PLOT When Godzilla returns to Japan, he's opposed by a giant version of the Frankenstein monster...

COMMENTARY After missing out on fighting King Kong and the Human Vapor in Japan, perhaps it should come as no surprise that Frankenstein also almost fought Godzilla. And, while Toho's last two near-misses with the Frankenstein monster probably influenced the idea, more than anything, it was the monumental success of *King Kong vs. Godzilla* that inspired the bout with Frankenstein. As it was, the 1962 film was the biggest hit Toho had ever had, and so the idea of pitting Godzilla against another famous monster seemed like a no-brainer. And the best thing of all: Frankenstein was in the public domain, which meant Toho wouldn't owe anyone a hefty rights fee to use the monster. The only question was, how to make the monster gigantic?

The rather ingenious—though others might say ludicrous—idea was that the Frankenstein monster's heart was transported to Hiroshima, Japan, for research purposes during the waning days of WWII. There the heart was blasted with radiation upon the dropping of the Atomic Bomb. And, for this reason, the heart mutated into a giant monster... which later defends the country against Godzilla.

If this whole synopsis sounded similar to 1965's *Frankenstein Conquers the World*, that's because *Godzilla vs. Frankenstein* served as the basis for that film. Oddly, Toho's production partner, United Productions of America, felt that Godzilla distracted too much from Frankenstein and requested that a new monster that eats people replace Godzilla. The underground burrowing monster

Baragon was created, and the film was shot in Japan as *Frankenstein vs. Underground Monster Baragon*. In the film, after the peaceful Frankenstein monster escapes from the lab, the underground monster Baragon shows up and begins eating people. Frankenstein is wrongly accused of Baragon's feast of human flesh, and so the military vows to destroy him. In the end, Frankenstein clears his name by battling Baragon. Though Frankenstein kills the beast, he sinks into a hole in the ground made by Baragon and is never seen again. For the most part, the film is very similar to *Godzilla vs. Frankenstein* aside from a few key differences which we will soon discuss.

But, before we examine the story, it's important to note that the origins of *Godzilla vs. Frankenstein* are quite nebulous. It's possible that either Toho commissioned an American writer to come up with a story, or that an American writer pitched the story to Toho on their own. What we know for certain is that future *Star Trek* writer Jerry Sohl wrote a treatment entitled *Godzilla vs. Frankenstein*, which this author has read. Sohl's *Godzilla vs. Frankenstein* treatment was then revised by Toho writer Kaoru Mabuchi into a full shooting script.

Sohl's 17-page treatment is similar to Toho's later script, *Frankenstein vs. Godzilla* (yes, the names are flipped between Sohl's version and Toho's). It begins similarly to the completed *Frankenstein Conquers the World* during the final days of WWII. As U.S. forces (seen crossing the Rhine River Bridge in Germany) advance on a secret Nazi Laboratory, the still-beating heart of the Frankenstein monster is whisked away by the Nazis. It sounds quite similar to the finished film, with Sohl writing,

> Deep within the confines of the structure, where it has been kept for years, beats the heart of Frankenstein's monster. It is in a glass case two feet on each side, pulsating in its salt solution, triggered by long-life batteries contained in a section beneath the enclosure. It is alive, throbbing with rhythmic life as it has for years, waiting for the time when scientists could utilize it in a secret project. But the preparation for war, and then the war itself, has halted the proposed experiments.

The heart is loaded onto a truck at night, and soon after we find ourselves out at sea where a Nazi submarine hands the heart off to a Japanese military sub. Soon after, we transition to Hiroshima. There the heart is delivered not to a hospital but a secret Japanese lab hidden within a cave on the outskirts of Hiroshima. Sohl's version of this sequence is more elaborate than the one in *Frankenstein Conquers the World*, as he wrote a scene set on Tinian Island, showing the U.S. army boarding the *Enola Gay*. Among those boarding an observation plane to follow the *Enola Gay* is none other than a young James Bowen (the main character portrayed by Nick Adams in *Frankenstein Conquers the World*). Notably Sohl emphasizes Bowen by having him react in shock at the dropping of the bomb. In the secret lab, an "unholy light illuminates the laboratory" as the scientists turn to watch the explosion. The glass case containing the heart shatters against the wall. As we pan across the death and destruction, the heart, still for a moment, resumes its beating and begins to move...

Actually, that is not the last we see of the heart. After cutting to Bowen's still shocked reaction aboard the plane, we return to the cave to find a slug-like trail in the heart's wake. It has moved across the floor and is developing into a fetus-like shape with legs and arms. Therefore, in Sohl's mind, the heart regenerated into the body, whereas in the finished film it is implied that a starving orphan may have eaten it. Sohl writes, "The heart occupies the entire screen. In a lap dissolve, we see it subtly altered into a vague fetus-like heart with the semblance of a head, legs and arms."

Following this is another lap dissolve meant to show the passage of time similar to a shot in the finished film. In a grotesque scene, we return to the heart/fetus, which grabs a mouse and then eats it!

We soon are reintroduced to Dr. James Bowen, who studies the effects of radiation on the bomb survivors at a clinic in Hiroshima. Dr. Suehiko Yoshi enters the clinic and chides Bowen for working inside on such a nice, sunny day. She soon manages to convince him to go on a picnic with her. As she waits on him, she turns her attention to the television, where a news report confirms that Godzilla has been discovered hibernating in the Kurile Trench. A recommendation is issued that boats bypass the area, lest their sonar or other sounds awaken the monster. On their picnic, Bowen tells Sueko that "if little-used radiation at the short end of the electromagnetic spectrum is utilized in the right way, he could impart life into dead cells, such as one of his forebears, Dr. Victor Frankenstein, did many years ago in Bavaria." The duo also just happens to be picnicking in front of the secret cave lab from earlier in the treatment, meaning this is a forbearer to the scene where Bowen and Sueko find Frankenstein in a random cave in the final

Old blurb from *Castle of Frankenstein* magazine, illustrating the many pre-release titles attached to *Frankenstein Conquers the World,* such as "Frankenstein vs. the Giant Devil Fish".

film. A screaming child alerts them to the monster's presence. This iteration of Frankenstein is revealed clawing his way out of a hole, and Bowen recognizes the monster as something he has seen in his dreams (if Sohl is trying to imply that Bowen had a premonition about the creature is unknown).

From the following description, one could assume that Sohl wanted the monster to look precisely like the Universal Frankenstein: "...we see enough to know that the heart has grown/regenerated itself into the monster that once was and is again." Unlike the film, Bowen immediately identifies the monster as Frankenstein, as he heard rumors of the heart being brought to Hiroshima before the bomb was dropped. Bowen also makes clear that the radiation has altered the heart in some way, though this is never implied in the film. Frankenstein also takes a dislike to Bowen because he associates him with Dr. Frankenstein (if Sohl is trying to imply that Bowen is a descendant of Dr. Frankenstein isn't clear, either).

Sue takes care of the five-foot-tall Frankenstein, who quickly reaches eight feet in height within a few days. Bowen then wonders, when will the monster stop growing? This question is what motivates the rest of the story, and is even covered in the news (in the finished film, not much is made of the monster in the news, but this treatment would have emphasized the stir the monster causes worldwide). Bowen then orders a shortening of the monster's rations, which prompts him to break out of his cell and terrorize a zoo in search of food. (There is no scene of him fighting off guards or going to Sue's apartment in this treatment). Sohl even describes the monster as breaking into cages and eating the animals on site!

Fear grips the world, especially Japan, as to just how big the monster will get. Dr. Bowen is asked if the monster might eat humans, to which Bowen responds no, but the world isn't satisfied

97

with his answer. Next up is a montage of the military confronting the monster, with bullets causing no real harm as the wounds immediately heal. Sohl also scripts a scene where a passing train runs over the monster's leg (remember, he's not Godzilla-sized yet) and cuts it off. In Sohl's treatment, we watch the leg grow back before our very eyes.

It is at the point that the monster reaches 12 feet in height that the Japanese Government gets the "bright idea" to revive the much more destructive Godzilla to squash Frankenstein. (One could apply some logic behind their idea assuming the fear is that the monster will grow larger than Godzilla, hence the monster squashing Frankenstein sooner rather than later.) The plan is to use sonar and other sound devices to awaken Godzilla and then guide the angry kaiju to Frankenstein's vicinity, where he can "make short work of him."

Submarines, planes, and ships are sent out to agitate Godzilla, and Sohl envisioned the monster chasing and then catching a submarine. Following this, Godzilla would rise from the depths and roast the planes and boats with his atomic ray. Meanwhile, Bowen implements a more peaceful plan to keep Frankenstein in place away from populated areas by shipping him a steady supply of animals to eat. In a somewhat incredulous scene, Godzilla is lured to Frankenstein's area by a jeep loaded with "sound devices known to enrage the monster." The vehicle comes across a twenty-foot-tall Frankenstein, asleep on the road, and must come to a halt. Godzilla then destroys the jeep, which awakens Frankenstein, though the monster doesn't try to fight the much bigger beast, and simply wanders off.

Frankenstein, who only ran away because he was looking for food, heads to a city. Godzilla, incensed the smaller monster ran from him, follows. In a scene that predates a similar sequence from *King Kong Escapes* (1967), Sue runs to intercept Frankenstein before he enters the city. Like Kong, Frankenstein picks Sue up and then runs off with her. Bowen must be restrained as he watches Frankenstein abscond with his lady love. Bowen then wonders aloud that if Frankenstein were to be torn apart, would his body then regenerate into multiple Frankensteins?

In the woods, Frankenstein's hunger pangs get the best of him. He digs a cliff-side cave for Sue, places her in it, and then goes off in search of food as his growth spurt continues (last we heard, the monster was now as tall as a two-story house). Godzilla soon comes upon the scene and, like the T-rex in *King Kong*, spies Sue in her cave and approaches. Frankenstein, described as having grown again but not being as big as Godzilla, comes to the rescue and the climactic battle is on:

> Sue watches the battle of the behemoths, the ground trembling as they go at each other, their fight creating deep fissures in the earth shaking below them. It is a tremendous battle, up and down the terrain, near the sea, then inland, knocking over buildings, power lines, antennae, falling into lakes, streams. Every time Frankenstein gets hurt, his cells quickly regenerate the injured part. Godzilla cries out his rage at this thing that can't be killed. The cry echoes throughout the land.

The battle rages up to the summit of an unnamed volcano, which erupts due to the earth tremors. Frankenstein falls inside, his body consumed by the lava (therefore Bowen's fear of multiple Frankensteins is quashed). The lava spray knocks Godzilla backward until he tumbles down the volcano and into the sea. In an epilogue, Bowen continues his research with Sue. He now believes he can cure radiation cancer and other ailments due to the monster's regenerative properties. However, he must find a way to do so without the endless duplication of Frankenstein; otherwise, Frankensteins could overrun the world.

Mabuchi's full screenplay is much closer to *Frankenstein Conquers the World,* with the first 36 scenes being more or less identical aside from small differences. (And, to reiterate, *Godzilla vs. Frankenstein* is fairly structurally similar to *Frankenstein Conquers the World* itself, so there's no need for a recap.) In this version, Godzilla is frozen inside of an iceberg, which the Japanese government eventually frees him from to fight Frankenstein. Godzilla is then lured to the mainland with flares.

At the same time, Bowen, Sueko, and another doctor, Kawaji, have taken a trip to Mt. Fuji to see Frankenstein, the goal being to take a photograph of the monster before he is destroyed by Godzilla. While Sueko sits in the car as Bowen and Kawaji wander outside, Frankenstein picks up the car and tips it over so that she falls into his hand. From here, we cut to Godzilla following a whole fleet of ships to Japan. The fleet makes landfall that evening with the Big G in hot pursuit. When fireworks fail to distract the monster, a giant 'heat ray' light tower is then used to agitate Godzilla onto the shore. When Godzilla reaches the tower, that light is shut off and the next one is then activated.

Cover of *Famous Monsters of Filmland* with *Frankenstein Conquers the World* as the cover story.

This process continues ad-nauseam until Frankenstein appears to destroy one of the towers. However, as in Sohl's treatment, the two monsters don't begin to fight. Instead, they eye each other in the eerie light created by the military flares and then suddenly disappear. The next morning Bowen informs the military that Frankenstein has Sueko, who he does not believe will be harmed by the monster. He also reiterates the need to collect a sample of Frankenstein's cells.

Soon after, we get to the end battle, which is very similar to the one from *King Kong vs. Godzilla* in terms of tone and maneuvers. It all begins when Godzilla climbs a mountain and discovers Frankenstein above him. Frankenstein throws a boulder into Godzilla's chest, enraging him, and the chase is on. Frankenstein has run ahead of Godzilla to clear the opening of a makeshift cave. Sueko is inside, and Frankenstein motions for her to go free because Godzilla is coming. As Godzilla approaches he is caught in a landslide and falls down the mountain. At the bottom, he is buried in the avalanche up to his chest. Frankenstein then taunts him by laughing! Enraged, Godzilla frees himself only to have Frankenstein leap onto him. When Godzilla tries to bite Frankenstein, he stuffs a rock in Godzilla's mouth. Once Godzilla dislodges it, he blasts Frankenstein with his ray, causing his hair to catch fire. Frankenstein then does his best to put out the flames with sand and then goes to hide behind a giant rock. When Godzilla comes to investigate, the monster has disappeared. Enraged, Godzilla rips the rock from the ground revealing a volcanic fissure beneath it.

Here we cut back to military HQ, where Bowen insists on going out to look for Sueko. In some striking imagery, we cut to Mt. Fuji at sunset and then to a shot of Godzilla's silhouette in front of a background of deep red clouds. Next up, we cut to Sueko lost and afraid in the forest, but soon we return to the monsters. Godzilla has fallen into a hole, possibly dug for him by Frankenstein. Some classic boulder tossing ensues, and eventually, Frankenstein runs off as the shaft begins to steam—more fore-shadowing of the impending eruption.

In a wild scene, Godzilla spots Sueko amidst the volcanic forest and picks her up! The monster then sniffs her as though preparing to eat her until Frankenstein shows up. He bites Godzilla on the hand, causing him to drop Sueko, while Godzilla bites Frankenstein on the jaw. As in the finished film with Baragon, Frankenstein judo-throws Godzilla at one point as well. Godzilla

101

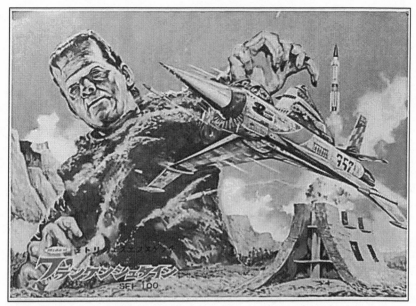

Old Japanese illustration depicting a giant version of the monster as he appeared in *Son of Frankenstein.*

soon blasts the forest, setting it afire just as Baragon does in the finished film. Bowen and Kawaji take Sueko away back to military HQ. Soon after, the ground shakes: Mt. Fuji is erupting! Godzilla and Frankenstein take their battle all the way up to the crater. Unlike Sohl's treatment, Frankenstein doesn't fall into the crater. He is swept off his feet and buried under a current of hot lava. Godzilla then falls down the mountain until he splashes into a raging river (of water). The final shot was to be of the erupting Mt. Fuji.

As stated before, Toho's production partner UPA asked that Godzilla be removed, which might've been for the best. As it was, Godzilla had recently become a hero in *Ghidorah, the Three-Headed Monster* (1964), and his villainous role in *Godzilla vs. Frankenstein* no longer worked.

In summary, *Frankenstein vs. Godzilla* makes for an intriguing title but was another film that was perhaps best left unproduced. Furthermore, *Frankenstein Conquers the World* is a much better version of the script.

10.
BATMAN FIGHTS DRACULA
A LOST FILIPINO HORROR

Released: June 3, 1967

(Lea Productions/Fidelis Productions)

Directed by: Leody M. Diaz **Screenplay by:** Bert R. Mendoza **Cast/Characters:** Jing Abalos (Batman/Bruce Wayne) Ramon d'Salva (Dr. Zerba) Vivian Lorrain (Marita Banzon) Nort Nepomuceno (Turko) Dante Rivero (Dracula) Rolan Robles (Ruben)

Academy Aspect, Eastmancolor, runtime unknown

PLOT A mad scientist uses Dracula to fight Batman...

COMMENTARY Though Batman and Dracula have tangled in animated movies like *Batman vs. Dracula* (2005), in an unauthorized production from the Philippines, they fought in live-action. One of the most sought-after lost Asian films of all time, *Batman Fights Dracula* is exactly what it sounds like. Directed by Leody M. Diaz,[1] the film presents a simple story—Batman Fights Dracula—in a rather comical fashion, perhaps copying the popular Adam West Batman series of the time. Though no footage of this lost film has ever surfaced, a bevy of advertising materials have at least been found, which help to fill in the blanks.

Even though they ripped off Batman for the movie, they apparently didn't want to touch any of the typical villains like Penguin or the Joker and so created their own: Dr. Zorba. In addition to being a mad scientist, Dr. Zorba is also a smuggler whose smuggling attempts have been foiled by Batman one too many times. Therefore Zorba and his henchman, Turko, come up with the brilliant idea to revive Dracula with electricity as though he were the Frankenstein monster. This results in a super-powered improved Dracula now impervious to crucifixes. Also, Dracula is easily controlled by Zorba...somehow. (Remember, not much is known of the production.)

103

Zorba operates out of a hidden underground lab located under a cemetery. Every so often, Dracula ventures out from the cemetery to drink human blood, which is apparently how the dynamic duo tracks him. Batman and Ruben (yes, that is this story's version of Robin) team up with a beautiful woman named Marita, the daughter of Dr. Banzon. Specifically, Marita helps the dynamic duo solve some sort of mystery involving Dr. Zorba's ultra-ray sunglasses. Marita is eventually kidnapped, and so Batman and Robin have to storm Zorba's lab. With Marita's help, they manage to turn Dracula against Dr. Zorba, who is killed by his vampire pawn. And that, unfortunately, is all we know.

As for surviving stills, at least one shot shows Batman and Dracula fighting in a cemetery, while the rest are typical fare for both characters: Dracula in his coffin, Batman using a grappling hook, etc.

Over the years, brave researchers have tried to find the film to no avail. The production companies involved no longer exist, many of the cast and crew are dead, and those that are still alive have no copies of the film, nor do they know where to look for one.

Chapter Notes

---

[1] Leody M. Diaz directed over eight films total, the best known of which was *The Bionic Boy*, about the wounded son of an Interpol agent who is given bionic powers and uses them to take revenge.

HAMMER ON TV

EVIL OF FRANKENSTEIN (1964)

Broadcast Date: January 2, 1968

Directed by: Freddie Francis **Screenplay by:** Anthony Hinds (as John Elder) based on a story by Peter Bryan **Special Effects by:** Les Bowie & Roy Ashton (makeup) **Music by:** Don Banks **Cast:** Peter Cushing (Baron Frankenstein), Peter Woodthorpe (Zoltan), Sandor Elès (Hans), Katy Wild (beggar girl), David Hutcheson (Burgomaster), Duncan Lamont (Chief of Police), Kiwi Kingston (the Monster)

Spherical, Eastmancolor,
84 Minutes (theatrical)
/96 Minutes (television)

In the late 1960s, three of Hammer's most prominent Universal horror films were picked up for broadcast on NBC. However, to be suitable for broadcast, certain scenes had to be edited out, making the films' runtimes shorter. To work around this, Universal actually shot new footage for the films years later so that they could fill a two-hour time slot.

On January 14, 1966, Universal filmed four new scenes to pad out *Evil of Frankenstein's* runtime. (At 96 minutes, that allowed for 24 minutes of commercials.) This version of the film premiered on January 2, 1968, almost two years after the new footage had been shot and four years after the film itself was in theaters.

The first thing one might notice about the TV version is that it changes the opening credits. Rather than having them roll over the Baron doing an operation, they are simply superimposed over a still background of the lab. Our first added scene occurs as we watch the mute girl begging in the streets. A reporter is watching her from within a doctor's office. Eventually, in walks the doctor and the duo have a discussion pertaining to the pre-credits scene, where a wood cutter's body was stolen. The reporter somehow knows that Baron Frankenstein took it but doesn't reveal how he knows this. The reporter then laments to the doctor that he wishes he had more time to stay and investigate, but he doesn't. As he walks outside, he sees some bullies harassing the mute girl, but the doctor stops him from intervening. He tells him that it would only offend the poor girl, here named Rena (she has no name in the film).

The doctor then proceeds to give the reporter the girl's backstory that she suddenly went deaf and mute at the age of seven. The scene ends, and this is the last we see of the reporter, as it turns out, so the TV cut certainly sets up some false expectations there. Fans will no doubt recall that *Evil of Frankenstein* has a lengthy, dragging flashback scene of Frankenstein creating the monster. It's even longer in the TV version, as it portrays seven-year-old Rena having a run-in with the monster in the woods. It comes across her as she's sitting in the forest playing with a doll. It doesn't do anything but walk by her and she screams and runs away back to her parents. To their shock, she can no longer speak. As for another detail, Rena's father is the owner of the sheep that we see slaughtered in the film. (As to those no doubt wondering, no, there really isn't any new monster footage. All we see of the monster are its shuffling feet, no headshots.)

While all this backstory is certainly interesting, it makes little sense in the context of the real film. The mute girl is nothing but affectionate towards the monster in the movie itself. If it caused her so much terror as a child, then it would seem odd for her to befriend it. But, back to the new scenes, after the monster falls off a cliff in the flashback, we were to cut to the doctor (from the earlier scene with the reporter) examining Rena, unable to explain how she went deaf and mute or how to help her. Our next and last new scene takes place 45 minutes into the film. It occurs after Hans and the Baron depart the carnival. In the scene, the doctor goes to see Rena's father, Johan, now a useless drunk (and presumably the reason why Rena has to beg for food). His wife had died long ago, and he says he rarely sees Rena anymore and that she spends most of her time in the mountains. As stated, this is the last we see of the doctor and Johan, leaving TV viewers to both ponder their fate and their presence in the story in general.

Evil of Frankenstein © 1964 Hammer Film Productions Ltd.

KISS OF THE VAMPIRE/KISS OF EVIL

Broadcast Date:
1966

Directed by: Don Sharp & Irving J. Moore (new footage) **Screenplay by:** Anthony Hinds (as John Elder) **Special Effects by:** Les Bowie **Music by:** James Bernard **Cast:** Clifford Evans (Professor Zimmer), Edward de Souza (Gerald Harcourt), Jennifer Daniel (Marianne Harcourt), Noel Willman (Dr. Ravna), Barry Warren (Carl Ravna), Jacquie Wallis (Sabena Ravna), Added Cast: Carl Esmond (Otto), Virginia Gregg (Rosa), Sheila Wells (Theresa), Horst Ebersberg (Anton), Walter Friedel (coachman)

Spherical, Eastmancolor,
88 Minutes (theatrical)/
92 Minutes (television)

In the case of *Kiss of the Vampire*, it was retitled *Kiss of Evil* and was broadcast in 1966. As opposed to *Evil of Frankenstein*, more production background exists on *Kiss's* TV cut, which credits Los Angeles TV veteran Irving J. Moore as the director. The new subplot for this version focuses on a family in the village with minor ties to Dr. Ravna's vampire cult. Specifically, the mother,

109

Rosa, is Dr. Ravna's robe maker! Her husband, Otto, is a shopkeeper, and her daughter, Theresa, desperately wants to attend the ball (no, she doesn't realize they are all vampires, though it might be more interesting if she did). Rounding out the new characters are Theresa's boyfriend, Anton, and Dr. Ravna's coachman (notably, an effort is made to match the wardrobe of the same character from the film). As it was, *Kiss of the Vampire* had more gore to trim than *Evil of Frankenstein*. As such, *Kiss of Evil* doesn't feature many of the more vivid shots, like the shovel driven into the coffin, Gerald making a cross on his shoulder out of smeared blood, etc. Unfortunately, most of the end scenes with the bats are cut because of the blood. To compromise, new stock shots of bats were added during the scene's buildup. What happens in the chateau had to be left to TV viewers' imaginations, and all that's seen is the less bloody aftermath.

This version is at least better at inserting the new characters into the proceedings. For instance, Otto and Rosa attend the opening funeral scene (via them, we also learn that Professor Zimmer's first name is Ernst). As a gift for making the robes, Carl Ravna sends the family a music box as well, which also means new music cues were composed for this version. And whereas *Evil of Frankenstein's* new characters disappeared once they had filled the necessary screen time, *Kiss of Evil* has a new epilogue showing the village as a much happier place now that they are rid of the Ravnas.

PHANTOM OF THE OPERA

Broadcast Date:
Mid-1960s

Directed by: Terence Fisher **Screenplay by:** Anthony Hinds (as John Elder) based on the book by Gaston Leroux **Special Effects by:** Brian Johnson & Roy Ashton (makeup) **Music by:** Edwin Astley **Cast:** Herbert Lorn (Professor Petrie/The Phantom), Heather Sears (Christine Charles), Edward de Souza (Harry Hunter), Thorley Walters (Lattimer), Michael Gough (Lord Ambrose D'Arcy), Added Cast: Liam Redmond (Ward), John Maddison (Dawson)

Spherical, Eastmancolor,
84 Minutes (theatrical)/
96 Minutes (television)

110

Lastly, there is the TV cut of *Phantom of the Opera*, which boosted the film's runtime from 84 minutes to 96 minutes! The subplot for this version centered around a pair of Scotland Yard inspectors named Ward and Dawson investigating the Phantom. The excruciating new scenes mostly just bashed viewers over the head by regurgitating plot details they already knew as the investigators discussed the goings-on.

Ultimately, these versions will only appeal to film historians and the most die-hard of Hammer aficionados. Though they were lost for a time after their broadcasts, they made their way online eventually. All three versions accompany their respective films' Blu-Ray releases from SCREAM Factory if one is interested in seeing them in full.

LA FURIA DEL HOMBRE LOBO

con
**PAUL NASCHY
PERLA CRISTAL
MICHAEL RIVERS
MARK STEVENS
VERONICA LUJAN**

DIRECTOR **JOSE Mª ZABALZA**
EASTMANCOLOR TECHNISCOPE

11.
NIGHTS OF THE WEREWOLF
PAUL NASCHY'S LOST WEREWOLF MOVIE

Release Date: 1968 (alleged)

Directed by: Rene Govar **Makeup by:** Paul Naschy **Cast:** Paul Naschy, Peter Beaumont, and Monique Brainville

Runtime Unknown

PLOT A professor manipulates his werewolf student to commit acts of vengeance on his behalf...

COMMENTARY Paul Naschy bears the unusual distinction of having been compared to both Lon Chaney Sr. and Jr., plus Roger Corman—odd bedfellows for comparisons to say the least. This is because Naschy had some serious makeup skills for the limited, Corman-sized budgets he had to work with. In his lifetime, the Spanish filmmaker appeared in hundreds of movies and produced many horror films of his own. Naschy's most famous films consisted of a dozen werewolf movies to star himself as the character Count Waldemar Daninsky. (Incredibly, he produced these films between 1968 and 2004!) The series debuted in 1968, with the 3-D horror *La Marca del Hombre Lobo* (*The Mark of the Wolfman*). Continuing the slightly heroic evolution of Larry Talbot, Naschy's Count Daninsky was a nobleman bitten by a werewolf, who then uses his werewolf abilities to fight evil vampires and another werewolf in the first film. The loosely connected series would get more far out with each entry, such as the third film, *Los Monstruos del Terror* (1970, AKA *Dracula vs. Frankenstein*). In it, aliens revive Frankenstein's monster, a mummy, a vampire, and Count Daninsky's werewolf to take over the world only to have the werewolf turn the tables on the aliens and fight the other monsters.

The second film in the series is lost—or believed to be lost as a few film scholars seem to doubt its existence. It was supposedly shot in 1968 and titled *Las Noches del Hombre-Lobo* (*Nights of the*

Alleged still from *Night of the Werewolf,* **though it could actually be from** *Fury of the Wolfman.*

Werewolf/Nights of the Wolfman). Allegedly the story had a professor character learn that one of his students suffers from lycanthropy and then pretends to help him. I say pretends because really he manipulates his abilities for nefarious ends via soundwaves. Under this sound control method, he uses the werewolf to get revenge on people who have wronged him, and that's all we know.

However, this plot sounds suspiciously similar to Naschy's 1970 film *La Furia del Hombre Lobo (The Fury of the Wolfman).* It is for this and several other reasons that some think *Nights of the Werewolf* never existed to begin with. However, Naschy insisted for years that his script for the film was actually shot, claiming in interviews that filming was done in Paris. During shooting, director Rene Govar was killed in a car crash one week after the print was sent off to the lab for processing. Because no one paid the negative costs, the lab held onto the footage as collateral. Unfortunately, they eventually misplaced it or discarded it altogether. More dubious than that, the actors that Naschy cited as appearing in the film, Peter Beaumont and Monique Brainville, apparently don't exist! Nor could Naschy ever recall the names of any of the other actors that appeared. Even the alleged French director of the project has no credits to his name. This is why some think the film never existed to begin with, theorizing that Naschy made it up early in his career to boost his resume. But that said, Naschy insisted that it existed until the day he died. Until the film is actually found, it looks like the adventures of Count Waldemar Daninsky will remain just one entry shy of a baker's dozen.

12.
DRACULA'S FEAST
OF BLOOD

Developed: March 1969

Screenplay by: Kevin Francis **Proposed Cast/Characters:** Dracula (Christopher Lee), Van Helsing (Peter Cushing), Dr. Seward [head of asylum], Renfield [asylum inmate]

PLOT Dracula returns to plague Van Helsing in London...

COMMENTARY After 1968's *Dracula Has Risen from the Grave*, and before 1970's *Taste the Blood of Dracula*, there was *Dracula's Feast of Blood*. It was submitted to Hammer by none other than *Grave* director Freddie Francis's son, Kevin Francis. Dated March of 1969, the 112-page script is reported to be a direct sequel to *Grave* but also utilized many heretofore unused elements from the Stoker novel, which surely would have pleased Christopher Lee had it been adapted. That's not the only thing to mourn about the film's nonproduction. It was even slated to bring Van Helsing back to the forefront as the main protagonist. And, for the very first time in a Hammer film, it would've introduced the characters of John Seward and Renfield.[1] *Feast of Blood's* storyline was reportedly similar to the original novel, taking place largely in London and including key scenes from the book that went unused by Jimmy Sangster for *Horror of Dracula*.

Most notably, Francis's script would begin with Dracula looking old and haggard as in the novel, something never before done by Hammer. But, like me, upon reading this you might be asking: How is this a direct sequel to *Grave* if it breaks continuity? Well, it doesn't necessarily break continuity, as the idea is since Dracula's last resurrection, he's gone too long without feeding, hence he's finally begun to age. (Besides, Hammer was pretty loose with the rules when it came to their Dracula mythos. Case in point: *Grave* stated that one had to pray at the vampire's moment of death to make the death final. No such thing occurred in previous entries, nor was that element reprised in sequels.)

115

Though he wasn't on set as Van Helsing, Peter Cushing was present for the filming of the finale of *Dracula Has Risen from the Grave* when Hammer was presented with the Queen's Award for Industry.

Francis envisioned the Count as having snow-white hair and a lined forehead (I'm not sure if he gave him a mustache or not).[2] As the story progressed and Dracula fed, he would become younger as in the novel. Locations would have included Castle Dracula, various locales around London (including Seward's asylum), plus the ship *Demeter* which Dracula uses to get to London. The climax would have seen Dracula perish on a ship at sea that catches fire. Sadly, it only took Hammer two months to decide they didn't want to adapt Francis's script, as they passed on it by May 19th. (Perhaps they felt it too expensive due to the ship scenes and the makeup needed to age Lee?) But that's not the end of the story, as allegedly *Feast of Blood* influenced *Taste*. And how did it influence it? Well, no one seems to know for sure, but Kevin Francis confronted Hammer over the fact that two scenes in *Taste* seemed to be lifted from his script. Hammer later paid Francis an undisclosed sum, so they must have agreed the two scripts were similar in some way. However, in his thesis on unmade Hammer, Keiran Foster explained that, "Comparing both screenplays (both held in the Hammer Script Archive) it is difficult to see which specific scenes Francis is referring to. Both screenplays feature the character Dracula, but other than this they are seemingly unrelated, featuring different characters and locations."[3] Also, Anthony Hinds, off another debacle after having overseen Hammer's *Journey to the Unknown* television series, wasn't keen on another. And so, after the controversy between *Taste* and *Feast*, he resigned from the company. And as for Kevin Francis, later, in 1974, he would announce the script again as a project for Tyburn! Once again, it went unmade.

Chapter Notes

[1] Technically, Seward is a throw-away character in *Horror* as played by Charles Lloyd-Pack and a Renfield-type character at least appeared in *Dracula – Prince of Darkness*.
[2] Lee would do a version of Dracula that same year, where he begins the film as an old man with a mustache as he slowly grows younger in Jesús Franco's *Count Dracula* (1970).
[3] Foster, Unseen Horrors, p. 104.

Staged publicity still of Weller reacting to Dracula.
Taste the Blood of Dracula © 1969 Hammer Film Productions Ltd.

13.
TASTE THE BLOOD OF DRACULA
WITHOUT THE COUNT!

Developed: 1969

Screenplay by: John Elder (Anthony Hinds) **Proposed Cast/Characters:** Lord Courtley (Ralph Bates), Dracula (Christopher Lee, flashback only)

PLOT When a nobleman by the name of Lord Courtley drinks the blood of Dracula during a ritual, he himself turns into a vampire...

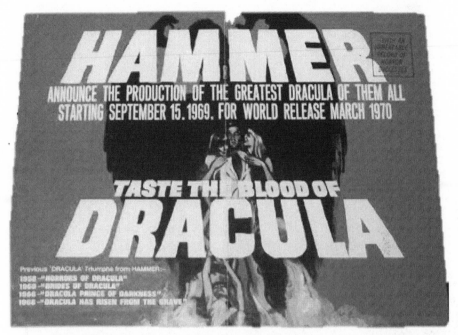

Tom Chantrell's advance poster for *Taste the Blood of Dracula,* which features the Lord Courtley character prominently. It was reused for *Scars of Dracula.*

COMMENTARY During the filming of *Dracula Has Risen from the Grave,* there had been much arguing with Christopher Lee over his salary. As such, at a Hammer board of directors meeting on June 24, 1969, the company decided to look for a replacement for Lee. Then, Brian Lawrence instructed Anthony Hinds to either write a sequel to *Grave* that didn't include Dracula, or to remove him from the current treatment. Hinds remembered in *Little Shoppe of Horrors* #13 that,

> Lee's agent was asking for more and more money for him, and Brian, in particular, became incensed about it, and asked me to see if I could write a Dracula story that did not actually have Dracula in it and so avoid having to pay Lee his 'astronomical' fee. So I did. It was accepted, and all seemed well until the US distributors discovered that Lee was to be absent, and dropped it. Panic! I had to rewrite the thing so that Lee could appear.[1]

119

VINCENT PRICE IN TASTE THE BLOOD OF DRACULA?

SUPPOSEDLY, VINCENT PRICE WAS ALSO ATTACHED TO THE FILM AT ONE TIME. SOURCES SUGGEST THAT PRICE WAS EITHER TO PLAY HARGOOD OR AN ADDITIONAL, FOURTH MEMBER OF THE PARTY WHO WAS LATER WRITTEN OUT.

The original story was the same as *Taste the Blood of Dracula*— only when the Lord Courtley character drinks the blood, he becomes a vampire—not Dracula himself. The only other big difference we know of is that during the ending Courtley cuts himself on a piece of stained glass from the church, which causes him to hallucinate the church as it was before it was desanctified. The holy images give him convulsions and he dies. Hammer had hoped Ralph Bates, who was to play Courtley, could then become his own popular vampire character and take over for the Count. However, Warner Bros wanted Lee in the film, and so negotiations began anew, and he finally relented. Because Bates was already cast, his character was retained with his death leading to Dracula's resurrection.

Director Peter Sasdy paints an entirely different picture of the film's development in *Little Shoppe of Horrors* #13. He implied that Dracula was always in the story, and the only discussion was the amount of days they had with Lee per his contract.[2] (Most likely, Sasdy simply came along after it was decided Dracula was in it.) Actress Linda Hayden, who played Alice, also offered a comment to the contrary in *Little Shoppe of Horrors* #13, where she told Bruce G. Hallenbeck that, "[Bates] wasn't really considered for the role of Dracula as Christopher Lee's replacement — although he probably could have done it."

Even after Dracula's integration, there are still some interesting changes to discuss, minor though they may be. For instance, the original version of *Taste* was to open with a travelling salesman character named Akermann rather than one named Weller. Like Weller, Akermann would've watched Dracula writhe in pain as he expires, but the title credits would play over this scene rather than after it. Instead of Lord Courtley, it was Lord Courtenay who would conduct the ceremony. Anthony Hinds envisioned Courtenay retching up great gobs of blood after he drinks from the goblet and this surely would've been too much for the censors. Rather than beating the choking Courtenay to death, the script called for Hargood to stab him to death instead. Lee objected to the idea of retching blood, noting it as "Disgusting" on his script. He also disliked that Dracula was resurrected by Courtley's death. (Perhaps he saw the flaw in the logic: why would the Count be angry that someone else's death has brought him life?) For some reason, when the Count reforms, it was visualized to have him still pierced in the chest with the crucifix from the last movie. (That, or perhaps it was some sort of flashback?) Rather than a single beating heart when he reforms, the idea was for there to be a whole cacophony of sounds as this happened (not dissimilar to the noises that Paul hears when he attempts to exorcise the church).

Though Lee often criticized the series for its lack of dialogue for Dracula, it was Lee himself who removed much of the Count's dialogue from this particular script. Originally, Dracula was a bit more chatty and polite. The script has him at one point say, "Hello, Lucy," to which Lee mockingly jotted down "Hello Dolly?" in his copy of the script. (This was Lee's way of saying Dracula wouldn't lower himself to greet one of his underlings.) Of the lines originally written for the love-starved daughters of Dracula's victims, Lee called them "appallingly comic." The lines written for Dracula during the climactic confrontation are, in a word, whiny. Dracula was to beg Alice not once, but twice to remove a cross from his view with dialogue like, "Alice, get rid of it! Alice, free me! Free me!"[3] Originally, Lee was also supposed to cackle a few times! He was to fall onto the floor rather unceremoniously, and Paul was to hold a crucifix in his face until he expired. The reinstated ending, where the church itself seems to kill Dracula (like it did Courtley) while Paul merely watches, is much better.

As it stands, the film is considered to be the last good Dracula sequel from Hammer. And, as good as it is, it certainly would have been interesting to see how it was received if it had stuck to the first version where Lord Courtley was the only vampire sans the Count. He might've even given Baron Meinster a run for his money!

Chapter Notes

[1] Meikle, "Anthony Hinds: The Man Who Made the Monsters," *Little Shoppe of Horrors* #32, pp.32-33.
[2] He also claimed that it was he who pressured Hammer to set the story in Victorian London (which could be true, the disciple of Dracula didn't have to be in London after all).
[3] Koetting, "John Elder, Christopher Lee and TASTE THE BLOOD OF DRACULA", *Little Shoppe of Horrors* #13.

TERRORIFICO!!
DESALMADO!!
SANGUINARIO!!

AMABA...
PARA MATAR!

•

CHRISTOPHER LEE
JENNY HANLEY

LAS CICATRICES DE DRÁCULA

DIRECCION ROY WARD BAKER   UNA PRODUCCION HAMMER PARA ANGLO·EMI

John Forbes Robertson as he appeared in *Legend of the 7 Golden Vampires.*
Legend of the 7 Golden Vampires © 1974 Hammer Film Productions Ltd.

14.
SCARS OF DRACULA
STARRING JOHN FORBES ROBERTSON

Developed: 1970

Screenplay by: Anthony Hinds (as John Elder) **Proposed Cast/Characters:** Dracula (John Forbes Robertson), Simon Carlson [male lead], Sarah Framsen [female lead], Paul [Sarah's missing brother], Klove [Dracula's servant], Tania [vampire bride]

PLOT A young man and his girlfriend go looking for her brother at Dracula's castle...

COMMENTARY As it stands, 1970's *Scars of Dracula* is usually considered the odd man out of Christopher Lee's Hammer Dracula cycle. The reasons are many, but first and foremost, *Scars* serves as the first sequel to break continuity with its predecessor. In *Taste the Blood of Dracula* the Count met his demise in England in the early 1900s. In *Scars*, we find his ashes present in Castle Dracula, and the setting appears to be at least 100 years before *Taste* based upon the costumes the characters wear.[1] Dracula is also uncharacteristically sadistic, violent, and talkative compared to previous outings, as though he's a different character entirely.

There is good evidence that Hammer was thinking of recasting a new actor as Dracula, hence the continuity break. As it was, Lee had seen a significant pay increase for *Taste*, which Hammer couldn't afford again. Furthermore, *Taste* had some financial backing from Warner Bros, but the backer for *Scars* was Britain's own EMI, which didn't have the same financial resources. (EMI had specifically requested a Dracula and Frankenstein film from Hammer, and so they obliged.) At the same time, Hammer was also doing what we would today call a reboot of its Frankenstein series. Upon receiving a spec script from writer Jeremy Burnham about Baron Frankenstein's younger days, they had naturally recast Peter Cushing with the younger Ralph Bates in what became *Horror of Frankenstein*. In the same way that *Horror of Frankenstein* was basically a remake of *Curse of Frankenstein*, the finished version of *Scars* was a quasi-remake of *Horror of Dracula's* first act at Castle Dracula. Film historian Bruce Hallenbeck is of the opinion that *Horror of Frankenstein* may have influenced a quasi-remake of *Horror of Dracula*. In *Little Shoppe of Horrors* #13, he wrote, "As SCARS was shot virtually back-to-back with HORROR OF FRANKENSTEIN, which was in fact a remake of CURSE OF FRANKENSTEIN, it seems to me that SCARS was pretty much intended as a remake of HORROR OF DRACULA."[2]

As to more evidence that Hammer was looking to recast Dracula, there is Tom Chantrell's concept poster for *Scars*. It notably featured a cartoonish Count in the background with what some supposed to be a younger, more attractive version of the character in the foreground being fondled by young women. (Unless this young man was meant to be the lothario Paul, perhaps being assaulted by a bevy of imagined brides as opposed to the finished film's lone vampire woman?)[3]

Christopher Lee himself espoused the opinion that Hammer had contemplated replacing him. After he signed on to do the film, he wrote a letter to his fan club president Gloria Lillibridge to inform her of the new project:

It's considerably better than the last one, but there's one extraordinary element in it and that is that no attempt is made at resuscitation. You remember that in all the previous pictures he's been revived in various weird and wonderful ways after being, so to speak, destroyed in previous episodes. In this one there's no attempt at resuscitation/resurrection, none whatever. I think I know the reason for this...

The reason they have brought the character back without accounting for his sudden appearance is, I'm quite certain, deliberately contrived in case I should say no and they can put in another actor (which they're always telling me they're going to do or will do one day) in which case there is no need for any further continuity. It doesn't have to be me, so they can start all over again with a completely new actor playing the part without having to explain the resuscitation because it isn't the same person.

You probably are aware of the fact that the next Frankenstein that they're making now is being made without Peter Cushing. I suppose they feel they can do without us now. I don't think really it's necessary for me to make any comment on this. I'm quite sure you can see this for yourself, but it's an old familiar story.

And indeed, as Lee said, the first draft script did not feature a resurrection scene, it was added in at the last minute.[4] Apart from that, not much is known about the first draft script other than that it was deemed unsatisfactory.[5] Supposedly, the treatment was written entirely within Anthony Hinds's notebook and was rather short. When it was offered to Roy Ward Baker, currently shooting *The Vampire Lovers*, there wasn't much time to revise it. As such, Baker scoured Stoker's original novel and added in as much material from it as he could. (This is where Dracula scaling the wall came from and a few other scenes).

The first draft that Baker fleshed out was only a little different from the final film. Much like the band of gypsies cut from *Revenge of Dracula/Prince of Darkness*, *Scars* originally was to begin with a whole band of gypsy servants at Castle Dracula, not just Klove. The servants were described as "big, slow moving dark complexed men."[6] When the villagers attack, the priest convinces all of the servants to free themselves and desert the castle, except for Klove who stays. And, though the castle looks the same in the film pre and post-fire, it was originally supposed to appear more vibrant before the fire, which makes sense.

The characters of Simon, Sara, and Paul are all present, but the relationships make a bit more sense. Whereas the final film has a strange, unexplained love triangle between the three, the first story was less complicated as Paul was Sara's brother rather than Simon's. In this version, Paul doesn't bed the Burgomeister's daughter, either. Instead, he gets in trouble with a prince. Specifically, Paul is set to photograph a notoriously ugly prince as a final test of sorts in his photography studies. If the prince is pleased with his portrait, Paul is more or less promised a good career. Paul, who disdains the rich and the upper class, stops off at Sara's birthday where he gives her a photo he took of her as in the film. He also shows her and Simon his portrait of the prince, which he has doctored to make him look handsome. Paul and Simon both despair over an obscenely expensive ring on the prince's finger. Simon then laments that such a ring could build two hospitals for the poor (Simon is studying to be a doctor).

Paul decides that he will steal the ring, and in a broad comedic scene does just that when he delivers the photograph. To escape, as in the film, Paul jumps out a window and into a stagecoach. This one has a driver though, who Paul bribes by saying he'll share with him the profits from the ring's sale. There's another humorous scene where they have to cross a border checkpoint, and Paul poses as royalty by wearing the ring. Eventually, the guards catch on that he's a fake, and Paul has to escape. From here, the story is basically the same, aside from very small details. For instance, the scene between Tanya, Dracula, and Paul is a bit different. The film re-edits the scene to have the Count stare oddly at Paul, but according to the script, he was angrily staring at Tanya. His first line was also to be, "I am Dracula." (Probably a nod to his first line in *Horror of Dracula*).

Initially, the priest character's PTSD (as we would now call it) was more heavily emphasized. In the film, he doesn't become fearful until he spots a bat overhead. In the first draft, he doesn't even spot a bat. Just walking to the castle is too much for him, so Simon eventually tells him to go back and watch Sara. Nor does the bat attack the priest in the end. Apparently he lives, and Sara wanders off while he's out of the room to head for the castle.

It was this draft of the script that would have starred a different actor as Dracula. This isn't just wanton speculation, the actor eyed for the role spoke about it to Wayne Kinsey in *Little Shoppe of Horrors* #32, devoted entirely to *Legend of the 7 Golden*

Vampires. You see, the actor approached was none other than John Forbes-Robertson!

Wayne Kinsey: How did you get cast as Dracula in *The Legend of the 7 Golden Vampires*?
John Forbes-Robertson: It was Roy (Ward Baker) again. Four years before *7 Golden Vampires*, he called me and said, "Christopher Lee's not going to do it (*Scars of Dracula*), and so we would like you to do it." I went down; but after messing about, Lee suddenly decided he would do it.[7]

And there you have it. As poorly as *Scars* was perceived, could you have imagined it with Forbes-Robertson? This may sound odd to say, because I love Christopher Lee, but considering that *Scars* was double-billed with *Horror of Frankenstein,* which had recast Cushing, I have to say it would have been rather intriguing to have seen *Scars* with Forbes-Robertson in the role...

Chapter Notes

---

[1] Actually, one wonders why Hammer even bothered to have Dracula resurrected, as they could have just considered this a prequel to *Horror of Dracula* where the Count has yet to die, which is arguably what this might actually be.
[2] Hallenbeck, "Scars of Dracula," *Little Shoppe of Horrors* #13 (Kindle Edition).
[3] In reality, it was simply *Taste the Blood of Dracula's* concept poster reused, and the fondled young man was Lord Courtley.
[4] Again, Hammer could have perhaps rectified this with some opening narration a la *Brides of Dracula* explaining that this film took place before Horror of Dracula in 1885. But, back then prequels were an odd concept, nor were they very common.
[5] Adding to the confusion, according to some sources, the *Scars* script was actually written before *Taste*! When exactly, I don't know.
[6] *Scars of Dracula* audio commentary by Constantine Nasr and Ted Newsom, SCREAM FACTORY.
[7] Kinsey, "Interview with John Forbes Robertson," *Little Shoppe of Horrors* #32 (Kindle Edition).

Peter Cushing as a vampire in *Tender Dracula* (1974).

15.
VAMPIRE VIRGINS

Developed: 1971

Screenplay by: Tudor Gates **Proposed Cast/Characters:** Count Karnstein (Peter Cushing), Kurt [vampire hunter], Johan [vampire hunter], Wanda, Trudi, Maria, Imogen [daughters of the village elders/vampire virgins]

PLOT Two young vampire hunters, Johan and Kurt, are hired by a village to rid their lands of the dreaded Karnstein family. The hunters kill all the vampires (or so they think) and return to the village only to find that the villagers won't pay them! Kurt seeks retribution on the villagers by kidnapping the daughters of the village elders. Kurt's brash act sets off a series of unforeseen events that will ultimately lead to his own undoing...

COMMENTARY When I first heard of this unmade Hammer horror under the title of the *Vampire Hunters*, I immediately thought it must have been an aborted Van Helsing movie. Fueling this theory was the fact that reports said Peter Cushing was to be the star. To my shock, I later learned that Cushing was slated to play the vampire for a change instead of the vampire hunter! As it turned out, *Vampire Hunters*, better known as *Vampire Virgins*, was a precursor to the final entry in the Karnstein trilogy, *Twins of Evil.*[1] Unlike many lost Hammer titles, which were little more than an idea backed by a Tom Chantrell poster, *Vampire Hunters/Virgins* has an excellent 14-page treatment circulating.

But, before delving into the story, let's backtrack a bit. If you'll recall, the final shots of *Lust for a Vampire* (1971)—the second entry of the Karnstein trilogy—oddly showed Count Karnstein to be alive and well amidst the burning castle. Considering that earlier in the film another character said that fire was useless to destroy the vampires, Hammer was trying to tell us something: that Count Karnstein would be back. As it turned out, Count Karnstein was the planned big bad of the third Karnstein film, where Carmilla wouldn't even appear. However, Hammer didn't have enough faith in actor Mike Raven, who played the part in

Lust, and planned to recast him with Cushing as the Count as stated earlier.

Vampire Virgins was to begin with an exciting pre-credits sequence similar to the one in *The Vampire Lovers,* albeit much more elaborate. Cushing, as Count Karnstein, would look down from atop his castle to watch as the various Karnstein vampires rise from their graves outside. Suddenly, the two young titular characters (if you're going by the *Vampire Hunters* title, that is) burst from the shadows and begin decapitating the vampires as they come out of the ground! Count Karnstein rushes to the graveyard only to be repelled by a handy cross from one of the hunters. The two men ride off on horseback with the severed heads of the vampires. Karnstein looks on with hatred and vows revenge; cue the opening titles...

The scene following the credits would take place within a village meeting house (the period accouterments showing us that it's the mid-nineteenth century). The villagers are complaining that the vampire hunters they've hired have yet to return from their job. (They seem more concerned with the down payment they gave the hunters to kill the vampires than they are the vampires themselves!) The two youths then burst through the doors, with sacks full of severed vampire heads. We learn from this scene the dynamics of the relationship between the two young hunters. Kurt is the hotheaded fire and ice character, while Johan is the calmer one (and reportedly the brains of the operation). The villagers then claim they cannot pay the 100 marks per head for the 11 vampire skulls! Kurt throws a fit and storms out angrily, while the compassionate Johan is more forgiving. (One could presume here that Johan kills vampires for the sake of doing good, while Kurt does it for money, an interesting dynamic.)

The duo discusses their problem over at a tavern. While Kurt angrily gets drunk, Johan decides he will go to negotiate again with one of the village elders, though Kurt tells him he's wasting his time. When Johan meets with the chief elder, he is also introduced to his beautiful daughter, Wanda. Unfortunately, Kurt was right; Johan's efforts are in vain, and they won't be getting the dues owed to them. As Johan negotiates in vain, a drunken Kurt goes from house to house kidnapping the beautiful daughters of the elders. This includes Wanda, who he abducts after Johan has gone.

Kurt then tosses the girls into the dungeon of Karnstein Castle— his plan being to ransom off the girls to the elders. (But we have to ask: isn't Kurt aware that there's one vampire by the name of

Count Karnstein hanging around the castle? It's possible that he isn't aware of this, as the treatment specified that it was Johan who warded off the Count with the crucifix in the pre-credits scene. But still, wouldn't a professional vampire hunter tell his partner that one got away?)

Whether Kurt is aware of Karnstein's presence or not, he leaves the girls in the dungeon. Wanda, the most proactive of the bunch, climbs out a window to escape. As she drops to the ground below, she falls into the waiting arms of the count! From here we would cut back to the village to check in on Kurt, who, still drunk, brags to the barmaid Gerda that the villagers are in for a nasty surprise in the morning. We would then cut back to Wanda being wined and dined by Cushing's charming vampire. The scene would end with him leaning in for a kiss only to bite her on the neck.

The next morning, the village is in an uproar. Initially, Kurt is so hungover that he can't recall that he's to blame for the commotion. When he does, he becomes ashamed, too ashamed to tell Johan what's happened. He immediately sets out to free the girls but is disturbed to find them all gone. Eventually he encounters Wanda, who is rather friendly with him considering what he'd done, and offers to show him how they escaped. Wanda then tricks Kurt into the cell, which she locks him in. Wanda, now under Karnstein's spell, is using Kurt as bait to catch Johan. Back at the village, Johan is being berated by the elders, who think the vampires have taken their daughters. Johan assures them that the vampires are all dead. (This would seem to imply that Johan thinks the Count is dead, even though the treatment said that Johan simply drove him away with a crucifix!)

We would cut away to a scene that would showcase the titular vampire virgins hanging around a stream, scantily clad. Several men working in a field notice the pretty girls and approach them. You can guess what happens next: a little seduction followed by some serious neck-biting. (The script noted that we were to see the aftermath of the attack in the form of blood running down the stream.)

In one of the following scenes, Johan encounters one of the vampirized virgins, Maria, and kills her. Johan returns to the village carrying the dead body and is accused of murdering her. When Johan tries to tell them that she was vampirized, they will hear none of it. Johan is put on trial, and testifying against him are the surviving three girls: Wanda, Imogen, and Trudi! The girls all claim that Johan was in cahoots with Kurt when they were

131

kidnapped, and furthermore, there never were any vampires, the villagers were swindled! Johan is sentenced to death by hanging.

In a scene meant to throw the audience, we would cut to a body being dropped from the gallows only to reveal that it was just a practice dummy (once the shock subsided, of course). The scene was apparently to take place at night, because it is revealed that Count Karnstein himself is the executioner! In a last-ditch effort, Johan begs to kiss the cross before he dies (knowing that the appearance of the cross will expose the vampires). The girls all cry for the execution of their captor, and the officials oblige them. The noose is put around his neck, and Karnstein throws the switch.

Johan begins to drop, when suddenly, an ax thrown through the air severs the rope! Lucky for Johan, while Karnstein was away, Kurt escaped and has come to his friend's rescue. Kurt rides his horse to the bottom of the gallows to rescue Johan. The duo fends off the villagers with the ax, and Johan again asks for a cross so that he may expose the undead. However, the vampires have all mysteriously vanished.

Kurt and Johan try to rustle a posse of villagers to go with them to Karnstein Castle, and only one man, Franz, answers the call. And what's special about Franz? Well, you see, Franz offered his help in order to impress the pretty girl next to him in the crowd, which just happens to be Imogen! The girl coerces Franz into a darkened corner...

When we next see Franz, he has two bite marks on his neck, and is riding with the vampire hunters to Karnstein Castle. Back in the village, the priest decides to test Johan's theory when he sees Imogen. In front of spectators, the vampire girl recoils from the priest's cross. The villagers hold up their own crucifixes until Imogen is surrounded. They realize the two men were telling the truth all along.

Back at the castle, the vampire hunters are not only being shadowed by Franz, the vampire double-agent, they are also walking into a trap. Karnstein and his human flunky Drax[2] have booby-trapped the castle corridor with a set of impaling spikes. In the hallway, Franz finally makes his move trying to bite Kurt. Johan pries him off and flings him into the wall, setting off the booby-trap which pierces Franz through the heart.

The men then ingeniously use Franz's dead body to set off any further traps until they get to Karnstein, Drax, and his remaining vampire virgins. When they do, Trudi momentarily entrances Kurt, while Johan chases after Wanda and Karnstein who disappear down a secret corridor. Kurt snaps out of his trance in time to

132

stake Trudi through the heart. However, Wanda and Drax soon appear. As Kurt stakes Wanda, Drax sneaks up behind Kurt and slices his shoulder with an ax. Mortally wounded, Kurt calls out for Johan, who doubles back for his companion. Johan finds Drax standing over his friend and so throws an ax at him, which decapitates Drax. Karnstein watches from the shadows as Johan kneels by the dying Kurt. Karnstein goes in for the kill and the final fight begins. Though emotionally charged, the finale doesn't really deliver an interesting killing blow to the vampire compared to, let's say, the crossbow decapitation scene from *Vampire Circus.* Amidst their struggle, Kurt simply stakes Karnstein, who had pounced on top of him. The vampire count gurgles up some blood and dies.

Johan goes back to the side of Kurt, still conscious. As it turns out, Kurt will live... as one of the undead! When Johan expresses some hopefulness at the fact that Kurt is still conscious, Kurt shows him the bite marks on his neck, which we didn't know about until now. During the chaos, Wanda got him. A tearful Johan knows what must be done for his friend and sends a stake through his heart.

In the epilogue, like a western hero, Johan mounts his horse and prepares to leave the village. The villagers thank him for what he has done, and the friendly barmaid begs him to stay. But no, there are more vampires to slay, and Johan rides off.

The ending presented here isn't your typical Hammer fare. As it was, Wanda was set up as the female lead. In Hammer vampire movies, the damsel in distress usually overcame her vampirism upon the death of the head vampire. I was assuming Wanda and Johan might live happily ever after when the story concluded, but obviously not as Kurt killed Wanda before this could happen. Because of this, one could argue that the central relationship in the story wasn't the romance between boy and girl as was usually the case with Hammer, but rather the brotherly bond between the two vampire hunters.

Overall, this is a very solid story, dare I say better than the Karnstein films that we got, a few of which were wonderful. It is also much tamer; unlike *Lust* and *Twins of Evil,* there are no arcane ceremonies, nor is there any sex (though the enticement of the men by the stream had possibilities for that, I'm sure). Had the script been revised for shooting, it's possible that Hammer would have added nudity. But, at the same time, the BBFC had become wise to Hammer's usual tricks in terms of how they managed to slip things past them. Hammer may have felt that it was now impossible to get anything too risqué past them, who knows?

Other than Cushing, it's unknown who else Hammer had an eye on for this production.[3] For the two young vampire hunters, it wouldn't be surprising if Hammer utilized Ralph Bates for the hero as he was popular at the studio at the time (even if he did usually play villains for them). Other likely choices included Simon Ward (*Frankenstein Must Be Destroyed*), Anthony Corlan (*Taste the Blood of Dracula; Vampire Circus*) and Shane Briant (*Frankenstein and the Monster from Hell*). As to the vampire virgins, previous *Vampire Lovers* stars Kate O'Mara, Pippa Steel, and Madeline Smith would have been fantastic.

To backtrack to something I said earlier, it seems unclear whether or not this treatment preceded or followed *Twins of Evil*. Odds favor it preceding it and I might be so bold as to speculate that Hammer possibly eyed the Collinson twins (Mary and Madeleine) for *Vampire Virgins*, then perhaps decided to tailor a whole movie around vampire twins. Just my own speculation, which could be wrong. In any case, *Twins of Evil* went on to become the favorite for many when it came to Hammer's Carmilla trilogy. However, James Carreras was no fan of the series, not to mention the last two entries didn't perform as well as the first, *The Vampire Lovers*, had in 1970. If *Twins of Evil* had performed better, and if James Carreras had some affinity for the films, it's quite possible that *Vampire Virgins* would have been resurrected to be the fourth Karnstein film.

Chapter Notes

---

[1] However, some sources state that this may have been a sequel to *Twins of Evil*, but more likely it preceded it.
[2] I don't know when Drax first appeared in the script, but like Klove and Dracula, Drax is Karnstein's human slave.
[3] Cushing did read the script, as he made a notation on it as to what he wanted Count Karnstein's hat to look like!

16.
BLOOD FROM THE MUMMY'S TOMB
STARRING PETER CUSHING

Developed: 1971

Directed by: Seth Holt (partial footage) **Screenplay by:** Christopher Wicking based upon the book by Bram Stoker **Proposed Cast/Characters:** Margaret Fuchs/Queen Tera (Valerie Leon), Julian Fuchs (Peter Cushing)

PLOT An evil Egyptian Queen is slowly reincarnated...

COMMENTARY By 1970, it had been three years since Hammer's last Mummy movie, that being *The Mummy's Shroud* from 1967. For reasons unknown, James Carreras began itching for another Mummy film and ordered a new screenplay. Unfortunately, no one knows what the 1970 pitch entailed. All we know is that it was to be co-written and directed by Jimmy Sangster. See the letter written by Anthony Hinds to Jimmy Sangster on April 17, 1970, below:

135

Publicity stills of Valerie Leon. Michael Carreras wanted another woman to play the part: Deborah Grant, a performer in the Royal Shakespear Company. Grant recalled in an interview with Jonathon Sothcott that she did a screen test for the film with Valerie Leon. She recalled that she wore Elizabeth Taylor's costume from *Cleopatra*. According to Grant, Leon won due to her "frontage". This would appear to be true, as Leon had very little in the way of acting skills. Furthermore, her real voice isn't even heard in the film. She was, in fact, dubbed by a "middle-aged actress" whose name isn't given.

Dear Jimmy: Jim Carreras has asked me to write a 'Mummy' script. I gather that Hammer was pleased with your performance as director [on *Horror of Frankenstein*]: If you have been bitten by the bug and fancy doing more of it, maybe you'd like to work on the script with me. You will appreciate I have no influence at Hammer anymore,[1] so this is not a contract!"[2]

Talks didn't last long. James Carreras canceled the production on April 22nd when he failed to garner any interest from investors. He sent the following letter to Sangster:

Dear Jimmy. I have today told Tony Hinds that there is very little interest in a MUMMY subject. Under the circumstances, therefore, we will have to forget it.[3]

The lack of interest wasn't necessarily surprising. Of all Hammer's monster properties, the mummy films were the least sexy of the bunch at a time when sex was selling Hammer's films to a greater extent. True, cleavage had always been an aspect of Hammer horror, but 1970's *The Vampire Lovers* had featured an abundance of nudity and had been a sizeable hit. By comparison, the Mummy franchise was kid stuff. Perhaps then, it should come as no surprise that it took a pretty girl to sell the next Hammer mummy movie.

Later in 1970, press agent Howard Brandy pitched James Carreras the idea of adapting Bram Stoker's 1903 novel *Jewel of the Seven Stars*. Often obscured by the shadow of Stoker's seminal *Dracula*, *Seven Stars* concerned an archeologist's efforts to revive the ancient Egyptian mummy, Queen Tera, whom he has fallen in love with. Brandy told Ted Newsom in an interview that he gave Carreras a brief outline of the story and that Carreras loved it. "It's a mummy movie with a pretty girl, and [Carreras] immediately said yes."[4]

As Hammer had a three-picture deal already set up with EMI, the *Jewel of the Seven Stars* adaptation became one of those projects. However, Carreras disliked that title and felt it would fare better with "Mummy" in the title. After all, it had an Egyptian aspect to it, so why not? Specifically, according to Christopher Wicking, Carreras placed all the keywords relating to Mummy movies like "blood," "shroud," "tomb," etc. and came up with the title *Blood from the Mummy's Tomb* (though "Bosoms from the Mummy's Tomb" may have been more appropriate).

Wicking's first draft of the screenplay was entitled *Bram Stoker's Blood from the Mummy's Tomb* and was "unusable" according to Howard Brandy. According to Brandy, the draft was very short, and when asked to do a rewrite, Wicking refused.[5] Wicking, on the other hand, claimed that Brandy had a falling out with his agent and that this was the cause of the drama. Whatever the case, the chosen director (recommended by Wicking himself) was Seth Holt, who had directed *The Nanny* (with Bette Davis) for Hammer in

137

1965.[6] As to stars, Peter Cushing would return to the series for the first time since 1959's *The Mummy*. He would, however, be playing a new character, Professor Fuchs, while Valerie Leon had been cast as his daughter Margaret.

Though *Blood from the Mummy's Tomb* was completed, it should have ended up as a very different film if not for several unfortunate tragedies. Following the drama with Wicking, there was an actor's strike that threatened to hold up the production, among other things. However, two tragic deaths impacted the project irrevocably: that of director Seth Holt's and Peter Cushing's wife, Helen Cushing. Christopher Neame, the production manager, remembered in issue #20 of *The House That Hammer Built* that the crew was aware that Helen Cushing was sick. As such, shooting was scheduled around Cushing so that he could not only get all of his scenes out of the way in general, but also leave early each day of shooting. "We wanted him to have as much time as he could with her and we'd planned to work with him primarily and get rid of him during the day as soon as possible."[7]

The first day of shooting comprised of the scene where Professor Fuchs, as currently played by Cushing, gifted daughter Margaret Tera's ring on her birthday. Filming was slow due to Leon's inexperience, so not much was shot.

After the first day of shooting was over, that night, the second assistant director called Cushing to let him know the schedule for the next day. Cushing informed him that, tragically, Helen was not expected to make it through the night. She didn't, and Hammer knew Cushing wouldn't be able to finish the film. With only one day's worth of footage shot, it was decided that it would be easiest to recast Cushing. Hammer did so in only one day, getting Andrew Keir to play the role of Fuchs.[8]

Keir recalled the incident in an interview with Stephen Laws at the Manchester Festival of Fantastic Films in 1993. Keir said that Carreras called him on a Friday night to inform him of the tragedy of Helen Cushing, and asked if he could take on Peter's part in the film. Keir, a good sport, traveled overnight to Wales without even having read the script to join shooting. Keir remembered, "Peter had marvelous qualities and as the part was written for Peter, it could only really be Peter in that role."[9]

In an interview, Leon recalled her sadness at not being able to work further with Cushing. When interviewed by Tim Greaves in *Little Shoppe of Horrors* #12, she said:

Still of Peter Cushing on set with Valerie Leon on his one and only day of shooting.
Blood from the Mummy's Tomb © 1971 Hammer Film Productions Ltd.

We actually did shoot the scene when he gives me the ring right at the beginning of the film, I remember that very well. And I was really sad when he had to drop out. Not only is he a really nice man, but obviously better known that Andrew Keir.[10]

Four weeks later, the next major tragedy occurred when Holt dropped dead of what was presumed to be a heart attack. Again, the production was faced with a seemingly insurmountable obstacle. Shooting had progressed far enough that it wouldn't be worth it to reshoot the whole film. Don Sharp, who had directed *Kiss of the Vampire* in 1963, was considered, but it would end up being Michael Carreras himself who stepped in to finish the job.[11]

139

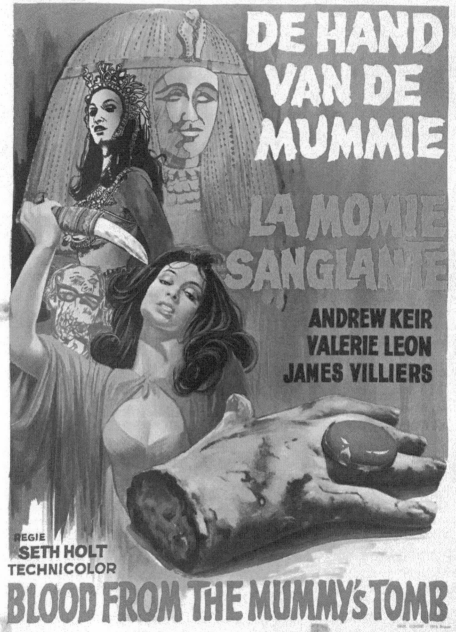

Blood from the Mummy's Tomb © 1971 Hammer Film Productions Ltd.

During a telephone interview conducted by John Hamilton with Christopher Neame on April 3, 2010, Hamilton asked Neame just how different he thought the film would have been had Cushing played Fuchs and Holt had finished directing/editing.

Neame said, "It would have been better. I have always found Peter Cushing a more watchable actor than Andrew Keir, who did a good job, but Peter was a bigger name."[12]

There were other reasons behind Neame's statement that "it would have been better". For starters, Holt didn't keep editorial notes. "[Holt would] shoot certain things and I'd ask, 'Why are you shooting that?'" remembered Neame. "He'd say, 'Don't worry, I know what I'm going to do with that. I can't wait to get my hands on this in the editing room.'"[13] Also, Holt's death meant that his usual editor, Oswald Hafenrichter, wouldn't be working on the film (actually, because Carreras fired Hafenrichter).

Carreras himself recalled the problems with taking up for Holt, stating that the main one was that Holt had shot the main portion of many scenes—just not the characters entering and exiting! Therefore Carreras had to restage many scenes to complete the task. Nor was any effort made by Carreras to emulate Holt's style according to some, though Carreras told *Fangoria* that he "tried to copy Seth's work as much as possible."[14]

Despite its setbacks, the film was received better by critics than many previous Hammer films had been in the past and is fondly remembered today by many as "the second-best Hammer Mummy film" behind the 1959 original.

Chapter Notes

[1] Anthony Hinds had sold off his interest in Hammer by 1970.
[2] Hallenbeck, "The Making of the Hammer Classic *Blood from the Mummy's Tomb*," *Little Shoppe of Horrors* #24, p. 84.
[3] Ibid.
[4] Ibid, p.85.
[5] In addition to being short, Wicking's script also had several explicit nude scenes that were removed.
[6] Before Holt, Gordon Hessler and Peter Duffell were considered.
[7] Neame as quoted in "The Making of the Hammer Classic *Blood from the Mummy's Tomb*," *Little Shoppe of Horrors* #24, p. 89.
[8] This wasn't the first time that Keir replaced Cushing. He also did so on *Dracula – Prince of Darkness*, as the early drafts featured Van Helsing until it was learned that Cushing was unavailable. Therefore, a new character was created for Keir: Father Sandor.
[9] Hallenbeck, "The Making of the Hammer Classic *Blood from the Mummy's Tomb*," *Little Shoppe of Horrors* #24, p. 90.
[10] Ibid.
[11] Actually, Carreras offered Sharp the opportunity to direct from scratch, in other words scrap the shot footage, but Sharp declined.
[12] Hamilton, "Christopher Neame Interview," *Little Shoppe of Horrors* #24, p.82.
[13] Ibid, p.93.
[14] Ibid, p.94.

142

An Indian Summer for the Prince of Darkness!

The Unquenchable **THIRST**of **DRACULA**

Dancing Ledge Productions presents a Hammer adaptation for Radio 4   CERT X

STARRING
NIKESH PATEL · KULVINDER GHIR · MICHAEL SHEEN · MEERA SYAL · ANNA MADELEY · AYESHA DHARKER
SAGAR IM ARYA · RAJ GHATAK · NATALIE KIMMERLING AND LEWIS MACLEOD AS COUNT DRACULA

SCREENPLAY BY   ADAPTED FOR RADIO BY   PRODUCED BY   DIRECTED BY
ANTHONY HINDS · MARK GATISS & LAURENCE BOWEN · LAURENCE BOWEN & PETER ETTEDGUI · MARK GATISS

A DANCING LEDGE PRODUCTION FOR BBC RADIO 4 © 2017

17.
THE UNQUENCHABLE THIRST
OF DRACULA

Developed: 1970, 1977

Screenplay by: Anthony Hinds (as John Elder) **Proposed Cast/Characters:** Dracula (Christopher Lee), Penny Woods [travelling heiress], Prem [travelling musician], Babu [Indian merchant], Lakshmi [Prem's sister], Maharajah [Dracula's servant], Maharani [Thuggee cult leader], Majordomo [Maharajah's servant]

Projected runtime: 86 minutes

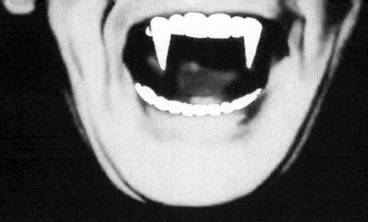

THE UNQUENCHABLE THIRST OF DRACULA

A LIVE reading of an UNFILMED

HAMMER™

SCREENPLAY

written by

ANTHONY HINDS

(TASTE THE BLOOD OF DRACULA, DRACULA HAS RISEN FROM THE GRAVE)

performed by

LAUREN CARSE - HARPAL HAYER - SOHM KAPILA - SHAJAIT KHAN
JONNY PHILLIPS - SABRINA SANDHU - JAS STEVEN SINGH

narrated by

JONATHAN RIGBY

(ENGLISH GOTHIC, CHRISTOPHER LEE: THE AUTHORISED SCREEN HISTORY')

BROADWAY CINEMA, NOTTINGHAM

7.30, SATURDAY 17TH OCTOBER 2015

www.broadway.org.uk/Mayhem

MAYHEM
FILM FESTIVAL

broadway

BBC CREDITS

ADAPTED TO RADIO BY MARK GATISS AND LAURENCE BOWEN
BASED ON THE SCREENPLAY BY ANTHONY HINDS
PRODUCED BY LAURENCE BOWEN AND PETER ETTEDGUI
DIRECTED BY MARK GATISS

NARRATED BY MICHAEL SHEEN
FEATURING
ANNA MADELEY AS PENNY
NIKESH PATEL AS PREM
KULVINDER GHIR AS BABU
MEERA SYAL AS THE RANI
AYESHA DHARKER AS LAKSHMI
AND LEWIS MACLEOD AS DRACULA

PLOT A young heiress named Penny Woods journeys to India to find her sister, last seen entering a mysterious cave near the palace of the Maharajah and Maharani. Little does Penny know, but Dracula is the secret ruler of the palace...

COMMENTARY This is easily one of the best-known aborted Dracula sequels of the Hammer pantheon. It is also one of the most confusing to research. In fact, I wasn't exactly sure just where to place it in this book, as it technically did begin in 1970 as *Dracula – High Priest of the Vampires*, though the version of it which we are about to discuss wasn't fleshed out in full until 1977. Nor is this actually connected to the slightly better-known *Kali – Devil Bride of Dracula,* which is only tangentially related due to the fact that both stories are set in India. (*Kali* was a direct prequel to *Legend of the 7 Golden Vampires* and will be discussed in its own chapter.)

Though Hammer initially had difficulty in luring Christopher Lee back to the role of Dracula, by the late 1960s, he was playing the Count regularly in films like *Dracula Has Risen From the Grave* (1968) and *Taste the Blood of Dracula* (1970), both of which were moneymakers for Hammer and Warner Bros. The plan going forward was to aim for one Lee Dracula picture per year! *Scars of Dracula,* also released in 1970, was not a hit, however. Perhaps Dracula wasn't welcome with audiences twice in one year? Or, maybe audiences simply didn't like the slightly more sadistic version of Lee's Dracula that appeared in the film. All Hammer

DRACULA – HIGH PRIEST OF THE VAMPIRES

DRACULA: HIGH PRIEST OF THE VAMPIRES IS BASICALLY THE SAME AS *UNQUENCHABLE THIRST*, EXCEPT FOR THAT IT IS COY ABOUT THE DATE. NO REFERENCE IS GIVEN TO THE YEAR, BUT THERE IS A CAR CHASE, AND PENNY IS DESCRIBED AS WEARING JEANS IN ONE SCENE! PERHAPS JEANS WAS A HASTY MISTAKE ON HINDS PART AND IT SHOULDN'T BE TAKEN TOO SERIOUSLY. HIGH PRIEST ALSO FEATURED NUDITY, WHEREAS *UNQUENCHABLE THIRST* DOES NOT—IRONIC CONSIDERING THAT IT CAME LATER.

knew was that they wanted to get the series back on track, and they also wanted to impress Warner Bros. And so they asked Anthony Hinds to pitch a story.

Though no longer officially a part of Hammer, Hinds was not averse to still writing screenplays for Hammer. Three months after he left the company, he turned in the treatment for *Dracula–High Priest of the Vampires* (AKA *Dracula in India*) in August of 1970. Michael Carreras met with Norman Katz of Warner Brothers in January of 1971, and they passed on the project. Instead, Warners suggested a modern set Dracula based on the success of *Count Yorga, Vampire* (1970), and so *Dracula A.D. 1972* was born.

As we all know, *Dracula A.D. 1972* and its sequel sounded the death knell for Hammer's Dracula series. In 1975 came the moderately successful *Legend of the 7 Golden Vampires*, which Warner Bros requested an India-set sequel to (but only as a way of using a cache of frozen rupees they had there). Hinds' old Dracula in India idea was briefly considered, but Warner Bros wanted something more action-oriented, so *Kali-Devil Bride of Dracula* was born... and then died. After the death of the Kali project, for whatever reason, Carreras returned to Hinds' old *High Priest* project and asked Hinds to give it an update in January of 1977. By February, Hinds had done so. *High Priest* was dusted off and rebranded *The Unquenchable Thirst of Dracula* in 1977. Though it never became a film, 40 years later, it became a 2017 radio play produced by the BBC based upon the script.

Thanks to the BBC radio play, which was incredibly well-done, we can get an idea of just how this prospective film would have compared to the Count's other outings. It's also very apparent that this version of Dracula was written for Christopher Lee and no other. (Even if chances were slim to none of him returning in 1977, remember that this story was originally written in 1970 when he was still attached to the role.) To a degree, *Unquenchable Thirst* is the same type of Hammer Dracula story, only in a different setting but with all the usual plot devices and tropes: A sibling seeking to avenge their lost/dead brother/sister (check), a female heroine placed in danger by Dracula (check), a group of travelers become trapped within Dracula's castle (check).

The unmade screenplay also predates 1984's *Indiana Jones and the Temple of Doom* to an uncanny extent, hidden passageways in the palace, an underground cult in a giant cave with men pounding drums, a hypnotized Maharajah, etc. And rather than a pit of lava as in the Indiana Jones film, Dracula has a "bottomless" pit patented after the real "Black Hole of Calcutta"—a small dungeon in Fort William, Calcutta. Speaking of that, ten years earlier, Hinds had planned to film *The Black Hole of Calcutta* as a follow-up to *The Stranglers of Bombay* (1959). So this idea had been percolating in Hinds' mind for some time. This would have also have been the most modern take on Dracula yet, set in the year 1934.[1] (*Dracula A.D. 1972* had yet to be produced when the story was first written in 1970.)

To discuss the story in-depth, let's start at the beginning. Not all Hammer productions opened with fairy-tale-like narration, but this one, like *Brides of Dracula*, would have. The narration explains that Dracula hasn't been seen in Transylvania for some time. Government officials believe him dead, while superstitious peasants think otherwise. They are right. Because of the advances in technology and western civilization, Dracula has traveled to the East. Not as far as Chunking, that would come later, but to India...

After the narration sets up that Dracula has moved eastward due to westward expansion, we would cut to a train station in India. There we would meet our heroine, Penny Woods, the focus of the story as opposed to previous male leads. As stated earlier, Penny is a wealthy heiress out to explore the world (similar to Julie Ege's character in *Legend of the 7 Golden Vampires*). On the train, Penny meets our other, very likable characters. First, there is kindly old Babu, who offers to take her into his home when he learns she is travelling alone.[2] And then there is brother and sister duo Prim and Lakshmi, who are travelling to perform at a palace. Penny and Prim, not surprisingly, are attracted to one another, setting up the first interracial romance thus far in a Hammer Dracula film. (Again, the first time going by the 1970 treatment. When the 1977 script was fleshed out, the first interracial Hammer romance had been between Leland Van Helsing and Mai Kwei in 1974's *Legend of the 7 Golden Vampires*.)

Also on the train, Penny glimpses a strange man with a "dead look" in his eye along with a scarred servant. (At first, I thought perhaps this was Dracula and Klove, but not so.) As it turns out, the man is the Maharajah himself, who drives Prem and Lakshmi to the palace while Penny goes to stay with Babu. Upon arriving at the palace, the first clue that something strange is afoot is that all the windows are barred shut. In this regard, the story is similar to a routine visit to Dracula's castle (locked doors, barred windows, etc.), only now set in a palace in India. At dinner, Prim expresses his great honor at getting to perform for the Maharaja and Maharani. The Maharajah disdainfully informs him that is not the case; they were brought here to perform for someone else. At that point, out of the shadows, Count Dracula makes his entrance and introduces himself.

Regally, Dracula watches the girl dance in the company of the royals. When the Maharani asks Dracula if the girl pleases him, it is clear he is not just a guest; he clearly rules the roost, so to speak. When Prim becomes drunk at dinner, he is taken away to his room and Lakshmi is then forced to dance sensually for Dracula alone. We cut back to Prim, who is racked with spasms of pain—it's now clear he was drugged. (Hinds is taking a page from his *Kiss of the Vampire* script, where the male lead is drugged at a party so that his wife may be alone with the head vampire.) As Lakshmi continues her sensual dance, we cut back and forth between her and Penny, who seems to be seeing the dance in a dream. As Lakshmi is bitten by Dracula, Penny for some reason, can feel the same happening to her. (It's very similar to the scene of Jessica Van Helsing dreaming of her friend's death in *Dracula A.D. 1972*, so perhaps the idea was actually lifted from the 1970 *High Priest of the Vampires* treatment? Or, vice versa, perhaps Hinds remembered the scene from *A.D.* when he was turning *High Priest* into *Unquenchable Thirst?*)

Poor Lakshmi isn't just bitten by Dracula. Next, she is taken away by the Maharani to a temple deep underground. (Just envision a slightly less grand version of the titular "Temple of Doom" from the Indiana Jones film and you get the idea.) Lakshmi is killed during the ceremony, which enrages Dracula when he finds out. It seems the idea that the Maharani was under Dracula's spell was actually a 52 fake out! It is actually she who controls the cult, not Dracula. The Count then does something undignified that Christopher Lee likely would have refused to do: get on the floor and lick up Lakshmi's blood!

The next morning, Prim is awakened and ushered quickly out of the castle, being told that his sister has elected to stay there. (Again, this is similar to *Kiss of the Vampire*.) Prim smells a rat and this, of course, sets into motion the usual Hammer plot of the brother out to rescue his sibling. (This was a recent plot device used in the previous two films as Paul had to avenge Lucy in *Taste the Blood of Dracula*, and Simon had to avenge his brother Paul in *Scars of Dracula*.)

As it turns out, that same day we also learn that Penny is out to avenge her missing sibling as well! The story she told on the train about using her newfound inheritance to travel for fun was a lie. She is really in India investigating the disappearance of her sister, Lucy (another common name from Hammer's name-bank!), last seen at caves near the palace. Penny explores the caves and comes face to face with a King Cobra. Prim is also snooping around the cave and arrives just in time after Penny is bitten by the cobra on her upper thigh. This leads to a semi-exploitive scene where Prim must suck out the poison. In the process, Prim learns that like him, Penny is looking for her missing sister as well. They continue their exploration of the underground cavern and eventually find Dracula sleeping in a white coffin. He awakens to incapacitate Prim and then tells Penny, "Don't worry. He is still one of the living." Dracula then utters a cackling laugh (which Lee probably would have rightly refused to do—his Dracula was no cackler). That said, the laughter is played to good effect, as Dracula has disappeared and now all Penny can hear is the cacophony of his cackling throughout the chamber. As he had in *Scars of Dracula*, the Count displays new supernatural powers here: everywhere that Penny turns to run he appears blocking her way.

When Penny asks him where her sister and Lakshmi are, he takes her to a caged-in underground chamber. Within it are hundreds of undead vampire brides (perhaps this inspired the vampire bride chamber seen in *Count Dracula and His Vampire Bride*?). Penny recognizes her sister Lucy among the poor imprisoned girls. If Dracula has his way, Penny will join her sister, though the Maharani has other plans. Considering Lakshmi to have been an "unclean sacrifice" due to Dracula's having fed on her, she now wants the "pure" Penny for that purpose. Dracula refuses the Maharani both Penny and Prim as sacrifices.

Dracula and the Maharani then have an exchange of dialogue where once again the power balance seems off-kilter. Though the Maharani thinks she still has some remnant of power, Dracula doesn't see it this way. To her their relationship is symbiotic, but

149

to him, he is the master of the palace. Dracula becomes violent when she says she will take Prim, grabbing her throat and making it clear that he will accept nothing less than total obedience.

In the end, Dracula takes Penny, but the Maharani defies Dracula to sacrifice Prem in one of her ceremonies, as he is still untouched by the "unclean one" (Dracula). Dracula is informed of this by the Maharajah, more loyal to the vampire than his own wife. Dracula then stops the ceremony, saving Prem—so that he may kill him himself—and he impales the Maharani on a sharp lingam. At the same time, Babu, who came to rescue Penny, fires off a gun, frightening the cultists into a panic. In the chaos, Prem and Penny are able to escape. During this same scene, Dracula makes the "Unquenchable Thirst" title literal, killing and draining as many of the cultists as he possibly can. Because of this and the fact that he killed their leader, the Maharani, Dracula becomes public enemy #1 in the eyes of the acolytes. As such, Dracula and the Maharajah flee the palace.

The story's climactic portion begins in the unlikeliest of ways—for a Hammer Dracula film, that is—in the form of a car chase when the Maharaja drives Dracula, safe in his coffin, away in his Rolls-Royce! Prem, Babu, and Penny follow in a Morris automobile until they crash during the frantic chase. But the Maharajah isn't out of the woods yet. He drives straight into the Mohabbat celebration, a religious festival involving a large chariot. (This would have certainly been another expense for Hammer due to the exterior period setting and the large group of extras required.)

The Rolls Royce has to force its way through the crowd. The Maharajah and his servant, the Majordomo, get out of the car to try and beat the crowd away, but this backfires and incites the crowd to mob violence. The Majordomo is beaten to death, and the crowd pushes the car out of the way down into a ditch. The Thuggee cultists, wanting revenge on Dracula, also descend on the ceremony, and see to it that the Maharajah is crushed under the wheels of the sacred carriage called the Jagannath (the focus of the ceremony).

Later that night, via her connection with Dracula (she was bit, remember) Penny is able to track the vampire king down just as he emerges from his coffin in the car wreckage. But, unlike Dracula's previous vampire brides who were subservient once bitten, Penny is somehow immune to Dracula's commands. In *Dracula Has Risen from the Grave* and *Taste the Blood of Dracula*, the damsel in distress fawned over Dracula's every move until they felt they were rejected in some way and switched alliances back to their boyfriends. Penny breaks the mold in this sense.

Dracula tries to make Penny feed upon a young boy so that she may become a full-fledged vampire, but she refuses. Prem then shoots Dracula in the shoulder, and he runs away, with his cape giving him the appearance of "wings" according to the script! (If Hinds was truly trying to make Dracula fly or not is unknown, but *Scars of Dracula* had certainly upped the Count's supernatural powers.)

Dracula finds solace at a sacred spot called the Tower of Silence. (This is a real location, by the way, built by Zoroastrians who would pile their dead at the top of the towers so that vultures could pick the bones clean. Can you see where this is going for Dracula?) At the tower, the enraged acolytes attack Dracula with sharpened bamboo lances. (Again, in this sense, the climax is a bit like that of *Kiss of the Vampire,* wherein evil destroys evil as the acolytes are in no way meant to be sympathetic.) Dracula fends off the men, but their sheer numbers force him back to the tower, which he then scales! (The scene was likely written because Dracula scaling his castle, also a scene from the original novel, was successfully pulled off and well-received in *Scars of Dracula.*) As he climbs the walls, Dracula dislodges a brick that tumbles down onto the Thuggee cultists below.

Once he's safely atop the tower, a mass of people, not just the acolytes, crowd around to ogle the trapped vampire. In fact, they do so all night! Just before sunrise, an army of vultures descends upon Dracula, with the King vulture knocking him over first. In trying to escape as the birds rip him apart, Dracula hurls himself over the side of the tower, landing on several of the acolyte's bamboo sticks impaling himself. In something of a triple-whammy as the sunlight then strikes him, causing Dracula to disintegrate. Like the first film, one of the last shots was to be of Dracula's signet ring glinting in the sunlight. Hinds was once quoted as saying that he "gave extra thought to highly visual ways to do in the Count" and this certainly rings here. However, if I had to criticize one aspect of this climax, it would be the pacing. Once at the top of the tower we know Dracula is done for. Instead of ending it right there and having the vultures begin feeding on him, we stretch out the scene all night!

Despite what I said earlier about this being the same story in a different locale, the epilogue breaks the traditional Hammer mold when Penny and Prim return to the palace to get her sister. What

Interior of a Tower of Silence

THE INSATIABLE THIRST OF DRACULA

AFTER 1973'S *COUNT DRACULA AND HIS VAMPIRE BRIDE*, LEE FINALLY MADE GOOD ON HIS THREAT TO LEAVE THE ROLE. IN SPITE OF THAT FACT AND THE FILM'S BOX-OFFICE FAILURE, ANOTHER SEQUEL WAS PENNED IN 1974! IT WAS ENTITLED *THE INSATIABLE THIRST OF DRACULA* AND WRITTEN BY ANTHONY HINDS. SOME THINK THAT THIS WOULD HAVE CONTINUED THE CONTEMPORARY SETTING FROM THE LAST TWO LEE DRACULA FILMS. THIS WOULD HAVE BEEN UNWISE AS THERE WAS REALLY NOWHERE LEFT FOR THE COUNT TO GO AFTER TRYING TO DECIMATE ALL OF HUMANITY WITH A PLAGUE! (WHAT WOULD HAVE BEEN NEXT, DRACULA GETS THE NUCLEAR LAUNCH CODES?) I THINK IT MORE LIKELY MYSELF THAT *INSATIABLE THIRST OF DRACULA* WAS A REVISION OF *THE UNQUENCHABLE THIRST OF DRACULA* SET IN INDIA. THE BOOK *HAMMER COMPLETE* ALSO CONCURS THAT THIS WAS JUST AN ALTERNATE WORKING TITLE FOR *UNQUENCHABLE THIRST OF DRACULA*, AND NOT A NEW IDEA.

happens is truly shocking. You see, much in the same way that the Bond series has a "sacrificial lamb," or secondary Bond girl that often dies midway through the movie, Hammer's Dracula films often had something similar: a female victim of Dracula's that dies while the heroine lives. There was Zena in *Dracula Has Risen from the Grave* and Lucy in *Taste the Blood of Dracula*, for instance. Here, Penny returns to the palace to find that all the vampire brides have reverted back to human form! (Furthermore, the "freed prisoners" aspect again predates *Indiana Jones and the Temple of Doom.*)[3] It seems we are truly on the verge of a happy ending.

But then the story really got me! I'd been duped. It's not a happy ending, not by a long shot. This is actually the biggest departure from typical Hammer horror where good triumphs over evil and all is well with the world. As the female brides surround Penny, Prem begins to feel uneasy. Penny reassures him that all is well—and then sinks her fangs into his neck! It's a tragic end for Prem who becomes dinner for the horde of female vampires, who seem to regard Penny as their leader. The story ends on the grim realization that the army of vampire brides is about to overrun the nearby town where Babu and his wife wait, unsuspecting. Though this ending surprised me, and it was refreshing, I still prefer the good ol' fashioned good prevails over evil ending. (It's unknown how Hinds' 1970 draft ended, but it's possible this ending was

153

inspired by recent horror films with downbeat twist endings and was unique to the 1977 version.)

As stated before, the 1970 treatment didn't go anywhere because Warners and Hammer wanted to try their hand at a modern take on Dracula. Why Michael Carreras later wanted to dust off a story clearly tailored for the Christopher Lee version of the Count in 1977 is anyone's guess. But, in any case, we're glad he did. Because if he didn't, then we may have never gotten the wonderful BBC adaptation of *The Unquenchable Thirst of Dracula*. The radio play was well-received, and we can only hope that a few more of Hammer's unproduced screenplays might receive the same treatment one day.

Chapter Notes

[1] And on that note, *Indiana Jones and the Temple of Doom* was set in the year 1935 itself!

[2] I halfway wonder if Michael Ripper would have been put into some type of politically incorrect makeup to play one of the parts of the Indian locals! If not for being Indian, the character of Babu seems to fit Ripper to a tee. (I should add this would have only applied if this was filmed by 1971 or so, as Ripper left Hammer in the early 1970s.)

[3] I must feign ignorance for a moment here and wonder if *Temple of Doom* and *Unquenchable Thirst* both had a similar source material to inspire it?

18.
VICTIM OF HIS IMAGINATION

Developed: 1972-1994

Screenplay by: Don Houghton **Proposed Cast/Characters:** Bram Stoker (Shane Briant), Henry Irving/Dracula (Christopher Lee), Doctor [Stoker's doctor], Florence Stoker [Stoker's wife], Terry [actress]

PLOT Bram Stoker is plagued with visions of Dracula on his deathbed...

COMMENTARY By 1972, Hammer was celebrating its 25th anniversary, and Michael Carreras was keen on announcing a special project to commemorate it.[1] The proposed film was called *Victim of his Imagination* and served as a bio-pic for Dracula's creator Bram Stoker, who had passed away 60 years ago in 1912. And yes, the film was still going to feature Christopher Lee as Dracula, but with a twist: Lee would play the dual roles of Dracula and British actor Henry Irving, one of the real-life figures who inspired the Count. Stoker was the bookkeeper and manager of Irving's theater troupe for many years. As Irving was a superstar in his day, Stoker based much of the Count on Irving like he did Vlad the Impaler. And while Lee would play Irving/Dracula, as for Bram Stoker, Hammer was thinking of Shane Briant for the role, who had recently starred in several Hammer films like *Frankenstein and the Monster from Hell.*[2]

Don Houghton wrote a 29-page treatment laying out the story in January of 1972. The proposed film had Bram on his deathbed as he's plagued by visions of all the literary monsters he's created over the years. This intriguing story device was essentially Hammer's way of having their cake and eating it too. Even though Dracula was a fictional character, visions of the monster plagued his creator—in Hammer's proposed story at least, whether or not that happened in real life is unknown. As the film flashed back to the past, we would track the key moments of Bram's life, with an emphasis on the creation of Dracula, who would visit Bram in night terrors throughout the story. In addition to Dracula, the story would also focus on Bram's relationship with his wife Florence, as well as Irving.

Actually, rather than the film being bookended by the 1912 segments at the beginning and end only, they would pop up sporadically throughout the narrative. In the 1912 scenes, an unnamed doctor would look for clues in Stoker's works which he hopes can help him ease Bram's suffering. As to this odd structure, Keiran Foster said of it in his thesis that, "Even at treatment stage, it is difficult to see how the ambitious narrative structure would have translated on to screen. Not only is there a flashback structure at its center, but it also introduces dream sequences (usually tied thematically with the narrative), which incorporate scenes from Stoker's works."[3]

For anyone who wants to read it in full, the 29-page treatment appears in Wayne Kinsey's wonderful *Legend of the 7 Golden Vampires Scrapbook*. There is no teaser sequence of any kind to open the proposed film. It begins with the credits, which play over various nightmare images. These images begin in a distorted red form until they take on various shapes and outlines. Naturally, there are plenty of skulls and vampire fangs at play in the montage, but at least one image was supposed to bring to mind the titular creature from *Lair of the White Worm*, one of Stoker's lesser-known novels when compared to *Dracula*. As the title sequence concludes, we would do a jump cut to a screaming Bram Stoker, awakening from the nightmare we've just witnessed. As stated before, an unnamed doctor character is present along with Florence, his wife. The doctor goes to give Bram a sedative, but he brushes his hand away, knowing that it will put him to sleep and return him to the nightmare-land from which he just came.

The main setting for this portion of the narrative is Bram's home in St. George's Square, London, in the year 1912. The camera would pan around the room that Bram lays in, revealing memorabilia from his life, notably a large, signed photo of Henry Irving and a copy of *Dracula*. (There was also to be a picture of Florence when she was younger, wearing a crucifix.) After establishing the contents of the room, we would listen to Bram rant and rave to the doctor. No dialogue is given, as it's just a treatment, but Bram would get the idea across to the doctor that he can't figure out the cause of his nightmares. Bram would then begin to recount his life, not from the beginning, but from the year 1876.

Bram Stoker c. 1906.

Shane Briant as he appeared in *Captain Kronos: Vampire Hunter* **(1974).**
© Hammer Film Productions Ltd.

The scene is set within a gay afterparty at the green room of the Theater Royal in Dublin. The center of attention is Henry Irving, hot off a successful performance in 'The Rivals'. Bram is there, invited only because he wrote a favorable review of the play. Florence is there too, notably wearing the golden crucifix necklace. She is talking with none other than Oscar Wilde, a former flame who gave her the necklace before she became engaged to Bram. When Wilde asks for the expensive item back, despite being engaged to Bram, Florence informs him that she shall keep it always! (Houghton in his treatment says this is Florence's way of reminding Bram that she is still desired by other men.)

Bram, meanwhile, is transfixed by Irving, who eventually goes to speak to the young critic, telling him that he loved his review. What's more, he'd like to make a place for Bram in his inner circle. A happy Bram would then cast a glance in Florence's direction, and become somewhat sour at seeing her talking to Wilde. We would cut from here to two years later, on the day of Florence and Bram's wedding. Notably, Wilde is a scowling guest there, though Florence still wears the golden crucifix necklace over her wedding gown. Nor is there time for a honeymoon, as Irving has sent for Bram to begin his duties as his acting manager as soon as possible.

That night, Bram and Florence board a ship for Birmingham. (A stormy exterior shot of the ship would seem to suggest Dracula's stormy voyage aboard the *Demeter*.) Back inside, Bram, rather than making love to his wife, is extolling his hopes and dreams to her, especially his desire to write. Florence beckons him to bed. Houghton writes, "Whether it is the storm, whether it is a latent impotence in BRAM, or whether it is the sight of OSCAR WILDE'S tiny golden cross still around her neck – a sudden, inexplicable fear stabs at him."[4] Bram then begins what is apparently his first nightmare on his wedding night, with Florence herself turning into a horrific vision of a wraith-like woman in white. What happens next? Well, we don't really know how the rest of their wedding night plays out since we flash back to the present of 1912, where Florence is wiping the sweat from Bram's brow.

Realizing that Florence's appearance snapped Bram out of his journey into the past, the doctor gently asks her to leave them, as the doctor is now thoroughly entranced by the mystery of Bram's nightmares. We fade back to Birmingham in 1878. The Stokers are caught up in the wild world of Irving's celebrity. As we focus on Florence at yet another party, it's clear that her wedding night with Bram on the ship did not end well. All her focus appears to be on the handsome Irving, along with the young men in his inner circle. Clearly, Florence has given up on the marriage in a sense but will stay with Bram just the same. However, the duo did apparently make love, for she eventually becomes pregnant with Bram's son, Noel. (Oddly enough, Bram's son is never mentioned again in the treatment, and the focus remains on Florence and Irving in terms of Bram's relationships.)

Despite the exciting circle he belongs to, Bram is more driven by his desire to write than anything else. He reads Sheridan Le Fanu's *Carmilla*, as well as non-fiction titles on the occult and vampires. *Dracula* is gestating slowly, aided along by the charming figure of

Irving, whose star continues to rise. During a performance of Hamlet, Bram becomes mesmerized by Irving, literally. During the performance, we would focus on Irving's hands as Bram digresses to the nightmare of his honeymoon. The strange wraith woman returns, accompanied by flashes of various images, most notably tortured hands, a blazing sun in the sky, and "ominous whitewashed crosses painted on black doors."[5]

Back in the present, the doctor picks up on these three images, wondering how they might unravel the mystery of the nightmares. Bram then looks to his bookshelf, to a collection of horror stories he wrote for children called *Under the Sunset*. We cut back to Bram's office in the Lyceum Theater in London in 1882, and there Bram shows Irving the page proofs for the book, which is soon to be published. Irving is impressed but considers them far too dark for children. Irving, who you should remember would have been played by the richly voiced Christopher Lee, begins to read a passage from the story. As he does, we would see the passage from "The Invisible Giant" play out in some animated form. The story has a little girl observing a spectral giant approaching her town, with the giant representing the coming plague. There would have been an emphasis on the thing's hands in the animated vignette. Irving soon puts the manuscript down and informs Bram that he plans to tour America next.

We would cut back to 1912, where Bram looks to yet another of his books on the shelf, this one called *A Glimpse of America*. We flash back to Irving's American tour in the year 1883. There Irving enjoys whirlwind success, while Bram is thrilled to meet Walt Whitman, who advises Bram on his horror stories. Bram shares the troubles of his reoccurring nightmares with him, and Whitman encourages him to put the nightmares to paper in hopes that it might ease them.

Our next historical vignette takes place in 1885 when Bram is back home. Exhausted between the tour, prepping Irving's next theatrical run in England, and his own burgeoning writing career, he turns to Florence for comfort. In a strange scene, Bram seems to conquer his sexual frustrations, and the couple begins to make love. However, as Florence's hands caress Bram's body, they become worm-like. Another vision strikes Bram of himself at his desk writing away, concocting *Lair of the White Worm*. Houghton doesn't really decide upon which scenes or images from the book we would be privy to here. He more or less just tells us what the book is about: an ancient dragon buried beneath the surface that takes on the form of a beautiful woman, Lady Arabella. So, in

160

essence, just as Irving is used as a model for Dracula, it seems that Florence is Lady Arabella! As Bram's vision concludes, we would see Florence sleeping satisfied in bed. (Bram must be quite a multitasker to not only satisfy Florence but to plot his next novel in the process!)

Back in 1912, the doctor plucks *Lair of the White Worm* from off the bookshelf and reminds Bram it was only published last year, in 1911. Bram tells him that the story had been festering in his brain for years, and he only finished it recently. He mentions it was the last thing he wrote at Cruden Bay. The words Cruden Bay then trigger another flashback and off we go to that very place in the year 1893. Bram had to take a retreat there after becoming exhausted working for Irving. There he observes Slains Castle, which perhaps inspired Castle Dracula (though Houghton doesn't imply this). Bram comes back invigorated from his short vacation and tries to tell Irving and Florence about the magic of the place. However, the only person who really listens to him is actress Ellen Terry, with whom he has formed a friendship over the years.

One evening something fateful happens at Irving's most recent dinner party. One of the guests is Professor Arminius Vambrey, "Master of Oriental Languages at Budapest University," and also an expert on vampires. In fact, Vambrey believes that vampires are real. Notably, he believes that Vlad the Impaler, also known as Voivode Drakula, was a vampire. Irving brushes off such ideas as fantasy, and for the first time ever, Bram loses patience with his friend, clearly taken by the stories. Overall, this had the potential to be one of the film's more interesting scenes. (It's worth pondering that Hammer might have wanted to cast Peter Cushing as Vambrey since Vambrey was the inspiration for Van Helsing. If so, this would have made for quite a scene for Cushing and Lee!)

That night, after the dinner party, Bram has his most horrific nightmare yet. His nightmare appears to take place in Cruden Bay in the year 1850 in the middle of a plague. The familiar three images come into play heavily again, with the tortured hands, the sun, and the crosses on the doors. The dream ends with a young boy screaming, which turns into Bram, who awakens in Florence's arms. From here, we return to 1912, where the doctor would spout off the necessary exposition to help the audience connect the dots that we are closer to solving the mystery.

In what Houghton calls an optional sequence, Bram expresses fears to the doctor that his works will be forgotten after his death. The doctor assures him that this won't be the case, and then picks his own favorite of Bram's works from the shelf: *The Squaw*. One of Bram's final works, *The Squaw* illustrated his fascination with the real-life torture device the Iron Virgin of Nuremburg, essentially a sarcophagus laden with spikes that would impale its victims when closed. Bram's story concerned a visiting doctor stepping into the sarcophagus only to have it accidentally shut upon him. However, as with *Lair of the White Worm*, it's not clear if Houghton anticipated a recreation of the story or just included a description of it for historical background.

In any case, the segment ends with the doctor shuddering at the thought of the story's climax. He closes the book and puts it back onto the shelf, right next to *Dracula*. This marks the end of what Houghton noted as the "Optional Sequence". Bram returns to his mutterings, expressing a fear that if he doesn't solve the mystery behind his nightmares, he may suffer eternal damnation upon his death, which he fears will be upon him before the dawn.

Our next flashback takes us to 1896, where Bram continues to toil away for Irving, now more successful than ever. Ellen, his actress friend, makes the comment to Bram that Irving "feeds" off of his good nature. As though the phrase "feeds off of" stirs something in his mind, Bram seeks out Professor Vambrey again to learn more about vampires.

There's no scene description to tell us about Bram and Vambrey's meeting, and the next sequence takes place in Cruden Bay later that year. Bram is beginning to write *Dracula* and has a vision of a tall, slender man wearing a cloak. His fingers drip with blood, but as he comes closer and closer into view we see that the man has no face. A montage would follow of Bram writing the book, the pages piling up as food on his desk remains untouched. Bram has to return to London before it's finished, but on his ride back, Bram was to look out at the passing scenery and imagine it to be Transylvania. (The screenplay has several visual parallels with scenes in the book, so this would likely represent Harker's journey to Castle Dracula.) Bram's head sinks down as he falls asleep on the journey, and we would cut back to 1912, where he has also fallen asleep.

The doctor leaves him and goes to speak with Florence. He expresses the opinion that the secret to Bram's nightmares lies somewhere in the book *Dracula*. Florence doesn't disagree exactly but puts forth her own opinion that the specter of death has always haunted Bram. She thinks this is best emphasized in his work 'The Burial of the Rats'. As Florence quotes the final passage of the story, where a man is consumed by rats, Houghton noted that the scene should be dramatized with Stoker as the main character. As the scene ends, Florence subtly expresses her own belief that Bram has always been a deranged man.

We flash back to 1896, where Bram had fallen asleep on his journey back to London. He is in the middle of another nightmare. It is the same plague dream as before, set in 1850, where Bram is the young boy living in fear. In this scene, glass suddenly breaks, the glass shards hitting the boy's mother, which represents Bram's own mother, Charlette. As his bloody mother holds out her arms to embrace him, the train whistle wakes Bram. Upon first opening his eyes, through blurry vision, he sees Dracula sitting across from him. But, as his vision clears, he sees it is simply a woman in a dark cloak. Bram gets up as the train has reached its destination.

Back at the theater, Irving and Terry are enthralling the audience with a performance of Othello. As Bram too becomes caught up in their performance, he suddenly looks down at his half-completed manuscript for *Dracula*. It is as if a lightbulb has just gone off in his head as he looks at his actor friend: Irving is the face of Dracula that had been missing! On stage, in Bram's mind's eye, Irving transforms into the Count, filling in the missing puzzle piece of the novel.

It is at this point that we finally would have seen Lee/Irving as Dracula. In a hallucinogenic visual, Bram imagines Dracula stalking a female victim, Ellen Terry, in his castle. Behind Dracula are his two vampire brides, who look just like Bram's wife and mother. Dracula bites into Ellen, and after he's done feeding, outstretches his hands toward Bram. Bram screams to his mother and wife to save him as Dracula moves closer and closer to him, but they only laugh maniacally.

Audience applause for Othello snaps Bram out of his dream-like state and he watches Irving and Terry bow before the audience. Disgusted by the strange scene he's just witnessed in his mind, he shuffles off into the night. Back at home, in his study, Bram holds the papers for *Dracula* in his hand and looks at a burning fire in the fireplace. For a moment it would appear that he wants to burn the book he's worked so hard on. But, instead, he sits back down to continue writing. A bit later, Florence comes in wearing a white nightgown and looking just like the vampire in his vision. However, nothing is said of Bram's reaction, and we would dissolve back to 1912. We are only hours from the dawn now, as Florence and the doctor listen intently to his story.

Side by side comparison of Henry Irving (left) and Christopher Lee (right).

It is now the winter of 1898. *Dracula* has been published and become quite a success, though Bram is reluctant to bask in the spotlight. Oddly, Irving has read the book and greatly dislikes it, calling it vulgar but failing to recognize himself in the Count. Irving is now also 60 years old and losing his luster. One night, Bram is awakened with the news that the Lyceum warehouse is burning, which destroys a great deal of the theater's sets and wardrobe. As Bram watches the building burn, he knows Irving's company is not long for the world.

That morning, the news hits Irving quite hard. Though Houghton doesn't explain how this would be expressed, he notes that Irving feels in some way that Bram's successful book has something to do with his bad luck and decline in popularity. The next sequence would be a montage of sorts, set between England and America, showing Irving's company in decline between the years 1900 and 1905. Ellen Terry leaves Irving's company while at the same time *Dracula* goes into its sixth printing. As his health and finances continue to decline, Irving finally notes a distinct similarity between himself and Dracula and seems to develop a certain sympathy for the vampire.

Rather abruptly, Houghton inserts another *Dracula* dramatization here, that being the book's ending. However, Houghton doesn't go into too much detail, perhaps knowing Hammer couldn't recreate the rather elaborate ending of the book (a chase in the snow to Castle Dracula). Instead, it seems more reminiscent of *Horror of Dracula*, with Van Helsing chasing after Dracula with a crucifix into the sunlight to meet his doom. (Had Hammer really been on the cheap, they could have simply reused the ending of *Horror of Dracula*, one supposes. Or, if they filmed it anew, it would provide an interesting remake of *Horror of Dracula's* ending in a way.) Regardless of how this scene would have been portrayed, Houghton notes that it needed to have the crucifix and the blaring sun to be consistent with Bram's other nightmares.

The next portion would deal with Irving's death. As the actor becomes frailer and frailer, he refuses to retire and keeps on performing. Then, on October 13, 1906, Bram receives a summons to come to the Midland Hotel in Bradford at once. Upon arrival, he finds Irving sprawled out on the floor taking his last breaths. Bram is greatly saddened as his old friend looks up at him and dies. Bram envisions himself as Van Helsing at the end of *Dracula*, plunging a stake into the Count's heart as he lies within a coffin. Sickened, Bram runs into the night. We would fade back to 1912 as Bram weeps at the memory of the event. He wonders aloud if he secretly hated Irving for the hold he had on him. Did Irving feed off of Bram's energy and kindness the same way that Dracula fed off others' blood?

As Bram gasps in agony, Florence implores the doctor to administer a sedative so that he may die in peace. But the doctor knows Bram must solve his enigma before he dies and asks him again to recall the reoccurring nightmare of the plague village. He asks Florence where Bram grew up, and she responds that it was in Sligo on the west coast of Ireland. Upon hearing this, the doctor realizes Bram's reoccurring dream in Cruden Bayt was never Cruden Bay at all; it was Sligo. And, it wasn't about the plague; it was about the Cholera outbreak of the 1850s. (This explains the crosses on the doors in Bram's visions.) The doctor leads Bram on to finish telling the story.

Bram recounts how he and his family had fled to Sligo to escape the Cholera outbreak. However, when they arrive in the village, the first case of Cholera pops up, and the other villagers blame the outsiders, thinking they brought it with them. Bram's father barricades his family in the home as the town spirals out of control. Eventually, bodies pile up in the streets, but the Stoker household remains untouched by the epidemic. One night, while Bram's father is away looking for food, a mob descends upon the Stoker house. Bram peeks out the window and watches as a woman in the mob collapses from the epidemic. Her body

A NEW HAMMER PRODUCTION
VICTIM
OF HIS
IMAGINATION
THE STORY OF BRAM STOKER

shudders, but no one goes to help her. Instead, she is trampled by the violent mob as they approach the house. This is the wraith woman so often seen in Bram's nightmares.

As Bram describes the horrific scenes, prodded on by the doctor, we would occasionally cut to Bram in bed in 1912 to heighten the sense of urgency. In the flashback, a man with the yellow face of death plasters himself across Bram's window. He breaks through the glass, his bloody arm flailing like a serpent. This is the source of the bloody hands and the white worm. Charlotte takes a knife and stabs at the man's arm in self-defense as blood splatters across her dress. Houghton then suggests that various images suggestive of the climaxes of Bram's novels be inserted, such as the man being overcome by rats, the man in the Iron Virgin, and the death of Dracula. Specifically, he wanted to show Bram as Dracula, clawing at the stake in his chest.

The sequence reaches its crescendo when Bram's mother, Charlotte, finally hacks the arm clean off, and it falls to the floor. She then goes to comfort Bram, but she looks like the specter of death as she does. However, this doesn't lead up to Bram's exact moment of death in 1912. Though I thought this final macabre shock might do our protagonist in, instead, we cut to Bram in bed looking to be at peace now that he and the doctor have put the puzzle together. He knows now that his horrific creations all sprang from that one event. Now at peace, Bram Stoker passes away, presumably free of the hellish afterlife he feared. Houghton then notes to superimpose the image of Dracula decomposing in his coffin as this happens. Florence weeps as the doctor pulls the bedsheet over Bram's face. He then turns to the bookshelf, picks up *Dracula*, and quotes from the portion of the book where Dracula proclaims that he will return again and again. The light of the dawn breaks into the room at that moment, and the doctor reflects that vampires cannot abide the light of day...

As to why the treatment never progressed into a screenplay, that's because Hammer had made a special arrangement with Warner Bros whereas their Dracula films were concerned, and Warners was more interested in the pair of contemporary Dracula flicks they had Hammer developing. (One thing's for sure, this film would've pleased Christopher Lee more so than *Dracula A.D. 1972*!) And yet, this was not the death of the project, which would gestate at Hammer for the next twenty years. In May of 1992, Carreras did his best to revive the film, though he was no longer at Hammer. Carreras first reread Houghton's old script, which he heavily annotated before writing a new, 15-page treatment of his own. Carreras's new version kept most of Houghton's three-tiered structure of the 1912 deathbed scenes, the flashbacks, and the night terrors. However, Carreras did attempt to streamline the treatment by having each flashback partially revolve around one of Irving's different plays. Carreras was at this time also writing his own historical novel on Stoker. As such, his treatment had much more historical detail than Houghton's. For instance, originally in the 1912 segments, the character was simply known

167

as "the doctor", but Carreras made him Professor Arminus Vambre.

This time around, Carreras didn't have visions of grandeur for the project. Instead of a high-budgeted theatrical feature, he thought of it as a prospective TV movie or mini-series. A wise promoter, Carreras knew that the publicity for Francis Ford Coppola's upcoming Dracula film could help get his project off the ground. And, if it was successful, then perhaps it could launch a series of biopics devoted to horror writers like Edgar Allen Poe and others.

For a time, things looked bright for the treatment, as Hammer had recently signed a new production deal with Warner Bros. When Carreras was setting up his interview for *Flesh and Blood: The Hammer Heritage of Horror* (released in 1994, but compiled before that), Hammer's Ted Newsom told Carreras that his pitch was well-received by Hammer and Warners. Ultimately, Hammer's production deal with Warners came to naught, and Carreras sadly passed away from cancer in 1994.

Chapter Notes

1 Though there was no way the film could get done that year, it was still announced in 1972.
2 Though not released until 1974, it was shot in 1971.
3 Foster, "Unseen Horrors", p. 108.
4 Page four of the treatment, as reprinted in *Legend of the 7 Golden Vampires Scrapbook*, p.24.
5 Page seven of the treatment, Ibid, p.25.

19.
RICHARD MATHESON'S
DRACULA

Broadcast Date: February 8, 1974 (U.S.)

Directed by: Dan Curtis **Teleplay by:** Richard Matheson based upon the book by Bram Stoker **Music by:** Robert Cobert **Special Effects by:** Kit West **Cast:** Jack Palance (Count Dracula/Vlad the Impaler), Simon Ward (Arthur Holmwood), Nigel Davenport (Abraham Van Helsing), Fiona Lewis (Lucy Westenra/Maria Tepes), Murray Brown (Jonathan Harker), Penelope Horner (Mina Murray), Pamela Brown (Mrs. Westenra)

Spherical, Color, 98 Minutes

PLOT Dracula terrorizes London in search of his lost love...

COMMENTARY In 1973, great television horror producer Dan Curtis finally adapted *Dracula*. I say finally because he had done not one, but two famous adaptations of vampires previous to this. The best known was *Dark Shadows*, where Barnabas Collins essentially became the TV version of Dracula in the late 1960s. Later in 1973 had aired his *The Nightstalker*, about a reporter pursuing a vampire through Las Vegas, which became the highest-rated TV movie of its time. Later that year, Curtis finally turned his attention to the original vampire, Dracula. But, whereas Curtis's previous three horror adaptations of *Dr. Jekyll and Mr. Hyde*, *The Portrait of Dorian Gray*, and *Frankenstein* had been filmed on videotape, his version of *Dracula* would be a much higher budgeted production, shot on film and made for British television. To that end, it was even lensed on location in England and also caught some authentic exterior footage in Yugoslavia. Written and shot as a three-hour masterpiece, CBS insisted that the film be edited down to a one-night, two-hour timeslot. Remarkably, that this version is much shorter than originally intended is not evident.

Jack Palance as Dracula.

Roughly, the story is similar to the novel and goes as follows: When Jonathan Harker arrives at Castle Dracula to oversee a real estate deal, his host Count Dracula becomes obsessed with a photograph of his friend, Lucy Westerna, who looks exactly like the Count's long dead wife. Harker is vampirized by Dracula's brides as the Count leaves for London to court Lucy, engaged to Arthur Holmwood. Dracula feeds on Lucy until she dies, despite the best efforts of Holmwood and vampire hunter Van Helsing. When Lucy rises again as a vampire, Van Helsing stakes her before

Dracula can come to collect her. Upon seeing Lucy's staked body, he becomes enraged and sets his sights on Mina as an act of revenge. After making Mina drink of his blood, Dracula returns to Transylvania. Using Mina's psychic connection to the Count, Holmwood and Van Helsing follow him. At Castle Dracula they dispatch the vampire version of Harker, and then expose Dracula to sunlight. In Dracula's helpless state, Van Helsing drives a lance through his heart, ending the Count's reign of terror.

Writer Richard Matheson said, "[It] turned out quite well, I thought, but it was even better at the three hours originally shot. I wrote a script for three hours, and Dan shot a three-hour version, but the network would give us only two hours. So Dan had to edit it down. I would have loved to have seen it at three hours."[1] Unfortunately, all the extra footage shot was lost sometime in the 1980s, meaning that a director's cut was impossible for home video. The full screenplay is at least preserved in Mark Dawidziak's 2006 book *Bloodlines: Richard Matheson's Dracula, I Am Legend, and Other Vampire Stories*.

As such, what we are about to discuss isn't the three-hour version as shot by Curtis, but Matheson's original script, which required some censoring for television. Our first major difference is that Matheson wanted to mimic the book, with Dracula's first scene as an old man with pointed fingernails and a white mustache, while in the film Dracula is the same throughout. (There may not have been room in the budget for this, and so in the film, Dracula looks the same age at all times.) It would only be

171

after feeding on Lucy that Dracula would revert back to a youthful appearance, which would mean a man in his forties in this case since that's what Palance was about then. Furthermore, when Dracula is denied feeding on Lucy, he would begin to age once again.

A notable deleted scene had Dracula arriving to save Harker from his vampire brides by offering them a gift: a squirming sack in his hands. In it is a "half-dead little girl" which the women pounce upon. It's not surprising the scene was cut, as it was a bit too horrific for television. (A similar scene had been cut from an early version of *Dracula's Daughter* back in the 1930s.) There would have been a follow-up to the scene too, where the little girl's parents show up outside the castle demanding her return, and Dracula sets the hounds upon them!

As for more elements that would have been too much for TV, Matheson envisioned the vampirized Lucy tempting Arthur Holmwood (her fiancé in this version) by baring her breasts. In the film, Lucy's death is fairly graphic, and in the uncut version, blood comes from out her mouth when she's staked. (Matheson even wanted to see her decapitated.) Later in the script, Dracula would also kill Lucy's mother, who figures into this version of the tale. In the film, she survives her encounter with Dracula, where he barges into a hotel where she and Mina are staying.

The story ends like the book, with Van Helsing and Holmwood attacking Castle Dracula. The film notably had Harker pop back up as a vampire at the end, but Matheson's script had him escaping the castle earlier so that this didn't happen. Matheson envisioned some things that were outside the scope of the budget, such as Dracula's hordes of rats. And, when Dracula is staked, Matheson envisioned gold coins falling from his pockets as in the book.

What Curtis added to the script later was the flashbacks, which predated similar though more ambitious flashbacks in Francis Ford Coppola's 1992 *Dracula*. It was also Dan Curtis who added the *Horror of Dracula*-like moment where Van Helsing rips down the curtains to expose the Count to sunlight.

Anyhow, though we might all lament the fact that the three-hour cut of Dan Curtis's Dracula is lost, the two-hour version is still quite spectacular.

Chapter Notes

1 Pierson, *Produced and Directed by Dan Curtis*, p.21.

20.
THE SEVEN BROTHERS
(DON'T) MEET DRACULA

Release Date: July 11, 1974 (China), October 6, 1974 (U.K.),
June 1979 (U.S.)

Directed by: Roy Ward Baker **Screenplay by:** Don Houghton
Special Effects by: Les Bowie **Music by:** James Bernard **Cast:**
Peter Cushing (Professor Van Helsing), David Chiang (Hsi
Ching/Hsi Tien-en), Robin Stewart (Leyland Van Helsing), Julie
Ege (Vanessa Buren), Shih Szu (Mai Kwei), Chan Shen
(Kah/Count Dracula's host), John Forbes-Robertson (Count
Dracula), Lau Kar-wing (Hsi Kwei/archer), Huang Pei-Chih (Hsi
Po-Kwei/spearman), Wang Chiang (Hsi San/twin swordsman),
David de Keyser (voice of Count Dracula)

Panavision, Eastmancolor, 89 Minutes

In the tradition of
The 7 Samurai and
The Magnificent 7,
Hammer *now present–*

PLOT Professor Van Helsing teams with a band of Kung Fu fighters in China to battle a vampire cult...

COMMENTARY In 1974 was released one of Hammer's most ambitious—and most unusual—vampire films in the form of *Legend of the 7 Golden Vampires*. A co-production between Hammer and Shaw Brothers of Hong Kong, it saw Peter Cushing's Van Helsing traveling to China in 1904 and battling a horde of vampires in a small village. The vampire sect is ruled over by none other than Count Dracula, played by John Forbes Robertson rather than Christopher Lee.

Many fans, myself included, have argued that *Legend of the 7 Golden Vampires* would have been better off as a Van Helsing solo film (which it essentially is) sans Dracula entirely. Apparently, Michael Carreras was of the same mindset, and the first draft of the script did not feature Dracula at all. Originally, the film was to simply begin with the flashback of Hsi Tien-en killing the seventh vampire, with the scene specifically set in 1780. We would not see Van Helsing, but the audience would surely recognize the voice of Peter Cushing and know who it was as he narrated the flashback. The credits would be integrated into the flashback as well. After the flashback was over, we would see Van Helsing giving the lecture one hundred years later, in 1880. Other than this, the film would have played out exactly the same aside from climaxing with the destruction of the final vampire. (The story didn't even include the character of Kah, the vampire priest, at this point.)

However, the Shaw Brothers' main caveat was that they wanted Dracula in the picture. Therefore, writer Don Houghton went back and bookended the script with scenes containing the Count, which, at that time, would only appear in the Shaw's version of the film. As such, the new version of the script, completed in July of 1973, didn't entail a heavy rewrite. Houghton simply inserted Dracula into the beginning and ending and retitled it *Dracula and the 7 Golden Vampires.*[1] The first iteration of the script to add Kah/Dracula also had the Seven Golden Vampires in need of resurrection as though they were all destroyed, something that doesn't happen in the film. The prologue in the script is only slightly different from the finished film, with Kah traveling to Castle Dracula (and along the way several children throw stones at him). Upon meeting Dracula, Kah explains how the Seven Golden Vampires are just effigies now in need of resurrection, which he hopes the Count can oversee. Furthermore, he hopes that Dracula will turn him into a vampire as well. Incensed, this

175

DELETED SCENES

> ONE DELETED SCENE THAT WAS SHOT INVOLVED LEYLAND VAN HELSING AND MAY ROSE GOING SKINNY DIPPING TOGETHER IN A LAKE. (ROBIN STEWART CONFIRMED THAT IT WAS FILMED AND THAT HE AND SHIH SZU WERE IN FACT COMPLETELY NAKED FOR THE SCENE.) AFTER THEY FINISH THEIR SWIM, THEY EXIT THE LAKE AND LAY BEHIND A SMALL BUSH TOGETHER, WHICH ROBIN FELT DIDN'T OBSCURE ANYTHING. HE PHONED HIS AGENT AND ASKED THAT HE LOBBY FOR THE SCENE TO BE CUT.

is where Dracula decides to take on Kah's form for an extended vacation. Houghton then explains in the short, three-page memo that from this point forward that "far eastern audiences" would know for the rest of the film that Kah is really Dracula. In other words, because the Dracula scenes would only be present in the Shaw cut, when English-speaking audiences saw Kah, they would only think him to be the high priest, not Dracula in disguise. The ending was rewritten to suit this as well. Kah would never revert back to Dracula as he did in the final film. Van Helsing would simply fight Kah, with one throw-away line added in for the Shaw version where Van Helsing realizes Kah and the Count are one and the same. After staking Kah, he would revert back to his Dracula form, but again, only in the Shaw cut.[2] In the Hammer version, Kah is simply shot in the back by Kwei, the arrow through his heart destroying him.

There was also to be an epilogue after the fight in the temple. Van Helsing, Leyland, Miao Kue, and the other surviving brothers return to the village. There the villagers are looking happier already, and the fires from earlier have died down. The dead brothers and Vanessa are laid out respectfully, and the remaining brothers collect their dead siblings' weapons. They then toss their own weapons onto the heap as though they may never pick them up again. The camera would then pull back slowly and then pan upwards for the credits to roll. (The film simply rolls the credits outside the temple.)

As for other odds and ends, due to issues of time rather than budget, several scenes were cut from the script. One concerned a Chinese sailing junk in Hong Kong harbor. At least one character, said to be patented after Major Holly in *She*, was also removed entirely. (The character would have been a British military officer of some sort.) The other differences are fairly minor, such as the zombies in the cave turning to dust after the conclusion of the battle. (Probably realizing the zombies were needed for the climax, they retreat instead in the film.) Before the final battle commences,

ABOVE: Still of the deleted skinny dipping scene. LEFT: Eva Rueber-Staier, former Miss World 1969, was the original choice for Vanessa Buren.

Van Helsing was to give a rousing speech, but it was never filmed. Also, the early scripts wisely left the events undated so as not to cause continuity problems (the dates 1804 and 1904 were superimposed into the final cut).

As to why Dracula appeared in both versions of the film upon release, this was because when Carreras approached Warner Bros about the picture, they also wanted Dracula.[3] Speaking of the Count, conflicting sources state that Christopher Lee either was or wasn't approached to play the part again. If he was, he obviously said no. And why shouldn't he have? The part for Dracula in this film is the most unnecessary of the whole series. As such, Lee's backup for *Scars of Dracula*, John Forbes-Robertson , was pressed into service at the request of director Roy Ward Baker. And so, for the one and only time in Hammer's history, an actor other than Lee played Dracula. Forbes-Robertson, aside from the makeup job, which wasn't his fault, does pretty well as the arch vampire. However, his original performance might have been better. You see, he was dubbed as Dracula, which he was none too happy about. He told Wayne Kinsey in *Little Shoppe of Horrors* #32 that, "[the new voice] just changed the whole characterization — my characterization of Dracula."[4]

However, if Forbes-Robertson was angry about that, then he would have really been mad at Michael Carreras for cutting him out of the entire film, which by his own admission, he did at one

178

IN 1975, BRUCE LEE'S ENTER THE DRAGON BECAME A MONUMENTAL HIT FOR WARNER BROS. YOU WOULD THINK THEN THAT THEY WOULD BE EAGER TO DISTRIBUTE HAMMER AND SHAW'S KUNG-FU VAMPIRE FILM, WHICH THEY ALSO PUT UP 25% OF THE BUDGET FOR! IN A MIND-BLOWING DECISION, WARNERS DECIDED TO WRITE THE FILM OFF AND NOT RELEASE IT AT ALL. MAKING MATTERS EVEN WORSE, THEY MADE IT INCREDIBLY DIFFICULT FOR OTHER U.S. DISTRIBUTERS TO PICK UP THE FILM. CARRERAS LAMENTED ON THIS FACT THREE YEARS LATER IN *HOUSE OF HAMMER* #17, SAYING, "WARNER BROTHERS, FOR INSTANCE, HAVE GOT THREE OF OUR FILMS JUST SITTING ON THE SHELF OVER THERE, INCLUDING LEGEND OF THE SEVEN GOLDEN VAMPIRES. THAT DID VERY WELL ALL OVER THE WORLD BUT IT'S NEVER BEEN RELEASED IN AMERICA. WARNER BROTHERS ARE JUST WAITING NOW FOR A TELEVISION SALE." A BEACON OF HOPE APPEARED IN THE FORM THE CANNON GROUP, WHO EXPRESSED INTEREST IN DISTRIBUTION. HOWEVER, THEY EVENTUALLY PASSED AND SENT THE PRINT OF THE FILM THEY HAD TO SAMUEL Z. ARKOFF OF AMERICAN INTERNATIONAL PICTURES. AIP WOULD HAVE BEEN PERFECT TO DISTRIBUTE THE FILM, AND AS LUCK HAD IT, THEY INTENDED TO. THEY NOT ONLY RE-EDITED THE FILM FROM 88 MINUTES TO 84 MINUTES, THEY ALSO HIRED SPECIAL EFFECTS VETERAN JACK RABIN TO SHOOT ADDITIONAL FOOTAGE FOR DRACULA'S DEATH! IN THE FALL OF 1976, WARNERS ISSUED SOME LAST MINUTE DEMANDS OF AIP THAT MADE DISTRIBUTION DIFFICULT, AND SO THEY DROPPED THE PROJECT. ULTIMATELY, THE FILM WAS PITIFULLY RELEASED AS *THE SEVEN BROTHERS MEET DRACULA* BY DYNAMITE ENTERTAINMENT IN 1979. IT NOT ONLY SHORTENED THE FILM TO AN EVEN GREATER EXTENT THAN AIP PLANNED TO DO, IT ALSO RESHUFFLED FOOTAGE AROUND SO AS TO MAKE IT ALMOST NONSENSICAL.

point. Yes, that's right, after filming was completed, Carreras still assembled a cut of the movie that eliminated Dracula despite the wishes of Warner Bros! In Carreras's own words in *House of Hammer* #17:

What happened when we saw the finished picture was that we thought the Kung Fu parts of the film were much more exciting than the Dracula sequences so we cut a version without Dracula at all, and what we had was a very good Chinese action- adventure Kung Fu frolic but unfortunately in that form it was too short so we had to put Dracula back in.

It's too bad this cut isn't available for examination as it would be interesting to watch. However, something seems fishy about Carreras saying the picture was too short. John Forbes-Robertson has less than ten minutes of screen time, easily. In fact, he might have less than five minutes! Cutting out Dracula shouldn't have made the film too short. And if it did, then why not add some of the extra kung-fu scenes alleged to exist in the Shaw Brothers version? As it stands, there is a rumor that the Shaw Brothers version of the film ran longer with extra kung-fu scenes. Because the Shaws disliked Baker's direction of the fight scenes, they inserted some new fight sequences into the movie. The Shaws also had their own director Chang Chech do the fight scenes for much of the picture. If online rumors are true, the Shaw Brother's cut of the movie runs at 110 minutes! Maybe Carreras didn't have access to that extra footage; who knows? Or, more likely, Dracula was left in at the insistence of Warner Bros.

Upon release in the East, particularly in Singapore, the film did bang-up business. However, that was the Shaw's territory, and thusly their profits. In Britain, the film opened at the #3 spot at the box office. Though this was encouraging, it dropped off by its second week and didn't make much of a splash. The real problem was that in the States, Warner Bros suddenly decided to shelve the film at the height of the kung-fu craze! (See the sidebar for more.) Had this film been distributed in 1975 by Warner Bros as it should have been, similar films, like *Kali: Devil Bride of Dracula*, may have followed.

Chapter Notes

1 However, in an interview in *House of Hammer* #17 Carreras said that "Houghton also had Dracula popping up in the middle" which is not the case in the finished film. Was Carreras misremembering or is there a deleted scene we don't know about?
2 In a slightly revised version of the scene, Dracula was to knock Van Helsing into a gong which alerts the others to the fight in the temple, and so they return to aid Van Helsing.
3 Hammer only put up 25% of the film, with the other 25% coming from Warner Bros, and the full %50 from Shaws.
4 Kinsey, "Interview with John Forbes Robertson," *Little Shoppe of Horrors* #32 (Kindle Edition).

■ ■ ■ ■ ■ ■ ■ ■ ■ ■ ■ ■ ■ ■ ■ ■ ■ ■ ■

21.
BLACK THE RIPPER

■ ■ ■ ■ ■ ■ ■ ■ ■ ■ ■ ■ ■ ■ ■ ■ ■ ■ ■

Shot: 1974-1976
Proposed Release Date: Memorial Day 1976

Director: Frank R. Saletri **Screenplay by:** Mike Finn **Credited Cast:** Marva Farmer (Carla), Hugh Van Patten (Mike)

PLOT A mysterious killer targets black prostitutes, and it's up to a karate instructor to stop him!

COMMENTARY In the early 1970s, a new genre called Blaxploitation Horror was created upon the release of *Blacula*. As the title implies, the film was more or less about an African version of Dracula, specifically a prince vampirized by the Count. Like *Dracula A.D. 1972* and *Count Yorga, Vampire*, it had a contemporary setting. It was also a huge hit with audiences spawning one sequel (*Scream Blacula, Scream!*) and a handful of imitators like *Blackenstein* and *Dr. Black, Mr. Hyde* (1976) to name a few. But, as Yoda so eloquently and enigmatically put it in *The Empire Strikes Back*, "There is another..."

Rumors claim that not only was another Blaxploitation Horror movie planned in the mid-1970s but it may have also been shot. As such, it's not an unproduced script, but a lost film. And that film is *Black the Ripper*. The story was created by attorney-turned-screenwriter Frank Saletri, who had also concocted *Blackenstein*. Thanks to an old issue of *Variety*, dated May 8, 1974, we know that the movie had begun filming back in March of that year. There was nary a peep about the film again until two years later when a February 25, 1976, issue of *Variety* had an ad stating that *Black the Ripper* would see release on Memorial Day 1976 for Dimension Pictures. Obviously, it never did.

For forty years, fans were left wondering if the film was actually ever finished. Then, in the 2010s, screenshots of the purported film began surfacing online. Eventually, a very rough cut of the movie, sans the ending credits, surfaced, which ran a scant 57

SALETRI'S OTHER SCREENPLAYS

minutes. Though it lacked the end credits, it did at least have the opening credits, which proved this was indeed *Black the Ripper.* Naturally, the opening credits feature a groovy theme song with lyrics that go "He's back! He's black! Black the Ripper!" It was sung by *Blackenstein*'s Marva Farmer, credited here as Marv Farmer for some reason. Actually, the credits are quite scarce, only acknowledging two actors, the director, and the writer, identified only as "Mike Finn".[1]

Allegedly, after the credits, the film opens in a karate studio and focuses on an instructor named Mike. He soon receives a phone call that sets the plot into motion, where one of his students informs him that his sister has just been murdered. The unnamed student goes on to tell Mike that he thinks he knows who did it: a shady pimp named Sideback that he told his sister to avoid. (Apparently she was a prostitute.) As is usual in a 70s vigilante crime thriller, the police are of no help, and so Mike has to take on the case himself.

During a scene where Mike questions a prostitute about the murder, he suddenly hears a voice call out to him.[2] From the darkness, Sideback appears, and a fight ensues between he and Mike. The men are both arrested, and while they are being taken to jail, another murder occurs which clears Sideback from suspicion. The murder even had a witness of sorts in the form of a blind man, who heard the killer say, "You deserve everything you're going to get, strumpet." At this point, the story shifts to a "mild-mannered" white accountant named Todd, who we are introduced to as he awkwardly attempts to flirt with his African American secretary, Carla. We know he's the titular character when she turns down his invitation to go on a date, and he says to himself, "You deserve everything you're going to get, strumpet."

Next up, we observe Todd dreaming that he's picking up a black prostitute in Victorian London! The narrative then shifts back to

"BLACK THE RIPPER"
(FRSCO Prods.)
Prod.-Scr. — Frank R. Saletri
Hugh van Putten, Bole Nikoli, Renata Harmon, Marva Farmer, Dale Bach
(Started March 4 in L.A.)

Mike, who has now convinced the police to take on the case of the new Jack the Ripper. (Some think there was a missing scene explaining this.) At about this time, Carla, the secretary, calls in to report that her boss has been acting suspiciously.

After this, Carla and Mike are seen together, implying they have either began a relationship or already had one, and it just wasn't established due to another missing scene. While Mike is at Carla's place, Todd comes calling. Unfortunately, he arrives while Mike is gone to get food. Todd kills Carla's roommate first and then turns his attention to Carla. Mike returns, fights Todd, and the would-be-Jack the Ripper is thrown from a third-story window. Mike and Carla embrace, and the disappointing sounding film ends.

Needles to say, there's a lot of odd things about the story. While I don't find the idea of a white villain in a blaxploitation film to be out of place, it doesn't fit the title or the formula as established by *Blacula* and *Blackenstein*, where the titular characters were black. Let's also consider the lyrics of the opening song, which supposedly state, "He's back! He's black! Black the Ripper!" As you can see right there, the lyrics imply that the titular character is black. Was this incompetence on the filmmaker's part, or is there something more fishy going on?

As it stands, there's a very significant hurdle to jump when it comes to proving the *Black the Ripper*'s existence. The main source for the film is a Daily Grindhouse article published on April Fool's Day of 2013. Was it all a joke? Even though they published screengrabs from the film, perhaps they were taken from an obscure, existing film? However, a Lost Media Wiki user had this to say about that,

> So, after adding the images from the The Daily Grindhouse article that was in the sources, I realize that the article came out on April 1st, 2013. It is entirely possible that this whole thing was an April Fool's joke, and I just got played.

However, when I usually see a web article that is made for April Fools Day, they make it appear legitimate for the day, and then edit in a disclaimer the next day to keep people from repeating the lie. I don't see that here. Also, The Daily Grindhouse has done some articles on April 1st that appear to be entirely legitimate.[3]

Since Daily Grindhouse has never retracted their story, perhaps it was real after all? Furthermore, if the *Variety* article was real, and not concocted as part of the joke, then that also means that there really was a *Black the Ripper* planned. Is it possible that the real *Variety* article was used to perpetrate an April Fool's Day Hoax? For now, like the identity of the real Jack the Ripper, it remains a mystery.

Purported screengrabs from *Black the Ripper*, though they may have very well come from other films entirely if it's all a hoax.

Chapter Notes

---

[1] Some sources think this is really Michael Finn, who directed *The Black Connection* and who lived in Las Vegas, a place that director Saletri had connections to.

[2] Those who have heard the voice claim it sounds like actor Antonio Fargas.

[3] lostmediawiki.com   /Black_the_Ripper_(lost_blaxploitation_horror_film;_existence_unconfirmed;_1974-1976)

This page and following: Tom Chantrell's exciting poster art for *Kali – Devil Bride of Dracula.*

22.
DRACULA
AND THE CURSE OF KALI

Developed: 1974-1977

Treatment by: Don Houghton **Proposed Cast/Characters:** Dr. Louis Van Helsing (Peter Cushing), Lt. Ashwood [Benghal Lancer], Esther Van Helsing [Van Helsing's daughter], Ranji Hissar [Afridi Prince], Dracula (unknown, possibly John Forbes-Robertson), Lal Gomal [Indian Professor], Shinwar Khan [Kali Temple Priest] Hugh Fennell [Anglo-Indian politician], Bahrud Singh [Sepoy Sergeant], Lalamir [kidnapped girl],

PLOT Professor Van Helsing faces off against Dracula in India...

185

COMMENTARY Before *Legend of the 7 Golden Vampires* failed to see release in the U.S. as anticipated, Warner Bros was already asking Hammer to begin work on a sequel to be set in India. This had nothing to do with the earlier discarded *Dracula – High Priest of the Vampires,* though, and had everything to do with the fact that Warners had a cache of frozen rupees that could only be used on a film shot in India. And because Warners was at the time impressed with *Legend,* they wanted a similar action-oriented sequel. This is the reason, I would presume, that Warners rejected *High Priest of the Vampires* when it was offered to them in March of 1974. Plus, that script was tailored more to Christopher Lee's Dracula, and it was unlikely that another actor could carry the weight of Dracula's scenes in that script. As such, a brand new sequel, more so in the vein of *Legend* was cooked up. Actually, sequel isn't really the right term. On the surface, the logical thing to do would have been to have Van Helsing and Leland travel from China to India, where they again meet a resurrected Count wanting revenge due to events of the last film. Instead, a prequel was cooked up that took place not only before *Legend,* but before *Horror of Dracula* as well!

The reason for this wasn't because anyone was itching for a prequel, but more so because Don Houghton wanted to set his story during the time period of the Indian Mutiny of 1857, in which an attempt was made to overthrow British rule. In fact, Houghton's twenty-page treatment, *Dracula and the Curse of Kali,* begins with a full page of historical background on the mutiny and Kali as the goddess of death.

Set in 1856, one year before the mutiny, the treatment gets off to a tantalizing start to say the least. Houghton sets the scene in India's Northwest Frontier just outside of Peshawar, near Khyber Pass at the British outpost of Fort Meerabad. A lookout spots a horse and rider galloping frantically towards the fort. The gates are opened in the nick of time as the horse barrels past them. Two local villagers try to calm the horse as it rears up and its rider falls from its back. Upon inspection, the other soldiers realize that not only is the rider a fellow soldier, but his dead body has been mutilated horribly. The man's eyes have been gouged out, and his heart has been removed! The two soldiers that examined the body turn away in revulsion as an eerie wind begins to howl. It is accompanied by a strange wailing... it is the Devil Wind! (Historically speaking, "The Devils Wind" was the name given to the mutiny by Sepoys, the Indian soldiers under the rule of the British.)

Although Houghton doesn't say it, I would guess that here is where the music would reach a crescendo, and perhaps the title credits would begin. In any case, the next portion of the treatment is labeled "Background" and introduces us to this film's version Van Helsing. Whereas previously we had met two different iterations of Van Helsing—Lawrence in *Horror*, *Brides*, and *Legend*, and his great-grandson Lorimer in *Dracula A.D. 1972* and its sequel—here we would have met Lawrence's father, Dr. Luis Van Helsing. Therefore, this would have been Cushing's third variation of the character. And, whereas the last film also introduced Van Helsing's son, Leyland, this story introduces a daughter, Esther, creating an interesting parallel between this treatment and *Legend*. But I'm getting ahead of myself.

Dr. Luis Van Helsing is scouring the Valley of Sugrakurram for the lost Temple of Kali, rumored to be located in a hidden cave. Along to help him are some Punjabi bearers and some friendly Afridi-Pathan guards. (The Afridi were a tribe of people living near Khyber Pass.) Van Helsing's introductory scene is more evocative of Cushing's character John Banning in *The Mummy* (1959), or better yet, Indiana Jones. We find Van Helsing very excited at the discovery of an ancient stone slab. Cryptically, it features a carving of a six-legged spider wrapped around a bat (Tom Chantrell used this image on a concept poster). Though Van Helsing is excited by the discovery, his aides are not. To them it is a bad omen, but Van Helsing decides to take it back to his tent anyways. As the stone is moved, the Devil Wind blows. The eerie moment passes upon the arrival of soldiers from Fort Meerabad. They are shocked to see Van Helsing alive in the wilderness. The leader, Captain Purnell, tells Van Helsing they had given him up for dead long ago. Purnell then informs him that he has need of him back at the fort at once, and more or less orders him to come with him. On the journey back, Van Helsing converses with Lieutenant Ashwood, who is essentially this film's equivalent of Leyland. (Or, that is to say, he's the young male lead to engage in the action scenes that would have been too taxing for the older Cushing.) Ashwood informs Van Helsing that due to rumors of his death, that his two children, Esther and Lawrence, are in Peshawar awaiting his return. (Houghton notes that it is clear that Ashwood has become quite taken with Van Helsing's beautiful daughter.)

 **RUMORS**

BEFORE THE EFFORTS OF KEIRAN FOSTER AND WAYNE KINSEY, MUCH SPECULATION ABOUNDED REGARDING KALI – DEVIL BRIDE OF DRACULA. THIS AUTHOR REMEMBERS READING AT LEAST ONE SOURCE THAT CLAIMED THIS WOULD BE A SEQUEL TO LEGEND WHICH BROUGHT BACK LEYLAND VAN HELSING ALONG WITH HIS FATHER. ANOTHER REPORT CLAIMED THAT THE STORY WAS TO BE BOOKENDED BY THE OLDER VAN HELSING, WHO EXPLAINS HOW HE FIRST ENCOUNTERED DRACULA IN 1870'S INDIA, WHERE HE FOUGHT HIM WITH THE AID OF BENGAL LANCERS (OR, VAN HELSING WAS HIMSELF A BENGAL LANCER, IT'S NOT CLEAR). HOWEVER, I CAN FIND NO SOURCES TO VERIFY ANY OF THOSE STORY VARIATIONS.

When the regiment returns to Fort Meerabad, they find it completely deserted. More sinister yet, they find two dead soldiers impaled onto a wall, their eyes torn from their sockets and their hearts missing. Though Purnell thinks it the work of revolting Sepoy soldiers, Van Helsing points out the ritualistic nature of the killings. Angrily, Purnell orders Van Helsing and Ashwood to ride to Peshawar to report the incident. After this, we would cut away to the hidden Temple of Kali, similar in certain ways to the titular locale of *Indiana Jones and the Temple of Doom*. Inside the huge, dome-like cavern, we would find all the Sepoys and villagers of Fort Meerabad who were abducted. The men are in chains, while the women are kept in a cage hanging above them (this features in Chantrell's poster). Similar to *Temple of Doom*'s Mola Ram, or perhaps we should say in place of Kah in keeping with the *Legend* comparisons, we have a character named Shinwar Khan in the role of the evil high priest. His goal is to somehow incarnate Kali in human form (and no, we don't know how). Before going any further, it should be noted that there is a gigantic statue within the temple of Kali (similar to the one from 1973's *Golden Voyage of Sinbad*).

What happens next seems a bit over the top. First, the shrouded figure of a woman, not clearly discernable, walks into the temple to sit upon a prominent throne, and it appears as though she has six arms! Is this Kali in human form? No dialogue is given to address this matter, and the audience would be "in the dark" so to speak, just like the prisoners watching the strange figure approaching the throne. After the men gasp in awe at the figure they've just seen, the temple guards place a metal collar with a bell on each of the men, so every move they make will cause the bell to sound. Then, out of the shadows come this treatment's equivalent to the zombies from the last picture. To make them distinct, they are lacking their eyes and their hearts, a great visual to say the least. (They too feature prominently on Chantrell's concept poster.) As the captured men tremble in fear, the eye-less ones, as they are called, respond to the noises made by the bells and approach the terrified prisoners. The poor captives then get their eyes gouged out by the zombies, who then rip their hearts out so that they may join their ranks!

Back to Van Helsing, he and Ashwood arrive in Peshawar where they find Esther and the young Lawrence, who would've gotten a quick cameo. Along with them is a colleague of Van Helsing's named Professor Lal Gomal. As Van Helsing brought the strange stone slab with him, Gomal helps him to translate it while Esther assists. (I suppose in this way that also makes Esther a bit like Jessica Van Helsing from the two 1970s-set entries.) By dawn, Van Helsing and Gomal have come to a dark realization, though Houghton doesn't reveal what it is yet. Van Helsing asks Ashwood if he could arrange a meeting between him and the Brigadier in charge. Ashwood arranges this, and Van Helsing tells the Brigadier he has every reason to believe that the Sepoys didn't revolt at Meerabad. Instead, he thinks the ancient cult of Kali is responsible and that it is slowly moving westward. At the same time, Van Helsing has heard reports of another strange creature moving eastward. In its wake are a trail of victims drained of all blood from Turkey into Persia and Afghanistan.

Of course, this creature is Dracula, and though not named, this is the first time he's hinted at in the treatment! Also, keep in mind that this being a prequel, that Van Helsing has never met Dracula. Furthermore, for a reason that's not terribly well explained, Dracula is heading east to marry Kali. How was this arranged? Again, the treatment doesn't say, but in later iterations, Michael Carreras would request a new scene, similar to the one that kicks off *Legend*, where an envoy arrives at Castle Dracula to pitch the marriage idea. In this iteration of the story, the whole idea falls into the realm of "mysterious prophecy" territory, with an old piece of script that Van Helsing found with the slab revealing that the approaching Devil Wind is Dracula set to marry Kali. The stone slab, they figure out, is meant to represent the marriage between Kali (the spider) and Dracula (the bat).

Just as *Curse of Kali* was a repeat of *Legend of the 7 Golden Vampires* in many ways, even the action would repeat itself with Van Helsing battling zombies with torches. On the note of Van Helsing, Cushing said he'd be willing to go on playing Van Helsing for as long as they liked (though he joked future roles might have to be written with the character in a wheelchair). Legend of the 7 Golden Vampires © 1974 Hammer Film Productions Ltd.

Naturally, the Brigadier brushes Van Helsing and his theories off, insisting it's simply the start of a rebellion. However, Van Helsing's words don't entirely fall on deaf ears. Listening in is a local political advisor, Hugh Fennel. Half Anglo and half Indian, he agrees to aid Van Helsing on his quest, as he knows of the Thugees and the Cult of Kali. Currently, a new regiment of soldiers is being sent to Fort Meerabad to quelch the uprising, complete with a cannon. Fennel arranges for Professor Gomal and Van Helsing to return with Ashwood as official investigators on his behalf. Esther also convinces her father to let her go too, while young Lawrence must sit out what would have been his first vampire hunting excursion (he stays with Mrs. Gomal).

Finally, on page 11, Dracula makes his first appearance. In his introductory scene, he is the esteemed guest of a merchant and his family in Afghanistan while he is on his way to Khyber Pass. (As this was an 1856 prequel, he required no resurrection scene.) At dinner, the merchant drinks too much wine and passes out. Dracula then glides stealthily through his house until he arrives at the bedroom of his beautiful daughter. What happens next isn't unlike what we'd seen a thousand times before and is perfunctory more than anything else. After Dracula finishes feeding, he exits the house accompanied by a flock of bats. He then mounts a black stallion and rides off into a thunderstorm, which is a nice visual at least. (After this, we won't see Dracula again until the end of the treatment!)

The next portion of the treatment is also repetitious of the formula established in *Legend*, where a great deal of time was spent trekking through the wilderness on the way to confront the vampire cult. In this case, Van Helsing traverses the Indian wilderness with Bengal Lancers rather than kung-fu fighters across China. And, rather than Chinese bandits, they are attacked by a rogue group of Afridi warriors. The Afridi suddenly cease their attack upon the orders of three mysterious men who ride into the fray. Two of the men Van Helsing recognizes as two of his Afridi helpers from earlier. The third man is introduced as an Afridi prince named Ranji Hissar. (Like Dracula, this rather important character is thrown into the narrative a little late in the game.) Hissar has sought out Van Helsing because his love, Lalamir, was kidnapped by Shinwar Khan and his Thugees. (In this way, he's a bit like Hsi Ching, the lead brother from the last film.) Knowing Van Helsing has a background in ancient cults, he thinks he can help him confront the Cult of Kali.

The group makes it back to Fort Meerabad, where Captain Purnell is waiting. Upon regrouping, the main regiment of soldiers sets out to search for the missing Sepoys, while Van Helsing, Esther, Gomal, Hissar, and the two Afridi make a separate journey to search out the Temple of Kali. The formula repetition of *Legend* continues with something of a reprise of the cave scene. If you'll recall, preceding the final battle in that film, Van Helsing and co. were accosted by the zombies and a few of the vampires in a cavern. Here, the group is making camp for the night outside. Esther has a strange feeling not that she's being watched, but listened in on. As the group huddles around the fire, it would be revealed that three eyeless ones are listening in from behind some rocks. The zombies attack the group, with bullets proving harmless on them. Van Helsing becomes aware of their hunting by sound and also that they are homing in on him because of a ticking watch in his pocket. Using the watch, Van Helsing guides the creatures to the fire. When they walk through it, they combust and are destroyed. Though the monsters have been dealt with, Hissar lets out a "roar of fury" upon seeing Shinwar Khan atop a cliff. He is flanked by temple guards and more eyeless ones. Escape is futile, and our heroes have been captured. (That, at least, deviates from Legend's formula.)

Back at Fort Meerabad, Ashwood is frightened for Esther and her father since they have yet to return. He asks Purnell if he might take a regiment of Sepoy soldiers with him to look for them, but Purnell says the Sepoys have grown disobedient and are no longer trustworthy. However, a Sepoy sergeant, Bahrud, overhears this and offers to escort Ashwood into the valley. Cut to inside the temple, where Van Helsing and his friends have been chained to the walls. Shinwar Khan informs them that they will not be killed yet, and that they have the privilege of being witness to the impending wedding of Dracula and Kali. The scene is quite atmospherically staged, similar to Temple of Doom, as the glowing cavern resounds with drumbeats. It also has something Temple of Doom didn't have: urns full of disembodied hearts and snakes! (Presumably, these might have been cobras, but Houghton doesn't specify.)

Back outside, Ashwood and his troops find the remains of the camp's fire. Conspicuously, Ashwood notices Van Helsing's watch on the ground, which he thinks was a clue intentionally left behind. (The idea is that Van Helsing's watch points to the direction of the cave, which is good and well, but a simpler solution for the story would just be to have the group find the hidden cave because of the drum beats.) Back inside the cave, a procession carries Dracula's coffin to the front of the temple with great ceremony. (Though a neat visual, where did the coffin come from? Last we saw Dracula, he was riding a stallion and had no way of carrying a coffin with him, though surely he had to.)

Ashwood and his men trek into a passage leading into the main cavern. Before they can breach the main room, they are accosted by temple guards. Ashwood beseeches Bahrud to escape and bring reinforcements. The man gets away as hoped, though Ashwood is captured. He is brought into the main cavern just as the wedding is kicking into high gear. To both he and Van Helsing's horror, Esther is being led to the dais where Kali's empty throne also sits. (And what is her role in the wedding? Well, that's not exactly clear. Her role in the story is to serve as a mutual damsel in distress for Ashwood and Van Helsing, of course, but her actual function in the wedding isn't clear.) Eventually, the shrouded form of Kali approaches her throne, while Dracula emerges from his casket. As this happens, a statue of the deity Shiva, Kali's sometimes husband, ominously crumbles into dust. All the temple guards gasp in shock. The snakes in the urns even rear up and hiss as though Dracula's presence is an afront. Maybe marrying Kali off to Dracula wasn't such a good idea after all...

As all this happens, Van Helsing eyes a torch on the wall nearby. If only he could get away and grab it. Gomal follows his gaze and gets the idea. When the time is right, they will make a break for it to grab the torches. Dracula approaches the throne of Kali and unveils his bride-to-be. Upon doing so, Dracula and Hissar both let out a cry of disgust, but for different reasons. Hissar recognizes "Kali" as his missing lover Lalamir, who is a zombie similar to the eyeless ones, only she still has her eyes. She is without her heart, though, and in the hollowed-out spot where it once resided "four giant serpents" which are her other four "arms" as it turns out. (How Hammer would have pulled this off is unknown, considering they could barely bring to life the tiny snakes making up the hair of *The Gorgon*!)

Dracula becomes angry because he expected Kali incarnate, not a makeshift imposter in her image. Shinwar Khan then brings the Count the woman's still-beating heart on a platter. What is he supposed to do with it? Houghton doesn't tell us, but Dracula tosses the platter aside in a rage. Since he can't feed on the undead Lalamir, he focuses his attention on the luscious still living Esther. Enraged, Ashwood manages to break free and makes a run for the dais. At the same time, Van Helsing and Gomal somehow do the same, grabbing torches to battle the eyeless ones. As Ashwood and the two Afridi fight their way to Dracula, the Count calls down a horde of bats from the ceiling to assault the heroes.

To kill the zombies, Van Helsing tosses torches into the snake urns containing their disembodied but still-beating hearts. Once their hearts burst into flame, the eyeless ones claw at their chests and begin to disintegrate. Hissar makes his way towards Lalamir while Ashwood wrestles with Dracula. Hissar becomes enveloped in the literal snake arms of Lalamir, as Houghton writes, "The coils of the massive snakes entwine the young Prince and drag him to Lalamir's body..."[1] Similar to Hsi Ching and Vanessa's death in *Legend*, Hissar manages to roll he and Lalamir into an all-consuming fire in a joint suicide.

Despite the destruction of the Kali imposter, the forces of good are slowly being overwhelmed as Shinwar Khan encourages his guards and the remaining eyeless ones to destroy the "defilers." Just when all hope seems lost, and similar to the ending of *Temple of Doom*, Bahrud returns with a group of Bengal Lancers. As they fire their rifles into the temple, this distracts Dracula, who has been fighting with Ashwood. During the distraction, Ashwood pulls Esther from the stone altar. At the same time, Gomal rescues the women from the cage and encourages them to flee the temple.

And if you're wondering just what Van Helsing gets to add to the exciting finale, just wait. Though he has zero interaction with Dracula—rather odd—Van Helsing does lead the charge out of the cave as he and the women are chased by more zombies and temple guards. Outside, a group of Lancers on horseback charge past Van Helsing and co. in the opposite direction, spearing the guards and zombies. Van Helsing then runs towards a cannon stationed outside, which he plans to fire on the cavern once everyone is out safely.

Inside, Dracula eyes Shinwar Khan angrily now that the tide of the battle has turned. It is through Khan's dialogue that we get at least some inclination of the plot here. Apparently he was to revive Khali so that Dracula could marry her, and then they would take over all of India and the Far East. Khan assures the Count that he can still resurrect Kali, but Dracula isn't buying it and sets a swarm of bats loose on the man. At that moment, Van Helsing has the cannon fire into the mouth of the cavern. As it shakes, Dracula pays it no mind and continues giving Khan a death glare. Eventually, the multiple cannon volleys into the temple causes it to crumble. In the process, the massive six-armed Kali statue falls over, and one of the swords impales Dracula and Khan both. The last shots would be of Van Helsing and the heroes watching the cavern collapse from outside and Dracula decaying from within.

Though certain visuals are undeniably interesting, there were some fairly serious problems with this treatment. For instance, the idea of Dracula joining forces with another evil entity via marriage has interesting possibilities, but we really don't know the parameters of the relationship. Furthermore, like the last film, Dracula might as well have not even have been in the story as he does next to nothing. The fact that he and Van Helsing share no dialogue in what is technically a prequel about the first time the doctor encountered the arch vampire is also strange and distracting. Nor does Van Helsing get to directly deliver the death blow to the Count! However, the fact that Kali kills Dracula wasn't just supposed to infuse the script with irony; it was actually Houghton's way of having his cake and eating it too. There was a chance that the Indian government would reject the script due to its treatment of Kali, hence Houghton making her seem to be the villain until the very end when the statue kills Dracula and Khan. Therefore, it could be argued that the Thugee cult was killing in the name of Kali, which Houghton hoped would appease the Indian government.

Despite the story's flaws, Houghton felt he had outdone himself compared to *Legend* and wrote a note to Brian Lawrence stating that his story was "Same format as '7 Vamps' – but I feel a much better and stronger storyline."[2] The treatment was submitted in May of 1974, and in all, between May and November of 1974, Houghton crafted three different drafts of the *Kali* story plus one brief, four page synopsis according to Keiran Foster in "Unseen Horrors". Upon reading the first treatment, Carreras gave a few brief suggestions, including the new title *Dracula and the Blood Lust of Kali* in June of 1974. It next became *Kali–Devil Bride of Dracula*, its better-known title. In October, Warner Bros was pushing Hammer to fast-track the treatment into a full screenplay. Warners also suggested that the script needed more horror than what was present in the treatment so that it would be 50% Hammer horror and 50% Bengal Lancers type adventure. Carreras then suggested two revisions, one minor and one major. The first was a prologue similar to *Legend* with emissaries from India trekking to Transylvania to propose the idea of the wedding to Dracula. The second, more significant revision was that Kali be an actual incarnated character in the story and an outright villain. Carreras also felt there needed to be more screen time for Dracula, and encouraged more scenes of Dracula and his bats causing chaos as he traveled east, and perhaps even Kali creating carnage as she and her followers traveled north. Furthermore, Carreras wasn't exactly sure how to portray Kali, though the idea of the six arms infatuated him. He seemed to go back and forth between portraying her as something beautiful yet horrific, or something akin to the Mummy. Carreras was also doubtful that a human being could play the part and envisioned some sort of working mechanism or animatronic to play the multi-armed villainess! In *Little Shoppe of Horrors* #10, a Carreras quote as stating, "Kali is really an animated stone figure with six arms, so there won't be any actress in the leading role for this; there might be someone under the stone, working the mechanisms, but it is not a castable part."[3]

Houghton was not happy with these requests, possibly because he feared the consequences of portraying Kali in such a negative light culturally speaking. In a response to Carreras, Houghton explained that these changes would create a great deal of work for him. And with Kali as a goddess incarnate, he wasn't sure how to kill her. He joked that he certainly couldn't have her and Dracula walk hand in hand into the sunset together.

In November of 1974, Houghton turned in a new version of the story simply called *Devil Bride of Dracula*. It added in the Transylvanian prologue as requested and shifted the setting to 1899. As such, it was still a prequel to the last film. (Why they didn't just make it a sequel where Van Helsing travels to India is anyone's guess.) The prologue scene was similar to *Dracula A.D. 1972* in that it opened with Van Helsing destroying Dracula with a stake to the heart. By the end of the prologue, Dracula is resurrected and vows vengeance on Van Helsing. Kali is gone entirely, hence the absence of that name in the new title. In her place is the fictional Snake Goddess and her Cult of the Cobra that cuts a swath of destruction through India in anticipation of her marriage to Count Dracula.

Houghton left the project after this treatment was rejected, and the next writer to take over was George Trow, who penned *Unholy Dracula*. This new story offered some interesting innovations, infusing it with elements of a treasure hunt. It too came up with a new villain in the form of the goddess Durga, who can only fully manifest her powers and wed Dracula after 13 jewels are tracked down and placed on a certain statue. As such, the protagonists and antagonists have to outwit one another in their quest to find the jewels first. And while the other treatments didn't offer much explanation as to why Dracula would want to marry Kali outside of world conquest, here, if he marries Durga, he will be able to walk in the sunlight again. At the story's end, when Dracula and Durga are destroyed, when they decompose, so too does a statue of the evil deity.

Carreras disliked this treatment, particularly a scene where Dracula was to laugh maniacally like some cartoon villain. Next, Carreras brought in Christopher Wicking, who simply called his three versions of the story *Devil Bride*. It reset the story back to 1856, but with Abraham Van Helsing in the lead (he's another new one and is again presumably Lawrence's father). The story begins with Van Helsing observing an Indian cult ritual devoted to the goddess Diva. Van Helsing suffers a hallucination during the ceremony and passes out, only to awaken later handcuffed to a hospital bed. In the hospital, he is then recruited by the East India Trading Company to track down and expose the Cult of Diva, which has been killing off high-ranking East India officials. As the last of the trio of writers, Wicking utilized elements from both his predecessors. Many of the scenes in Wicking's story were lifted from *Curse of Kali*, but with the jewel subplot from *Unholy Dracula* added in. Notably, Wicking's unfinished script left off with Van Helsing inspecting the safe of a man recently murdered by the Thugees. Unfortunately, Wicking's drafts were undated, so we don't know when they were written. What we do know is that *House of Hammer* #4 reported the following in 1977:

Devil Bride For Dracula.
Following on from the success of *Legend of the 7 Golden Vampires*, India will be the exotic locale for this latest adventure of the arch-vampire. Who will play the role of Dracula? All we can reveal at this point is that the answer will be a terrific surprise!

This little blurb confirms two things. Firstly, even though Warner Bros was still sitting on *Legend*, Hammer was still developing *Kali*. Another rumor that the item confirmed was that a new younger actor would take the place of John Forbes-Robertson to play the Dracula part—presumably because this was a prequel. In *Little Shoppe of Horrors* #32, Wayne Kinsey asked Forbes-Robertson if he'd ever been approached for the project.

Kinsey: Did Hammer ever discuss another Dracula picture with you? They were planning one in India.

Forbes-Robertson: That's the first time I've heard of that. That was never contemplated with me at all.[4]

Then there was the following conversation between *Starlog* writer Steve Swires and Michael Carreras at a Famous Monsters convention in 1975 where Carreras told Swires:

I will not, to be perfectly honest, offer the part to Christopher Lee. We will be treating this Dracula as a young and virile sensual character, because he will have to have a romantic involvement with Kali, the goddess of the thuggees. With all due respect to Christopher and his talents, he would not suit this particular interpretation.

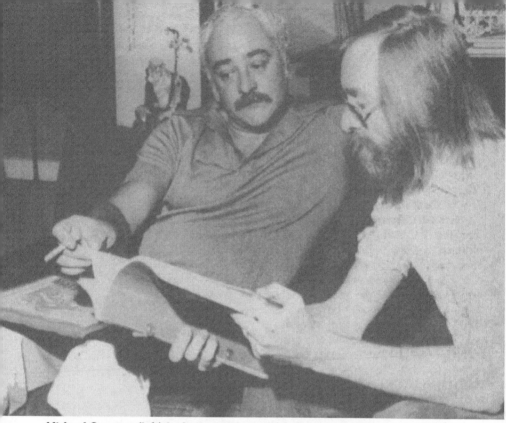

Michael Carreras (left) looks over the script for *Nessie* with Chritopher Wicking, who did one of the rewrites on *Kali – Devil Bride of Dracula*.

That said, I don't think this entirely ruled out Forbes-Robertson again so much as I think Carreras was trying to illustrate why he didn't need Lee, knowing full well he'd turn the part down if asked.

However, Warner Bros eventually lost interest. Carreras explained,

> I worked that out for Warner Bros. They had an enormous amount of blocked rupees in India, and wanted to use them to make a film.... I went to India, and researched the material. Suddenly, while we were in pre-production, the Indian government changed its monetary policy and gave Warner Bros, all their blocked rupees. Consequently, they didn't want to make a picture in India any more. Since the script was specifically tailored for India, it couldn't be adapted to another location.[5]

VAN HELSING'S LAST HURRAH

INSTEAD OF THIS FILM, VAN HELSING'S LAST APPEARANCE FOR HAMMER ENDED UP BEING IN THE HAMMER ENDORSED MAGAZINE, *HOUSE OF HAMMER*, WHICH FEATURED A COMIC CALLED "VAN HELSING'S TERROR TALES" AND DEVIATED FAR FROM TYPICAL HAMMER FARE. FOR INSTANCE, VAN HELSING RELATES AN OLD LEGEND ABOUT A KNIGHT WHO SLAYS AN ACTUAL DRAGON. SAID DRAGON TURNS OUT TO BE A SHAPESHIFTING WOMAN. ANOTHER TERROR TALE TOLD OF A ZOMBIE, ANOTHER FEATURED A MUMMY, PRETTY MUCH EVERYTHING BUT VAMPIRES. FURTHERMORE, AT LEAST ONE OF VAN HELSING'S TERROR TALES TOOK PLACE IN THE 1950S, SO APPARENTLY IT WAS LORIMER VAN HELSING TELLING THE TALES RATHER THAN LAWRENCE!)

This was by no means the last canceled Hammer Dracula film, however, as there were many more rumored throughout the late 1970s...

Chapter Notes

[1] *Peter Cushing Scrapbook*, p.214.
[2] Ibid, p.213.
[3] Davies, "The Un-Filmed Hammer: An A to Z Guide," *Little Shoppe of Horrors* #10 (Kindle Edition).
[4] Kinsey, "Interview with John Forbes Robertson," *Little Shoppe of Horrors* #32 (Kindle Edition).
[5] Maxford, *Hammer Complete*, p.898.

23.
INVISIBLE MAN
VS. THE HUMAN TORCH

Intended Release Date: 1976
Draft Dates: May 5, 1975 (first draft script); October 24, 1975 (second draft script)

Screenplay by: Masahiro Kakefuda & Jun Fukuda (second draft only) **Producers:** Tomoyuki Tanaka & Fumio Tanaka **Proposed Director:** Jun Fukuda **Proposed Cast/Characters:** Shiro Saijo [detective/invisible man], Koichi Shimada [research engineer/flame human], Taeko [Shimada's wife], Yoshiro Iwakura [President of Iwakura Co., Ltd.], Kajiura [Iwakura's assistant], Tsukisaka [Club owner], Tachibana [Club manager], Anesaki [gangster boss], Marumi [gangster boss], Sachiko Kagawa [Anesaki's employee], Teranishi [Saijo's partner]

PLOT A detective with the ability to turn invisible tracks a man with the power to become a human flame...

COMMENTARY Earlier in this book had been mentioned Toho Studios' "Transforming Humans" series of the late 1950s and early 1960s. By the mid-1970s, these films were playing on Japanese television to renewed success. As such, Toho producer Tomoyuki Tanaka decided to do an update on the franchise. In June of 1973, Tanaka announced plans for a new slate of "Strange Human Sci-Fi Series." Immediately, ideas were thrown around for a new invisible man and also a "plant man", which apparently never got past the story pitch stage. Tanaka's first real attempt was a semi-gothic horror called *The Human Torch* (or *Flame Human*). The story was a supernatural murder mystery set within the gothic mansion of a wealthy Japanese family. There, a flaming human kills off members of the family one by one. Tanaka liked the flame human, but apparently didn't feel that it was enough of a draw by itself. As such, *Invisible Man vs. Human Torch* was born, with Jun Fukuda slated to direct.

Back in 1960, Fukuda had directed *Secret of the Telegian*. Fukuda loved the film and considered it one of his favorites but was often relegated to directing entries of the Godzilla series, which he disdained. An interview with David Milner of Cult Films implied that Fukuda had written a "sequel" to *Telegian* in the mid-1960s, where an invisible man fights a flame human. However, Fukuda might have been misremembering as all evidence points to that concept only being developed in the mid-1970s. Whether Fukuda was revising an earlier idea or not, his new script was co-written with Masahiro Kakefuda. The resulting *Invisible Man vs. the Human Torch* was essentially a dark, gritty Yakuza film with sci-fi elements.

It begins with our main character, Detective Shiro Saijo, and his partner, Teranishi, engaged in a car chase with several bank robbers. Saijo fires at the men from his car, and the getaway car crashes into a wall, bursting into flames. The robbers, who jumped out at the last minute, run into the Shirikawa Chemical Plant, where Saijo and Teranishi pursue. Saijo follows one of the robbers into a room containing a cyclotron—a particle accelerator—where they scuffle over control of the robber's gun. The gun fires a bullet into the cyclotron, causing it to malfunction. The robber gets away and kicks Saijo into the cyclotron. Roll opening credits.

Saijo awakens in the hospital surrounded by his boss, Sugiyama, and Teranishi, who informs him that he has been unconscious for five whole days. They congratulate Saijo as a hero but remind him he needs at least a month's worth of rest. Saijo, completely wrapped in bandages, is given some medicine to accelerate the healing process, and he goes back to sleep. Saijo awakens alone. Wanting a cigarette, he begins to unravel the bandage on his hand. To his shock, his hand is gone! He unravels more bandages to find his whole arm gone. Saijo steps in front of a mirror and is horrified to find that his whole body is now invisible. A nurse walks in on the sight of the bandages crumbling to the floor and screams. The nurse leaves the room and Saijo rematerializes, leaving the other nurses to find Saijo out of bed. They make him lie back down, and Saijo begins to think the medicine given to him may have caused a strange reaction. Saijo settles into bed to read the paper and is shocked to see the news that his old friend, Koichi Shimada, has died in an accident while testing a new type of race car at the Fuji Speedway. Saijo stands at his window, watching the sunset, as he sadly reflects upon his friendship with Shimada.

Saijo attends Shimada's wake at his home in Tokyo, where he meets Shimada's wife, Taeko. Also in attendance is Shimada's boss, Yoshiro Iwakura, President of Iwakura Co., Ltd. Saijo wishes to see footage of the accident to determine if there was any foul play. Though he can't be sure foul play was involved, Saijo becomes suspicious when he observes a mysterious woman from the wake, Sachiko Kagawa, watching the accident on the video. The same day as the wake, Taeko told Saijo that Shimada's diary was stolen from their home. Saijo goes to Sachiko's place of work, where he confronts her on the suspicion that she stole Shimada's diary. A man with a scarred face attacks Saijo, while Sachiko runs away. Saijo overpowers the man and catches up to Sachiko, who confesses she stole the diary for a man named Takeshi Anesaki, a gangster.

Sachiko takes Saijo to Anesaki's hotel, where Anesaki is down in the boiler room reading Shimada's diary. A man made entirely of flame appears before Anesaki and strangles him with his flaming hands. Saijo tries to put out the fire on Anesaki when he walks in, but it's too late. Anesaki is already dead. Saijo picks up pieces of the charred diary for investigation. Meanwhile, Taeko has been invited to the mansion of Mr. Iwakura, also her uncle in addition to being her late husband's boss, who expresses concern for her wellbeing and extends an offer to live with him. Back at his office, Saijo tells Teranishi that he believes foul play was involved in Shimada's death while Teranishi is sure that it was just an accident. Saijo wants to keep investigating Anesaki and goes to a club owned by his partner, Marumi. Saijo spies on Marumi and his men, but he is caught, beaten, and captured.

Saijo awakens tied to a chair, alone in a room with the contents of his coat scattered across the floor. He spies some of his medicine and recalling what happened the last time he took it, rocks his chair onto the floor, using his tongue to lick up one of the pills as he hears footsteps approaching. When Marumi's goons enter the room, they are shocked that Saijo has disappeared. The invisible Saijo then begins to beat up the men, who are terrified and confused by what is happening. Saijo leaves and goes to see Taeko to ask if she had ever heard Shimada speak about the gangsters. While there, an intruder breaks into Shimada's old office, but when Saijo opens the door, the man is gone. Saijo runs outside to follow the man, who hops into a car and speeds away. Saijo gets in his car, and a chase ensues. The intruder's car crashes and bursts into flames on a bridge. The driver emerges on fire, much to Saijo's shock. To escape Saijo, the burning man jumps into the water and disappears.

Saijo collects strange black ashes found at the scene as well as a lighter that has Shimada's initials carved into it. Saijo takes the lighter to Taeko who recognizes it and says they bought it on a trip to Sweden. Saijo also has the strange black residue analyzed in the police lab. The technician tells Saijo that the residue is human and proceeds to tell him a story about coal miners whose skin became so saturated with coal that they themselves became flammable. The tech tells Saijo that this sample contains sulfur, ammonia, methane, and hydrogen, which is not normally found in humans. The two theorize a burning man is on the loose who can ignite his own skin without harming himself.

Meanwhile, the gangsters reconvene at the club and come to the conclusion that Shimada is alive. As they fear, that night Shimada comes to exact his revenge on the men. Even their bullets have no effect on the flaming Shimada, who subsequently kills the club's owner, Tsukisa. Saijo arrives on the scene and calls Shimada's name. The flame man ignores him and runs away from Saijo and into a waiting car. Saijo shoots at the driver of the car and is sure he nicks them in the arm. Saijo then breaks the news to Taeko that her husband is alive. Saijo is somewhat distraught with the callous manner in which Shimada murdered the gangsters, though Taeko begs him not to arrest her husband. Before he goes, Taeko reveals to Saijo a letter she received requesting she come to a warehouse in Tokyo Bay. Saijo goes there, but Taeko secretly tails him there. Saijo is attacked, and Taeko is kidnapped by the gangsters, who take her away and question her about Shimada's whereabouts. Saijo, in his invisible form, ambushes the men and they retreat. Instead of materializing, Saijo spies on Taeko as she dresses a wound on her right arm. He realizes she was Shimada's mystery driver and has known about her husband's ability all along!

Saijo follows Taeko to a swampy marsh and materializes as she gets out of her car. He tells her he has investigated Shimada's past and found out that his father was killed by the mob fifteen years ago. Saijo confronts Taeko about knowing Shimada was still alive all along. At that point, Shimada walks out of the shadows, revealing himself to Saijo. Shimada tells Saijo of his tragic past, where the mob killed his father by trapping him in a barn and burning him alive, which Shimada witnessed and barely escaped himself. Saijo reassures Shimada that he will see to it that those men go to prison but Shimada says that is not good enough for him and intends to kill them all. Saijo draws his gun on Shimada to arrest him. Shimada tells him that five years ago, he modified his body to be immortal and that his bullets will only spark flames

203

Alleged piece of concept art for the Human Torch.

from his skin. The two men begin to fight and rain falls from the sky. Saijo takes another capsule and disappears before Shimada's eyes and the fight continues. However, Shimada can track Saijo's movements by watching his feet splash in the mud. Shimada shouts to Saijo, "You have modified yourself just like me!" Shimada shoots Saijo in the arm and blood drips onto the ground as Saijo runs away. Shimada shouts that no matter what, Saijo will not stop him from fulfilling his purpose.

Saijo returns to Shimada's home and finds a secret underground room with a strange machine—the device Shimada used to turn himself into a flame human. Back at the club, Yoshihiro Iwakura and his secretary, Kajiura, are meeting with Tsukisaka. As it turns out, Iwakura is in cahoots with the mob. Shimada causes a gas line to explode in Tsukisaka's office, killing him, though Iwakura gets away. Saijo, who has been tailing Shimada, materializes in front of him and confronts him for trying to kill Iwakura. Shimada reveals that Iwakura was always in league with the mob and he will kill him no matter what. Saijo and Shimada fight again and Shimada dives into the water to escape. Taeko pulls up in her car next to Saijo, who proceeds to tell her that he thinks Shimada only married her to get close to her uncle, Iwakura, to kill him. Taeko then surprises Saijo by telling him that she knows this because she also wants to kill her uncle as he had killed her father as well. Saijo warns her that he overheard Iwakura saying he has invented a new gun that can kill Shimada so he must arrest Iwakura to save Shimada's life. Taeko argues against this and says, "If a man lives for nothing other than revenge, if you take that from him, he will be left with nothing." Saijo won't relent and says he is going to arrest Iwakura. Taeko then slips a pistol from her overcoat and shoots Saijo in the arm before she disappears into the fog.

Taeko goes to Iwakura to take him up on his offer to stay with him for safety. That night, she sneaks into his room to kill him, but Iwakura is wise to her plan and stops her. Next, Iwakura learns that Tachibana, one of the club managers, has been feeding Shimada information all along. He forces Tachibana to call Shimada at his usual time to tell him that Taeko is being held prisoner in Iwakura's mansion. Tachibana tells him he will let him in through a secret underground tunnel. When the call is over, Iwakura has Tachibana shot in the head.

As planned, Shimada walks into a trap in Iwakura's mansion and Iwakura pelts Shimada's arms with the special fire gun that can harm him. Just when Iwakura is about to deliver the death blow, Taeko jumps in front of him and takes the shot, dying instantly. Outside, Saijo breaks into the mansion in his invisible form and makes his way downstairs where he knocks the fire gun from Iwakura's hands.

Another fight breaks out between Saijo and Shimada, who shoots Saijo, again drawing blood. With Saijo down, Shimada returns his attention to Iwakura, setting him ablaze and killing him. Saijo fears that Shimada will never stop his killing spree and

GODZILLA VS. THE DEVIL

SHORTLY AFTER THIS PROJECT'S CANCELATION TOHO BEGAT PLANS TO REVIVE GODZILLA. ONE OF THE FIRST TREATMENTS TO LAND ON THEIR DOOR CAME FROM THEIR OLD PRODUCTION PARTNERS FROM UPA, WHO HAD CO-PRODUCED *FRANKENSTEIN CONQUERS THE WORLD* (1965) WITH THEM, AND ITS SEQUEL, *WAR OF THE GARGANTUAS* (1966). IN THE AFOREMENTIONED FILM, FRANKENSTEIN'S CELLS SPAWN TWO NEW MONSTERS, THE GARGANTUAS. UPA PITCHED TOHO TWO IDEAS. THE FIRST WAS *GODZILLA VS. GARGANTUA*, WHERE GODZILLA FIGHTS A SURVIVING FRANKENSTEIN OFF-SHOOT, MAKING IT A REVIVAL OF THE *GODZILLA VS. FRANKENSTEIN* CONCEPT IN A WAY. PERHAPS EVEN MORE INTRIGUING FOR HORROR FANS WAS UPA'S OTHER PITCH: *GODZILLA VS. THE DEVIL*. JUST AS IT SOUNDS, THE FILM WAS TO END WITH GODZILLA BATTLING A GIANT VERSION OF THE DEVIL. IT WOULD HAVE BEEN PRECEDED BY THE BIG G BATTLING A GIANT FISH, BIRD AND SPIDER SPAWNED FROM THE "EVIL OF MANKIND." THE TWO TREATMENTS WERE GIVEN TO TOHO IN 1978, AND TOHO ANNOUNCED AN UNTITLED "U.S.-JAPAN GODZILLA CO-PRODUCTION" THAT NEVER MATERIALIZED.

gives him one last chance to turn himself in as Teranishi and the rest of Saijo's squad arrives. Shimada shoots at the detectives, so Saijo grabs the fire gun and kills Shimada. The flaming form of Shimada attacks Saijo as he dies, eventually melting away into nothing. A depressed Saijo walks away into the sunrise.

Though undeniably interesting, the script has a few problems. The biggest one is the origins of the two mutant humans, which are never adequately explained. In Saijo's case, the fact that he fell into a cyclotron seems to be enough information for the audience as to why he is invisible. That it is Saijo's prescription drugs for his injury that cause him to disappear, and that he is unable to turn invisible without them is interesting, though. However, there isn't even a single scene of Saijo consulting a scientist friend to explain his transformation. That said, this is only a minor quibble compared to the lack of emphasis on Shimada's origin. The story might have been better to make Shimada's flame powers supernatural and tie them in with his father's horrific death. At one point, Shimada has a line about having "already died once" and "having been to hell"—whether these lines were meant to be metaphorical or literal is unknown.

The Invisible Man element of the script is fairly well utilized, especially in the suspenseful scene where Saijo is bound and tied to a chair. One of the better scenes also had Saijo approaching the gangsters in classic invisible man garb: a trench coat and bandages, which he slowly peels off one by one until he is invisible. He keeps smoking his cigarette, however, which he puts out on one of the thug's faces. (Why he was wearing the trench coat and bandages, other than to make a cool visual entrance for the audience, really makes no sense.)

Overall, the script is full of 70s tropes that nostalgia buffs would love. There are the overly dramatic happy flashbacks to Shimada and Saijo playing football together (and presumably running and laughing in slow motion). Then there are the colorful gangster characters, such as Tsukisaka, owner of the "Oriental Club," who has a glass eye. The action scenes also have a style and flare to them that are distinctly 1970s, like a well-described scene where Saijo spots an attacker approaching from behind through his reflection in a glass bottle. And like any good crime noir film, there are twists galore. For instance, though it's no big surprise that Shimada is the flame human, it is a big surprise that his grieving wife was in on the secret all along.

Ironically enough, the reason this film didn't end up being produced was partly to blame on Hammer Films. At the time, Toho and Hammer had entered into a partnership to produce the big-budget *Nessie*. The unceasing problems with that burgeoning production eventually led to the cancellation of *Invisible Man vs. the Human Torch*. Before that happened, the film was announced in the 1976 Toho lineup with this tagline: "Strange human series first bulletin! Wrapping the whole body with a flame of grudge one after another brutal revenge! A detective who became a transparent human in a cyclotron follows!" The final nail in the film's coffin likely occurred when Toho begat plans to revive Godzilla in 1978, and at that point, all of their focus shifted from the invisible man to their trustworthy giant monster.

Vlad the Impaler.

24.
DRACULA:
THE BEGINNING

Developed: 1974-1993

Screenplay by: Brian Hayles Proposed **Cast/Characters:** Vlad Tepes [Transylvanian warlord], Ilonya [Vlad's wife], Benedek [monk] Istvan [Vlad's son], Milista [witch]

PLOT Penny Woods is a young heiress, using her newfound fortune to explore the world

COMMENTARY By 1974, Michael Carreras was realizing that the good ol' days of run of the mill Dracula movies were behind Hammer. Now they needed gimmicks to help keep the series afloat, such as the modern-day setting of *Dracula A.D. 1972* and the Kung Fu element in *Legend of the 7 Golden Vampires*. In the Spring of 1974, Carreras happened to catch a radio play called *Lord Dracula*. It was written by Brian Hayles and combined the legend of Vlad Tepes and Dracula more thoroughly than Bram Stoker did. Essentially, the radio play showed how Tepes actually became Dracula through the lens of fantasy.

In the radio play, Tepes starts out as the brutal Transylvanian warlord and is arrested for war crimes early on. During his prison term, Tepes falls in love with a woman named Ilonya, who cares for him during his incarceration. Tepes even pledges himself to God under the guidance of a monk named Benedek. After being released, he returns to his castle in Transylvania with Ilonya. There he informs his oldest son, Istvan, that he and his new wife are expecting a child. However, the baby is stillborn, so Tepes turns against God and begins another reign of terror, with Benedek forced to watch. Tepes is eventually seduced by a witch named Militsa, who coerces Tepes further down the path of the dark side. Through a ritual, Tepes becomes a vampire and bears the new name of Dracula. But, because Vlad is now undead, he and the witch Milista decide they need to find a way to retain his vast fortune and so leave it to Vlaachim. And who is Vlaachim, you ask? It's Vlad's heretofore unknown baby brother, who even son

Istvan didn't know existed. With his father dead and look-alike younger brother suddenly in his place, Istvan and Benedek exhume Vlad's grave. When they find it empty, they conclude Vlaachim is a rejuvenated Vlad. They are right, of course, and Vlad is confronted by Benedek and Istvan. A battle ensues, and Militsa is killed. During the fight, through sorcery learned from Militsa, Dracula makes it appear as though he's been beheaded when really it was a random monk named Jacob. Dracula escapes, Benedek and Istvan are arrested for killing the monk, and the duo is executed.

In *House of Hammer* #17, in 1977, Carreras spoke of when he first came across the play:

> It was put on by the BBC about two years ago and was the most exciting piece of horror writing I'd ever heard. It's very literary. It has the flavour of *A Man for All Seasons* and is historically correct. Actually I didn't hear the original broadcast [on April 27th] but two people rang me up the next morning. One was Tony Keys, the film producer, and the other was my middle son Jimmy and they both said: "Did you listen to that play?" So due to these two recommendations I got in touch with Brian Hayles and had him send me a recording. I received it at the office but I must confess I didn't play it right away, instead I took it home and finally played it the following Friday night. I had some people for dinner and afterwards I asked them to listen to *Lord Dracula* with me. I told them I had no idea what it would be like, so we turned the lights down and we listened . . . and we were mesmerized! It was one of the most marvelous broadcasts I'd ever heard. It was tremendous! So I quickly rang Brian, we met and did a deal.[1]

Carreras actually tapped Hayles himself to write the screenplay, which was titled *Dracula: The Beginning* at this stage. Being written by the original author, it is basically just a screenplay version of the play with only one minor difference. In the end, Tepes/Dracula frames his son and the monk for the death of his wife and child. And while the monk is executed, his son lives but is imprisoned. In October of 1974, Carreras offered the project to director Ken Russel. The director seemed open to the possibility but disdained the end "bloodbath" as he called it, and wanted to revise the third act, which Carreras was agreeable to.

However, much like one of Vlad's unfortunate victims, the project was destined to die a slow death over the next five years. First, there was the devastating axed U.S. release of *Legend of the 7 Golden Vampires*, which Warner Bros suspiciously shelved at the last minute. The Vlad project was also hindered a bit by Warners initially wanting a sequel to the aforementioned film that they declined to release in the form of *Kali – Devil Bride of Dracula*. Had Hammer not been distracted by *Kali*, they might've given more attention to *Dracula: The Beginning*. Worse still was the non-event that was *Nessie*, which was Carreras's top priority. Eventually, he gave up on *Kali* as his burgeoning Dracula project and shifted his emphasis to the Vlad the Impaler pic. For instance, while working on *Nessie* in 1976, he was trying to court Germany's Constantin Films to be another partner along with Toho. In his discussions with them, he also brought up the possibility of them co-producing a Vald the Impaler biopic that he called *The Blasphemer*. Needles to say, the deal with Germany didn't come through. A year later, when interviewed by *House of Hammer* about *Nessie* in 1977, he also mentioned *Dracula: The Beginning* and how the production would be another big-budget event film like *Nessie*:

> I want to go absolutely first class with this picture and it will be four, if not five, times as expensive as any single Hammer film. We are now fully scripted and we are at the moment, casting it. We've sent the script to people like Richard Burton and Richard Harris but we don't know as yet who will play the lead I haven't even selected a director yet. I'd love to direct it myself, having worked so closely on it with the writer, but I know I'm not talented enough to do it. I'm waiting to see who will play the lead and then jointly we'll find the right director. We are aiming for a production date of October November this year.[2]

Carreras also revealed that he had already scouted locations and had wanted to film in Yugoslavia. "The Romanians turned us down flat when we asked if we could film in their country because apparently Vlad Tepes is a national hero, though don't ask me how anyone can have as a national hero a man who impaled over fifty thousand people," Carreras said in *House of Hammer*. Among other interesting comments he gave in the interview, he admitted that the picture was going to be some kind of historically accurate biopic. Carreras said, "We are bending the truth... instead of saying that this was a live man who later inspired a writer, Bram

211

Stoker, to create Dracula we are saying that Vlad became Dracula. I think it will be a hell of a movie."

And it might well have been, but by 1979 Carreras was removed from Hammer, which was finally officially dead. Years later, in 1987, in an interview with Steve Swires of *Fangoria*, Carreras said that the script was still his "prize possession" and that "I will never give up the idea of doing it. If we were allowed to make one more film, Vlad the Impaler would be it."

Chapter Notes

[1] *House of Hammer* #17.
[2] Ibid.

PART II:
THE REMAKE ERA

25.
KEN RUSSELL'S
DRACULA

Developed: 1979

Screenplay by: Ken Russell **Proposed Director:** Ken Russell **Proposed Cast/Characters:** Dracula (Mick Fleetwood, Peter O'Toole, Lawrence Olivier), Lucia [opera singer] (Sarah Miles), Mina [Lucia's secretary] (Mia Farrow), Dr. Seward [Lucia's suitor] (Michael York), Jonathan Harker [Mina's fiancé], Quincy Morris [cowboy] (James Coburn), Renfield [inmate at asylum] (Oliver Reed), Van Helsing [Seward's mentor]

PLOT An immortal artist known as Count Dracula sets out to save a famous opera singer from a terminal illness by turning her into one of the undead...

COMMENTARY The late 1970s saw a resurgence of interest in the Dracula story, with no less than three films released on the Count: *Love at First Bite* (1979), *Dracula* (1979), and *Nosferatu* (1979). There was also one other major adaptation that didn't go forward: Ken Russell's *Dracula*. Russell, of course, was the famed director of *Women in Love* (1969) and *The Devils* (1971), among others. Russell's main inspiration to tackle the story was that he took umbrage with the fact that the Count would suddenly travel all the way to London just to seduce a young woman. He felt Dracula needed more purpose in traveling so far and so came up with another reason. Russell's unique angle had Dracula as an artist who reinvents himself once a generation. When Dracula learns that Lucy—in this version a celebrated opera singer—is dying, he makes the journey to London to make her immortal. (However, despite what Rusell says, in both his version and Stoker's, Dracula is already heading to London before he sets his sights on Lucy, so his argument isn't actually plot-hole proof.)

In the end, Russell's version wouldn't be produced because of the Mirisch Company's *Dracula* remake starring Frank Langella as the title character and Sir Laurence Olivier as Van Helsing. Ironically, before this happened, Russell had hoped Olivier might play Dracula in his version! Later he envisioned Peter O'Toole in the part and also Mick Fleetwood[1] (yes, that Mick Fleetwood of Fleetwood Mac)! Of all his choices, Mick Fleetwood might have been the best, as he looked as though he could be Vlad Tepes with the right makeup and wardrobe. In regards to the other players, Russell envisioned Peter Ustinov as Van Helsing. Oliver Reed, a frequent performer in Russell's films, was envisioned as Renfield, while Sarah Miles and Mia Farrow would respectively play Lucy and Mina. Michael York was to be Jonathan Harker, and frequent Western star James Coburn was to be cowboy Quincy Morris. (The only character without an actor attached was that of Dr. Seward.)

Behind the scenes were also involved John Hawn and his screenplay development company. Michael Nolin, an acquisition consultant at Columbia pictures, was also a driving force in the production (therefore, we could also assume Columbia would have been the distributor). Nolin had even given Russell a copy of *The Annotated Dracula* by Leonard Wolf to look over for inspiration.

Aside from meetings regarding the cast (Russell met Fleetwood after a canceled concert, for instance), John Hawn bought a two-page ad in *The Hollywood Reporter* (and possibly *Variety* as well) announcing Ken Russell's *Dracula*. And that was about as far as the film got. Lucky for us, Russell's screenplay has been published and is available to read for anyone who wants to see it.

The first visual was to be of a crowded Transylvanian street in the middle of a strange celebration. There would be marionette bats operated by puppeteers plus a giant effigy of Vlad the Impaler belching smoke and firecrackers. Walking through the jubilee is Jonathan Harker, searching out a coach driver. When Harker finds the coachman, he tries to persuade Harker to stay and enjoy the festival for the night. However, Harker wants to attend to his business with Count Dracula at once. When he presses the coach driver on his reluctance, he asks Harker if he knows what day it is. Harker's patience at a loss, he replies, "The Fourth of May, 1925. And unless we get a move on, it will soon be the Fifth." (This was Russell's sly little way of letting us know the year, which he's moved up from the original setting of the late 1890s to the 1920s. Similarly, the Frank Langella *Dracula* was set in 1913.) The coach driver tells Harker that it's the Eve of St. George's Day, and at midnight all the evil in the world will be out in full force.

This script's purported top pick for Dracula: Mick Fleetwood.

Harker shows compassion rather than contempt for the man's beliefs, but urges him on just the same and the driver relents. Before departing, Harker throws a coin to some street urchins who, in return, place a rosary in his palm before they dart away. (How do the children know where he is going or that he will need it? We never find out, but they give it to him just the same.) Russell deviates from the novel in the next sequence, which seems to be loosely inspired by *Dracula's Guest*, a deleted chapter from the novel turned short story that had Harker encountering numerous horrors on his way to Castle Dracula. As they travel through the woods, Harker is at first enchanted by the medieval beauty of it all—until he catches a fleeting glimpse of a heinous pagan ceremony where a woman is killed in the woods. He beseeches the coach driver to take him back to town to alert the police, but when he turns to look back to the coachman next to him, he's transformed into a werewolf! (What could be a werewolf figures into *Dracula's Guest*, hence my comparison earlier.) Harker grabs his whip and tries to keep the beast at bay. A struggle ensues on the back of the carriage, and eventually Harker manages to kick the wolf-man into the dirt as the carriage races on.

The scenes of horror continue. Harker next passes a woman being bitten by a gargantuan vampire bat. As he comes nearer to Castle Dracula, in a nod to Vlad the Impaler, he finds dead bodies impaled on huge stakes leading up to the castle gates. Worse still, a pack of ravenous wolves are in hot pursuit of him (that's the main reason he didn't stop to help the peasant girl being attacked by the bat). Harker continues to race towards the front of Castle Dracula, where he sees a man in black who doesn't seem the least bit concerned about the wolves. Harker shouts a warning to him regarding the wolves as he comes to a stop, but the man still isn't worried. He greets the wolves as they approach and it becomes evident that they are his pets, which he feeds cubes of sugar to. He introduces himself as Dracula and welcomes Harker to his home. Harker informs Dracula of all the horrible things he's just seen, and the Count reveals that it was an elaborate practical joke to welcome him.

Lazlo, the coachman, drives up in a Rolls Royce still dressed as the werewolf. Next to him is the peasant girl earlier being feasted upon by the bat. She waves to him as Lazlo takes off his mask and laughs. Dracula is in the middle of holding a huge party at the castle. Harker walks inside with Dracula and is astonished. Despite its medieval appearance outside, inside it as modern as any 1920s era mansion! Inside the Count wines and dines Harker, who takes in the sights of the celebration. (It's not ever clear if this is a secret vampire gathering à la *Kiss of the Vampire* or just the area's rich and famous.) Dracula takes Harker to a special art room devoted entirely to the works of Aubrey Beardsley, the most controversial artist of the Art Nouveau era. Dracula expresses his regret at having never met Beardsley before bidding an exhausted Harker goodnight with a glass of wine. As Harker gazes at one of Beardsley's erotic paintings featuring three nude women, they suddenly seem to come alive. These, of course, are Dracula's

217

brides. Harker isn't alarmed, either due to something in the wine or because he simply thinks it's just another joke. As usual, Dracula comes in and rebukes the female vampires for attempting to feed on his guest and drives them away. Because Harker appears to be so drunk from the wine, Dracula doesn't worry about what his guest has just seen.

After this, the screenplay follows the usual tropes from the novel, including the poor baby offered to the brides and then its mother yelling for its return at the bottom of the castle. It is at this point that Dracula crawls down the castle wall to feed on her as well. The next morning comes the scene of Harker talking to Dracula as he shaves. As usual, Harker takes note of the Count's lack of reflection and cuts himself. Dracula briefly loses control of himself and reaches for Harker, but his hand accidentally comes into contact with the rosary gifted to him by the children and he snaps back to his senses. The scene ends with Dracula telling him that after they have had lunch, they can finish their business. As they dine, Schubert's unfinished symphony plays in the background, and Dracula accidentally lets slip that he's disappointed that he didn't help him finish it. (Schubert should have been dead before Dracula was alive to aid him, hence the slip-up. In any case, it's just another way that Russell demonstrates Dracula's affinity for artists.) Eventually, the two get to talking about the real estate deal, but rather than London, the property the Count bought is from Southampton. (Russell changed the locale because he had lived there himself.) Dracula has also bought a little chapel there, and he casually asks if it's still sanctified. To his relief, Harker replies that it's not.

Dracula signs the deed concluding their business, and Harker plans to leave immediately. Dracula says he hopes it's not due to the joke the night before, and Harker reveals that he is getting married. The Count comments that he should have married her before leaving and brought her to Transylvania on their honeymoon. Harker responds that she couldn't get away as she is the secretary of the famous opera star Lucia Weber. (As stated earlier, this script's version of Lucy is a famous opera singer. This rings back to why Russell said it seemed silly why Dracula would have gone all the way to England for a simple girl, as now the girl is an artist that Dracula greatly respects. Not only that, but Lucia is dying. Right away, it's easy to connect the dots that Dracula wants to go to England to make her an undead like him so that she can live forever. Quite an interesting twist on Russell's part even if Dracula had already purchased property in London anyways.)

With his new, expedited travel plans in mind, the Count informs Harker that he cannot leave today, as it's St. George's Day, and there's no public transportation. He tells Harker that Lazlo will take him into town first thing in the morning. Dracula leaves Harker alone, and we find Harker is not as gullible as we think. As it turns out, he did see Dracula ward off his brides the night before and attack the woman outside. Harker merely acted drunk in front of the Count out of fear, though he made a mortal mistake in revealing his personal details to Dracula in regards to Mina and Lucia. In any case, Harker immediately sets out to escape Castle Dracula. As in the book and many other iterations of the story, Harker must climb down one of the castle walls. On his way down, he accidentally falls into a chapel. In it, he spies a mural of Dracula as Vlad the Impaler along with his three brides, and he begins to connect the dots that the Count is an ancient monster. He continues his exploration and eventually comes across the Count slumbering in his casket. Knowing nothing of what it takes to kill a vampire, Harker stabs Dracula with a knife rather than a stake. The vampire awakens and pulls it out, then tries to stab Harker with the knife. Harker bolts out of the room just as a band of gypsy servants come in. (These gypsy servants were an important part of the novel and were often left out of film adaptations.)

Harker escapes to another room where, from a window, he can observe caskets of earth being loaded onto wagons in preparation for Dracula's journey. Just when he thinks he is home free, Harker is accosted by the vampire brides, who hypnotize him. At the last second, Harker, who has either snapped out of the trance or was only pretending to be hypnotized, punches one of the brides! His first hit does nothing to harm the undead woman, and he, in turn, is tossed across the room. Harker then wraps the beaded rosary around his fist, and this time his punches do damage thanks to the rosary (one even knocks one of the bride's fangs out). Harker hangs the rosary on the door on his way out, effectively trapping the brides inside so that he can get away.

In the next room, Harker finds a macabre museum of sorts where Dracula's mummified victims, most of them romantic couples, sit on display. Horrified, Harker rushes to the window overlooking a river. Taking his chances, he jumps in, and we would then dissolve into Dracula's coat of arms. It is a stencil on Dracula's casket as it is lifted and placed on board a vessel bound

219

for England. After the ship sets sail, we would cut to an image of a similar ship on the box cover of a book of matches, being handled by none other than Renfield. The box contains no matches, though, only flies. After popping a dead fly into his mouth, Renfield looks out his peephole and spies Lucia being taken on a tour of the sanitarium by Dr. Seward. There is some brief banter between the trio about Renfield and his flies before Seward covers the peephole. It is also soon apparent that this version of Seward is romantically entangled with Lucia. (He is also a younger iteration of the character compared to other film adaptations, which made him older than he was in the book, where he was also one of Lucy's three suitors.)

Lucia asks him what Renfield is doing there, and Seward explains that initially he met Renfield to try and treat him for leukemia, and he later descended into madness. Specifically, Renfield went off to Transylvania looking for a cure, and that's when he came back insane. Renfield pipes in again, overhearing, singing a strange song that more or less tells of Dracula's impending arrival, though he doesn't name the Count. At another point, Lucia breaks down in tears regarding her looming farewell performance, and Renfield chimes in again, telling her that she should carry on as though she will sing forever. An irritated Seward bids his poor beloved goodbye, then tells Renfield that he has 48 hours to dispose of his nasty flies. Renfield thanks him for his kindness, and remarks that he is almost as kind as "the master."

At that remark, there would be a slow dissolve to the *Demeter* sailing at dusk. Dracula emerges from his coffin and crawls on deck. We would then cut back to the asylum, where after a brief exchange between Renfield and Seward, one of Renfield's pet spiders traps a fly in its web and begins to feed on it. Artistically, we would cut to what appears to be a web on the *Demeter*, but it is really some rope netting, and resting against it is an unconscious sailor that Dracula is feeding upon, just like the spider and the fly. This intercutting between Renfield catching prey in his cell and Dracula stalking victims aboard the *Demeter* continues. One visual of particular note would see the Captain and his men inspecting a dead sailor when suddenly blood drips on them from above. They look up to see Dracula hanging upside down like a bat from the masthead, blood dripping from his fangs.

Had this script went before cameras it would have reunited Oliver Reed and Sarah Miles (seen here in 1978's *The Big Sleep*) as Renfield and Mina.

Eventually, we would cut to Lucia sitting on the shore, watching the *Demeter* approaching as she chants to herself, "Who shall I take as my last lover?" A bit odd, considering that earlier she seemed perfectly content with Seward. However, her little monologue reveals she has another suitor in the form of none other than Quincy Morris. (There is no version of Arthur

Holmwood in this script. I assume Russell chose Texan Quincy Morris because he would contrast better against Seward. In any case, it's nice to see Morris appear for a change as he was often left out of film adaptations of the novel.) Eventually, Mina, Lucia's secretary and Harker's aforementioned fiancé, comes onto the scene and joins Lucia. Talk between them turns from Quincy Morris to Mina's wedding with Harker, who should have been home yesterday. But, the duo is soon distracting by the *Demeter*, which is literally speeding into port. As you can guess, Dracula has killed the entire crew as usual, and the ship crashes into the dock. (In this case, it does so in the middle of an outside concert where a live band performs.)

Quincy gets his introduction in this scene when he shows up and tells the Harbormaster that he'd better get on board and turn the engines off before the ship explodes. The harbormaster doesn't seem concerned enough to suit Quincy, so he gets some rope, forms a lasso, and slings it around the flagpole. He then climbs up onto the ship and runs to shut off the engine. (Quincy also has a not so honorable intention in doing so, as maritime law of the era permitted the first man on board able to claim a deserted ship's contents, which Quincy intends to do.) Meanwhile, Dr. Seward attends to the injured, and Mina reminds Lucia that both her boyfriends are quite gallant.

The harbormaster asks if Seward will come on board with them to inspect the ship. When Lucia and Mina ask to go too, Seward vouches for them as nursing assistants, and off they go. Inside, there is a typical scare where Quincy hears a noise, and when he draws his gun, it turns out to be a black cat. As the scene progresses, the cat seems to spy on the investigation. (However, it's never revealed if the cat is, in fact, Dracula in disguise.) Eventually, all of the characters meet up with Quincy as they investigate the ship. They find only one man dead and clutching a rosary. (All the other bodies were presumably tossed overboard by the Count.) Suspiciously, they find that the ship's logbook is incomplete, with certain pages torn out. They also deduct that someone still living had to steer the ship to port, as the man at the helm had already been dead for too long. Later, after the others have left, Quincy pries open the boxes in the hold and is bemused that they hold nothing but dirt. Dracula appears in the doorway and announces himself as the owner of the crates, which he acts as though were shipped to him (rather than him accompanying them). Quincy lets the Count take what is his, and the duo basically has a brief, pleasant exchange.

James Coburn in one of his many Westerns.

The next scene is Lucia's farewell performance at the opera, where she plays Joan of Arc. Dracula is there watching too, and Lucia takes special notice of him. Next up is an after-party at Lucia's luxurious estate. Dracula is part of the crowd but keeps his distance, watching Lucia dance with Seward through some opera glasses. At one point, it appears that Seward is proposing to Lucia. Quincy notices this and has the band begin to play a lively,

223

jazzy tune to ruin the moment. He uses the new music as an excuse to pluck Lucia from Seward and take her out onto the dance floor. Eventually, Seward and Quincy get into a fistfight, and Lucia runs away crying.

When she is alone, Dracula comes upon her and tells her that he'd prefer to remember her as Joan of Arc rather than Ophelia. Lucia takes to the mystery man right away and feels that she knows him somehow. We learn through the duo's dialogue that Dracula has attended Lucia's performances across the globe for many years, and though they have never met, Lucia recognizes him. Dracula says that he couldn't stand to watch her from a distance any longer and had to finally meet her. Lucia intones that it's too late now, as she's dying—unless he happens to be a miracle worker. Dracula then leads her on to believe that he is a specialist of sorts that hails from Transylvania. (This ties into Seward telling Lucia that Renfield was somehow cured in Transylvania, which she remembers.) Dracula explains that he has helped other dying artists with similar ailments, though he cannot divulge who they are. Lucia becomes entranced by the Count. They begin to dance, and he gives her the kiss of the vampire, which puts Lucia into a trance where she imagines herself to be at the Fountain of Youth.

We would fade out to Mina searching for Lucia in the garden. She finds Lucia alone near a fountain, as if dancing with an invisible stranger. Mina snaps Lucia out of her trance, and she is disappointed to find that her "lover" is gone, though a flitting in the trees signals to us that Dracula has flown away as a bat. Mina leads Lucia back inside to go to bed, and then notices the strange marks on her neck. There is a quick scene of Renfield watching Dracula in bat form sail past his window, and then we would cut to the next morning. The scene is set at a train station, where Seward awaits the arrival of his old friend and mentor, Professor Van Helsing. Mina comes to get Seward, but is separated from him by distance. He stands on one platform outside, and she on the other. She shouts to him that she is concerned for Lucia, who she says must be attended to at once. Before she can explain further, the train comes in, drowning out all other noise. Seward greets Van Helsing, who is described as having a round cheery face and long silver locks.

Seward again converses with Mina from a distance in the carriage set to take him and Van Helsing to the sanitarium. She is in a carriage opposite him, as she is leaving to see Harker, who has just returned and is in poor health. She does her best to get the urgency of the situation across to Seward as to Lucia's condition before their two carriages take them their separate ways.

Back at the sanitarium, though Lucia is pale, she is well enough to walk under her own power and goes to see Renfield, knowing that she and he share the same "master" now. She asks Renfield how she might see Dracula, but Renfield just rants on about how the master has deserted him and says nothing of real consequence to her. Seward arrives about then as Lucia begins to faint, and he picks her up in his arms. Van Helsing stays behind to examine Renfield (examining Renfield was the purpose of his visit to begin with, by the way), while Seward sees to Lucia. The verbal banter between Renfield and Van Helsing is well done, especially when one imagines Oliver Reed in the role as planned. Though Renfield starts off the conversation seeming to be out of his mind, as it progresses, he composes his words quite intelligently to the professor's shock. Van Helsing is no fool either; he picks up on the fact that Renfield isn't into eating bugs so much as he wants to drink blood. Renfield begs Van Helsing to see to his freedom or suffer the consequences, more or less, but the doctor doesn't budge. Renfield will stay put, and Van Helsing bids him goodbye for the moment.

A bit later, Van Helsing oversees a blood transfusion from Seward into Lucia. As the two men converse, it becomes apparent to Seward that Van Helsing is formulating a theory that he's not yet willing to share. Van Helsing concedes this, stating Seward would not believe him and that he needs to consult some books in a special London University library before he feels confident enough to share it. And so off Van Helsing goes to London via motorcar, with Dracula watching from the shadows with a smile. The Count then turns his gaze to the gardener and his young son outside of the asylum. Clearly, he's plotting something devious for them.

We would next cut to Renfield, who attacks his orderly when he brings him his supper. Renfield escapes and makes way for Lucia but finds Seward in his way as he examines her. Renfield sinks his teeth into Seward's wrist, and the doctor kicks Renfield in the groin. Renfield then proceeds to lap up the bit of Seward's blood that spilled to the floor. Seeming to be sated by the blood, the orderlies are able to take him back to his cell. Upon leaving Lucia in her room to recover, Dracula appears at the window with a blazing red sunset behind him. Lucia smiles at the sight of her lover and goes to open the window, but she is too weak. Besides, Dracula has mysteriously disappeared.

Along with Ken Russell's *Dracula* was this bizarre musical *Dracula Fever* from the late 1970s which was never produced.

We cut to Renfield's cell, where he is whispering to Dracula outside, and it is apparent Renfield is jealous of Lucia. That is why he attacked her earlier. He knows the Count is going to give her immortality, which is a gift he feels he deserves first. (Renfield and Lucia both are only in a half-vampire state, not yet fully transformed.) Renfield seems to know vampire lore and refuses the Count entrance into the asylum. What happens next comprises this screenplay's most controversial element. Dracula opens his cape, revealing the young gardener's son. It is never explicitly stated how old he is, but he is presumably very young, and for some reason, he is also naked. (By making the boy naked, there seems to be a perverse sexual inclination to the scene. The boy is meant to be food for the blood-crazed Renfield, much like the baby was for the brides, but by presenting him nude, this changes the scene in a troubling way. Had this actually gone before cameras, the studio most likely would have forbidden the nudity, and wisely at that.) In any case, Renfield succumbs to the temptation of the blood and invites Dracula in. As Renfield suckles the boy's blood, Dracula flies into the asylum in a red mist. (Lucia seemed more than willing to let Dracula in, why then did he need to appeal to Renfield? Perhaps it was because Lucia was too weak to open the window, but all Dracula really needs is the invitation to come inside. Once he received the invite from Lucia, he could have presumably broken through the window on his own.)

The next scene is comparable to the so-called "vampire wedding" from the 1979 *Dracula*. Similar to that scene, which also came from the novel, Dracula enters Lucia's room and opens a vein in his chest, which she drinks from to some swelling music. (This, in effect, makes her a full vampire, which is what Renfield is not.) We would cut to the next morning, where the first light of dawn awakens Seward in his room. He rushes to check in on Lucia, as if having had a premonition that something terrible had happened. He finds the room empty and asks the nurse where she's been moved to. The nurse informs Seward that Lucy died at 4:30 that very morning.

We would then cut back to Quincy on the deserted ship that he claimed earlier. The black cat is still following him as he instructs an accountant to give him an inventory of everything on board and its worth. Before the man leaves, Morris asks him if he knows the meaning of the multiple flags being flown above. The man doesn't know, and Morris makes it his mission to find out (correctly assuming that they were some kind of distress symbol).[2] Quincy is likewise perplexed by the strange man who had the boxes of

227

earth shipped to him. He gets his address—a property still called Carfax despite the slight shift in setting—and goes to spy on him. (This has nothing to do with Lucia's death, by the way, as he is still unaware of it.) Quincy's sleuthing leads him to the old deserted chapel on the property. He takes cover when he hears someone coming. It turns out to be Renfield, who escaped the night before and is carrying the dead boy. He calls to his master even though it is daylight, again begging for immortality. Then, somehow, he senses the presence of an intruder and attacks Quincy with superhuman strength. Renfield drags Quincy to Dracula's casket, which slowly begins to crack open as it is now dusk.

Strangely, light pours out of the casket, and when the lid opens, Quincy would see Dracula's skeleton shining within his body like an X-ray! Dracula rises, and just as he's about to put the bite on Quincy, it's Van Helsing and Seward to the rescue along with orderlies and some Doberman Pinchers. (One can deduct that they used the dogs to trace Renfield's scent to Carfax, and their rescuing of Quincy was simply luck.) Before Dracula turns into a bat and flies off, Quincy shoots him with his revolver several times. The men stand in stunned silence at what they've just seen. We would cut to some time later in a study lit by a fireplace. As Quincy sulks, drinking by the fire, it's clear he's been told Lucy is dead. Van Helsing, meanwhile, is poring over one of the books he acquired in London. Next is the usual song and dance where Van Helsing explains the parameters of the vampire to a skeptical audience, in this case, Seward and Quincy. Van Helsing explains the means necessary to defeat Dracula and suggests they begin by sterilizing the boxes of earth Dracula brought with him. When Quincy asks why Dracula brought so much dirt with him, Van Helsing explains that he thinks Dracula plans to take over all of England with an army of newly created vampires, an interesting addition to the story.

Before setting out to acquire the needed Holy Water, wooden stakes, and the usual paraphernalia, Quincy asks to pay his last respects to Lucia. Seward begrudgingly agrees to take him to her (Lucia's death has done nothing to bond the two together). In the morgue, Quincy and Van Helsing look over Lucia while Seward receives an urgent phone call from Mina, who tells him that Harker has news for him. Seward has no idea that Harker has met their mutual nemesis and brushes off the phone call as quickly as he can, talking to her just long enough to assure her he'll have a room waiting for them at the sanitarium. Quincy, meanwhile, seems to have finally come around to the idea of Lucia being a vampire (he did, after all, witness Dracula turn into a bat). Van Helsing explains to him that so long as the crucifix necklace remains around her neck, she cannot rise again as an undead, nor can Dracula lay a hand on her.

The next scene would show all the caskets of earth being burned, while Quincy laments that one is still missing. Elsewhere, Mina has arrived at the sanitarium and is awaiting Seward's arrival. Lucia then makes a surprise appearance despite what Van Helsing said about her not rising again due to the cross... or so it seems. As no one told Mina that Lucia is dead—that we know of at least—she doesn't seem overly surprised to see her friend alive, though she is surprised to see her well enough to be walking. The two catch up on recent events, discussing everything except what's really relevant. Mina doesn't say a word about Harker's escape from Castle Dracula, and Lucia naturally doesn't reveal that she died and has risen again as a vampire. But, Mina is not as clueless as we might think. As the two women enter a room together, Mina goes to get Lucia a shawl from a closet so that she may be warm. Suddenly, she shoves Lucia into the closet and locks the door so that she may not escape. Immediately, she sets out to find Seward. (We can presume Harker told her of the vampire danger afoot, and perhaps someone at the asylum told Mina of Lucia's death upon arrival.)

Not able to find the doctor, Mina approaches an orderly. When the man turns around, the prospective audience would recognize him as Renfield, who Mina has never met. Not knowing any better, she lets the madman lead her to a darkened room where a lecture is taking place. Via an old projector, on the screen is the image of a heart. The lecturer is speaking about blood in a scientific discourse. The man giving the lecture is Dracula, of course. (However, it's not entirely clear who is listening to the lecture. Are they normal people, or the inmates of the asylum?[3]) In any case, towards the end of the lecture, the attendees all begin chanting that "the blood is the life"—so whoever they are, they are under Dracula's spell. Mina herself becomes hypnotized by the Count and approaches him as her clothes "melt off her body" and he puts the bite on her in a scene that might have still been too racy even for 1979.

Outside, Seward, Van Helsing, and Quincy are just finishing up with the burning caskets when they see a man running through the woods. At first, they think it's Renfield as he's wearing a straitjacket. But it's not. It's the orderly from the morgue, and he

229

is wearing Lucia's golden cross. Seward and Quincy angrily interrogate the man, who confesses that he stole the cross from Lucia's dead body and that when he did, she arose as a vampire. According to him, she knocked him unconscious, and when he came to, he was trapped in the straitjacket.

The script's next scene continues its nude streak that would surely have curtailed its actual filming, as we find a naked Lucia feeding on Harker. Van Helsing comes to the rescue, shining a golden cross in her face. With the help of Quincy and Seward, Lucia is confined to a straitjacket, and when the cross is placed back around her neck, she passes out. Despite her being our female lead, in the very next scene Lucia is staked by Quincy and Van Helsing, effectively destroying her. With Lucia now dead for good, the female lead then shifts to Mina, which, though necessary, is also a bit odd. (As it is, we don't have a great deal invested in Mina compared to Lucia. Had this script gotten a second draft, some more scenes for Mina might have been in order leading up to this. Likewise, it's somewhat interesting how this script began with Harker as the protagonist, lost sight of him in the middle, and now he's the romantic male lead again for the final third now that Lucia, attached to Seward and Quincy, is dead.))

In any case, like in other adaptations, Mina serves as a psychic link to Dracula, who we learn is sailing away. We could cut away to see Renfield swimming in the water behind his ship, pathetically begging to be taken along. Eventually, Renfield weakens until he sinks beneath the waves and dies. As in many other adaptations, Van Helsing soon deducts that Mina's psychic link can lead them to Dracula, who he theorizes is probably returning to Transylvania. Van Helsing decides that they should spilt up, lest one of their methods of transportation be delayed somehow. Quincy and Seward will go together, while he, Harker, and Mina will go their own way. Not long after this is decided, we spare any type of traveling montage and cut to the trio in a car speeding through Vienna. Van Helsing is trying hard to get Mina to concentrate to know just where Dracula is. (Yes, they know he is headed to the castle, but they want to know how far along he is on his journey so they can intercept him before he gets there.) Just in the nick of time, the travelers manage to board a train that they believe Dracula's casket is on. However, matters are complicated when Harker observes that the casket is being guarded. (By who exactly? A simple paid employee of the shipping company instructed to do so? A half-vampire slave like Renfield? We don't know.) Mina concocts a plan to pull the communication chord to stop the train. Her reason, which she will deliver to the guard in tears, will be that her hat with a diamond brooch flew out the window. The plan goes into effect, the train stops, and Harker and Van Helsing get to opening the casket while the guard is away. But, to their horror, it is empty. The guard, who has been arguing with Mina, is shocked to see gypsy bandits on horseback approaching the train. Mina's plan wasn't to aid Harker and Van Helsing; it was to aid Dracula in escaping all along. It is now dusk, and when another train passes by on the tracks parallel, the strobing lights of the other train illuminate Dracula looking in at Mina through the window. He thanks her, and she goes to join him. (I have to admit, this is a satisfying twist. Initially I thought it odd that Mina had no romantic attachment to Dracula as is the norm.)

The bandits not only get away with the casket, they also shoot at Harker and Van Helsing, hitting the latter. Dying, Van Helsing beseeches Harker to leave him to go after Mina. Harker kisses Van Helsing on the forehead and sets out on his own to find Mina as the train trudges on. (Yes, Van Helsing does die as this is the last we see of him.) Elsewhere, the gypsies have stopped to make camp near a beach, where Dracula stands on the shore with Mina. Even though she's not an artist, Russell notes that Dracula has taken a special liking to Mina. (I'm not entirely convinced by this as Dracula was enamored more so with Lucia. In fact, we haven't even seen Dracula react to Lucia's death! Overall, I would say a script doctor would have been required to better balance this element of the story as the sudden romance with Mina seems abrupt.) During this scene Russell touches upon something very, very interesting, though. There are many who believe that certain elitists within the entertainment industry have sold their souls to the devil. (There are more than a few musicians out there who openly admit to it.) Dracula alludes to this in the scene where Mina remarks that becoming a vampire will separate her from God's love. Dracula then goes on to describe God as teasing man with delights that he cannot savor for long in his short lifespan. Dracula intones on that God likes to cut down artists in their prime and cites Shakespear and Michaelangelo as examples. The Count then states that he and his vampire brethren began to "fight back", and that today some of the world's best known artists are actually vampires who must keep their identities secret. Dracula then takes things a step further and asks Mina if she's ever noticed the physical resemblances between certain artists. He says that once a lifetime they reinvent themselves so that they can go on

231

making art. He then hints but doesn't confirm that he himself is among several of those artists. (The only one he confirms himself to be is Cassanova.) The scene ends with Dracula and Mina in a passionate embrace.

Our next scene takes place in a small rural church during mass. Harker bursts in begging for the priest to bless the bullets in his gun (per some old instructions from Van Helsing). However, Harker is yelling in English not Romanian, and none of the congregation, save for one man, understands him. The man conveys Harker's odd request to the priest, who refuses to carry it out until Harker becomes violent and fires off a shot in the church. The odd scene is quasi-comical and played for laughs, as is the following one. In it, Quincy is speeding across the countryside in a 1920s era sportscar with Seward looking miserable and clearly fearing for his life. Seward eventually yells at Quincy to stop as he's sighted the Count's procession sailing down a river on a makeshift raft of logs. The two men then ponder the best way to do in Dracula, seeing as how Van Helsing and Harker have obviously failed to do so. Remembering an explosion they heard off in the distance earlier, they decide a quarry must be nearby. As such, they will procure some dynamite and blow the Count to kingdom come. They acquire the desired explosives and then do their best to race the log raft to the castle, which in the sports car isn't too difficult (aside from not jostling the explosives on board too hard).

The two find a spot overlooking the river, and unaware that Mina is on the raft, begin lobbing sticks of dynamite at it. Their explosive volley doesn't destroy Dracula, but it does sink the raft and the coffin. Seward warns Quincy that it's not over yet; come nightfall Dracula will rise again. After some time has passed, we would pan into the depths to the casket resting on the river bottom. Bubbles spew from a crease as it opens slowly. Dracula's pale fingers struggle to lift the lid until suddenly he transforms into a water rat and swims to the surface. The rat crawls into the reeds and transforms into a bat, and then flies for the castle. (Before going any further, it's important to note that it is not yet night, but a very cloudy sunset.)

In a spectacular shot, Mina is standing atop the battlements of the castle, watching as the bat approaches. Suddenly gun shots ring out. Harker has been waiting to ambush the Count. His shots fail to hit the bat, and Mina attacks him. Just when all hope seems lost, a cloud parts and a final ray of light from the sunset strikes the bat. Dracula transforms into a naked man in midair, his arms flailing as he is now powerless due to the sun's ray. He then falls into the trees below, being impaled like so many of his victims back when he was known as Vlad the Impaler. Mina screams and collapses into Harker's arms. There's no sudden comeback for Dracula, by the way, and this is his method of defeat. (Though there's not a great deal of build-up to it, it was still a unique way to kill him which hadn't been done before.)

This ending also surprised me, as I assumed Russell would take an anti-religious stance geared at conjuring sympathy for the vampire, but he doesn't. Instead, it's the opposite. As Harker carries Mina down a stairwell, one of the vampire brides runs towards him. He pulls out his gun and shoots her, ending her undead existence. As she falls, she drops an oil lamp onto some heavy drapery which ignites into flames. The other two vampire women then run in and implore Harker not to shoot. Their sister was running to thank him, not harm him. Thanks to him, they are free of Dracula's power. One says that to live an eternity without love was the true meaning of damnation, and the two sisters begin to chant, "He did not love us." Mina, understanding the horrible fate that almost befell her, utters, "May God forgive you. May He forgive us all." Mina and Harker exit the castle just as Quincy and Seward pull up in their motorcar. They get in the vehicle and they drive away. The last shot would be of Dracula, now aged 500 years, watching his beloved castle burn amid his death throes.

Like all the other unproduced scripts in this book, there are plenty of pros and cons to mull over. As to the positives, Dracula reimagined as an artist is a fantastic angle on Russell's part. The 1920s setting as opposed to the late 1890s was another fun innovation, as was including Quincy Morris for a change. This script's most problematic aspect from a narrative angle is how it shifts its characters between the three acts. The first and last act have Harker as its protagonist, while the much longer middle act had Seward as the hero. Therefore, when Harker becomes the hero again after being offscreen (or off-page in this case) for so long, it's rather odd. As it is, Seward also has more to prove as a man than either Harker or Quincy, his competition for Lucia. The more interesting end to the story might have been having Seward prove his worth over Quincy by defeating Dracula and saving Lucia's soul.

Even odder is the switching of focus between the female leads.

Since the focus was on Lucia from the start, I can't help but feel the shift to Mina in this script was a bit too sudden. It might've

233

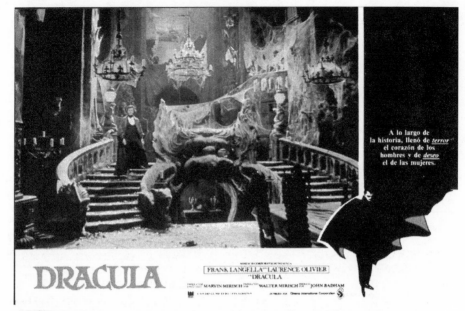

Lobby Card for the 1979 *Dracula* which ultimately led to this film's undoing.
© 1979 Universal Pictures

been better if Dracula put the bite on Mina first just to feed on her, or even use her as a way of getting closer to Lucia, with his efforts to get to the artist he desires being continually thwarted until the last act. This could have provided a satisfying character arc for Lucia too. In Mina's case, she gets a happy ending once her vampirism is reversed. Had this happened to Lucia, she would revert back to a mortal state where she is soon to succumb to leukemia. In essence, Lucia would give up her immortality in the end so that she wouldn't be damned. In any case, the character functions needed the help of a script doctor.

Ultimately, though this author ultimately enjoyed the Frank Langella *Dracula* that helped cancel this one's production, the Ken Russell *Dracula* is still a fun 'what if' to mull over for fans.

Chapter Notes

[1] Though Russell has been quoted that he eyed Fleetwood, other sources act as though they had to twist Russell's arm to even consider Fleetwood, who he was very reluctant to cast.
[2] This subplot is eventually forgotten.
[3] Much later, it's alluded to that these were the inmates.

26.
REMAKE FROM THE BLACK LAGOON PART I
KNEALE AND KIM'S CREATURE

Developed: 1981-1983

Screenplay by: Nigel Kneale & Evan Kim **Proposed Directors:** Jack Arnold & Joe Dante **Proposed Cast/Characters:** Cassie Quin [environmentalist], Matt Garoll [biologist], Paul Shriver [Navy captain]

PLOT The Creature is captured in the Amazon and brought to a military base in California, where he meets another Creature and escapes...

COMMENTARY In the early 1980s, Universal got a wild hair to remake 1954's *Creature from the Black Lagoon.* And why the Creature as opposed to Frankenstein or the Mummy? I would have to guess that the success of *Alien* as a creature feature had something to do with it. Actually, what really got the ball rolling on the *Creature* remake was an aborted remake of *The Lost World* in 1981. *Creature from the Black Lagoon* director Jack Arnold was supposed to helm it, with John Landis producing. Universal felt that Arnold couldn't bring *The Lost World* in on the proposed $10 million budget, and they switched Arnold over to a 3-D remake of *Creature from the Black Lagoon.* Was this because Arnold was the original *Creature* director? Was it because Universal had done some pre-production location scouting in South America, where *Creature* had also been set? We're not sure. As is usual in these cases, a conflicting story states that Arnold proposed the *Lost World* remake after Universal commissioned him to do a *Creature* remake![1] Regardless of the project's origins, we do know that a script was completed, and it was written by none other than Nigel Kneale, creator of Britain's popular scientist Bernard Quatermass. (Made even more famous by Hammer films like *Quatermass and the Pit* in 1967.) After Kneale completed his version, actor/writer Evan Kim (Dirty Harry's partner in *The Deadpool*) wrote a revision to better integrate 3-D effects into it. Only the first half of the script references 3-D effects, though, and then seems to forget that was a major part of the concept.

Colorized still from the original *Creature from the Black Lagoon.* © 1954 Universal Pictures

236

Rick Baker was slated to create the Creature, and it sounds as if the remake would have been produced except for one thing: Universal decided to make the third Jaws movie in 3-D instead! Allegedly John Landis had some 3-D test footage for the *Creature* remake shot. He claimed that when MCA head Sid Sheinberg saw his *Creature* test footage, he exclaimed, "What a great idea! But why do the Creature? Let's do *Jaws 3-D!*" Ironically enough, *Jaws 3-D* borrowed quite a few ideas and gimmicks from *Revenge of the Creature* (1955), also released in 3-D, and quite possibly, Kneale and Kim's script as well.

Very similar to *Jaws 3-D*, the first scene was supposed to illustrate the 3-D effects right away, with various fish swimming around in front of the camera. The Creature's hand suddenly pops out and grabs an eel, at which point the title would come on screen. The first real scene takes place in a village along the Amazon, which is essentially a tourist trap selling fake trinkets to gullible travelers. (One woman, Mrs. Parker, buys a shrunken head, and her husband points out to her that it says "MADE IN KOREA" on the bottom.) A woman named Cassie Quin, who is writing a thesis on the destruction of the rainforest, begs the boat captain, Miguel, to take them out deeper into the "real rainforest," to which he begrudgingly agrees. He takes them deeper upriver, where they eventually find themselves stranded in the Black Lagoon when the boat gets entangled in some roots. While Miguel works to free them, a tourist named Suzie goes for a swim. Right away, this remake gets to recreating the series most evocative imagery of the Creature stalking a woman under the water. As the boat is freed and ready to go, the others call out for Suzie, who has just noticed the Creature swimming beneath her. She screams and Miguel dives into the water to help her, but he is killed as Suzie makes it back to the boat. Cassie manages to snap a few pictures of the Creature before it slips back into the Black Lagoon and out of view. The boat makes it back to Iquitos, where the tourists inform the press of the monster they saw in the water. Dr. Matt Garroll of the Wonderlife Foundation of Florida approaches Cassie and asks for the photos in her camera. Once Matt figures out that Cassie is a fellow intellectual, he invites her to become a part of his expedition to capture the Creature, and she accompanies him back to his research vessel.

As one of the crew develops Cassie's photos, Matt tells her how the Creature has been reported off and on for many years. While this is a tenuous reference to the original series at best, when he adds that once one was captured thirty years ago, this all but confirms that this isn't a remake; it's a sequel! Couple this with the fact that the Creature is never given a clear description in this script and it's fairly safe to assume this was simply meant to be another member of the Creature family from the first series, if not perhaps the original Creature himself.

The vessel sails into the Black Lagoon, where Matt and a crewman named Carlos go diving and plant cameras on the lagoon bottom. The Creature then systematically disables them one by one in a display of intelligence. Matt, Cassie, and five others then go scuba diving into the lagoon. One of the spooked members, Wally, shoots a fish when he mistakes it for the Creature. The Creature was watching, though, and becomes enraged, attacking and mutilating Wally. (The Creature is displayed in this draft as some kind of protector of marine life. This is good and well, but doesn't exactly gel with the Creature snagging the eel in the first couple of shots!) Cassie stays behind to observe the Creature as Wally is taken back on board the ship. To Cassie's shock, the Creature appears to be trying to talk to the dead fish! She tracks the Creature to the opening of a cavern that looks to have been carved by an intelligent species of some sort. The Creature then surfaces into a room full of skulls lined with beings like him. (This interesting detail isn't really explored any further, though.)

Back on the ship, having observed the Creature's intelligence, Cassie asks Matt to let her try and communicate with it. Matt obliges, and believe it or not, Cassie is successful in her endeavors. The Creature does speak to her in a sense, though it basically just repeats the same word over and over again. Matt wasn't entirely honest with Cassie, though, and uses her experiments to trap the poor Creature in a shark cage. Cassie is angered by this and immediately sets it free. Matt then uses soundwaves to incapacitate the Creature. Next, Matt locks up Cassie in a cabin, dopes up the Creature with tranquilizers, and sets sail from Iquitos back to the States. Once they are safely at sea, Matt lets Cassie out of her chambers to come see the Creature in its tank. He informs her that according to correspondence he's had with the foundation, the Creature and his ilk were the first beings to walk upright.

While caught in a storm, the Creature's vitals begin to plummet and so they lessen the amount of tranquilizers being given to him. The Creature wakes up when no one is around and breaks free of his tank. He then walks around the ship until he comes to the engine room. He kills several crewmen and then destroys the engine because the noises it made were making him angry.

(Remember, he's sensitive to certain sounds.) This strands the ship in the middle of the storm, which is a very interesting concept. (Before this set-piece, the film was mostly retreading the first movie and *Creature Walks Among Us*, but now it's in fresh new territory. In fact, if one wanted to, the whole rest of the film could have been about the characters trapped on the ship with the killer Creature if they wanted.)

When Carlos goes to the flooded engine room, the Creature bursts out of the water, attacks him and then drowns him. Matt manages to lock the Creature within the engine room at least, so that he won't pose a threat to the rest of them. The storm begins to dissipate, and a helicopter descends on the stranded ship. It is the U.S. Navy under the command of Captain Paul Shriver, though they aren't there to help the stranded crew as much as they are to capture the Creature. The military quickly subdues the Creature with gas grenades and then seals him up in a special container. Captain Shriver then more or less drafts Matt and Cassie to become a part of his research team and flies them to the Long Beach Naval Base in California, where the Creature will be studied.

In another fun twist, we then meet a second monster. It turns out that Shriver is in the business of capturing creatures. The one in the adjoining tank next to the Creature is a larger, walrus-like monster captured off the coast of Alaska called Homo Horribillis. It was one of three and is the only survivor as the other two died in captivity. The second creature also isn't described very well, and it's not certain if it has tusks despite the comparisons to a walrus. All we know for sure is that it's blubbery like a walrus and has skin like one. As this is more a sequel than a remake, the addition of a new Creature species is quite welcome overall!

Shriver considers the creatures to be "men of the wrong day," created on the fifth day of Genesis rather than the sixth. Shriver soon has the veil lifted between the two tanks so the creatures can see one another. Rather than acting confrontational, the Creature tries to communicate with Horribillis. Shriver takes Cassie and Matt to a dolphin tank and explains that they've been trying and failing to train dolphins for military missions. Rather than attempting to train the Creature, Shriver thinks that the Creature could be the key to communicating with the dolphins!

That night in Cassie's room, Cassie and Matt ponder why the other two Horribillis specimens died in captivity. Then they rather abruptly make love! (One of the main complaints leveled at this script is a lack of character development where the two's romantic relationship is concerned.) Next up is a scene evocative of *Revenge of the Creature*, where an experiment is performed on the Creature, who has been implanted with some kind of pleasure and pain stimulator in his brain. When the pleasure centers are stimulated, Cassie tells the Creature "good," and when the pain receptors are stimulated, she tells him "bad". Disgusted by the experiment and convinced that Shriver is crazy, Cassie and Matt decide to leave. The military won't allow this, though, and detain the duo. Back at the containment facility, the Creature is beginning to communicate with the stronger but less intelligent Horribillis. The Creature gets Horribillis to dislodge some support beams, which enables them to escape their enclosure. (Many people who have read this script compare the two creatures to George and Lenny from *Of Mice and Men*.) Horribillis kills two guards who come onto the scene, and the two creatures eventually bust out of the wall and escape. (On his way out, the Creature does stop and talk to the dolphins, though, mainly to remind us that he has the ability to communicate with other sea life.) Humorously, the Creature and his companion are blocked from the ocean by the freeway, and so they must walk through the urban landscape. Naturally, this provides fodder for some of the script's more fun scenes.

For instance, the Creature walks through a grocery store parking lot and causes a woman to faint. In another humorous scene, we next find the Creature and Horribillis frolicking through the sprinkler system of a suburban yard at night. When a car approaches the house, the Creature runs out back to hide, while the less intelligent Horribillis tries to hide behind a shrub too small to conceal it. When the man sees the form hiding behind the bushes, he begs what he assumes is just a large man to take whatever he wants, fearing him to be a robber. The man has a weak heart and apparently dies of fright once he actually sees Horribillis in full. (A rather needless death which is tonally inconsistent with the humorous nature of the scenes.) Elsewhere, Shriver loans Cassie and Matt his convertible Porsche to go out and look for the Creature.

In the next scene, the Creature and Horribillis take a dip in a neighbor's pool. The owner of the pool dives into the water, not knowing the Creature is there, and he dies as well. (Again, very tonally inconsistent. It was one thing to have the Creature kill intruders in his territory in the Black Lagoon or to kill his captors when escaping, but to kill innocent people on their territory makes the monster less sympathetic, and this script wants us to sympathize with the Creature.) Eventually, Navy helicopters spot the monsters, and they evade them by running into the forest. They eventually make their way to a waste treatment plant, where they see cascades of water. The Creature realizes what the place really is and tries to stop Horribillis from jumping into the toxic waste, but he does anyways and gets stuck in the sludge. The Creature runs and hides upon the military's arrival, and though he gets away, he apparently gets struck with a bullet or two during his escape. Horribillis, on the other hand, is shot and killed (since he's stuck in sludge, it seems like they could have recaptured him pretty easily). Afterwards they burn the body, and that's that for poor Horribillis.

Meanwhile, Matt and Cassie come across an old bag lady who saw the Creature stumble into a nearby park. Cassie is guided to the wounded Creature, who chokes out the word "good" upon seeing her again. Shriver reports to his admiral about the escape and promises to destroy the Creature. (Considering we oddly don't see the admiral's face, this almost seems like a set-up for a sequel since the character is kept so mysterious. Usually when a character is teased in such a way, it's to leave an intentional plot thread dangling for a follow-up.) Elsewhere, Matt and Cassie have kept their discovery a secret and have transported the Creature to an aquarium. In the water, Matt walks the monster to revive him. When the Creature revives, it puts out a call to all the sea life in the aquarium à la Aquaman or Tarzan! It is morning at this point, and the aquarium is in full swing with a sort of water rodeo going on. (In attendance are none other than Mr. and Mrs. Parker, the humorous tourists from the beginning of the script!)

The military arrives and knocks Matt over the head with a pistol just as the Creature gets away. (Oddly enough, this KO's the male lead for the rest of the script! However, one could consider the Creature to be the actual male lead anyways...) Just when we think Shriver has the Creature cornered, it jumps into the waters of the orca tank. Killer Whales then jump out of the water to shield the Creature from the bullets! (Why are they willing to die for the Creature they've only just met? This would need to be addressed or changed in some way. Plus, do we really want to see Killer Whales getting shot to save the Creature?) Though the last bit with the whales was a bit problematic, the next bit is fun at least, as an orca bursts out of the water and eats Shriver! After this, there's another shot of Cassie cradling the unconscious Matt, and then the final shots comprise of the Creature escaping into the ocean and being escorted away by dolphins.

As you can see for yourself, the script was an interesting little amalgamation of all three past Creature films. The first bits in the Black Lagoon did a good job of paying homage to the first film in three major ways. It featured the underwater ballet scene, it had the Creature's cave, and it had the Creature captured within the lagoon. In terms of what was new, it had a boat of tourists in the Amazon, which was rather interesting. The second portion of the story played a light homage to *The Creature Walks Among Us*, with the monster transported across the ocean on a ship. When the Creature is situated on the military base, those scenes are reminiscent of both *Creature Walks Among Us* and *Revenge of the Creature*. The second Creature, which is basically a cold water mammalian counterpart to the Creature, is probably the script's best innovation/addition to the mythos. (On that note, could the smoother skinned Horribillis have been a nod to the altered Creature in *Walks Among Us*?) Finally, the last act mostly mirrors *Revenge*, with the Creature loose in civilization and later running amuck in a water park. Unfortunately, this ending is also something of a weak spot for several reasons. Again, the characterization of the Creature needed a bit of work, as he had killed too many innocent victims to end this picture on a truly positive note. The fix to this problem would be simply to revise the bits where the Creature and Horribillis ran amuck in suburbia, not killing anyone there and just frightening them (as with the woman in the parking lot earlier). And though it's a fun idea for the Creature to cause the orca to kill Shriver, it's also a bit odd that the Creature himself doesn't do in the villain and just gets away. With some more revisions, this could have been an excellent fourth Creature film.

Ultimately, of the three proposed Creature remakes covered in this book, Kneale and Kim's version came the closest to actually being produced. And as stated before, it actually played into the development of *Jaws 3-D*. Initially the plan was to film the third Jaws as a spoof called *Jaws 3, People 0*. Universal decided against this and hired Richard Matheson to do a straight sequel. His concept was that a giant shark becomes trapped in an inland lake. Upon the meddling of studio executives, it was decided—thanks to the 3-D *Creature* remake—to make the third Jaws a 3-D feature and the lake setting was shifted to a water park... just like in the *Creature* script. As mentioned earlier, both the *Creature* script and *Jaws 3-D* start off with underwater scenes of fish swimming towards the camera to show off the 3-D effects. *Jaws 3-D* also has a scene where the lead characters walk a comatose monster (a

As odd as this might sound, the *Creature from the Black Lagoon* remake ended up inspiring the birth of *Jaws 3-D*. © 1983 Universal Pictures

baby monster shark in this case) through the water to gets its gills working again. And, the *Creature* script and *Jaws 3-D* end with a water park in chaos during a big event, and both also have heroic dolphins that play into the climax. Coincidence? In Hollywood, I doubt it...

Chapter Notes

---

1 Joe Dante was on standby as a backup director if Arnold passed on the project.

Nakajima's werewolf in a behind the scenes still of *Legendary Beast Wolfman vs. Godzilla.* © Shizuo Nakajima

27.
LEGENDARY BEAST WOLFMAN VS. GODZILLA

Developmental Period: 1983-Present
Intended Release Date: Summer 2016

Directed by: Shizuo Nakajima **Screenplay by:** Shizuo Nakajima
SPFX Director: Shizuo Nakajima **Music by:** Akira Ifukube (stock
tracks) **Known Cast:** Ema Ishihara (love interest)

8mm, Color, Uncompleted

PLOT Godzilla battles a giant werewolf...

COMMENTARY Earlier in this book we covered Godzilla's
cancelled battle with Frankenstein. While that never came to pass,
in the 1980s, Godzilla did for a fact battle a giant werewolf. A few
of you have no doubt heard of this, or perhaps seen a still from
the film. However, those of you who have never heard of it are
probably asking why, if this was filmed, has it never been seen?
Well, that's due to Godzilla's status as a registered trademark of
Toho Co., Ltd. in Japan and *Legendary Beast Wolfman vs. Godzilla*
is not a Toho film. *Wolfman vs. Godzilla* is a fan film, technically,
though it's much more ambitious than most fan films considering
it has a $100,000 budget!
   The film was the creation of Shizuo Nakajima, a Toho production
assistant on films such as 1975's *Terror of Mechagodzilla*. At that
time, it was thought that the 1975 film might be the last Godzilla
movie ever made. As the years pressed on with no new Godzilla
sequels, Nakajima took it upon himself to craft his own Godzilla
movie. Initially envisioned as a short film that paid homage to
Hammer's *Curse of the Werewolf* (1961) and *King Kong vs. Godzilla*
(1962), it eventually evolved into a full-fledged feature. Fortunately
for Nakajima, he was popular with the Toho staff, and they gave
him two puppet Godzilla props. On top of this, Nakajima then built
his own Godzilla and Wolfman suits, plus miniature sets. The
resultant giant monster footage looks as though it was taken
straight from the 1960s. However, the werewolf transformation

scene is clearly influenced by 1981's *An American Werewolf in London*. For that matter, it is incredibly well done. It concludes with the Wolfman walking outside, still human sized, to confront the military while holding his love interest in his arms.

And just how does a human-sized werewolf become gigantic to battle Godzilla? Well, that's tough to say. As it stands, right now only Nakajima knows the details of his fan film as he's still editing it together to this day (though all of the footage has at least been shot). Of the ten hours of shot footage, some snippets have since materialized on YouTube. Of the human footage showcased, the first snippet shows a man entering what appears to be an Egyptian tomb. Then, there is footage of scientists studying a Wolfman statue in a lab as Godzilla approaches which implies that they are trying to induce a transformation (perhaps a gigantic one?) from the Wolfman to battle Godzilla. The footage even comes complete with fleeing extras. There's also a fairly ambitious car chase scene where some Yakuza appear to capture the Wolfman in his human form. Said Yakuza ward off the pursuing police vehicles with a bazooka!

So basically, the film's story seems to be that an explorer found the statue of an ancient werewolf, which itself somehow transforms the male lead into a giant wolfman. The giant wolfman then becomes a hero by battling Godzilla... eventually. Before the title bout, though, as is customary in a Japanese giant monster movie, the giant Wolfman fights the military. Footage of the giant Wolfman battling the military is just like similar scenes in many other Toho films. As the hairy beast wanders through the forest, a bevy of tanks and helicopters approach, and Nakajima even filmed a few shots of a real military jeep and soldiers traveling down the road. This footage is most evocative of *War of the Gargantuas* where the beast is blasted by maser tanks. In another nod to that film, the Wolfman pursues a low flying chopper through the forest.

The film first came to the attention of western fans when curious photos of this strange "lost" film showing Godzilla battling a furry whatsit appeared online. Said fans then went wild with speculation. Was the furry kaiju a stand-in for the 1962 King Kong costume?[1] Was it some obscure kaiju from a TV show posing with Godzilla? Eventually, one fan, Mark Jaramillo, got curious enough to do some serious digging and that western fans even know about this film is predominantly thanks to this super fan. Jaramillo, who saw stills from the film on the internet, printed them out, and then began an investigation of sorts by taking the stills to Tetsu Shiota, owner of the Anime Jungle in Little Tokyo, Los Angeles. Amazingly,

Shiota managed to connect Jaramillo with the film's director Shizuo Nakajima, who was elated that an American fan was curious about his film. This led to Nakajima giving Jaramillo stills of the film and even a clip to take to G-Fest—an annual Godzilla convention held in Chicago—in 2012.

American fans got to see even more footage of the film when Shizuo Nakajima came to G-Fest XX in 2013 to a very enthusiastic reception. In 2016, Nakajima implied that the film would receive a DVD/Blu-ray release that summer, but unfortunately it never panned out. Fan esteem for the film remains high, and Godzilla and Wolfman chibi figures have even been produced by fans. Not only that, the film even spawned a fan-made spoof called *Rabbitman vs. Godzilla!* Hopefully one day the film will be completed and released to DVD with some sort of approval on Toho's part. Until that day comes, the film will unfortunately remain unfinished.

Chapter Notes

[1] This is because *Wolfman vs. Godzilla* utilized a suit modeled after the Godzilla suit from *King Kong vs. Godzilla*.

VLAD THE IMPALER

Developmental Period: 1979-1997

Screenplay by: Arthur Ellis & John Peacock **Proposed Cast/Characters:** Vlad Tepes [Transylvanian warlord], Ilonya [Vlad's wife], Benedek [monk], Istvan [Vlad's son], Milista [witch]

PLOT The story of how Vlad the Impaler became the dreaded vampire Dracula...

COMMENTARY After Michael Carreras's removal from Hammer in the Spring of 1979, the creditors put Brian Lawrence and Roy Skeggs in charge. (Both men had plenty of previous experience with the company and were by no means newcomers.) The two produced no films for Hammer but were eventually able to repurchase the company for $100,000. During this transaction or shortly after, they produced the television series *Hammer House of Horror* and began to consider new film projects. (However, since the TV series was their main priority it would heavily impede upon the theatrical features.)

The first project that Skeggs and Lawrence went back to was *Dracula: The Beginning*, now called *Vlad the Impaler*. John Peacock was brought on to handle the rewrite of the earlier treatment. He did not rewrite it himself, though, and approached another writer named Arthur Ellis to do so in either 1982 or '83. Under Skeggs and Lawrence, they wisely decided to finally stray away from the Gothic trappings of Hammer to go more so in the direction of the *Omen* franchise, which was by then winding down with *Omen 3: The Final Conflict* (1981). And modernize the script Ellis did, bookending it with a modern-set prologue and epilogue.

The exciting prologue, apparently a bit like the teaser of a James Bond movie, was action-centric and had a vampire hunter (not Van Helsing) storming a dilapidated old house. Within it he clears out a nest of vampires, and after that begins to reflect on the origins of the vampire curse. This would serve as the set up to flash back to the Vlad the Impaler section, which, it is said, is basically the same as Hayles' draft.

Ellis makes some interesting additions to Hayle's script. These additions don't change the narrative structurally, they just infuse it with a bit more of the supernatural. Case in point, Vlad has a horse straight from Hell named Salamander! Other than that, apparently the two screenplays were very similar. As to the modern epilogue, it was essentially a sequel set-up for what could have been a "Vlad the Impaler 1984 AD"! (Don't quote me on that, that's just my own funny little title for it!) Upon concluding his meditation on Vlad/Dracula, the vampire hunter was to mutter, "Oh where shall we meet, my sad Lord Dracula... that we may duel once again."[1]

Actually, this line does more than set up a potential modern-day sequel, but also implies that the vampire hunter has dueled with Dracula before. In any case, it was ironic that even though the new Hammer wanted to shy away from the failings of the 1970s that they were planning a sequel similar to *Dracula A.D. 1972*.

As to how Ellis's new script was received, Skeggs and Lawrence ironically removed the Omen-like elements that they had requested! They struck out all sections containing the hellish horse, but did retain the modern bookends, which apparently were Ellis's only remaining contributions to the script.

What put the brakes on this project more than anything wasn't script issues, though. It was a burgeoning deal to produce a second TV series with 20th Century Fox to be called *Hammer House of Mystery and Suspense*. *Vlad the Impaler* would lie dormant until the late 1980s when *Screen International* reported in July of 1987 that the film was to be a co-production between Hammer and U.S.-based producer Steve Krantz. By December of 1988, John Peacock had created a new draft that totally discarded every addition by Ellis. The main alteration this time was Vlad's leaving his estate to Milista rather than non-existent baby brother Vlaachim. (Personally, I find this to be a mistake, as the presence of Vlaachim created a nice little parallel to the original novel where Dracula appears to grow younger as he feeds.)

With this fairly minor change set into place, a shooting schedule was prepped for production. For reasons unknown, the project didn't happen. But *Vlad the Impaler* wasn't staked yet. In 1993, Hammer entered into a new and exciting deal with Warner Bros to not only remake some of their classic library, but also make all-original films. One of the better-known remakes was to be a Joe Dante directed *The Devil Rides Out*, while the original project was *Vlad the Impaler* again. And, considering that *Bram Stoker's Dracula* was a huge hit in 1992 and also utilized historical flashbacks to Vlad the Impaler, the project's chances of production increased.

American writer Jonas McCord was hired to revamp the script yet again, and shooting was to take place in Romania under a $12 million budget. McCord turned in two drafts. The first was dated November of 1993 and kept the original title, while the second was retitled *Vlad Dracul* (and was actually identical to the first in terms of content).

McCord reinstated the Vlaachim subplot and also beefed up Ilonya's part. In this version, Ilonya is thrown from her horse during a boar hunt with Vlad. Upon hitting the ground, she sees an angelic-looking girl that we would later learn to be the witch Milista. This accident leads to Ilonya's death in childbirth, which sets Vlad on the dark path to vampirism. It also makes it clear that events are being manipulated to turn Vlad into a vampire. Finally, Hammer had a script they were satisfied with, and production was still being advertised in February of 1995, with the budget upped from $12 million to $18 million. The wheels of production turned slowly, with director Xavier Koller announced for the project a year later in 1996.

However, progress on the proposed Hammer remakes was stalled when it couldn't be determined who actually owned the rights to them![2] Furthermore, Skeggs was approaching retirement around this time, and his desire to produce more films seemed to be waning. The last official mention of *Vlad the Impaler* still being a planned production was in March of 1997. After that, the project was never mentioned again.

Chapter Notes

---

[1] Foster, Unseen Horrors, p.190.
[2] A remake of *Quatermass and the Pit* was one of the primary troublemakers in this regard.

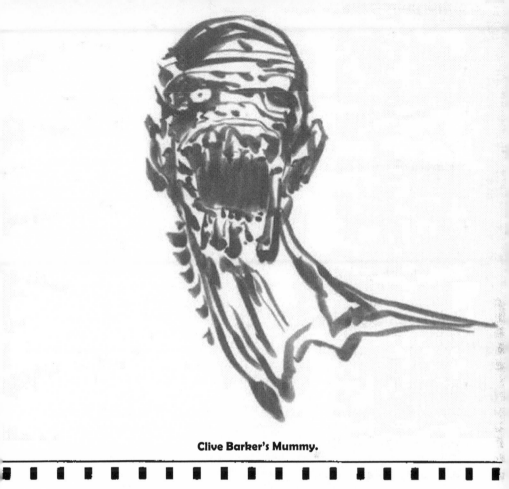

Clive Barker's Mummy.

29.
CLIVE BARKER'S MUMMY

Developed: 1992

Proposed Director: Clive Barker **Screenplay by:** Mick Garris

PLOT A new exhibit on ancient Egypt opens a portal to space aliens...

COMMENTARY In 1999, for the first time in many, many years, a Universal Classic Monster movie became a major moneymaker in theaters. That film was the Stephen Sommers directed *Mummy* remake. However, remake isn't really the right word, as the film was more of an Indiana Jones-type action film than a horror movie. For some purists, this was off-putting, but audiences loved it. But, as it turns out, Universal had been contemplating a Mummy remake for the past ten years, and the pitches that preceded Sommers' Mummy were quite strange.

When I first began researching *Mummy* remakes, I assumed the impetus for their production was the success of *Bram Stoker's Dracula* in 1992. However, according to an old *Fangoria* article, the Mummy remake had begun gestating in the late 1980s. Screenwriter Abbie Bernstein was instructed by Universal to write *"The Terminator* only with a mummy"! So, even back then, Universal appeared to be contemplating a more action-driven approach to *The Mummy*. Furthermore, they wanted the Mummy to be off killing people by the very first page! Bernstein decided that page one was too soon for that, but managed to get the Mummy on screen by page four. (Upon reading this, the producers then felt that was too fast and had the Mummy appear on page 15 instead!)

Though Bernstein could have simply had the Mummy hunt down desecrators of the tomb Terminator-style (which, in a way, was what Kharis did anyways), in her story the Mummy is searching for a MacGuffin that will bring about the apocalypse. Specifically, it is an artifact called the Tear of Sechmed, which will poison all life on Earth if dropped in the ocean.[1] (This was therefore in keeping closer to *The Terminator*, which also revolved around the apocalypse.) Details on the exact outline are nebulous, but apparently the Mummy and the Tear of Sechmed would be found together in Egypt. After their discovery, two different teams of scientists study the Tear and the Mummy. The team studying the Mummy uses a new type of brain-stimulating equipment meant to help paraplegics on the dried-up corpse! (This idea would also bleed into many later *Mummy* remake treatments.) This Mummy awakens and escapes the lab. As it has a psychic connection to the Tear, it sets out to obtain it and drop it into the ocean. As the Mummy moves along chasing the heroes, it slowly loses its bandages. As such, it has to replace them and does so in scavenger-like fashion by replacing them with barbed wire, phone cables, chain mesh, and anything it can get its hands on. Though a bit silly, it does fit with making the Mummy more Terminator-like! Bernstein described it as a "skeleton of 20th Century wrappings"[2] which you have to admit is an interesting visual. For whatever reason, Berstein's treatment of the late 1980s was scrapped, and talks of a Mummy remake didn't heat up again until the early 1990s.[3]

I am unaware of who exactly pushed for the above-described Mummy remake, but the one that began in 1992 was the brainchild of producers James Jacks and Sean Daniel. And while this was not coincidentally the same year that Francis Ford Coppola's big-budget *Dracula* became a hit, Universal apparently didn't want to risk much on *The Mummy*. Instead, Universal was only willing to put up a $10 million budget for what they thought could become a low-budget horror franchise, which were still popular in the early 1990s. The producing duo first courted *Hellraiser* director Clive Barker to helm *The Mummy*. (Some sources even imply that his *Mummy* script started out as the third *Hellraiser* sequel until Barker felt he could rework the premise into a *Mummy* remake.)

Barker's reimagining wouldn't be set in the 1930s, but the 1990s. A basic description of the story will simply tell you that the head of a contemporary art museum turns out to be a cultist trying to reanimate mummies, but it's actually much stranger than that. The full screenplay was written by Mick Garris. "In a way, it was a little bit like Clive Barker meets Erich von Däniken," Garris said. "The Mummy itself is a suspended animation creature from long ago and far away with alien protectors that come to life. It is housed in the brand new museum built in the heart of Beverly Hills." He goes on to say that on the night of the grand opening that "creatures from beyond our planet" begin to attack.[4] Apparently, there wasn't even a traditional shuffling mummy in the proposed movie!

Years later, Barker would muse that the project probably would have been impossible in the pre-CGI era in which it was conceived. (CGI did exist by then, but it was not widely used.) However, the ambitious special effects scenes were the least of his concerns when it came to pitching the story to Universal. In 2015 he told *Fangoria* that in the first scene, a "strange boy-child is born, under circumstances—high howling winds and a ferocious thunderstorm—that suggest something unnatural is afoot."[5] The story would then jump ahead about 20 years into the future with sacred Egyptian artifacts being brought to America for an exhibition "that would put the Tutankhamen exhibit to shame."[6] As the story progresses, an "uncommonly beautiful woman" seduces her way through the male characters leaving a swath of murder in her wake. (Unfortunately, Barker doesn't really reveal her mission or intent in the interview.) Barker says that it would be revealed in the third act that this woman was the "strange boy-child" born in the first scene, now turned into a woman. Barker told *Fangoria* that,

> We loved the idea, so much so that we put the mystery surrounding this ambiguous creature and her extraordinary secret at the heart of our story. Our creation was not welcomed at Universal, needless to say. The script, which Mick had labored hard over, working in a diminutive hotel room in London, which I visited daily for story conferences, was eviscerated by the script readers and our producers. How could we expect to get away with something so weird? Nobody in America, we were told, would accept such a ridiculous premise.[7]

How does this character tie into the aliens and the mummy? We don't know, as Barker didn't say. In any case, after a few meetings, Barker and Universal both seemed to lose interest in him directing, and so he was off the project.

Chapter Notes

1 In the film's mythology, Sechmed was a goddess sent to earth by the gods to pacify and dominate mankind, but instead she tried to destroy them and so the gods put her to sleep, more or less.
2 Screenplay Archaeology Podcast, Episode 27: The Mummy, (June 11, 2017).
3 Bernstein supposedly spoke with George Romero over the phone about this project, but he didn't like the direction it was going in.
4 So, in a way, this was actually a precursor of sorts to *Stargate*, which also combined ancient Egyptology with ancient aliens.
5 bloody-disgusting.com/movie/3441008/george-romero-clive-barker-almost-directed-mummy-remakes-90s/
6 Ibid.
7 Ibid.

30.
REMAKE FROM THE BLACK LAGOON PART I
JOHN CARPENTER'S CREATURE

Developed: 1992-1993
Script Date: May 8, 1992

Screenplay by: Bill Phillips **Proposed Director:** John Carpenter
Proposed Cast/Characters: Abel Gonzales [diver], Cirri
Thompson [Green Peace activist], Pete Hazard [crazy government
official], Jake Hayman [doctor], Mary Peirson [Canadian botanist],
Bobby Whitaker [ornithologist], Adolpho Palminteri [crew
member], Jean Claude Gaston [botanist]

PLOT A strange fish-man is found within an ancient underwater
pyramid...

COMMENTARY After the success of *The Thing* remake in 1982
and the more recent *Memoirs of an Invisible Man* in 1991,
Universal President Tom Pollock offered director John Carpenter
the chance to remake one of their pictures. Carpenter immediately
picked *Creature from the Black Lagoon,* which had apparently been
forgotten since *Jaws 3-D.* Before he had his own script written, he
did at least look at the previous attempt, telling *Starlog* that he
had read the Nigel Kneale script and talked to John Landis about
it. "Nigel wrote a very interesting script, but it was written for 3-
D," Carpenter said in *Starlog* #177 in 1992. "[Kneale's script] was
also written nearly ten years ago, and things have changed since
then... but we may use aspects of Nigel's work. He wrote some
pretty neat scenes, but we're going to redo them."
   As this interview took place before the script we're about to cover
was written, it's unknown if any early drafts did use any of
Kneale's ideas. One thing Carpenter would do, as with the
previous script, was keep the Creature the same... basically.
Specifically, Carpenter said that he had spoken with famous
makeup man Rick Baker about making the Creature look "less
rubbery."[1] But otherwise, he and Baker would stick to the original
design as closely as possible.

The first draft was written by Bill Phillips, best known for *Christine* (1983). It begins with an homage of sorts to the original film, showing the Earth from a distance as the credits begin to roll.[2] The camera zooms past the clouds until we are in South America, where we would hone in on an airplane flying over the Amazon River (some superimposed text would have also informed us that the year was 1988). The two men in the plane comprise of Richard Conroy, an American, and Pete Hazard, an Australian. The plane encounters a fierce storm at the same time that Richard, the pilot, notices a bad fuel leak, which causes them to crash-land right into the Black Lagoon.

The two men flee the plane once it's down, thinking it will explode, only it doesn't. Richardthinks that all the fuel must have leaked out during the descent. He goes to inspect the plane while Pete begins to photograph the jungle. Richard soon calls his attention to a strange megalithic rock with hieroglyphics on it jutting out of the water. As the men get closer in a raft, they realize that it is actually the tip of a huge pyramid hidden under the water. As they circle it in their raft, a clawed hand explodes from the depths and grabs Richard by the face in what sounded to be a good scare. Pete screams as Richard is pulled under, never to be seen again. Pete paddles as fast as he can back to the plane, where he radios for help. The last shot of the sequence is of a huge shadow falling over Pete before he can finish relaying his message and he screams.

We would fade out to five years later, where we would focus on the expansive, 60-foot long research vessel *El Dorado II*, which even has a helicopter on deck. The vessel is already parked in the Black Lagoon near the tip of the pyramid. Among the crew are plenty of characters/victims to choose from. In the lead is American Abel Gonzales (32), followed by Jake Hayman (47), a narcissistic Long Island M.D., Jean-Claude Gaston (30), a French botanist, Bobby Whitaker (27), an ornithologist, Hector Ramirez (40), an Amazonian Indian who has a Ph.D., Mary Peirson (49), a Canadian botanist, and Adolpho Palminteri (35), a snazzily dressed Italian.

In addition to the mysterious pyramid, the crew has also found the crashed plane and puzzle over the fact that they can find no bodies. However, they don't spend too much time debating what happened to the plane's occupants, as the sunken temple is far more interesting. Mainly they are astounded because rather than looking like it became submerged in recent years, it looks like it was built underwater. Though there is some talk of getting a

256

professional archeologist to come down and investigate the pyramid, they decide to go and explore it themselves. Before they do, into their midst comes the beautiful Cirri Thompson, a 29-year-old Greenpeace activist on the run. (She was arrested for her efforts to thwart the cutting of the forest.) The group unanimously agrees to take Cirri in on the condition that she be their sound recorder during their filming of the pyramid. That same night, Jake tries to put the moves on Cirri, telling her that he used to be a member of Greenpeace in Iceland. Abel comes in to make sure that Cirri is situated, and in the process, Cirri politely hints that Jake was on his way out to get rid of him. Later that night, Cirri slips out on deck when she can't sleep to stare at the pyramid in the water. She thinks she sees something stir in the water, but before she can contemplate what it was, Jake saunters on deck and tells her that she looks like Ava Gardner in *Mogambo*. Jake tries again to put the moves on her, while down below the water, something watches them. Cirri is saved by Abel again, who also can't sleep. He says that he can't wait to get into the pyramid to explore. Overall not much of importance happens in this scene except that we further establish the characters and get a POV shot from the Creature watching them.

The next morning, Bobby and Abel dive into the lagoon with a camera. A pink dolphin darts past their camera, which the crew of *El Dorado II* sees on a live camera feed. Hector then tells of a legend that at night the pink dolphin transforms into a man. He then jokes that the legend was created to explain "mysterious" pregnancies. (This little myth is naturally meant to foreshadow the Creature in some way.) Back under the water, the scuba divers pass a school of piranha on their way into the pyramid (some expositional dialogue tells us that the piranha won't attack unless they sense blood in the water). On the feed, Hector confirms that he sees Incan writing on the temple and one symbol in particular stands out that reads "danger". Abel swims inside even though he knows it will anger Jake, who still wants to wait for someone more qualified. Inside, Abel finds various markings depicting underwater life, along with stone furniture, altars, goblets— basically everything you would expect to find within an ancient temple. He grabs a goblet to take back up to the surface when a large shadow passes over him. It's not the Gillman though, it's a Pirarucu, the Amazon's largest fish. When Abel surfaces with the goblet, it appears to be pure gold. He wants to go back for more, but Bobby convinces him not to, and they return to the ship.

Back on board, they debate again whether or not the pyramid was built specifically to exist underwater or not. Hector then mentions the legend that there was a race of fish people who lived underwater who surfaced once a year to procure a maiden so that they could have a child. (This was the same legend that inspired the writing of the first *Creature* movie by William Alland. So clearly, Phillips was aware of the project's origins.) As Hector explains the legend to Jake and Mary, Cirri, Abel, and Jean Claude explore the interior of the pyramid. Because there is also an audio feed, the boat crew hears what sounds to be a scream! After they hear it, they all notice that suddenly Jean Claude is gone. Mary goes to the top of the pyramid—which the crew had earlier discovered an opening into—and shines a distress light signaling that Cirri and Abel should surface at once. They look frantically for Jean Claude and then surface as ordered.

Upon surfacing, they tell Mary that they have no idea what happened to Jean Claude, and so immediately head back down to look for him. They swim deeper into the pyramid discovering various bones and remains as they search for their missing comrade. From the darkness, the Creature watches, though we still don't know what he looks like. Eventually, the duo finds their way into an air chamber shaped like a trapezoid. As such, they take out their regulators and stand in the water, which is only three feet deep. They call out for Jean Claude while the Creature stalks them via POV shots in the shallow water. Not finding Jean Claude, they decide to go, and lucky for them, the Creature is still too timid to approach.

Back on board *El Dorado II*, they watch the video footage once more. It doesn't show Jean Claude's disappearance, just the sound of his scream. They wonder if he might still be alive considering they found an air chamber within the pyramid and agree to search again later. But first, they decide to call for help. We cut to a Brazilian government office in Sao Paolo and get quite a surprise: Pete Hazard is working there! (No, we don't ever find out how he escaped from the Creature in the first sequence, but obviously he did.) Pete receives a phone call from the expedition and tells them not to do anything until he arrives. On the other end of the phone Hector is none too happy that "some asshole from the government" has told them to wait before searching the pyramid. Knowing that Jean Claude can't wait that long, Abel, Cirri, and Bobby go on a search and rescue dive anyways. Bobby and Abel head down a tunnel to the left, while Cirri deviates and takes a tunnel to the right without their knowing it. Cirri finds another room/air chamber, though the water is deeper and the room is larger than the one before. She has been followed in by the Creature, who watches her from a distance.

The script finally gives us a description of the Creature here, and he appears more or less as he did in the original films. The main deviation is that he's described as having very sharp teeth, and is colored a shade of translucent green, with some silver around the gills. Notably, the eyes are said to have hints of intelligence and emotion. As Cirri swims, we get a recreation of the famous underwater ballet from the first film, only here taking place within the temple rather than outside in the lagoon. As the Creature swims beneath her, he can't help himself and touches her leg. When Cirri looks beneath her, he is already gone. Soon after Cirri reconnects with Abel and Bobby in another chamber.[3] Abel is irate at Cirri for putting herself in danger by separating from the group and they leave the temple.

Cut to Pete flying down the river in a rusty old motorboat as "Sympathy for the Devil" blares on the soundtrack. As a monkey chatters at him, he whips out his pistol and shoots it to remind us what a bad apple he is. (Today it's the sort of character perfect for Danny McBride, but some claimed Kurt Russel was eyed for the part at the time.) Back in the Black Lagoon, Jake, Adolpho, and Hector have joined Cirri, Abel, and Bobby within the temple in the main air chamber. Outside, Pete arrives at *El Dorado II,* where only Mary remains. The more reserved Mary and the crude, boisterous Pete make for some interesting interactions, both comical and uncomfortable, as we're not sure just what we're supposed to think of Pete yet. (Is he an otherwise good-natured fire and ice character there for laughs? Or does something more sinister lurk beneath the surface?) We leave Pete and Mary on a humorous note before cutting back to the interior of the pyramid. There, Bobby stumbles on something, which turns out to be submerged human remains. There are many, and among them is Richard—Pete's pilot companion from the opening. We would cut to Richard's remains being laid out on the deck of *El Dorado II* as Pete chastises the group for being dumb enough to explore the pyramid. They argue that Jean Claude could still be down there, to which Pete replies, "Or what's left of him."

Pete flies into a rage and goes outside, firing his gun at the temple and screaming that he's going to kill the Creature. When the others ask him to calm down, he goes on and on about how fearsome the Creature is and how it will rip the flesh from your bones. To illustrate, he rips open his shirt to show a wound caused

259

by the Creature, then tells them how he was found by the Yanomame Indians after the attack. Pete more or less tries to order the group to leave, and Hector asks to see Pete's I.D. Pete obliges, and Hector informs him that even if he is a government official, they were given jurisdiction by the University of Brazil. Therefore his orders for them to leave are moot. Pete becomes enraged, then tosses a grenade at the temple. The crew is horrified as the blast naturally damages the ancient structure, and they beg him to stop. Pete tells them it's always been his goal to destroy the pyramid; he just didn't know how to find it again after the Creature attacked him. (Therefore there's not a plot hole as to why he waited five years to return, since he didn't know where it was after the attack. But, if you're wondering why the Creature didn't kill him, that's never explained.) However, the group manages to palaver a truce with Pete. He'll help them explore the pyramid to find Jean Claude, and he can kill the monster with a harpoon gun rather than explosives when they find him.

The next segment is something of a calm before the storm and mostly comprises of various character moments with the crew bonding with Cirri. (More than anyone else, it's the relationship between Cirri and the standoffish Mary that the script emphasizes. On the subject of Mary, it's important to note that she has an elaborate lab below deck which includes animals in cages.) The action picks up again when it's discovered that *El Dorado II's* radio has stopped working, and they all wonder if Pete may have done it. They agree that while they are in the pyramid with Pete tomorrow someone should stick around and get rid of his explosives. As planned, the next day when everyone explores the temple, Mary enters Pete's boat to grab the explosives. However, she can see that he's boobytrapped the cabin to shoot anyone who enters, and so she gives up. Inside the pyramid, the group finds a brand new chamber that appears to be a graveyard of sorts. Within it, they finally find Jean Claude, a deep gash across his chest and one of his arms torn off. They take his body with them back outside the pyramid. When they see Mary, she shakes her head as a nonverbal way of telling them that her mission to grab the explosives wasn't a success.

That night, Cirri goes to Abel's cabin to discuss Jean Claude's death. The scene ends with Abel consoling her as she cries and mostly serves as a way of furthering along the obligatory romance. The next day, the core group meets to talk about Pete in secret. With Jean Claude's body found, they have no more need of Pete, but as Americans they feel they can't arrest someone from the

Brazilian government. As such, Adolpho sets out on a smaller boat down the river to go and get someone else from the government to help. Little does he know, Pete is waiting and ambushes him, shooting poor Adolpho in the head. Back at the ship that night, Cirri can't sleep and goes to watch the last video of Jean Claude one more time. She freeze frames it when she thinks she sees something in the background and runs to get Mary. She is shocked to find her in the company of Jake. (From what everyone can see on the surface, they hate each other, but not so according to their sleeping arrangements!) After studying the image for some time, they can make out a vague human shape in the background. The realization begins to dawn on them that Pete may not be wrong after all.

The next day, Cirri and Abel explore the pyramid again. This time they find hieroglyphs that seem to depict a half man half fish creature. Then they find a strange skeleton with a webbed hand (a nod to the hand in the original film). They decide to take a sample back to the boat, but someone has blocked the only way in and out! Just when all hope seems lost, Pete and Jake come to the rescue, dislodging the debris. They all regroup with Hector and Bobby, and Cirri shows them the strange skeleton. From a distance, the Creature watches them interact and takes special note of Cirri's growing affection towards Abel. Rather than being jealous, the Creature seems intrigued.

Later, the group decides that anthropologists and archeologists are needed at the site right away. This angers Pete, who can tell that the group is more concerned with capturing the Creature rather than killing it. Pete, Hector, and Abel take to the jungle using the helicopter and finds more remains of the same pyramid on land. They decide that it must be a three-part structure that extends underground to the land rather than entirely being located in the lagoon. Eventually, they find an above-ground entrance into the temple to confirm this. Meanwhile, Bobby, Jake, and Cirri have returned to the pyramid armed with harpoons. They manage to find a secret passageway into the grandest room yet. In addition to being a bigger room, it appears that it might be bottomless in its depth, and it even has a few small islands dotting the waterscape. Onto one of these islands crawls the Creature, and it is revealed that he more or less has separate land and water modes. As he stands on land, water pours from pouches in his arms and legs, and his skin changes color subtly as his lungs begin to inflate. Lastly, his eyes even lose the fishy film and

Unfortunately, the closest we ever got to a Creature remake was 1987's *Monster Squad*, which featured a Gillman-type character.

become more human-like. (Was this a nod to *The Creature Walks Among Us?*) Though they don't see the Creature, Jake can hear it breathing in the distance. At about this point, the three are joined by Hector, Abel, and Pete. As the group searches for the Creature in the water, he watches from the island, a strange octopus-like ink oozing from his forehead. The Creature finds a hiding place in the rocks, and eventually the group gives up on searching the depths for him. They come onto the very same island and Bobby receives a scare when an iguana drops onto him from a tree. A bit later, Bobby comes face to face with the Creature in the dark. Its claws extend, and it slashes Bobby across the face. Hector hears Bobby's scream and runs to his side, but it's too late; the Creature has dived into the water. Pete pursues the Creature, caring only for revenge, while the others prepare to get Bobby out of the pyramid.

We follow Pete down a passageway which leads into a shrine room of sorts devoted to the race of the Creatures. As Pete marvels at the ancient structure, the Creature hides within some reeds. Not finding the monster, Pete leaves. Back on the *El Dorado II*, Hector has found a poisonous root of some sort that will knock out the Creature if ground up and placed into the water. Hector mentions that many locals simply use it for fishing, but that in this case they have "increased the dosage." (This plays homage to a method used to catch the Creature in the original film.) They drop the powder into the biggest chamber where they saw the Creature last, but he can sense the toxins and swims away. However, they are able to spot the Creature swimming away from the area, and Jake is a good enough aim to harpoon him in the torso. The Creature tires as the harpoon was also laced with the sedative substance. The Creature begins to slow, allowing another member of the expedition to hit him with their harpoon as well. The Creature succumbs to unconsciousness and floats to the surface.

They soon ensnare the Creature in a big net, and right away, Pete prepares to stab him. Hector whips out a revolver and makes it clear to Pete that they are taking the Creature alive. The Creature is next placed within a cage in Mary's lab. Cirri enters and remarks how pitiful the waking Creature looks and Abel reminds her that he killed Jean Claude and Bobby. (This is the first confirmation we get that Bobby didn't make it.) Meanwhile, in an amusing little character moment, the Creature sees his reflection in the mirror for the first time and is initially frightened of himself. A bit later, when Abel and Cirri share a flirtatious moment, this time the Creature doesn't like it. He feels that Cirri should be his and becomes agitated in the cage. The monster begins to rage so hard that he makes progress in damaging the steel bars. The rest of the crew runs inside as Cirri tries to calm the Creature to no avail. As a last-ditch effort, Hector shoots the Creature with another sedative-laced harpoon, knocking him out again. Under the circumstances, they decide to leave the lagoon as soon as possible and get the Creature to the University of Brazil. This news doesn't sit well with Pete, as he feels transporting the monster is suicidal.

Below deck in the lab, Mary is alone with the Creature. Unbeknownst to her, the sedative wears off sooner than anticipated and the Creature is smart enough not to let her know it. He's also intelligent enough to know how to get her nearer to his cage. Stealthily, he reaches his arm through the bars of the cage and grabs a broom. With it, he pushes a packet of Mary's gum towards the edge of the counter. (A running gag throughout the script is how much Mary loves gum, and apparently, even the Creature has noticed.) Mary accidentally knocks the gum off the counter, and it lands near the cage. When she bends down to pick it up, the Creature grabs her and pulls her through the narrow bars into the cage with him! (It's a rather gruesome death for an overall likable character.) With no witnesses, the Creature begins to bend and break the bars. Just as he gets out, Hector rushes in. Upon seeing the monster loose, he shuts the door to the lab, locking the Creature inside. The monster flies into a rage, knocking over Mary's various chemicals until it starts a fire and also sets the animals in the cages free. He then breaks through the window by throwing his cage out of it, followed by the mirror. The Creature gracefully dives off the deck back into the lagoon, and Pete begins chucking grenades at him in a vain effort to destroy the monster.

Hector, Jake, and Pete set out on the chopper to look for the Creature in the jungle for some reason. The two intellectuals still don't want to kill the monster because it could be the key to evolutionary secrets in their minds, while Pete is still deadset on killing it. (This is one spot where character motivations needed to

One of the only known photos of John Carpenter and Rick Baker's Creature design.

be better defined. For instance, what was Pete's relationship with Roger that made him so hellbent on revenge? Though the two seemed to be friends in the opening scene, they didn't seem to be close to the extent that Pete would devote his life to avenging him. Or is Pete simply angry that the monster gave him a scar across his chest? As for Jake—who is devastated over Mary's recent death—you would think he would be more gung ho about killing the Creature now, but apparently not.)

Abel and Cirri have remained on *El Dorado II* putting out the flames. The two share a tender moment and go in for a kiss when the Creature bursts inside, knocks Abel out of the way, and takes Cirri with him back into the lagoon. As the helicopter approaches, Pete shoots at the monster just as it submerges with Cirri out of sight. Abel, Jake, Hector, and Pete set off to rescue Cirri in the underground lake cavern (which they have quicker access to via the hole in the jungle). As for the Creature and Cirri, the former finally becomes aware of the latter's inability to breathe and basically kisses an air bubble into her mouth. The Creature has to repeat this process a few times, and it seems that Cirri has become comfortable with it, understanding that the monster means her no harm.

The Creature, Cirri, and their pursuers eventually surface in a beautiful grotto outside of the temple in the jungle. The four men split up, going in separate directions to cover more ground. Jake finds Cirri behind a beautiful waterfall, while Pete lags behind. Upon seeing the Creature, Jake shoots him again with another harpoon (this one isn't laced with sedatives, though). He manages to hit him a second time, but as he's reloading, the Creature slices Jake's head clean off. (After this, the script more or less describes him as a chicken running around with his head cut off.) Abel and Hector hear the commotion and run towards it, while Pete follows the Creature. Upon arriving at the waterfall, Hector pauses to look at Jake's headless body while Abel runs on after the Creature. However, the Creature is still there and comes up behind Hector, crushing his spine.

By this time, Abel and Pete have regrouped and heard Hector's scream. The men find the carnage then run behind the waterfall.

A CAMEO FOR JOHN AGAR?

IN HIS INTERVIEW WITH *STARLOG*, CARPENTER MENTIONED WANTING TO WRITE IN A SUPPORTING ROLE FOR FORMER *CREATURE* STAR JOHN AGAR. HE TOLD STEVE SWIRES IN *STARLOG* #177 THAT "I RECENTLY SAW [AGAR] IN A PICTURE, AND HE WAS TERRIFIC. HE HAS AGED AND BECOME AN INTERESTING CHARACTER ACTOR. IT WOULD BE FUN TO TRY TO GET HIM INTO THE FILM AS A REAL CHARACTER, AND NOT JUST IN A CAMEO. I WOULD LIKE TO GIVE HIM SOMETHING TO DO RATHER THAN MERELY HAVE A WALK-ON. AGAR WAS ALWAYS MY FAVORITE OF THE SCIENCE-FICTION STARS." WHICH CHARACTER SEEMED SUITED FOR HIM IN THIS DRAFT? YOUR GUESS IS AS GOOD AS MINE.

Cirri isn't there, and there are two different passages to follow. They split up going their separate ways. Pete is the lucky one who finds the Creature, currently pulling spears from his torso. Pete fires his gun into the monster and is shocked to find that he shot the mirror from the boat! (The Creature, infatuated with the reflective surface, had brought it back to his lair.) The Creature then steps out beside Pete and grabs him. They lock eyes with Pete realizing that the animal he's been hunting is more human and intelligent than he imagined. The Creature crushes Pete's face and then pounds his head down into his shoulders! (While Pete deservingly received this film's most gruesome kill, keep in mind that the other characters never learned that he murdered Adolpho, which seems like an unclosed circle in the plot.) The Creature tosses Pete's carcass into the water, which attracts piranhas that devour his body entirely.

Elsewhere, Abel finally finds Cirri, who is being stalked by a 45-foot long anaconda! (And while very cool, this does indeed come out of nowhere—there's no real foreshadowing of giant anacondas being a thing in this script.) Just as it's about to tighten its coils, Abel shoots it with a harpoon. As the snake writhes in pain, Abel begins hacking at it with a knife. The Creature comes in about then and is touched by what he sees instead of enraged. Rather than killing Abel, he knocks him out of the way and begins to wrestle the snake. A bit like the scene in the 1976 *King Kong*, the Creature tears the snake in half and then approaches Cirri, who is in tears. He looks at her forlornly, as though he realizes that she doesn't belong in his world. Cirri isn't crying because she's afraid, though, she's simply overwhelmed by the whole situation. In an act of gratitude towards the Creature, she pulls out one of the

265

harpoons still embedded in his torso. He reaches out to touch her face and then stops himself. He then turns and walks towards the water where he belongs. Cirri goes to Abel, who was knocked unconscious and shakes him awake. As the two walk away into the dawn, the Creature peaks his head out of the water once more to watch them.

A second draft was completed by June of that same year. It reimagined Pete as a poacher and also included a scene where Abel, now a Brazilian, saves Cirri from authorities who are trying to arrest her Greenpeace group. In addition to these character changes, more scenes from the original *Creature from the Black Lagoon* were added. For instance, in one scene, the Creature catches on fire onboard the boat before diving into the water. In another, he loses a finger in a net, and in another, Cirri tosses her cigarette into the water—only since she's from Greenpeace, the cigarette is biodegradable![4] The new climax jettisons the Anaconda[5] and also has Abel stabbing the Creature in the stomach with a Bowie knife. And yet, the Creature still lets him go! However, there never was a third draft that we know of, and this is where Carpenter's *Creature* ended.

As to why the remake never went forth, the deal was supposed to be that Carpenter would do *Village of the Damned* for Universal, and in return, they would next give him the *Creature* remake... only they didn't. *Village of the Damned* was not the big hit that Universal had expected, being both a critical and commercial failure. Or, at least, that's the commonly accepted story, but Carpenter may have lost interest. Whatever the reason, of the three Creature remakes presented in this book, Carpenter's version was arguably the best.

Chapter Notes

1 Swires, "John Carpenter: Creature Features," *Starlog* #177 (April 1992) pp.30-31.
2 In the original film's case, they were showing the creation of the world, not so in this script, but the intent to show the world from a distance is the same I think.
3 There is an interesting visual where the wall behind Bobby is covered with spiders. He tells Cirri not to worry as he's sure they don't bite. Immediately after, the huge spider catches and eats a lizard!
4 In the first draft it is Jake who tosses his cigarette into the water. Cirri complains, and a crew member informs her that his cigarettes are biodegradable.
5 Ironically enough, *Anaconda* (1997) is itself a quasi-remake of *Creature from the Black Lagoon*, as the two have similar stories and settings to a degree.

31.
JOE DANTE'S
MUMMY

Developed: 1993-1994

Screenplay by: Alan Ormsby and John Sayles **Proposed Director:** Joe Dante **Proposed Cast/Characters:** Helen Grover [reincarnation of Anck-su-namun], Mike Razinsky [archeologist], Imhotep [ancient mummy] (Daniel Day Lewis), John Norton [expedition leader] (Christopher Lee)

PLOT An ancient mummy, Imhotep, is resurrected in modern-day Los Angeles...

COMMENTARY After Clive Barker's exit, the next director considered for *The Mummy* remake was Joe Dante, who envisioned Daniel Day-Lewis as his Mummy. Alan Ormsby was commissioned to write the first draft, which was later re-written by John Sayles. Like the previous two versions, it too had a contemporary setting, but this one was more in line with the original. It featured Imhotep, a female lead named Helen, and also had the reincarnation love story at its core. However, that is about where the similarities end. And though this script wasn't produced, Stephen Sommers did read it before making his *Mummy*, so you might notice a few similar ideas in it...

The story begins in 1963 in Egypt, where we meet our main character, Helen Grover, as a young girl wearing an oversized pith helmet. She is talking to her father as they look out over the Egyptian landscape. Cryptically, she says to him, "I used to live here, you know?" He thinks it's a simple child's fantasy, but little does he know the truth of the matter. A bit later, Helen's parents tragically die of Nile Fever before they can find the lost tomb of Princess Anck-su-namun, a priestess of Isis. As such, Helen is soured on Egyptology for the rest of her life. The story jumps ahead to 1993, where Helen is now a successful lawyer in America. Meanwhile in Egypt, another group of explorers has successfully found the lost tomb of Anck-su-namun. Along with Anck-su-namun, they also find a mystery body, not properly mummified and wrapped in sheepskin.[1]

When the artifacts and the mummy are brought to a Los Angeles museum, Helen is coerced into attending the grand opening, which is overseen by John Norton (to be played by Christopher Lee), an archeologist from Oxford. While there, Helen also meets the male lead, Mike Razinsky, who had been part of the expedition but split with them because he felt the mummies and the tomb should stay in Egypt. Notably, he shows Helen a picture of the pyramid in which the tomb was found, which is unique because the top is flat rather than pointed like other temples. He also tells her about the mystery mummy they found wrapped in sheepskin and sealed into the walls. Helen wanders off to be alone and finds herself in front of the unknown mummy. Curiously, she whispers the name Imhotep in front of it, and a small earthquake occurs. During the tremor, the mummy bursts out of its glass display case. Worrying it's been damaged, Norton orders the mummy taken to the university hospital where it can be scanned within an MRI machine. At the hospital, Norton finds a heart scarab above mummy's chest, and when he reads the inscription accompanying it, this unknowingly begins the mummy's resurrection (also aided in some way by the MRI machine, which was a carryover from the old "Terminator-Mummy" treatment). The mummy bursts from the sheepskin and immediately attacks Norton, absorbing his life force to partially regenerate until he achieves the appearance of a very elderly man. He then takes Norton's clothes, puts them on, and walks out of the hospital. (As he passes through an emergency room, he can see the ghosts of the recently deceased floating around, which has nothing to do with the story but is an interesting idea just the same.)

The ancient Egyptian walks out into the strange world of modern day L.A. One of the first things he takes note of is the "Walk/Don't Walk" signs on the streetlights, which reminds him of the hieroglyphics of old. He then wanders into a 7 Eleven, where he absorbs the clerk's life force, growing younger again. He continues his feeding frenzy, attacking a street punk and then a prostitute until he's fully regenerated into a man in his mid-thirties (Daniel Day Lewis's age in 1993). That morning, Imhotep hears Hebrew being spoken as he walks down the street and recognizes it as the language of the slaves. (He can only speak Egyptian and Hebrew at the moment.) He walks into a nearby Hebrew University and starts talking to a rabbi there, who directs him to the library. In the library, Imhotep somehow sucks the words right out of the books because they are all blank when he's done! (This, of course, is his magical way of learning English for the sake of the script.) On his way out, Imhotep then notices a poster on the wall for the exhibit and knows to go to the museum. By chance, on his way there, he stumbles across Mike and Helen on a date at the pier.[2] He goes up and strikes a conversation with the two and takes note of the fact that Mike has multiple religious symbols on his necklace, including the star of David, which makes Imhotep jokingly refer to him as a slave. (Sommers used the necklace idea for the character of Benny in his *Mummy*.)

Later, Mike gets a call that Norton has gone missing. Mike goes to the hospital's MRI room, where the shriveled body was found and mistook to be the mummy. Mike notices the crowns on the teeth and suggests they check Norton's dental records on a whim. As he continues his investigation, he also looks at security footage of the grand opening and notices Helen whispering the name Imhotep in front of the mummy. He goes to visit Helen and tells her what he saw on the video and that the name Imhotep was strangely scratched out of all the walls in the tomb. Meanwhile, Imhotep is at the museum and uses a scarab (hidden within his necklace) to attack the guard on duty. Just like in the 1999 *Mummy*, it burrows into his skin and kills him. Imhotep then performs a ceremony over Anck-su-namun's body, which draws Helen to the museum. He immediately deducts that Helen is Anck-su-namun's reincarnation, and he phases her through all her past lives. Mike shows up in the middle of the bizarre scene and uses his Ankh necklace to ward off Imhotep.

Bonded together by the strange experience, Helen asks Mike to stay with her at her apartment. A bit later, Imhotep communicates with the Anck-su-namun part of Helen's soul. She becomes strangely aroused by the experience and begins making out with Mike. When he sees that her face has changed to that of an Egyptian he understandably freaks out. This snaps Helen out of her strange, Egyptian trance. The next morning, while Helen is away at work, Imhotep stands on the beach using the sun to enhance his magic. As he does so he tries to make Mike stab himself to death with a knife. However, Helen's cat scratches Mike, snapping him out of it, and he then grabs his Ankh necklace for protection, which ceases the attack. That same day, Helen quits her job and wanders around in a haze until she finds herself on the same beach as Imhotep, who is wearing a speedo! He shows Helen all her past lives via the ocean like the pool in the original film (furthermore, a similar scene of Helen's past lives was shot and deleted from the original *Mummy* in 1933). Then, he shows her their shared history in Egypt, where he was once a general and she was a princess. Their love was forbidden, and so Imhotep made a deal with the evil god Set to be immortal with her. However, before he could inform Anck-su-namun of his deal, she let a poisonous asp bite her Cleopatra-style. Imhotep assumed Anck-su-namun's suicide was due to her despair over their not being together. When Anck-su-namun was being mummified, Imhotep went berserk and attacked the priests. Because he shed blood in the temple, Imhotep was sentenced to be buried alive. Back in the present, Imhotep eventually leaves Helen alone on the beach, where she is found later that night by Mike as the tide is coming in.

Back at the apartment, three policemen show up to arrest Mike. They think he is the one who murdered Norton (this in spite of the fact that it was Mike who suggested that they check his dental records to confirm that the dead body was his!). However, before they can haul him away, a scarab attacks one of the police officers. (Imhotep had apparently placed the scarab in Helen's purse.) As in Sommer's *Mummy*, it crawls into the cop's skin, and they save his life by cutting it out of him. They toss the bug to the floor, and it turns back to stone. One of the other cops shoots it, and it scatters into six pieces which then become six live scarabs that kill all three cops. Stranger yet, Helen's cat then eats the scarabs once they are done killing the cops! (Though not clear, the idea is similar to Sommer's *Mummy* where cats are feared due to their role in Egyptian mythology as magical creatures.)

Meanwhile, for some reason the Egyptian government has taken back all of the Egyptian artifacts from the museum. As they transport the artifacts through the desert outside of L.A. (presumably they are on their way to a private airstrip), Imhotep controls the sands and blocks the road. The scene would end with Imhotep standing before them with glowing eyes. (Later, the party is found completely drained and dead, but we don't see him kill them.) Imhotep then begins to build a huge pyramid in the desert under a certain solar alignment so he can draw energy from the sun to become stronger.

The final act has Helen separating from Mike, drawn to the pyramid. Having some knowledge in astronomy, Mike figures out where Imhotep built the pyramid and tracks Helen there. Inside the pyramid, Helen fully transforms into Anck-su-namun, Egyptian garb and all. Similar to the idea in the original *Cagliostro, King of the Dead*, Imhotep wants to take her soul from the new

271

healthy body and place it into the old, withered body, which he would then presumably regenerate somehow. (Whatever his plans, it all seems a bit convoluted.) With all her memories intact, Helen remembers that back when she was Anck-su-namun, she actually killed herself to avoid this very fate. Imhotep only believed she did it out of despair, when in fact she was aware of the deal with Set and wanted no part of it.

Mike has wandered into the pyramid by this point, and upon finding a room stocked with ancient weapons, picks up a sickle and goes to confront Imhotep. There's a hiccup though: Helen's cat is also there (it had hitched a ride with Helen in her car) and vomits up the scarab it ate earlier! The scarab then crawls into a baboon mummy that was part of the exhibit, which had included mummified animals. The baboon mummy comes to life and Mike has to fight it. (This is problematic because the cat had been heroic up to this point, which muddies the reader's perspective on the cat and distracts somewhat from the story. An easier fix would have been to simply have Imhotep bring the baboon mummy to life on purpose, rather than the cat vomiting up the scarab.) Anck-su-namun calls upon Isis to grant her magic powers and then turns her cat into a leopard which defeats the baboon. The leopard turns back into a cat upon defeating the baboon mummy, and Helen/Anck-su-namun battles Imhotep with magic. Eventually, Anck-su-namun turns Imhotep back into the dried-up mummy that he began the story as.

Anck-su-namun then tries to commit suicide, but Mike calls to Helen within her, begging her to keep living for his sake. Anck-su-namun reverts back to Helen, which comes at a bad time as Imhotep revives as the mummy again—just a mummy, mind you. Mike half-jokingly asks Helen if she can turn back into the princess for an instant to take care of the mummy, who Mike ends up destroying by simply lighting him fire, which seems a bit anti-climactic. The dramatic crescendo occurred when Mike stopped Helen from committing suicide, and perhaps that's where the story should have ended. In any case, the pyramid begins to collapse, and the lovers escape along with the cat. They walk off into the desert, and the story ends.

Things never looked particularly bright for the project, which was estimated to cost $25 million, but Universal would only allocate $15 for. The next problem was Universal head Sid Sheinberg. Steven Spielberg, a friend of Joe Dante's, loved his script and arranged a meeting with Sheinberg as they toured the set of *Casper*, currently filming. To their shock, Sheinberg said he didn't like the script. When Spielberg asked him why, he responded, "It should be a period picture like the first one." In an interview years later, Dante recalled,

I wanted to point out that the first one was not a period picture. That it looks like a period picture now, because it's made in 1933. And he obviously thought our picture should take place in 1933. And it didn't. And ultimately, that's the reason it didn't get made.[3]

Chapter Notes

[1] They take this to mean that the man was mummified alive (back then when they found a mummy in sheepskin they thought this was what it meant).

[2] Stephen Sommers referenced this scene when he made the comment that he felt this wasn't the Mummy because he walked around the modern world.

[3] Cairns, "I want to give you a piece of my mind: Interview with Joe Dante (Part 1)," (July 6, 2009). https://mubi.com/notebook/posts/i-want-to-give-you-a-piece-of-my-mind-interview-with-joe-dante-part-1

32.
GEORGE ROMERO'S MUMMY

Developed: 1993-1994

Screenplay by: Mick Garris and George Romero **Proposed Director:** George Romero **Proposed Cast/Characters:** Helen Grover [reincarnation of Anck-su-namun], Mike Razinsky [archeologist], Imhotep [ancient mummy], Kharis [Imhotep's slave], Eleanor [rich museum benefactor]

PLOT An unnamed American city is terrorized by two mummies in the form of Imhotep and his slave, Kharis...

COMMENTARY Of the main trio of directors[1] which were offered *The Mummy* before Stephen Sommers came along, the most eyebrow-raising name for most is George A. Romero. As the director of *Night of the Living Dead*, he seemed to be a perfect choice to direct what Universal essentially wanted to be a low-budget Egyptian zombie movie. A first draft, built upon the remains of the previous one, was completed by October of 1994. The first pass was by Romero himself, while the second was by Mick Garris, who had worked on a few of the previous drafts. The main character was again to be Helen Grover, who this time is the archeologist to discover the tomb of Imhotep in the city of Abydos. In this iteration, Imhotep is an Egyptian general from the time of Ramesses II. The remains of Imhotep and a few other mummies are brought to an unnamed city in the U.S. Like in the other drafts, Imhotep's remains are exposed to rays from an MRI scan in a high-tech forensic archaeology lab and he awakens.

Romero also tips his hat to the Mummy sequels as Imhotep next resurrects Kharis, his old slave! Kharis had rested next to his master and was also brought to the States and was installed in a museum. Through magic, Imhotep resurrects him and uses him to hunt and kill all those in possession of relics from his tomb. This is very interesting, as we would have the human Imhotep and the more zombie-like, undead Kharis in one film together, something that had never been done (and still hasn't).

The screenplay begins with a flashback to ancient Egypt. Imhotep and Anck-su-namun make love in his bed-chamber before commencing with a ceremony that will make them immortal per Set, as in the last screenplay. The priests of Isis burst into the room to save Anck-su-namun as Imhotep stabs her to complete the ritual.[2] The stab is not fatal, though, and Anck-su-namun orders him to be buried alive and that's that for the prologue.

Years later, Helen and Mike (yes, same guy as in the last story) find the tomb, including the items used in the ritual that opened the script. Eleanor, the expedition's main funder and the rich owner of a museum back in the States, wants the tomb transported in its entirety to the museum ASAP.[3] Cut to the opening night where we learn that the entire tomb was successfully transported to America except for the three items used in the opening ritual, which were mysteriously lost in transit. Mike makes it his mission to find the stolen items, which will be his main function for the rest of the story in addition to being a romantic rival to Imhotep.[4] In a nice touch added by Romero, when they go to open the sarcophagus for the first time, the still-unnamed mummy's fingernails are dug into the lid. Therefore, the mummy is lifted out with the lid itself! As in the previous draft, it is decided to do an MRI scan to see how well the body is preserved beneath the bandages. At the hospital, after everyone has gone, a tech named Colorado walks in and the mummy suddenly grabs him and drains his life force. (As in the previous draft, when his dead body is discovered shriveled and aged, authorities think that it is the mummy.)

The mummy, who we know as Imhotep from the previous draft, walks into a 7 Eleven and begins draining various people of their life forces. (However, unlike the previous iteration of Imhotep, this one shows remorse for draining some of his victims and hates what he's become. As for a few other pertinent details, in this version, Imhotep has to keep feeding to keep up appearances. Also, so much as briefly touching Imhotep will turn one's skin grey.)

Imhotep eventually visits the tomb exhibit and meets Helen, who he recognizes as Anck-su-namun at once. He points out to her that certain pieces are missing from the exhibit, which impresses her. Imhotep walks her home and as they talk she comes to believe that he's part of the antiquities service because he says he knew her in Egypt. In reality, he means ancient Egypt, but she thinks she must have met him in Egypt recently (hence her thinking he must be part of the antiquities service).

Afterward, Imhotep returns to the museum to revive Kharis. In a nice nod to the blacked-out eyes of Kharis in *The Mummy's Hand*, this version of Kharis literally has eyes that have been replaced with black stones. Imhotep then sets Kharis on a mission to find the stolen items needed to complete the ritual from the prologue. Elsewhere, Mike is acquiring some leads on the stolen artifacts, some of which trace back to Eleanor. Mike and Helen both go to Eleanor's so he can interrogate her about the missing items. She is having a social gathering at the time, and after they leave, Kharis shows up. First, the mummy knocks off the head of Eleanor's butler, then goes into the main party room and kills everyone there. (Not much was to be shown apart from an arm being thrown out a window, the rest would apparently be left to the audience's imagination.) As for Kharis's other killings, his next victim is a guy named Willie, who owns a pawn shop. Somehow he has acquired the chalice from the prologue and is drinking beer out of it! It later turns out that Richard Norton (not to be played by Lee this time) is the one fencing the items. Kharis kills him and chucks him into the sewer. (However, this killing is a little silly because the purpose of the killings is to retrieve the artifacts, and the dagger in Norton's possession is still in his office.)

Imhotep eventually shares his backstory with Helen, which is similar but not identical to the previous versions. (In this one, Set appeared to Imhotep in a vision when he was dying of thirst in the desert.) As Imhotep tells Helen his tale, they are attacked by a mugger whose bullet knicks Helen across the face. Imhotep kills him and then uses a special salve to heal Helen's wound. (In the Romero draft, he can reverse his energy-sucking abilities.)

After this, because Imhotep needs animal blood for his ritual, he goes to the zoo, wrestles a lion, then rips its throat out with his teeth! That night, Helen has a creepy dream where she sees all of Imhotep's recent victims. When Helen goes to see Imhotep, he tells her that he has something wrong with him that the doctors can't help. Two pages are missing from the script and what they contain is a mystery, but when we resume the action, Mike is looking for Helen and finds her in the company of Imhotep. Imhotep is then arrested by the police at Mike's insistence. In a weakened state, as he has not recently been rejuvenated, Imhotep is apprehended. In the back of the squad car he begins to convulse. One of the officers reaches back to touch him, and when he does Imhotep takes his energy and bursts from the squad car. Helen was also in the car, and so Imhotep pulls her out and takes her back to the museum. There he gives her a healing kiss to fix her injuries from the crash.

The script manages to surprise the reader towards the end during the ritual scene where Imhotep asks Helen to kill him and release him from immortality! Kharis shows up and Imhotep tells him that they are soon to be free. However, Kharis turns on his master and we get Kharis vs. Imhotep in a first! In Romero's draft, Mike and a ton of cops show up to fight Kharis using weapons from within the museum.[5] During the battle, Kharis loses one of his stone eyes, and is also burnt to a crisp, but like the Energizer Bunny, he keeps on going. His battle with the police results in a wing of the museum collapsing on him. But then, Kharis's hand pops out of the rubble (someone shouts out that "It's the mummy's hand!" in a nod to the film of the same name that introduced Kharis). Kharis bursts from the rubble and resumes the fight with Mike.

As this happens, Imhotep finally convinces Helen to stab him and save Mike (as stabbing him will kill Kharis by undoing the ritual from years ago). Helen does so, and the day is saved. Like in the original *Mummy*, Imhotep dissolves into nothing, and only his clothes remain.

Ultimately, Romero's vision for the project was also rejected as it was considered too dark and violent by producer James Jacks and Universal. Furthermore, Romero was also bound to a contract with MGM at the time, which hindered further development on the project. Universal wanted a "more accessible" (read: PG-13 rather than R) script for audiences and so commissioned a total rewrite. Mick Garris came on board next but left, and he was followed by Wes Craven, who eventually turned down Universal's offer. Then Stephen Sommers finally came along and pitched a version that Universal actually liked. In fact, they liked his Mummy meets Indiana Jones hybrid so much that they upped the budget from $15 million to $80 million!

Chapter Notes

[1] Supposedly, it was also briefly offered to Sam Raimi.

[2] In Garris's version, Kharis is guarding the door as this happens, and he is subdued and mummified (in the Romero draft he's not introduced in this way, he's simply dug up as a mummy).

[3] Between the two drafts, Eleanor is a character who differs greatly depending on the version. In Garris's draft, she is more sympathetic, as she is dying; hence the tomb being brought to America is one of her last wishes. She and Helen are very close in the Garris draft as well.

[4] We meet Mike for the first time in the Garris draft here as he was not part of the expedition. At the grand opening, he congratulates Helen on the find, but she's upset that the ritual items were lost in transit. In Garris's draft, his job is to find stolen antiquities hence his being at the grand opening.

[5] Gariss's draft did away with this scene, probably for budgetary reasons.

33.
REMAKE FROM THE BLACK LAGOON PART I
IVAN REITMAN'S CREATURE

Developed: 1994-1997
Script Date: March 27, 1996

Screenplay by: Timothy Harris and Herschel Weingrod **Proposed Director:** Ivan Rietman **Proposed Cast/Characters:** Laura [Olympic swimmer], Alex [marine biologist], Santos [policeman], Scott [teenager], Sean [Scott's father], Melanie [Scott's girlfriend], Greggor [Laura's trainer]

PLOT A vicious sea creature terrorizes a Florida island resort...

COMMENTARY After the failure to launch of the John Carpenter Creature, talks resumed in the mid-1990s with Ivan Reitman, producer of the *Ghostbusters* films, among other hits. Via his Northern Lights production company, he commissioned four script drafts from writers Timothy Harris and Herschel Weingrod, who had co-written *Twins* (1988) and *Kindergarten Cop* (1990) for Reitman in the past. However, what they came up with wasn't the least bit comical. Notably, their version, called *The Creature from the Black Lagoon* (some left off "The"), was the darkest version of the story yet.

While the first *Creature* remake helped inspire *Jaws 3-D*, this remake was itself very much inspired by the *Jaws* franchise[1] and the recent hit *Jurassic Park*. Case in point, the script is rife with underwater POV shots of the Creature stalking its victims in addition to many other *Jaws* tropes. And like the shark in *Jaws*, there is absolutely nothing sympathetic about the Creature in this version, which is a strange amalgamation of various underwater life. It has a tail, tentacles, can spew ink, and seems to be more of a reptilian/amphibian than a fish-man. In several instances the Creature is even compared to a velociraptor!

Furthermore, there are no scenes set at the Black Lagoon in the Amazon. In this version, the Black Lagoon is the name given to a lagoon on a Florida island resort! The script opens in the year 1990 when the resort is first being constructed on Pierpoint Island.

Dynamite is set off to clear some rocks from the lagoon in order to make a beach, and in the process the explosion jars loose a mysterious, football-sized egg from a nearby reef. The egg begins to crack open, giving the prospective audience a tiny glimpse of the Creature within. A large fish approaches the egg, and whatever is in it reaches out and grabs it. We would then jump ahead to five years later, after the Black Lagoon Reef Club has been completed. Several residents live there already, but the developers are still actively pursuing more. There are quite a few characters to keep track of right from the start, though not many of them are of any consequence. The first main character we meet is former Olympic swimmer Laura and her coach, Greggor. Currently there is friction between them because Laura wants to keep training while Greggor wants her to accept an offer to become a commentator at the Olympics. Of the other important players is the island's police officer, Santos, and Sean and Scott Hawkins, a father and son fishing duo. Fifteen-year-old Scott is enamored with a girl named Melanie Schultz, whose parents are contemplating buying a property on the island.

The story kicks off in earnest with another Creature teaser scene where a tour guide named Roger Thompkins is drunk and taking a leak into the ocean. He falls into the water and is ripped below the surface by the Creature, who we still don't see yet. A bit later, in a very *Jaws*-like scene, Susan Gillmore, the sales manager, tells tourists and prospective buyers that the reef acts as a natural barrier from ocean predators, making it "safer than your bath tub." Elsewhere, Laura and Greggor (who used to date, by the way) have just gotten into another argument when Greggor tries to get Laura to take performance-enhancing drugs. She gets mad and leaves to go for a swim in the Black Lagoon. As you can guess, the Creature looks up at her lustfully from the depths but, for whatever reason, doesn't attack her. (It should also be noted here that the way the Creature identifies Laura is by the white swimsuit that she wears.) In a scene not too long after, the Creature attacks a windsail in yet another *Jaws* nod![2] (The windsurfer gets away unscathed but certainly wonders just what made his board snap in half.) Meanwhile, Sean and Scott have gone fishing out in the ocean. Scott catches a large sail fish, but then the Creature gets it and tears it apart beneath the waves. Sean thinks it must have been a shark and wants to go out again tomorrow to catch it.

Eventually, Santos reports that Roger's severed leg has been found in the ocean, and they fear that a shark is on the loose, which ties into Sean's shark theory from earlier. (This is another *Jaws* trope, where a normal-sized shark is blamed for recent killings when a much more dangerous monster is responsible.) In a funny scene, Santos tries to entice a marine biologist named Alex from the mainland to come to the Reef Club to investigate the shark attack. Alex is more interested in his current studies until Santos mentions they are hosting the Sports Illustrated Swimsuit shoot that weekend. Jump cut to Alex

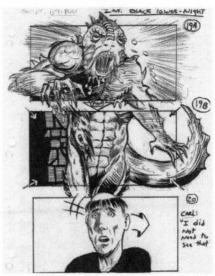

The Gillman's tail from this version managed to carry-over all the way into an unfilmed scene from 2004's *Van Helsing,* where the Creature was supposed to inhabit the moat of Dracula's castle. © 2004 Universal Pictures

there watching the models. (This is also a classic *Jaws* staple in that a big event must serve as the backdrop for the ensuing ocean monster massacre.) Alex eventually stops ogling the models and examines the leg which Santos was carrying around in an ice chest. He determines there are no bite marks, so it wasn't bitten off by a shark. Elsewhere, the Hawkins' fishing trip is in progress along with Melanie, who Scott invited. However, their definition of "fishing" is not what Melanie expects, as they lure sharks to the surface with bait and then shoot them with rifles. Santos comes by on his police cruiser with Alex, who investigates the dead sharks that the Hawkins have killed. He sees claw marks on their bodies similar to the severed leg. Now he knows a dangerous animal is afoot if it attacks even sharks. Meanwhile, Laura is out for a swim while the Creature watches from below again. (This time we would see his gills pulsating and his tail changing color to show that he's also a chameleon.) As the Creature stalks her, swimming nearer and nearer in a typical Jaws-type scene, the police cruiser pulls up. Santos and Alex insist that she come aboard at once due to the mystery animal in the water. Little do they know that same animal has grabbed ahold of the boat as it speeds away and leaves claw marks in the hull.

Later that night, the Schultz family announces they will buy the property after all, and the head sale rep notably doesn't inform them of the killer animal in their midst (similar to the mayor in *Jaws*). Elsewhere, the night is teeming with lovers. Alex and Laura continue their trajectory towards a romantic relationship while Greggor wanders off with one of the swimsuit models named Tanya (who he has loaned Laura's white swimsuit to). Lastly, Scott and Melanie strip to their underwear and set out in a sailboat. When it tips over, the Creature spies Melanie in her white underwear and mistakes it for Laura's white swimsuit, fueling his infatuation. He lets the teenagers be, though, when he notices Tanya in Laura's white bathing suit some distance away. The Creature attacks Tanya and Greggor both, dragging them underwater. He beheads Greggor, but a much worse fate awaits Tanya as it is implied that she is raped and killed by the Creature! (This is probably one of the reasons this script never got made.) The next morning on the beach, the camera crew wanders where Tanya is. Eventually she and Greggor's remains are found being picked apart by seagulls. The *Jaws* callbacks keep coming as Alex accompanies Laura to the morgue to identify Greggor's body. A detective named Garcia from the mainland has shown up now, too, thanks to the increasing body count. Due to the claw marks, Alex thinks the killer is a sea creature with seven digits—possibly some kind of early tetrapod that should have gone extinct millions of years ago. It is at this point that the residents are informed of the deaths by Garcia. However, because he thinks a human could be to blame, he forbids anyone from leaving the island because he wants to question everyone.

Alex brings in a researcher named Ian Poindexter to help, and Poindexter, in turn, brings along his high-tech research vessel. Onboard they reconstruct what they think the Creature could look like and they propose that it's a further evolution of the Acanthostega, a stem-tetrapod from the Devonian period. So, rather than a fish-man as in the original film, this Gillman is more of an amphibian along the lines of a salamander! On the research vessel, they get a ping on their radar and figure it's the creature swimming beneath them. When it disappears, they assume it has vanished into a cave. Onboard they just happen to have a specially trained seal named Molly used by the military to plant mines on Russian submarines. (Yes, you read that right.) Molly is outfitted with a camera and sent into the depths. She finds the Creature's cave which is littered with the skeletons of various undersea life plus some human beings. Meanwhile, Garcia has theorized that whoever killed Tanya was a stalker out to get Laura instead. And, as well all know, he's not wrong—he just doesn't know that the stalker is a monster. Garcia informs Laura of his theory, and as she leaves his office, the Creature watches her from the water. After Laura returns to her penthouse, it finally comes on land giving the prospective audience their first clear look at the monster. (It is at this point that the writers describe it as looking a bit like an aquatic velociraptor! As for color, rather than dark green, they describe the Creature as having the color of burnished metal. The face isn't dinosaurian, but more humanoid, with the script likening it to a Greco Roman coin of all things!).

The Creature walks across the golf course and kills the groundskeeper. However, the Creature spends too much time out of the water and passes out. Sean sees this, gets a harpoon net gun, shoots the comatose monster, and begins to drag it across the golf course. (Sean, upon seeing the Creature, rightly assumed that it was the killer. Due to the recent killings, Melanie and her parents are also leaving, which is difficult for Scott. As such, Sean thinks that if he captures the monster, maybe Melanie and her parents will stay.) As Sean hauls it across the golf course, the sprinklers come on, and the water revives the Creature. It then drags poor Sean to a nearby pool and kills him, and as he does so, shoots ink into the water like an octopus!

Things go from bad to worse when a storm approaches the island, leading Garcia to allow the evacuation of the remaining residents (some had already left on a ferry). Garcia transports Laura and some others in a van towards a bridge to the mainland, which the Creature destroys right before they are about to drive onto it. The van crashes into the water upside down. Of all the people swimming out, the Creature makes a beeline for Garcia and disembowels him. Alex comes along in a research submersible and attacks the Creature with torpedoes! This allows Laura to escape while the Creature attacks the sub, causing it to get stuck within the bridge's wreckage. Alex manages to pop the hatch and swim to the surface while Ian Poindexter distracts it with dynamite. Now the residents are all effectively stranded on the island, and Mrs. Schultz reminds everyone that it's Laura that the Creature wants, stirring up some animosity towards her.

As the storm also approaches, residents head to the upper floors of the resort in case it floods. The Creature breaks into the building by way of a connection between the spa and the lagoon (some sort of tunnel connected them due to the spa using water from the lagoon). It bursts through the wall of the men's room and kills two policemen. Next up, the Creature barges into the room of some newlyweds who manage to escape (the Creature then tears open their waterbed and moistens itself). On the top floor, the residents seem to consider just giving Laura to the Creature, but Alex, now Laura's romantic attachment, talks them all out of it. As the debate concludes, the Creature has learned how to push buttons and has traveled to the top floor in the elevator (they had barricaded the stairs but never assumed it might use the elevator). (This scene was probably meant to mimic the moment in *Jurassic Park* when the raptors learn to open doors.)

Santos and Alex see the monster and drive it away with a shotgun. They better barricade themselves inside, then a power outage occurs. It is around this time that Alex figures out the Creature wants to mate with Laura because she's the best swimmer. This is followed by a moment of suspense when they hear something in the bathtub, and it turns out to be Molly the seal. Meanwhile, the Creature is trying to get past a massive ventilation fan so that it can get into the air vents. He manages to disable it (though he does lose two fingers) and crawls through the vents. It bursts from a ceiling vent, and Alex and Santos shoot it again. Ian sneaks up to shoot the Creature with a harpoon gun, but it notices him and blinds him with ink. (The ink is also implied to be acidic, so this may have been inspired by the Dilophosaurus in *Jurassic Park*.) Knowing the Creature is sensitive to sound, Alex drives it off with the fire alarm.

Soon after this, Santos gets word that the storm is too intense for the rescue boat to get through at the moment. Feeling guilty since the Creature wants her, Laura takes the electric harpoon gun and sets off on her own to kill it. Laura and Alex set a trap in the parking garage, creating a circle of gasoline they plan to capture the Creature in. The monster breaks down the sea wall with its immense strength, flooding the garage and undoing the trap in the process. It snatches Laura and takes her to the Black Lagoon while Alex is incapacitated. In the meantime, the storm has dissipated enough that the Coast Guard can finally approach. In the lagoon, the Creature does a mating dance of sorts to try and impress Laura. She plays along with the game and manages to find a spare air tank in the wreckage blown in by the storm, along with a harpoon gun. She grabs the gun and shoots the Creature through the heart. Laura bursts to the surface to swim for Alex, who is on the beach waiting for her. The Creature surfaces behind her, but Santos shoots him again with his shotgun. The Creature drifts out to sea then sinks into the depths (which is pretty similar to the endings of the first two Creature movies). However, in the last shot, a seabird lands on the reef and pecks loose another egg for the hoped-for sequel.

It's unknown why Universal passed on the picture, but there's a good chance they didn't like the hard, R-Rated edge to the script. The main problem is mainly that this script takes the Creature's attraction to Kay in the original film too far. Yes, we all know what was implied in that first film, but nobody wants to see it. In that regard, this script seems more befitting of a hard, gross-out 1980s monster film rather than a mid-90s, post-*Jurassic Park* PG-13 monster movie. There's no way Universal would risk blowing a potential tentpole franchise on this script.

As for other problems, Rick Baker walked away from project because he felt they were overcomplicating the design. Case in point, at one point it's mentioned the Creature has tentacles! However, the writers didn't describe where these tentacles are on the body very well or how they worked. Furthermore, this Creature also had suckers on its palms like an octopus, too. Overall, this script was so un-Creature-like that they could have simply shot it as an all-original film.

A bit later, Universal either offered this script or the Creature-remake concept itself to Peter Jackson, who turned it down in favor of *King Kong*... which was itself postponed until the mid-2000s. And there the Creature remake would sit until after the success of the Stephen Sommers *Mummy* in 1999, but that's a story for another time...

Chapter Notes

---

1 Actually, I would say it reminded me of *Piranha II* more than anything else!

2 Or, more accurately in this case, *Jaws 2* and *The Last Shark*.

34.
SHERLOCK HOLMES AND THE VENGEANCE OF DRACULA

Script Date: October 5, 2000
Developed: unknown-1999

Screenplay by: Michael B. Valle **Proposed Director:** Christopher Columbus **Proposed Cast/Characters:** Sherlock Holmes [detective], Professor Moriarity [Holmes's nemesis], Dracula [vampire], Constance [Holmes's love interest], Watson [Holmes's partner], Van Helsing [vampire hunter], Lewellyn [Moriarity's henchman], the Mangler [Moriarity's henchman], Wojcek [Dracula's henchman], Mollie [vampire], Lestrade [Scotland Yard investigator], Mrs. Hudson [Holmes's housekeeper], Arthur Holmwood [Dracula's first victim], Dr. Seward [Dracula's second victim]

PLOT Count Dracula returns to London to take revenge on characters from the Bram Stoker novel, though his efforts are foiled by Sherlock Holmes...

COMMENTARY Sherlock Holmes encountering Dracula will be off-putting for some and a dream come true for others. But, since you're reading this book, the latter is probably true in your case. And nor will the story disappoint, as it is truly one of the best unproduced screenplays in this book. No, it's quite possibly the best unproduced screenplay in this book. And just how did this project come to be? The origins of this tantalizing title are unfortunately something of a mystery. However, this may be because it was a spec script by first-time screenplay writer Michael B. Valle. Perhaps that's also why it's so good. Spec scripts come from passion and imagination rather than soulless studio politics and meddling.

When Valle set down to write it, there was no interest in either Sherlock Holmes on the big screen or Classic Monsters (*The Mummy* had yet to be released). And yet, in spite of that, it sold to Columbia Pictures in the Fall of 1999 (and yes, *The Mummy's*

I HAVE HEARD SOME SOURCES CLAIM THIS PROJECT DATES BACK TO THE LATE 1970S, BUT I ASSUME THEY MIGHT BE CONFUSING IT WITH THE UNRELATED NOVEL (WHICH I ATTACHED AS THE IMAGE) AND THE HAMMER HOAX CALLED DRACULA WALKS THE NIGHT WHICH WAS ALLEGEDLY PITCHED IN 1974. ON THE LOST FILMS FANZINE FACEBOOK PAGE, WILLIAM WILSON MENTIONED THAT HE SAW A LISTING FOR THE PROJECT IN VARIETY IN 1993 WITH RICHARD FRANKLIN ATTACHED AS DIRECTOR.

success that summer may have had something to do with it). Columbia paid Valle $700,000 for his script, with another $300,000 to come if it was produced. That's $1 million dollars for a first-time screenwriter, if that gives you any indication of just how good the script was. It was nearly perfect for the late 90s/early 2000s as well, and had it been produced might've even outshined The Mummy. Like that film, it's high on laughs, scares, and excitement.

The script begins on a foggy night on the London docks in 1891. A ship has just docked at the pier, where several typical cockney-speaking dock workers unload a precious cargo. Eager to get a look at what's so valuable, they are disgusted when they find only a coffin, which one of the men then spits on and kicks. A few moments later, a bat swoops from out of the night sky and tears into his neck. Soon the man is beset by so many bats that they begin to lift his writhing body off the pier. The other men run away in fear just as the lid of the coffin begins to open. As they flee down a side street, an unseen snarling beast with glowing, red eyes chases them. Eventually, the beast catches one of the men and reveals itself to be a wolf. A moment later, when the man's companion looks behind him, he sees not a wolf, but a caped man with red eyes. He screams and we cut to the London Museum.

Inside we are introduced to Sherlock Holmes, on what is for him a typical case concerning the stolen Ling Tao Tapestry, which is being ransomed for one thousand pounds. Also there is Smythe, a museum official, plus Holmes's competition, Inspector Lestrade from Scotland Yard, and Watson, of course. The sequence is a bit like the opening teaser segment of a James Bond film as it really has nothing to do with the overall plot and provides Holmes with a quick mystery to solve. To everyone's shock, it doesn't take Holmes long to deduct that the tapestry has been hidden within the museum. Upon learning that painters had been there the weekend it disappeared, and upon seeing fresh paint on the pant leg of the very museum official that called him, Holmes deducts that the official and the painters conspired together. The painters brought in a fake wall to hide the painting, which Holmes chops through with a sword, revealing the missing Ling Tao Tapestry behind it. The official merely invited Holmes and the Scotland Yard inspector to avoid suspicion. Once the ransom had been paid, he would have taken his cut and the tapestry would be revealed to still be in the museum via a confidential source. Case closed.

Well, case closed until Smythe makes a run for it. Whereas the first half of this sequence had been a typical Holmes brain twister, the second half is an action piece. Holmes, Watson, and Lestrade each go off in separate directions to trail the assailant, who slipped away before they knew exactly where he went. Holmes traces Smythe to the roof where he's holding a maid at gunpoint. (The maid had gone onto the roof to eat a snack.) In their palavering, Holmes deducts that his arch nemesis, Professor Moriarity, was behind the scheme. (So, in that sense, this sequence is related to the plot, but only tangentially.) And though Smythe doesn't identify Moriarity by name, his description of him as an "eloquent man with a silver-topped cane. A huge black mastiff always at his side"[1] is all that it takes for Holmes to figure out that Moriarity was the mastermind.

Ingenious, as always, just as Smythe is about to shoot Holmes, he tosses a handful of breadcrumbs—from the maid's snack—at him. And what good is that, you might ask? The breadcrumbs suddenly attract a flock of pigeons that descend on Smythe. In the chaos, Holmes tackles him, allowing the maid to escape. As the two men wrestle about, they eventually tumble from the roof. Smythe falls to his death, but Holmes uses what is apparently a special kind of scarf he's wearing to more or less lasso a marble ornament. Holmes swings from the marble to let himself drop safely onto a ledge. At the bottom of the museum, Watson and Lestrade are examining the dead body when Holmes walks down the front steps calm and composed. Holmes fills his compatriots in on the fact that Moriarity was the mastermind behind the plot when the maid throws her arms around him in gratitude. An uncomfortable Holmes shucks her off and walks into the night.

Cut to Moriarity's lair at the ruins of the Featherstone Library of Mathematics and Science. Actually, much like Lex Luthor's luxurious lair in *Superman: The Movie* (1978), Moriarity's digs are located under the ruins. As he stands before a large blackboard, in true supervillain fashion, he rants:

> My daring ploy to kidnap the Duke of Windsor—nullified! My ingenious subterfuge to purloin the Crown Jewels—neutralized! And now my brilliant ruse against the British Museum—negated![2]

Listening to his rant are Moriarity's black mastiff, Samson, and "Mangler" McMann—basically this script's equivalent of a James Bond henchman. (His defining trait is his gigantic, almost ape-like hands, hence the name "Mangler".) Another member of Moriarity's villainous menagerie soon enters as well. This one brings to mind the Riddler, as he's dressed in an all-green suit and has tiny green emeralds embedded in his teeth! His name is Lewellyn, and it was he who orchestrated the painting of the museum.[3] Lastly, there is also Moriarity's turban-clad bodyguard and chauffeur, Sahid.

Sahid bids Moriarity into an adjoining room. There, strapped to a chair, is one of the dock workers (in fact, one of Moriarity's lesser thugs) from the opening scene. The man, Dawson, is the lone survivor of Dracula's attack (though he knows not the name of Dracula). Moriarity had hired Dawson to intercept what he thought was a highly valuable art shipment for his collection, not knowing it was actually the casket of Dracula. At first, Moriarity thinks Dawson is lying to him with his tales of a haunted coffin. To better judge the veracity of his tales, he sets his pet cobra loose on Dawson, which coils around his body. In his terror, Dawson doesn't change his story about the strange happenings at the dock. He passes out, and Moriarity has Mangler grab the cobra before it can strike the man dead. Moriarity orders his goons to get their various enforcers and pickpockets to get to the bottom of this mystery. In an effective cut, we go from Moriarity feeding his dog some cuts of prime beef to a mutt chowing down on garbage in an alleyway near Hyde Park. Through it strides an ominous cloaked man. The dog growls at him, only to have the man growl back.

Dracula peers into the window of a cozy little home in the area. Within it we are introduced to Agnes Bracknell and her daughter

Constance, who is working away at fixing a velocipede while her mother chides her for wearing trousers like a man. We learn why they are of significance when Arthur Holmwood (AKA Lord Godalming) walks into the room and Valle informs us that the two women are his aunt and cousin. The ensuing conversation focuses mostly on Constance, establishing her as the female lead. Similar to Holmes, she is a rare specimen who Arthur feels most men are too intimidated to court.

Arthur goes to his room, planning to retire, when he notices a strange chill in the air despite it being the month of May. It's so cold his window has frosted over. And, written in the cold glass pane is a single word: DIE. Similar to the old Universal films like *Son of Dracula*, a green mist seeps under the doorway and Dracula slowly materializes out of it:

COUNT DRACULA OF TRANSYLVANIA is a handsome man of indeterminate age, with chiseled European features and commanding eyes that flash with hellfire. Soulless, pitiless orbs.

DRACULA
I am pleased to see you in good health, Lord Godalming. Especially since I've journeyed across half of Europe to kill you...[4]

After this, poor Holmwood, one of the heroes of the original novel, succumbs to Dracula's advance and is killed. However, in true Universal fashion, we don't actually see his death, and dissolve to Holmes playing the violin. It is now morning, and as Holmes plays, Watson reads him the mail, noting an invitation to honor the engagement of Countess d'Mornay to the Duke of Rutherford. Holmes isn't interested though, and chides the event as "An insufferable evening fawned upon by mindless, shallow women fluttering about in all their ostentatious fashions."[5] This, of course, is to remind us of Holmes's lack of a romantic life. To further hit home his disdain of romantic relations, Holmes goes on to humorously list all the crimes of passion they've investigated in the last month alone.

Mrs. Hudson steps in to announce a visitor, which turns out to be Constance. She immediately informs Holmes that she enjoys reading of his adventures each month in *The Strand* and that she is a great admirer of his. "Of course you are," Holmes snidely replies and then goes on in his usual way of telling her everything about herself. In this case, he points out that he can see that she didn't ride her velocipede, as usual, this morning. Constance impresses him by replying in kind, "You undoubtedly observed the cherry blossom petals on my shawl which fell from the trees in bloom surrounding Hyde Park." She goes on to list a multitude of minutia that only Holmes would notice, which shocks him for a change. Finally, he has met a woman after his own heart, or mind, in this case.

Constance's composure is made all the more impressive when she reveals to Holmes the tragic purpose of her visit: the death of Arthur Holmwood, found hanging from the rafters. Though a suicide note accompanied the body, Constance is certain that it was a murder. Holmes initially dismisses her, but upon her insistence, agrees to take on the case. In the carriage ride to Hyde Park, Constance divulges some exposition relative to the events of *Dracula*, mainly that Lucy Westerna, Arthur's fiancé, died last year of a "rare blood disease." From this comment we know that Constance either doesn't know the truth or is hiding it from Holmes. (As the script progresses, we find out that it is a case of the former.)

In the house, Holmes finds Arthur still hanging from the rafters and it doesn't take him long to suspect foul play, just as Constance insisted. He takes special note of a dagger with runes on the handle that pinned the suicide note to the desk. Holmes knows the dagger must have been of significance, though we don't know how so yet. Holmes's next disturbing clue is when he sees handprints outside of the window. The oddest thing about them is that they appear as though someone crawled headfirst and downwards out the window! (You'll naturally now recall the famous scene from *Dracula* where the Count crawls down the castle wall.) Next, it is Watson who notices that Holmwood has been entirely drained of blood. (Rather careless of Dracula to do so when he went to so much trouble to make the death look like a suicide.)

Before departing, Holmes asks Constance if Holmwood had traveled abroad recently for any reason. This gives the script another good excuse to recap the events of *Dracula*, with Constance revealing that Arthur went to the Carpathian Mountains about a year ago on business he was "loathe to discuss." Upon Holmes's goodbye to Constance, we would cut to a "forlorn graveyard situated high on a bluff overlooking the vast London skyline."[6] This, of course, is Dracula's London lair. He also has a Renfield-like crony named Wojcek who lets Dracula feed upon him! Dracula spits out his blood in disgust upon finding that it is laced with opium. The Count is then given a good line when he berates his lackey's drug problem, stating, "You pathetic anarchists! You terrorize others to forge a world free from control, yet you lack control over yourselves."[7]

Actually, all of Dracula's dialogue is quite well done, as he goes on to lament how he's currently relegated to such poor quarters when he used to live a life of luxury. Wojcek informs the Count that the lots he wanted have been purchased and then goes on to call Dracula the Ubermach that Nietzsche spoke of. Dracula tells him to save his "boot-licking" and asks him if he's located Dr. Seward. Wojcek replies that he has, and that also Seward is still unaware of Dracula's arrival. Satisfied, Dracula looks over London in the distance and proclaims, "An unsuspecting city at my disposal—whispering with dark promise..."[8] He then dives off the cliff and transforms into a giant vampire bat on his way down. Dracula glides over various rooftops in this ghastly form before we fade to Holmes examining the dagger, which also contains images of bats. With Watson, he has deduced that the dagger—which is of Transylvanian origin—must have been related to Holmwoods' trip to the Carpathians, which Holmes also correctly thinks was linked to the death of Lucy Westerna. This had led Holmes to Lucy's obituary, which in turn led to mention of Dr. Seward. Thinking the good doctor might better inform their investigation, Holmes and Watson track him down at the Royal Academy of Science, where he is giving a lecture.

Actually, it's more than just a lecture. Seward is conducting a live autopsy on the corpse of a criminally insane man. For a moment, Seward thinks he recognizes Dracula in the audience, but he blinks, and the Count is gone. Seward chalks it up to his being tired and continues on with the demonstration. But, when he looks up a second time, Dracula is sitting closer, and hisses at him. (This might've been a tad much for a 90s version of the character, though it wouldn't have been out of place in the 1970s.) Things get worse when the cadaver suddenly comes to life and grabs Seward's arm, telling him that, "A rendezvous with Death is nigh."[9] A panicked Seward runs from the room, proclaiming that he must find shelter until dawn. (However, the whole thing was a hallucination on Seward's part, leaving the audience to think Seward has gone mad.)

Humorously, outside, Holmes tells Watson how he wanted to come to Seward's lecture on the insane anyway when Seward bursts out the front doors like a madman himself. He ignores

Holmes's pleas to stop, and quickly boards a taxi carriage. It takes off swiftly and so Holmes and Watson board another taxi to pursue him. As Seward's taxi races through a foggy street, Dracula steps from the mist and grabs the carriage's railing with superhuman strength. It comes to a violent halt. Impressively, Dracula strides between the terrified horses and then bashes their skulls together, killing them instantly. He rips the carriage door off by the hinges and greets Dr. Seward. His dialogue is something I think a great many of us would have enjoyed hearing Christopher Lee speak if he was still young enough for the part:

DRACULA
Good evening, Doctor Seward.

SEWARD
I thought—you were dead —

DRACULA
But I am.

Dracula reaches a clawed hand towards Seward. But the good doctor has been taking notes from Van Helsing and produces a crucifix. Dracula recoils in horror, but it's not over yet. The vampire picks up the carriage with Seward still in it and dashes it to the ground. Seward stumbles out of the carriage in a daze. At first, he doesn't see the Count, but then Dracula descends from above him out of the mist, his cape "unfurled behind him like silken bat wings."[10]
"You will not escape my vengeance so easily," he tells Seward and then we cut to Holmes and Watson arriving on the scene. Upon finding the crushed carriage, the driver is still alive and tells Holmes that the "fiend" has absconded with Seward. Holmes and Watson track Dracula to an alleyway where he's just finished feeding on Seward. Holmes tries to tackle Dracula, unaware of his supernatural strength and is easily dismissed by the Count. Undeterred, Holmes informs the man that he's under arrest for the murder of Arthur Holmwood/Lord Godalming. Dracula smiles and says to Holmes, "Well done. I took great pains to disguise my hand in Godalming's death. Was I that careless?"
There is some more banter before Dracula dematerializes in the fog and then reappears closer to Holmes and Watson, who unloads a revolver into him to no effect. It is at this moment that the

293

detective duo realizes they are facing a supernatural foe. Holmes asks Dracula who he is, and he responds, "I am your master." In a very Hammer-Dracula move, he then begins throwing cobblestones at the two men. Upon the arrival of some police bobbies on the scene, Dracula jumps onto a rooftop and disappears. Holmes and Watson regroup with Seward, still alive but in the process of dying. His last words to Holmes are to warn the doctor. (We, of course, know this to be Van Helsing, though Holmes and Watson don't know who he's talking about.)

The next scene takes place in Moriarity's lair, where he's playing the piano in a private recital for famous singer Mollie Mallone. After some comedic banter between Mollie and the Mangler, Lewellyn walks in to inform the professor that one of his informants has important news. We would dissolve to none other than Seward's coach driver telling Moriarity about the superhuman man he witnessed earlier that night. Moriarity is less concerned with the man's supernatural abilities and is more enamored with the fact that the man outwitted Holmes. As such, Moriarity wants this man as an ally. From there, we cut to Holmes and Watson being questioned in the office of Lestrade, who finds it hard to believe everything he's just heard. However, a bit later, Lestrade accompanies Holmes and Watson, along with Constance, to the autopsy of Seward. There they all observe the marks on the neck, which the coroner points out were also present on the body of Holmwood.

Later, the quartet of Holmes, Watson, Lestrade, and Constance do a deeper examination of Seward's crucifix in classic Holmes fashion—though Holmes is none too pleased that Constance is aiding in the investigation. Anyhow, the main takeaway for the group is that Seward carried the cross on his person everywhere, a curious habit to say the least. Watson is the first to finally use the 'V' word, but Holmes quickly dismisses him, coming up with a number of reasons why the blood could have been drained. This is rather silly on Holmes's part considering everything that he saw Dracula do earlier. He thinks someone wants them to think it's the work of a vampire. The scene concludes out on the street, where Holmes is bidding Constance goodbye. She wishes to help find the man who gifted Seward with the cross (an inscription showed that it was a gift). Holmes declines her offer, though, and the situation is made more awkward when a street photographer offers to take the "couple's" photo. Constance is amused at Holmes's embarrassment and bids him goodbye.

Whereas Holmes doesn't believe the vampire story, Moriarity does. Thanks to one of his henchmen following Wojcek back to Dracula's lair, the Count awakens from his slumber to find Moriarity lording over him. Mangler holds a wooden stake over Dracula's heart as the professor explains the purpose of his visit. Moriarity wishes to become one of the undead. When Dracula chides him for daring to command him, Moriarity tries to get Dracula to empathize with him as one with superior intellect! Moriarity says:

Men like us—possessed of superior intellect and ambition—are entitled, are destined, to rule the weak around us. Bestow upon me your power! Your immortality! My genius must not be bound by mortal constraints![11]

Dracula isn't having it, though. He causes a powerful wind to blow out all the candles in the room and swiftly disappears. Moriarity whirls around to find the Count standing behind him. Lewellyn shoots an arrow from a crossbow at Dracula, which he catches in mid-air. Amused, Dracula looks at Moriarity and says, "You are audacious. I almost regret having to kill you..."[12] Moriarity responds that he could prove to be a useful ally to the Count with all his connections. When Dracula continues to advance, Moriarity pulls a hidden sword from his cane and presses it into Dracula's chest. However, Dracula lets the sword pierce his undead flesh and walks nearer and nearer as he impales himself. All the while, Moriarity keeps listing all the benefits of this prospective partnership. Finally, he calls for his mastiff to attack Dracula. The vampire swiftly hypnotizes the vicious animal, which comes up to the Count and licks his hand. Finally, Dracula tells him, "Despite your arrogance, I admit your offer intrigues me." The Count pulls the sword from his chest, drops the blade at Moriarity's feet, and tells him that he has a "final act of retribution to attend to" before vanishing.

Meanwhile, Holmes has figured out that the cross belonged to Abraham Van Helsing. As with Seward earlier, this puts Holmes and Dracula on a collision course as the Count hurtles towards his next victim. We would cut to Van Helsing, who is described in this iteration as heavy-set and with a goatee. He is currently enjoying himself in a glass garden conservatory when all of a sudden it is besieged by a horde of rats. There are so many that the glass collapses from the weight of them, and Van Helsing flees to the safety of his adjoining study. Inside, Dracula is already waiting for him. Like a Bond villain, he offers a fake apology for demolishing his "quaint conservatory" in his effort to make a grand entrance. Van Helsing asks how this could be, and we finally learn how Dracula came back. Rather than the old Hammer method where an elaborate ceremony was used to resurrect the Count, here Dracula informs Van Helsing that he forgot to cut off his head. As it turns out, in this mythology, a stake to the heart isn't enough to kill the Count; it just slows him down. (However, Dracula does sow the seeds of his own destruction by telling Van Helsing that his head must be cut off to remain dead.)

Just as Dracula pounces on Van Helsing, Holmes and Watson come to the rescue, ordering "the fiend" to unhand the good doctor. Dracula calls Holmes a "tenacious hound" and then shoots a jet of fire from the fireplace at him. Holmes and Watson counter by flipping over a table and using it as a shield to charge the demon vampire. He brushes it aside, and Watson has another go at shooting Dracula. This time he aims for the head and takes out one of Dracula's eyes. The men watch in shock as the eye reforms itself and Dracula cackles. Van Helsing produces a handy cross and rebukes the demonic Dracula in the name of Jesus Christ, and so he has no option but to flee. Actually, he doesn't just flee; he explodes into a horde of bats and flies away.

On their way to a hospital in a carriage, Van Helsing brings Holmes and Watson up to speed on Dracula, identifying him as Vlad the Impaler turned vampire. Van Helsing delivers the necessary exposition all the way to the hospital and implores the duo to find Dracula's resting place just as he passes out on a gurney. Next, we check back in with Moriarity, who returns to his lair only to find that Dracula has now taken it over. Sahid has been vampirized, and Mollie is giving the Count a private dance as he sits at Moriarity's desk. Charmingly, he tells Moriarity that he admires his taste in finery. There is some banter between the two, again evocative of a Bond villain on Dracula's end, before the Count asks, "Tell me more about this man named Holmes." Moriarity goes on a complete rant about Holmes, which is interrupted by Mollie, who tells him that he's getting "too riled up" in front of their guest. Moriarty at this point notices that Mollie casually has his pet cobra draped across her shoulders as though it's harmless. His suspicion that she is a vampire is confirmed when she slips a forked tongue from her mouth like a snake. Moriarity is incensed to say the least. Dracula has turned his servants into vampires rather than he himself as requested! He confronts the Count about this afront, and Dracula tells him that he will grant his wish for immortality if he kills Sherlock Holmes. Dracula then departs with Mollie, leaving Moriarity to stew in his rage.

Back at Baker Street, Holmes and Watson are arguing about Dracula's existence. Holmes still thinks some form of trickery is involved, though Watson is rightly convinced that what they saw was a real vampire. Watson leaves in a huff, rightly irritated that Holmes refuses to see the truth. However, after Watson departs, Holmes does pluck a book off the shelf dealing with the undead. The next morning, over breakfast, Watson apologizes for his outburst, and Holmes apologizes for not being more open-minded. It's unclear if Holmes has come to believe they are dealing with a real vampire or just a man who believes himself to be one, but Holmes suggests they check shipping records for recent arrivals of boxes of earth from Transylvania. If they can find the boxes, they can find the vampire's lair.

The next scene serves as a montage of sorts where Holmes and Watson unsuccessfully try to entice dock workers into giving them recent shipping records. Holmes is pretending to be a preacher looking for a lost shipment of Bibles from Transylvania. He fails until Constance walks in unexpectedly and pretends to be the Reverend Holmes's goddaughter! Constance is able to get the needed records through her powers of persuasion. Outside, Holmes reminds Constance that she is his client, not his assistant. This leads into a conversation wherein Constance asks Holmes why he dislikes women so. Holmes explains that he finds women distracting, to which she responds that she'll take that as a compliment. Holmes really is distracted by Constance as he fails to notice that a random peddler has just thrown a bottle at the couple. Constance knocks Holmes over and saves them both as the bottle, containing some volatile chemical, explodes. There is the obligatory moment of the duo staring into each other's eyes on the ground before coming to their senses. Looking around the scene, the peddler is gone, and Holmes deducts the bottle was nitroglycerin. He also points out to Constance that this proves his point about being distracted and insists she go home. Rather than being angry, Constance seems flattered as she picks up on Holmes's growing attraction to her.

The next scene has Holmes and Watson arriving at an abandoned mansion, Dracula's new lair, armed with stakes and hammers. However, they don't find the Count, only Mollie sleeping in a coffin. Watson does a brief medical examination, announcing that the woman in the coffin is dead—until she opens her eyes.

Before Watson can stake her, she crushes the stake in her hands and jumps from the coffin. She pounces on Holmes and knocks him into the wall as Watson utters a line most Sherlock fans surely never expected to hear: "Holmes – your holy water!"

Holmes splashes Mollie with the fluid, which ignites her hair into flames. Holmes next rips out the planks boarding up the windows so that a beam of sunlight separates him from the vengeful vampire. With Holmes out of reach, Mollie pounces on Watson, knocking him into the wine cellar. As Mollie hunts Watson through broken glass in the cellar, Holmes does something truly ingenious. Through a very complicated relay system of refractive surfaces, he uses a mirror to bounce the sunlight off of one object into the next until the sun beam shines into the wine cellar. The light then hits the numerous glass shards, which create a light trap of sorts cutting Mollie to pieces. (This is truly worthy of a Sherlock Holmes-themed vampire movie!)

Back at Moriarity's lair, the professor watches as his once-trusted dog guards Dracula's casket as he sleeps. Upon waking for the evening, Moriarity gifts Dracula with a new, indestructible coffin that locks from within, guaranteeing the Count's safety as he sleeps. Dracula is impressed with the gift, but his mood sours when Moriarity's thug that tried and failed to kill Holmes earlier reports on his failure. Dracula then takes the spicket from a keg of alcohol and stabs the man in the heart with it. Dracula then uses the spigot to pour himself a nice glass of blood from the man's corpse! (An inventive scene to say the least!) Moriarity and the Count banter intelligently for a bit before the professor again asks Dracula to grant him immortality. The vampire reminds him he will only do so upon Holmes and Van Helsing's deaths. And that's when an idea hits Moriarity...

Meanwhile, Holmes and Watson are visiting Van Helsing in a hospital located on consecrated ground, meaning Van Helsing is in no danger of Dracula so long as he rests there. And though Dracula can't enter, he does spy on them from the window. Beneath him, he notices Constance walking up to the hospital, and so he materializes in front of her. (Remember, Constance has never seen Dracula, nor does she know his name.) Dracula turns on the charm right away, telling her, "It has been countless decades since I have savored such loveliness..."[13]

Constance doesn't dislike Dracula but isn't so charmed by him that she wants to waste any time talking to him and tells him she must be getting inside. The Count informs her that her friend Sherlock Holmes has just left—a lie—and that he would be delighted to escort her for the evening. At first, Constance seems to be ready to turn down the offer, but a look into the vampire's hypnotic eyes changes her mind. Cut to Constance and the Count walking down a business street, window shopping as odd as that sounds. Constance speaks of gender equality issues, and unlike Holmes, Dracula validates Constance's beliefs, thus endearing himself to her rather quickly. And with that, Constance has become the typical female love-interest/victim common to nearly every iteration of the Dracula tale. By the time Dracula has escorted her back to her home at Godalming Manor, he is making plans to one day show her his castle in Transylvania. (Of course, the way I have so simply summarized it sounds corny, but it's handled well enough in the script.) When Dracula leans in to kiss Constance, he gives her the kiss of the vampire instead. And like so many Hammer vixens, Constance leans into and enjoys it. Bidding the Count goodnight, she tells him that she awaits dusk tomorrow with eagerness.

As Dracula walks to the curb, Moriarity's coach pulls up. Moriarty invites Dracula to see what's inside, which turns out to be an unconscious Watson. (Moriarity's men had kidnapped Watson from the hospital during Dracula and Constance's outing.) "A delicious irony—Sherlock Holmes doomed by his most trusted friend!" Dracula proclaims.[14] The scene ends with the Count baring his fangs and putting the bite on Watson. In the next scene, Watson walks into Van Helsing's room at the hospital and tries to shoot an unsuspecting Holmes, who notices that something is off about his friend at the last moment. What happens next is rather interesting, as it touches upon an unsaid truth about Holmes and Watson's relationship. When Holmes deducts that Dracula has gotten his clutches into his friend, Watson answers that Dracula has shown him the truth:

> For years I have lived in your shadow. Always eclipsed by your conceited displays of deductive trickery. I never should have written those blasted stories. Now the whole world adores you—and I'm little more than your glorified secretary.[15]

"Watson, you must fight Dracula's malignant hold over you!" Holmes implores, and Watson answers, "Your condescending arrogance. Your colossal ego. You desire my company only to flatter you as some mindless sycophant!"[16]

Watson shoots again and Holmes dodges. The two men begin to wrestle, but Holmes becomes distracted when he sees the fang marks on Watson's neck. Watson gets the upper hand and knocks Holmes's head into the foot of Van Helsing's bedpost. Just before he loses consciousness, Holmes tells his old friend, "Watson, don't let Dracula control you!"[17] For a moment, Watson snaps out of his trance, but only for an instant. Soon Dracula's will tugs at his soul, but Watson fights it, moving his aim from Holmes to put the gun to his own temple. Just when we think the script is going to get a little too dark, Van Helsing comes in for the save, knocking Watson over the head with his bedpan. He then tells Holmes, "Your friend is under Dracula's power. There is but one chance left to save him!"[18]

In the next scene, Holmes and Van Helsing oust a doctor from an empty room so as to perform a blood transfusion on Watson. There's some great humor as the doctor calls the police. Later he can be seen telling Lestrade that, "They're both crazed – babbling about vampires! One actually insisted he was Sherlock Holmes and threatened me at gunpoint!"[19] Inside the operating room, Van Helsing explains to Holmes that now that Dracula has fed on Watson's blood, it makes him susceptible to his spell. To counter this, Van Helsing has infused Holmes's own blood transfusion with some holy water, which will hopefully dilute Dracula's hold. Things go from bad to worse when Lestrade enters the room to inform Holmes he is under arrest. It's not for pointing the gun at the doctor, though; it's for the murder of Dr. Seward! Ingeniously, Dracula and Moriarity planted evidence in Holmes's office (offscreen, by the way) to make it appear as though Holmes wanted to kill Seward so that he could publish his groundbreaking discoveries for himself! As Holmes is being escorted out of the hospital by police, he grabs a man's crutch and uses it to batter the bobbie beside him. He then knocks Lestrade in the stomach with it and makes a run for it. They eventually corner Holmes in a lab of some sort, but Holmes picks up two beakers of chemicals and dashes them onto the floor. Upon breaking and mixing together, the room fills with smoke and Holmes escapes out a window.

Out on the streets, Dracula materializes before Holmes and chides him about losing everything he holds dear. He then makes it clear that he won't kill Holmes because he wants to see him debased into becoming his "pathetic, unthinking slave." However, when Dracula bores his hypnotic eyes into Holmes, he's shocked to have finally met a mental match. He cannot hypnotize Holmes, and he knows it. He throws the detective to the ground and tells him that he won't be able to resist his powers once he drinks his blood. But Holmes, ever crafty, crawls his way to a building just across the street. Dracula is too busy chiding Holmes to notice what the building is, as he tells Holmes he knows his worst fear is to become "a mindless zombie" and that it "is truly a fate worse than death for you..."[20]

However, when Dracula takes another step closer, his body begins to sizzle. Holmes has crawled his way to hallowed ground, and a cross atop a church is reflecting the moonlight onto Dracula. Holmes commands the Count to be gone from this sanctified ground, and Dracula warns him, "I shall return, Sherlock Holmes— for your soul!"[21]

Dracula returns to Moriarity's lair in the form of a huge, enraged wolf. He quickly resumes his human form and berates Moriarity for failing to kill Holmes again. Moriarity argues that he's at least made Holmes a fugitive and that should earn him the right to be immortal. Dracula becomes even angrier and shatters Moriarity's chalkboard. The situation is diffused when Lewellyn and Mangler bring in a fresh victim for the Count to feed upon. Moriarity is disgusted by this, as he can see that all of his men now serve the Count.

At Godalming Manor, Holmes stumbles through the front door, exhausted (he did give a hefty amount of blood to save Watson). Constance helps him inside before he collapses. He awakens four hours later and finds something to be off about Constance. Her mother is nowhere to be found (she says she returned back home), and she has camera equipment laying all about the place. Holmes asks her about it, and she says it's a gift from her new friend the Count, who has a "special interest in daytime photography".[22] Upon hearing "the Count", Holmes grabs Constance roughly and checks her neck. As he feared, he finds the bite marks. "Dracula has enslaved you!" he proclaims.

She answers, "On the contrary. Dracula has set me free!"

Constance then goes on to berate Holmes for his repressed lifestyle, one she is now free of as she seduces him by the fire. Fearing the kiss of the vampire, Holmes at first wards off her advances. But he gives in to temptation and gives her a passionate kiss—one she does not reciprocate with a vampire bite, I might add. Holmes finally admits his feelings for Constance and is then bashed over the head from behind by Wojcek. Next comes the classic James Bond-type scene where the hero is left to his impending doom after the bad guy leaves him alone. In this case,

Holmes awakens strapped to a chair. Constance bids him goodbye with a kiss and Wojcek tells Holmes not to worry, that he promised Constance he wouldn't kill him. Keeping his promise, he dumps Moriarity's pet cobra onto the floor near Holmes, the implication being, of course, that the cobra will kill him in Wojcek's place.

In elaborate Holmes fashion, the detective knocks a coat rack over into the shelving containing the chemicals necessary to develop Constance's wet-plates for her photography. The flammable chemicals spill across the floor in the path of the slithering snake. Holmes then rocks his chair over and nudges himself to his overcoat, which had been tossed to the ground. He grabs his trusty magnifying glass in his teeth and uses it to project a sunbeam onto the chemicals, just in time to ignite them as the cobra slithers through them. With the snake now toast, Holmes only has to worry about unbinding himself (which he does with a shattered glass chard).

Back at Moriarity's lair, the professor makes one last attempt to gain immortality. He drugs his beloved mastiff so as to gain access to Dracula's coffin. His bit about it being impregnable was a lie, as Moriarity installed a hidden latch, and he opens it. Moriarity then takes out a syringe and draws Dracula's blood, which awakens the Count. Moriarity tells him it's no use attacking him right then because his powers are null in the daylight hours. He explains to Dracula that he will become a vampire by injecting himself with the Count's blood. However, Sahid tries to stop Moriarity, and in their struggle, it's he who accidentally gets injected. Sahid very violently transforms into a vampire.

When Llewellyn and the Mangler walk in, Moriarity commands them to help him restrain Dracula so that he may harvest more blood, but the two men reveal that their loyalty is now to the vampire. Dracula thanks Moriarity for showing him this new, more effective way of vampirizing people. Dracula reveals that he didn't just come to London for revenge. He also plans to vampirize the entire island nation and use the populace as his vampire slaves to take over the rest of the world! So, what started as a simple Holmes caper has now escalated into a world-saving scenario! Interesting indeed.

Realizing that the situation has spun out of control, Moriarty activates a secret trap door under his desk and uses it to escape in a steampunk-like pneumatic tube. Next comes one of the most amusing scenes in the Sherlock Holmes canon. As Holmes stakes out his residence on Baker Street from an alley, Moriarity approaches him from behind and tells Holmes that he dare not approach, as three policemen disguised as peddlers are lying in wait for him. Holmes asks Moriarity what evil machinations he's up to now, and Moriarity reveals that he too has been bested by Dracula and needs his help in defeating the demon. In an amusing scene, the two rivals begrudgingly strike a temporary truce to take out the vampire.

At one of Moriarity's hideouts known only to him, he and Holmes hash out a plan to find Dracula. "Do I smell ferrous oxalate?" Moriarity asks his nemesis. Holmes replies, "The result of an unwelcome encounter with an unfriendly serpent and some conveniently accessible photography equipment."[23]

At the mention of photography equipment, Moriarity tells Holmes that a photographer was killed recently and that it can't be a coincidence. Moriarity shows Holmes a newspaper clipping on the man's death, and Holmes recognizes him as the photographer who tried to take he and Constance's photo. Holmes theorizes that Dracula wanted the photographer's "sealed wagon" which contained a portable darkroom. It would be the perfect vehicle to transport Dracula's coffin. The duo agrees that if they find the darkroom, they find Dracula. Holmes next enlists his band of "Baker Street Irregulars" (a group of ragged street urchins) to help them find the sealed wagon. Cue a semi-humorous little montage of the boys scouring London for the carriage. Towards the end of the montage, one of the boys spots the special carriage heading towards a prison. (Considering that Dracula knows his blood can change people into vampires, and he's heading towards a prison, you know it can't be good.)

Back at the hideout, Holmes is concocting some sort of chemical deterrent to Dracula, while Moriarity has been constructing weapons suited for a vampire hunt: six bullets filled with oak, tear-gas canisters injected with powdered garlic, and a pesticide spray-pump filled with holy water. The duo then has some delightful banter about the irony of their relationship. It kicks off when Holmes tells Moriarity it's a shame he uses his genius to commit crimes, while Moriarity reminds him he mostly uses his genius to solve his crimes. Holmes then admits, "It is indeed ironic —our mutual rivalry seems to provide us with the intellectual stimulation we crave."[24] As the two reminisce about old cases, one of the Baker Street Boys comes in and informs the men that he spotted the carriage.

Just as Holmes added his Baker Street Boys to the fray, now it's Moriarity's turn. In his case, he hires three burly brawlers from Dorset Street to aid them in their quest. He christens them as

303

"Hungry" Hank Thompson, "Matchstick" Mullin, and "Winky" Greggs. The men are gifted with Moriarity's makeshift weapons, and off they go. While Holmes, Mullin, and Moriarity ride within the latter's expensive carriage, the other two brawlers sit up top. One throws his crucifix in the mud calling the whole vampire hunt silly just as Sahid lands on the roof. In his vampire form, he uses his talons to make short work of Greggs. Next, he punches his fist through Thompson's body in a scene so gory it might have lost the film the coveted PG-13 rating it would have no doubt desired. Next, Sahid rips the roof off the carriage and grabs Mullin. Moriarity and Holmes try to hold the man in place, but they are no match for the vampire's strength. Sahid rips the man's head off, leaving Holmes and Moriarity with his lower half. (Again, I'm willing to bet this would have been revised to keep it PG-13.) Sahid then tells his old master that he's here for him, making an interesting parallel to Watson's pent-up aggression towards Holmes earlier.

Adding to the suspense, the out-of-control carriage is riding along a cliff overlooking the sea. Sahid drops down inside to throttle Moriarity, and Holmes shoots him with some holy water. Burning, Sahid turns his attention to Holmes, making it Moriarity's turn to defend his enemy turned ally. Moriarity shoots at Sahid with the wooden bullets, which are only effective when shot through the heart. Due to the jostling carriage, Moriarity misses his mark. Sahid turns to him and tells him that he serves a new master now and knocks him out the door. Moriarity hooks his cane onto the carriage at the last moment, saving him from the perilous fall. Sahid turns his attention back to Holmes, who pulls the man's turban down over his eyes. Holmes then drops one of the garlic-laced grenades down Sahid's shirt. It detonates, searing Sahid's skin as Holmes kicks him out the door and sends him sailing off the cliff. Holmes stops the horses and then helps Moriarity back into the carriage. The scene ends with Moriarity stating that Dracula obviously knows they are coming as Holmes stares at the prison in the distance.

Back at the hospital, Watson has awakened and is himself again to Van Helsing's relief. Watson insists on sneaking out to help Holmes, and Van Helsing begrudgingly agrees to distract the police while he does so. Instead, Van Helsing is kidnapped by Wojeck, who carts him off to see Dracula while Watson observes this from a distance. Meanwhile, Holmes and Moriarity are planning to enter the prison when Holmes notices black smudges on Moriarity's neck. He asks about them, and Moriarity reveals that Sahid's hands were dirty with the smudge. The two men look off into the distance, where a huge factory also sits. It is the Rivington Gas Works, the city of London's main supplier of gas. The duo realizes that the prison isn't Dracula's target after all. Moriarity explains Dracula's ability to infect people with his blood and theorizes that he plans to interfuse his blood into London's gaslight network. The gas would seep into every home in London and vampirize the whole city!

Feeling overwhelmed, Moriarity suddenly chickens out of their mission, which greatly irritates Holmes. Before marching off on his own, he tells Moriarity:

Despite my dedicated efforts over the years to secure your incarceration, I have always harbored an underlying respect for your remarkable criminal talents. But I see now you are no better than the lowliest crook who acts out of selfishness and cowardice. You are undeserving of my admiration, sir -- only my contempt.[25]

The compliment/insult is just the encouragement that Moriarity needs, and so he follows Holmes into certain doom. As the duo approach the factory, they are greeted by the sight of corpses lit by gaslight. Suddenly, Moriarity's dog, Samson, attacks them. As much as he hates to, Moriarity has no choice but to kill his beloved pet by stabbing him with his sword. Samson doesn't die but seems to enlarge and become more vicious. As Holmes notes, the dog is now a vampire itself! Holmes busts the cap off a gas valve, which Moriarity ignites with a spark from his sword. The flames roast Samson, who runs off into the night on fire. Moriarity is now more disgusted than ever with Dracula, who soon steps before them accompanied by Mangler and Lewellyn. (For his final elaborate outfit of the script, Lewellyn is wearing a white suit, his teeth now laced with diamonds. On the note of Lewellyn's teeth, he now sports fangs, too.) Dracula greets the two men and says that he is "flattered to know that the threat of my power compels two such hated enemies to join forces against me."

Inside the factory, Dracula stands above a large metal vat and cuts his wrist over it so that his blood spills into it. "Soon a new Army of Darkness shall be spawned with my blood. The birth of the new Vampire Dynasty is upon us!" Dracula proclaims.[26] The Mangler throws an iron lever which begins to mix the blood into a gas, and Moriarity estimates that they have ten minutes to stop the ghoulish operation. From here, Valle begins to nicely close all his circles, as they say in the scriptwriting business. At this point,

Constance comes onto the scene looking beautiful as ever, while at the same time, Wojcek pulls up with Van Helsing. Dracula greets Van Helsing as the guest of honor, and Van Helsing asks if there are any limits to Dracula's "blasphemous villainy". Constance glides behind Holmes and tells him she warned him not to come. He beseeches her to flee, but she reminds him that the Count has freed her so that she is beholden to no man. Holmes then tells her, "But it is a hollow temptation! To sacrifice not only your soul, but your family—your faith — (with effort) and the love of a foolish man too proud to admit the depth of his true feelings for you..."[27]

The Count jealously chides Holmes, telling him that all that awaits him is a "painful and dramatic death" and then looks to the ceiling and shouts, "Heed me, my winged brethren!" As you can imagine, a horde of bats descends on Holmes, Moriarity and Van Helsing. The trio can do nothing but run as there are too many to fight. The men take cover under a tarp, which the bats proceed to rip to shreds. Just when all hope seems lost, the deafening blast of a steam whistle pervades the factory. The horrendous noise is too much for Dracula and the sensitive bats to handle. This, of course, is Watson's big moment in the climax, as it was he who saved the day. (Another circle closed on Valle's part, after all, he couldn't leave Watson out of the climax, even if it is rather stuffed with characters at this point.) "I couldn't let you face Dracula and his minions alone," Watson proclaims upon locking eyes with Holmes. The Count orders his three henchmen after the men. Moriarity faces Mangler, Van Helsing battles Lewellyn, and Holmes takes on Wojcek. Moriarity manages to trick the Mangler into a furnace, while Watson aids Van Helsing against Lewellyn (eventually Van Helsing stakes him with a broken shovel). Lastly, Holmes buries Wojcek under an avalanche of coal before facing Dracula. Of course, Holmes is no physical match for the Count, who tosses him around like a rag doll. Constance intervenes, begging the Count not to kill him because she loves him too much. Holmes is shocked and Dracula is enraged by this announcement, and he throws Holmes up onto an upper deck. Dracula then leaps up onto the platform, where he aims not to deliver a killing blow but the curse of the undead onto Holmes. What happens next will make any fan of either Sherlock Holmes or Brides of Dracula grin from ear to ear. All hope seems lost as Dracula sinks his fangs into Holmes's neck and drinks deeply of his life force. But then, Dracula begins to gag. Something isn't right. "You have poisoned me!" accuses the Count.

Holmes then reveals just what the chemical compound he was working on earlier was: a chemical solution comprised of holy water, silver nitrate and a pure garlic extract of *allicin sulphide,* which he infused into his blood. "A rather elementary precaution," Holmes coolly states.[28] With this solution having reduced Dracula to a mere mortal, the two men are on equal footing as Holmes delivers a beat-down on Dracula, who eventually tumbles into a coal bin below. The bin is for unground coal, and Constance flips a lever that starts the machinery so that it will grind it up. As Dracula screams in shock at Constance's betrayal, he disappears down the chute, churned into dust. The script could have ended there, but it doesn't.

Instead, Dracula rises from the dust as a green mist that solidifies back into his corporeal form.

DRACULA

You are too late! My blood has permeated the city's gaslines. Countless souls throughout London are already transforming into legions of vampires – and increasing my power a hundredfold![29]

He's not bluffing. We then cut to a London street scene showing several people collapsing from the gas, which sets off a montage of various shots of people being infected. Back at the factory, Dracula literally begins to turn into a giant vampire monster growing taller and sprouting bat-wings. Eventually he becomes a half-man half-bat and induces a thunderstorm. He uses the forceful winds to blow over all the main characters but Constance, who he still wishes to wed despite her earlier betrayal. He flies her up twenty stories to a catwalk as she screams at Holmes to help her. Holmes grabs onto a block and pulley chain in hopes that he can be propelled up to the catwalk, while Moriarity uses his mathematical genius to calculate an explosion that will destroy the factory and incinerate Dracula. Watson and Moriarity both beg Holmes not to go on the suicide mission to rescue Constance, but he won't have it. Up he goes while Moriarity preps the explosion.

On the catwalk, Dracula croons to Constance how she will be his vampire queen to rule their subjects. Just as he is about to put the bite on her, he takes note of a surprised look in her eye and turns to see Holmes ascending on the chain. Dracula calls down lightning to strike it, but Holmes jumps off in the nick of time. However, he loses his large, wooden stake in the process. A game of bat and mouse then proceeds between Holmes and the flying Dracula as our hero must not only dodge the giant vampire but his bolts of lightning as well. Eventually, Holmes regroups with Constance, and the couple are faced with Dracula across the catwalk. He tells Holmes to face oblivion when Watson and Van Helsing activate a huge fan on the catwalk from the controls below. Dracula laughs that the wind cannot harm him, but the jokes on him. Holmes picks up a wooden ladder, throws it into the fan, and it splinters into a hundred pieces. "Go thee back to Hell!" Holmes commands as the wooden stakes fly through the air and pierce Dracula's giant body. As at least one of the stakes went through his heart, he's done for.

But the Count isn't dead yet, Valle still has a few circles to close, and he closes them well. Dracula falls from the platform before Moriarity and beseeches him to remove the stake. If he does, he will grant him the immortality he seeks. Moriarity replies, "And forfeit my humanity? A vastly unequal transposition."[30] Moriarity then slices off Dracula's head, making the Count's death final. (Remember earlier Dracula himself told Van Helsing his head had to be cut off.) When this happens, the forces of nature go berserk. The heroes rush from the factory, dodging debris as they go. As they round the corner, Samson, now truly a hell hound after being lit on fire earlier, stops them in their tracks. Moriarity tells the others to save themselves. It was he who first abetted Dracula, and it is his dog, so he will distract it so that they may escape. "None shall mourn my death," he tells Holmes and adds, "but you have loyal friends who should be saved. Now go!"

"Our petty code of honor," Holmes replies, and off they go.

Intercut between Moriarity's battle with the vampire dog is the heroes' hasty escape. They find a quick exit via the coal transport tunnels on mine carts. Meanwhile, Moriarity stakes Samson through the heart with the spoke of a broken wagon wheel (shades of *Dracula A.D. 1972*, perhaps?). But it's of no use. He will still die as the factory begins to explode. As it does, the force of the explosion propels the heroes in the mine cart down the shaft at lightning speed. They emerge from the tunnel to watch the factory's continuing destruction, which finally seems to abate at the first rays of dawn. Back in London, another montage confirms that the populace have returned to normal, and seem to regard last night's events as a dream of some sort. Back at the factory, Van Helsing proclaims that Dracula is dead forever, while Constance thanks Holmes for saving her. Watson remarks that poor Moriarity couldn't have survived the blast and we would then cut to Dracula's indestructible coffin within the factory. It begins to creak open, and Moriarity's familiar silver cane begins to emerge...

The film's epilogue takes place at the hospital where Van Helsing sees to Constance's recovery. When Holmes expresses excitement over going to see her, Van Helsing delivers sad news: everyone who was vampirized by the Count that night is experiencing a form of short-term amnesia. In other words, they don't remember what transpired during the time that they were vampirized. As such, though Constance will still remember Holmes, she will only remember her time with him up to the point that she met Dracula. And it was after she met the Count that she and Holmes professed their love for one another.

Holmes and Watson enter the room to find Constance looking well but a bit worn out, as her mother, Agnes, watches over her. Watson invites Agnes out for tea so that Holmes may be alone with Constance. Though she is pleased to see Holmes, she clearly is no longer in love with him. He is nothing but a respected friend. She informs him excitedly that Van Helsing has made arrangements for her to recover in America, in the care of none other than John and Mina Harker. Holmes tries his best to hide his disappointment but puts on a strong front for Constance who is excited to be traveling abroad. (It's a rather heartbreaking scene, but I have a feeling that in the James Bond tradition, Valle didn't want Holmes tied to Constance in potential sequels so that there could be a new love interest in each entry.)

Back at Baker Street, the story comes to a close as Holmes and Watson decide that "The Case of the Vengeful Vampire" shan't be recorded as no one would ever believe it. Watson then apologizes for the things he said to Holmes while under Dracula's influence. Homes counters and says that that it is he who is "at fault for not expressing enough how deeply—and how often"[31] he depends upon Watson, his most trusted friend. The script then ends on a wonderful button, where Holmes asks for the day's mail and is handed a letter. His eyes gleam with excitement as he reads, "To my esteemed opponent: The truce has ended and the dance resumes anew—Are you up to the challenge?" Holmes shows Watson and then says, "It's signed, 'Your incomparable adversary—M.'"

Holmes and Watson get to scanning the papers for strange news and find a headline screaming, "Queen's Rembrandt Stolen From Buckingham Palace in Daring Theft! Scotland Yard Mystified by Unknown Criminal Mastermind." Just as the men are excitedly about to rush off to investigate, Mrs. Hudson comes in to express her disappointment that they will be missing dinner again. Changed by his experience with Constance and more mindful of a woman's feelings, Holmes plucks a red rose from a bouquet on his mantle, gives it to Mrs. Hudson, and kisses her on the cheek while apologizing. As Mrs. Hudson stands there in shock, Holmes and Watson rush out the door to counter Moriarty's newest plot. The camera would pan back as the two walk and talk excitedly down a crowded London street.

Overall, this script not only works as a great Holmes adventure but also as a wonderful sequel to *Dracula* itself. If one were to somehow remove the supernatural element and Dracula, this would still be a solid Sherlock Holmes vehicle. Likewise, but to a lesser degree, if one were to remove Holmes, this would still be a great *Dracula* sequel. All this makes it that much more of a shame that it was never produced.

As to why the script never went before cameras, there's a good chance that it would have done so if it were not for the Harry Potter film franchise just getting off the ground in 1999. *Vengeance of Dracula* was given to *Goonies* director Christopher Columbus and his 1492 Productions. The main problem was that Columbus wanted to direct the Holmes/Dracula pic, but he was already committed to *Harry Potter and the Sorcerer's Stone*, which would be completed and released in 2001. While Columbus worked on Potter and debated as to whether he'd direct the Dracula pic, a new writer was hired to polish the script. Actually, polish isn't the right word, as the script already has the sheen of a final draft. What was needed was someone to cut it down for the sake of both the run time and the budget most likely. Chosen for the job was horror filmmaker Rand Ravich, though to this day, no one has seen his script and it's unknown if it was ever finished. By March of 2001, Michael Valle had passed away, and after directing his second Potter film, for whatever reason, Columbus didn't resume work on the Dracula Holmes film.

With Sherlock Holmes more recently being brought to life by Robert Downey Jr. on the big screen, until he relinquishes the role for a reboot, it's unlikely that this script will be resurrected any time soon.

Chapter Notes

1 Valle, *Sherlock Holmes and the Vengeance of Dracula* script, p.8.
2 Ibid, p.10.
3 Throughout the script, Lewellyn changes the gems in his teeth to match whatever color suit he's wearing.
4 Valle, *Sherlock Holmes and the Vengeance of Dracula* script, p.15.
5 Ibid, p.16.
6 Ibid, p.25.
7 Ibid.
8 Ibid, p.27.
9 Ibid, p.30.
10 Ibid, p.32.
11 Ibid, p.43.
12 Ibid, p.44.
13 Ibid, p.65.
14 Ibid, p.68.
15 Ibid, p.69.
16 Ibid.
17 Ibid, p.70.
18 Ibid.
19 Ibid, p.71.
20 Ibid, p.75.
21 Ibid.
22 Even though this is a throwaway plot device, the idea that Dracula, a creature of the night, would yearn to see daylight, is interesting.
23 Valle, *Sherlock Holmes and the Vengeance of Dracula* script, p.88.
24 Ibid, p.91.
25 Ibid, p.102.
26 Ibid, p.105.
27 Ibid, p.106.
28 Ibid, p.110.
29 Ibid, p.113.
30 Ibid, p.118.
31 Ibid, p.126.

35.
THE BRIDE OF FRANKENSTEIN

Script Date: October 5, 2000
Developed: unknown-2000

Screenplay by: Laeta Kalogridis **Proposed Director:** Alex Proyas
Proposed Cast/Characters: Lily Pretorius [wealthy heiress], Ben
Morran [detective], Victor Frankenstein [brilliant scientist],
Hawkins [police investigator], Amelie [Lily's bodyguard], Septimus
Pretorius [Lily's father], Elizabeth Pretorius [Lily's mother]

PLOT In the future, Victor Frankenstein resurrects his fiancé Lily
Pretorius via nanobot technology ...

COMMENTARY Of all the scripts in this book, it is ironically this
one, which is the most recent one in terms of this book's time
frame, that the least amount of information exists for. How it came
to be written and why it was never made is unknown. Nor is this
is a simple *Bride of Frankenstein* remake, as it's more of a wild
reimagining. It also wouldn't appear to be connected to the recent
success of *The Mummy* as a family-friendly PG-13 action pic, as
this is more of a gritty *Blade Runner*-esque R-Rated romp. You
read that right: this script is comparable to *Blade Runner*! This is
because rather than the distant past, this version of *Bride* is set
in the future. (The script is also unusual in that it features almost
all of the characters common to the Frankenstein mythos except
for the monster himself—only the Bride appears in this one, so
don't be distracted wondering when the monster will come in.)
   The script was written by Laeta Kalogridis, the eventual writer
of tentpoles like *Laura Croft: Tomb Raider* (2001). Kalogridis got
her foot in the door when she sold a spec script to Warner Bros on
Joan of Arc titled *In Nomine Dei*, which went unproduced. She also
went on to work on projects like the notorious Halle Berry
Catwoman (2004),[1] the DC Comics live-action TV adaptation of
Birds of Prey (2002), and also an unmade version of *Wonder
Woman* for Paramount. As you can see for yourself, Kalogridis
specialized in female action heroes, and as it turns out, her *Bride
of Frankenstein* reimagining is more sci-fi action than gothic

horror. So, if you've ever wanted to see the Bride of Frankenstein character portrayed as a superhero in the future, this is the script for you!

Before we go any further, some world-building, or rather world explaining, is in order. As already stated, this story takes place in the future, but it's unclear if it's set in the future of the real world that we live in, or a fantasy world meant to mirror the one in *Metropolis* (1927). There is also a class system at play, with the upper class literally living in the crystalline skyscrapers called Tors, while the lower class exists on the street level. The upper structure is called "The Enclave," and the street level is called the "Lower Realm". Two of the most prominent wealthy families in the Enclave are none other than the Frankensteins and the Pretoriuses.

The first visual in the script established the futuristic setting, though it is stated that the towers still have a certain, gothic look to them. There are vaulted domes of pure crystal, shimmering spires that look like "monolithic icicles," and crystalline bridges that create skyways in between the towering buildings. It's a visually stimulating idea to say the least. After establishing the upper strata, we would get a peak down below at a playground that is described as dark and dingy. We can hear a little girl singing "Ring around the Rosey" to herself as she oddly plays by herself at night. In a fake-out type scare, she thinks she sees a monster approaching in the dark. But, it turns out to be a prostitute, mortally wounded, who falls in front of her and mutters some last words about how she "shouldn't have gone back" before dying. The little girl would scream, and we would fade into the next morning, getting a closer look at the seedy underbelly of the futuristic society's Lower Realm. There the homeless indulge in VR headsets as their futuristic drug of choice as they wander the streets, and "gigantic vidscreens" show constant ads while futuristic police cruisers glide through the streets. (Right away, you can tell this is going to be a very pricey production!)

Our first real scene occurs in the autopsy room, where the deceased prostitute is being examined by a doctor and a detective, Ben Morran. The strange thing about the body is that many of the internal organs have been removed. But what really gets Ben's attention is a brief glimpse of what he thinks to be advanced nanotechnology, which hides deep in the corpse upon his seeing it. Ben goes to get the forensic investigator, Hawkins, to study it further, but when the two men return, the body is gone. Suspiciously, it's already been slated for burial. We would then

313

cut to a graveyard scene which is befitting of a *Bride* remake, even if it is set in a futuristic society. Just like in an old Universal or Hammer film, a gravedigger sitting on the sidelines urges the priest doing the lonely funeral to hurry it up. The priest succumbs to the pressure and gets it over with quickly. The poor dead woman is then dumped unceremoniously into a pit with other dead bodies, onto which a strange white powder is dumped. The powder then rapidly decomposes the bodies into the dirt. As this happens, Ben and Hawkins run onto the scene, urging them to stop, but it's too late. Hawkins chides Ben for even caring about the case, as it was just another death in the Lower Realm. (Though we don't know why just yet, the case seems personal for Ben.)

We would cut to another aerial view of the Enclave at dawn, where we see the castle-like structures of the ultra-rich, namely Tor Pretorius, the tallest spire among the skyline. The Tor even has a family crest displayed, that of a phoenix rising from the ashes. On the balcony, the young and beautiful Lily Pretorius watches a falcon soar through the skies. Inside Lily's quarters, we would see that she is some sort of scientist, as papers are strewn across the floor and there are several computers with complicated readouts. Lily's personal bodyguard, Amelie, walks through the room and goes out to see her master on the balcony. However, from their banter it's clear that Lily regards Amelie as a trusted friend rather than a bodyguard, and we learn that Lily was up all night working on her research. The purpose of Amelie's visit is to show her a picture of Ben, who is visiting Tor Frankenstein. (Why is this relevant to Lily? We don't know yet.) And so off Lily and her bodyguard go to Tor Frankenstein, where Lily enters the lab of Victor Frankenstein. The lab is essentially the futuristic equivalent of the one from the Universal films one could suppose, complete with its own version of Ygor, here a half man half machine. In this case, Ygor was a mortally wounded man who Frankenstein saved via his advanced robotics. And yes, Ygor is described as being quite grotesque, with "worm-like scars" across his face, which is half flesh and half metal. However, Lily isn't afraid, and it's clear that the two know one another and are friendly. Ygor tells her that Victor will be pleased that she is there and goes off to fetch him.

Victor is studying a dead body with Ben, who regards the scientist with respect (it was Victor who designed the powder that decomposed the bodies earlier, for instance). Ben is hoping that Victor will know something of the nano-tech he thought he observed in the prostitute's body earlier. Currently, Frankenstein is experimenting with nanobots on the dead body of a child

314

because he's looking into the mysteries of youth. (This is legal, by the way, it's the experimentation of nanobots on the living that is forbidden.) As to Victor's appearance, he seems to be modeled after Colin Clive, being described as "unrelentingly intense" with dark, piercing eyes. Lily interrupts the lesson Victor is giving Ben, and Victor gives her a quick peck on the cheek before introducing her to Ben. Lily reveals that she's met him before, as he questioned some members of her father's company about the recent deaths in the Lower Realm where people turned up missing organs. (There is some tension, as Ben seemed to think it was possible that the people had been selling their organs to House Pretorius.)

Eventually, Victor tells Ben he's spared all the time that he can and needs to get back to work, and so Lily offers to see Ben out. The ensuing conversation exists not only to set up the inevitable romantic tension between the two, but also to deliver some exposition on nanobot technology, which Lily explains to Ben. We also learn here that Victor is her fiancé. When Lily tells him Victor's research is going to change the whole world, Ben replies that it's only going to benefit the Enclave, not the whole world. As Ben departs in an elevator, it's clear that the two know each other better than we think, but what past they share is still a mystery.

The next sequence comprises of Lily and Victor's engagement party in Tor Pretorius, where we meet the patriarch of the family, Septimus Pretorius and his wife, Elizabeth. These, of course, are Lily's parents. They are thrilled by the looming marriage of Lily to Victor because it will join together the two oldest (read: richest) houses in the Enclave. As Lily watches her father speak to Victor, her mother comes up beside her. Some exposition is delivered revealing a bit of the backstory of the strange future society, describing a distant uprising in the past. According to Elizabeth, it is only thanks to the Enclave—the winner of the war, obviously— that civilization as they know it has prevailed. As such, Elizabeth more or less confirms that the houses of Frankenstein and Pretorius rule the world, and it's Lily's duty to marry Victor, even if she's not sure that she loves him. A little later, there is a scene between Victor and Lily out on the balcony, where he tells her that her work with recombinant proteins solved a great deal of problems for him. Victor then reveals that his research has progressed to the point that his nanobots won't merely slow down aging, they will cease it altogether. This is because the nanobots regenerate human tissue on a molecular level (you can probably see where this is going to go later). Lily asks the question, "What if we aren't meant to be eternal?" which upsets Victor. Then comes

315

the trope of the "science going too far" debate common to the old Universal horror films, so it keeps up that end of the legacy.

Lily eventually decides to leave with Amelie, as what Victor has just told her is too much to handle on top of her looming nuptials. Amelie takes Lily on what we think is just a late-night drive, which becomes ominous upon the arrival of a thunderstorm. But it's not just a drive. Amelie is taking Lily to meet Ben in an old, abandoned church. As you might have suspected earlier, the two are secret lovers. Lily eventually breaks their kiss to say, "This isn't right."

Ben responds, "Marrying him? Or loving me?"

Lily goes on about how brilliant Victor is, how it's her responsibility to marry him, etc. Ben becomes angry, not just about the marriage, but the fact that he knows all of Victor's scientific advances will only benefit the Enclave. As their argument reaches its crescendo, and after Ben tells Lily she belongs with him, the violent storm busts out one of the stained glass windows. Lily runs from the church back to her futuristic car, where Amelie waits. After driving for a bit, Lily says she wants to get out and walk. (This is because earlier Ben told her that she's too detached from the "real world" beneath her.) Lily walks around for a bit and takes sympathy on a young girl selling virtual reality devices (as hinted before, virtual reality is implied to be this society's drug). Lily buys all of it so that the girl may go off and buy better clothes (she is dressed skimpily). Soon after, a mugger attacks them but Amelie wards him off rather easily, and they return to Tor Pretorius.

However, Lily doesn't turn in for bed. She goes to Tor Frankenstein to see Victor. He is angry that she left so suddenly, explaining that he told everyone she had become sick to avoid embarrassment. Lily tries as compassionately as she can to tell Victor she doesn't wish to marry him. He reminds her of all their scientific accomplishments together, and Lily says that "Sometimes, it feels like we share one mind, but not one heart." Victor grabs her, asking if it's really because she loves someone else. Unable to lie, Lily looks away, and Victor insists that Lily tell him his name. She relents and reveals that it was the very detective he met this morning. Henry becomes enraged and pushes Lily away from him. Though he didn't necessarily mean to, his push sends her careening into a glass partition that shatters. In the process, one of the glass shards pierces her heart and kills her.

Victor is beside himself for what he's done. Cut to his lab looking "medieval" in the darkness, as he readies his equipment to bring

Lily back from the dead with Ygor. (One of the more interesting visuals has Lily's body being injected from all sides by needles to implant her with the nanobots.) The nanobots repair the tear in Lily's heart, which Victor then tries to restart in a manic scene similar to the 1931 *Frankenstein*. Beseeching her to live, lightning strikes the spire of the lab and conducts itself all the way down to Lily. The impact of the electricity blows Victor backwards and also gives Lily a faint blue glow. Like the Karloff Frankenstein monster, Lily's hand raises slightly, and her eyes begin fluttering. It is Ygor who mutters the "It's alive!" line to Victor, who corrects him that it's not "it" but "she." Victor leans over to caress Lily's face, and she suddenly grabs him by the throat, saying, "It's not right." Ygor acts fast and injects her with a sedative that knocks her out.

While she's out, Victor uses the nanobots to perform surgery on her brain—one that will not only make her forget the past few hours but will also manipulate her hormones into loving him rather than Ben. Going a step beyond that, he erases the memory of Ben from her brain altogether. We would cut to Lily waking in bed, rather startled, the next morning. She runs her hand along her body, looking for scars but finding none. As she gets up to move, the script notes that she has a new "cat-like grace" to her. She walks over to Victor's lab and sneaks up behind him, placing her hands over his eyes. He spins around, grabbing her wrists, afraid that she is attacking him. But she's not. As hoped, she doesn't remember the night before at all.

Eventually, Lily's playfulness leads to full-on love-making with Victor in a scene that could have earned the film an R-rating depending on how it was directed. Notably, at one point, we would see Lily's veins glow blue, indicating that the nanobots beneath her skin are extra fired-up at the moment, so to speak. Later, Lily watches the dawn from the balcony, oblivious to how far off the ground she is as she lightly clutches the railing. Suddenly, she sees flashes of images from the night before consisting of bright lights, needles, and a blast of lightning. Lost in the images, Lily falls from the balcony headfirst just as Amelie walks in. However, she doesn't tumble far. With cat-like agility and super strength, she digs her fingers into the exterior of the Tor and manages to flip herself back onto the balcony, landing in front of Amelie. Both puzzle at Lily's newfound strength and agility, but Lily tires of Amelie's questions and asks her to stop.

We check back in with Ben, who is investigating another murder with Hawkins, where the victim is again devoid of specific organs. This time, Hawkins finds DNA under the dead woman's fingernails, meaning he can hopefully find the killer. Later that night, in a candle-lit chapel, Lily and Victor are married (making the title a bit more literal than the original film in that regard). As they have their first dance as man and wife, Lily catches a glimpse of Ben off in a corner. She is fascinated by him, and luckily Victor fails to notice. Victor is further distracted when his mother-in-law, Elizabeth, asks if she might have a dance with him, and he happily obliges.

Ben is not there for the wedding, though. He's there to ask for DNA scans on Enclave citizens. As it is, the DNA found under the dead woman's nails matched no citizen of the Lower Realm, meaning the killer may have come from the Enclave. This enrages Pretorius, who Ben is talking with. By the time that Lily makes it over to the corner, her enraged father is demanding that Ben leave. After Pretorius storms off, Ben congratulates Lily on her wedding, and she asks if they have met before. Sensing her sincerity, Ben asks Lily what is wrong and touches her hand. This elicits a very strange response from her, as though her body remembers him, but her brain does not. Some guards come along and throw Ben out, and a worried Victor rushes to Lily's side, asking if the man hurt her. Lily assures him that he did not and that he should resume his dance with her mother.

Lily goes outside to get some air and observes Amelie getting groped by a wealthy citizen. (Amelie lives in the Lower Realm and is politically powerless against the man, hence the fact she doesn't fight back.) Enraged, Lily steps in and breaks the man's arm to the point that the bone juts out of his skin. This act doesn't go unnoticed, and several of the wedding guests begin to scream. We cut to later, where Lily tells Victor that she doesn't know what came over her in the moment. Victor gives Lily a sedative to help her sleep, and at the same time draws a bit of her blood for examination. As Victor studies the blood sample, Lily dreams of the church she and Ben met in earlier, only now it is more ancient and gothic looking than before. Suddenly this turns into a memory of her "rebirth" the night before, and she awakens from the nightmare/flashback.

Lily goes to look at herself in the mirror and catches a fleeting glimpse of one of the nanobots scurrying across her eye before it disappears. With Victor gone, Lily sneaks out and tries to find the old church in the Lower Realm. A little girl stops her on the street and informs her that she has bought new shoes and clothes. It is the young girl from a few nights before, who Lily can't remember. She grabs the young girl by the arm and begs her for more information about herself, but the young girl becomes frightened. A stranger approaches and identifies Lily by name. She knows him as well. It is a man named Peter Ryosh who knows her family and attended the wedding. (He too is part of the Enclave, rightly making one wonder what he's doing down below like Lily.) He tells Lily that she should probably be getting home, and he offers to buy the terrified little girl some food. As Lily watches him leave, she notices his clothes have bloodstains. At first, Lily turns and walks away, but then she begins to connect the dots that this is likely the suspect that Ben was looking for!

Lily now realizes that the child is in danger, but by the time she turns back around, they are lost in the crowd. We would next cut to a bar, where a depressed Ben drinks with Hawkins, who tells him he's in trouble for what he did at the wedding. However, Ben is more upset by the fact that Lily acted as though she didn't know him. Lily runs past that very bar searching for the girl but fails to notice Ben. Suddenly, she hears the girl scream and manages to pinpoint her location via her new Bride of Frankenstein super powers. The little girl has just been pulled into a futuristic van, which Lily rips the doors off of as though she's Wonder Woman. Inside she finds a mobile lab of sorts, and the girl is already strapped into a chair. Ryosh tells Lily to get out and informs her that she's interfering with her family's own business! That's right, Ryosh works for Lily's father, who is in the business of procuring organs for research. (Ryosh at least implies that Pretorius is unaware of how the organs are collected, though.)

Lily makes short work of the three assailants, killing Ryosh and the other two (but she lets the driver escape). Lily isn't unscathed, though, and has been cut badly in certain spots. As Lily reaches to take the little girl's hand, the child reacts in fear and awe as Lily's wounds stitch themselves up via the nanobots. (The nano-stitches would presumably be evocative of the stitches on the original Bride.) Within an instant, the wounds are healed. By this time the commotion has attracted the police—including Ben. Lily runs down an alleyway but stops when she sees that Ben is her pursuer. When Hawkins comes onto the scene, too, she bolts again. With gravity-defying acrobatics and superhuman speed, she escapes. But soon more police are in hot pursuit, following her up a tall building. When she becomes cornered on the roof, she jumps from one building to the next. However, she only jumps far enough to cling to the side of the building. Soon a bullet finds its mark, and Lily falls. She crashes through a window and into a sweatshop-type factory that is making some kind of futuristic conduit. The women working in the factory stare at Lily, who survived a fall that should have killed her, in shock. The blood dripping from her wounds is also a strange, silvery blue.

As Lily runs from the factory, we cut back to Victor in the lab. He's alarmed by something he's observed in Lily's blood, but we don't know exactly why yet. We check back in with Lily, who is hiding from the police atop the ruins of an old, burned-down building outside of the city. Somehow Ben has managed to track her even though the others haven't. He sneaks up on her as she perches atop a beam, still in disbelief that she killed all those men earlier. When Ben questions her about it, Lily tells him to "check Ryosh's bloodprint" and he'll figure it out. Despite his love for her, he's still going to take her in and whips out some magnetic handcuffs. As Ben takes another step forward, a wooden beam splinters off and alerts the police below to their presence. They immediately begin shooting, and Lily dives into a nearby river.

Back home, Lily disrobes in the mirror and admires how lithe and muscular her body has become. She also notices the flattened slug of a bullet that impacted her body earlier. Then, beneath her skin, Lily can see the nanobots crawling about near an area of her skin that is becoming increasingly discolored into a bluish-black color, and she smashes the mirror in horror. In her lab, Lily runs tests on herself when she figures out that nanobots are now in her bloodstream. Just then, Victor walks in, and she tells him about her alarming discovery, which he already knows all about. Victor tells a slight fib, claiming that she fell to her death (but leaves out the fact that he pushed her) and that he injected her with nanobots to save her. Lily shows him the discolored patch of skin spreading across her chest. Victor admits that it's because the nanobots are multiplying exponentially, something they weren't supposed to do. However, Lily doesn't become too angry with him, and the scene ends with him trying to console her as she holds her head between her hands.

The next day, Lily confronts her father about the organ harvesting. He counters by claiming he thought Ryosh was getting them through legitimate means (in some cases, it was thought that people willingly sold non-essential organs to him). Lily then asks him about the eyes he'd been harvesting—since no one would dare sell their eyes as opposed to some of the other organs. He is shocked, and in her anger Lily slams her fist into his granite desk, cracking the stone. Eventually she storms out with nothing resolved. As she does so, a new guard that has replaced Amelie follows her (Amelie has been banned because of the earlier incident where the man groped her, even though it wasn't her fault).

Lily takes a nap in her room and is awakened by Ben, who snuck in and knocked out her guard. He does his best to get her to remember him, and while she doesn't doubt that she knew him, she still can't remember him. She does admit that she's had dreams about him, at least. Ben tells her that he wants to take her far away, to the "outer territories" if need be. She asks what will happen if she doesn't go. He responds that he will leave her alone with Victor if that's what she desires, but he will never stop loving her. In that moment, Lily leaps on him, pinning him to the ground for a passionate kiss. Upon the kiss, all her repressed memories come flooding back. Now she knows the truth of her and Victor's relationship again.

Suddenly a group of Tor Frankenstein sentries barges in with Victor. They apprehend Ben, and Victor asks Lily if she's hurt. She confronts Victor, telling him she knows what happened to her was no accident. But he plunges a sedative into her neck before she can do anything else and is rendered unconscious. As for Ben, while Victor could have killed him and solved all his problems—it seems like Enclave citizens can get away with anything—he banishes Ben back to the Lower Realm and informs him that his police license has been revoked.

In the next scene, evocative of the original films, Lily is found chained to a reclinable examination table that is currently flipped upright. Victor marvels at what the nanobots are doing to her body as Ygor looks on. Lily comes to and accuses Victor of turning her into a monster. He just looks at her admiringly, no longer as a woman so much as his prize creation. Lily's body has continued to change, becoming more lithe and discolored than before. She asks him if he can undo what he has done, and he affirms that he cannot. He then tells her to be grateful and that he is now more than her savior, he is her creator. Victor also lets slip that she suffered some irreparable brain damage to her temporal lobe, which regulates the emotional response—hence her inability to control herself when she becomes angry or aroused.

Victor tells Lily he is going to try and fix the problem. She surprisingly tells him that she doesn't want him to. She likes it. She tells him how much she liked it when she ended Ryosh's life and how she will enjoy it when she ends his. Cut to a panicked Victor looking for a more potent tranquilizer to subdue his bride. He theorizes that the nanobots are becoming adept at fighting off the sedatives. Meanwhile, Ygor shares an interesting character moment with Lily. He reminds her that the doctor hadn't invented nanobots when he saved him. While he is ugly, she is beautiful and nearly invincible. He tells her she should be happy and then reminds her that eventually the doctor will remove her memories again, and she will be in love with Victor once more. Lily replies she'd rather be free and bursts from her chains. A fight ensues between her and Ygor, who also has somewhat advanced strength due to Victor's experiments on him. The two slam each other into steel girders and break all kinds of typical lab equipment (glass beakers and the like) in what looked to be a pretty well-choreographed fight. As Victor watches, he alerts security. As the battle rages on, Ygor hits Lily in the face with a beaker of acid. As her face repairs, her eyes come back as gleaming green jewels, looking not unlike a cat's eyes.

She launches herself at Ygor, but he catches her neck in his metal hand and slams her against the wall. As he tightens his grip in an effort to crush her neck, she reaches out and tears off the metal portion of his skull. This agonizing move proves Ygor's defeat as he writhes in pain. Next comes in another regiment of Tor Frankenstein sentries, who chase Lily into a futuristic garage/hanger. She locks them out and flies out of the hanger in a "flittercraft". One of the guards shoots it down to Victor's dismay and it then crashes into another Tor and explodes. However, as the camera pans to the hangar door, we see Lily beneath it, having pinned herself in place with her fingernails. She sent the flittercraft on its way as a decoy. Next, Lily hops atop a futuristic elevator with two sentries within. She shatters through the glass ceiling and attacks them. She enters a room with even more sentries and battles them one by one. (At one point, Lily is described as whirling through the air like a pinwheel as she slams into the sentries.) Just when Lily appears to be outnumbered, Ben arrives to help in a last-minute save.

The two escape in a futuristic car and drive to an old clapboard house in the Lower Realm. It is Amelie's home as it turns out (apparently she and Ben had joined forces offscreen). Amelie tries to remove one of the bullets from Lily's skin but finds she doesn't need to when the nanobots push it out themselves, along with some strange silver-tinted blood. Using some medical equipment borrowed from Hawkins, Lily continues her self-examination that she had begun in Tor Frankenstein much earlier. To her horror, she realizes that technically her flesh is necrotic. Although her brain is alive, her body is dead, and the nanobots are rebuilding it from the inside out. Soon, she will no longer be human at all.

Lily begins to have a breakdown as she feels revolted by her changing appearance, which is amplified by the lights of a passing train.

Ben calms her, though, and tells her she's beautiful. The script notes that he's not lying, and though she is changing, she's still beautiful in an alien way. This is followed by yet another sex scene, this one by the fire. The next morning, Lily's father shows up (Elizabeth knew where Amelie lived). He's there as a caring father, though, and admits to her that even though he didn't know how the bodies were being procured, he knew it couldn't be good. He also reveals that he was getting them for Victor all along. Pretorius looks at his daughter's changed appearance. Her skin is more metallic, and beneath her veins can be seen crawling the nanobots. He then says, "I never thought the price for eternal life would be the only true immortality I have — my child."

He asks Lily for forgiveness with shaking hands. She rises and embraces him. A barrage of bullets suddenly hurtles into the home, killing him in Lily's arms. Amelie is hit too and dies as well. Lily grabs an M16 in Amelie's armory (she was a bodyguard, remember) and goes out to fight. She succeeds in mowing down many of the men, and then goes back inside right around the time that Victor arrives to speak with the officer in charge. Reinforcements then lay siege to the house, throwing in gas canisters and then firing another stream of endless rounds inside. Ben is hit in the leg by a bullet as the house catches fire due to the canisters. Eventually it collapses on itself, but Lily emerges unscathed carrying Ben, who still clings to life. As for Lily, she's gone full Terminator now. Her skin has been burnt off, so now she's made of pure metal.

Lily does her best to escape with Ben, jumping through the air in leaps and bounds to avoid being hit by bullets. One strikes her in midair, and she drops Ben while she falls into a moving train car full of scrap metal. The police swarm around Ben's body. They ask Victor if they can keep him alive and he replies that he can. However, to him, Ben is only bait. As Victor watches the train speeding away, he says, "Come for him, Lily. I'll be waiting."

A flying police cruiser hovers over the scrap car of the train. Lily's hand bursts from the metal and grabs the bottom landing gear, and she then hoists herself up into the craft. She takes control of the air cruiser, flies it to Tor Frankenstein, and jumps out of it. She does the typical superhero landing, crashing through shattered glass and landing on the floor in a crouching position.

She is already surrounded by a group of sentries, while beyond them she can see Victor standing over Ben on a gurney.

"Hi honey. I'm home," she says to Victor. He answers that he knew she'd come for Ben, and she responds that he's wrong. She came for him. What happens next is a more futuristic version of *The Matrix* as Lily battles the sentries within the beautiful crystalline building, with bullets flying and glass shattering. Lily manages to dismantle all the guards (she even uses a laser scalpel to cut one into pieces) and faces Victor. Lily lets him know that his horrible experiments are over, forever. Victor tries to convince her that she's a marvelous creation. His final mistake is reminding her again that she is his bride and that she belongs to him. Lily plays along for a moment as if his words have mesmerized her. She takes his hands gently, then crushes them as she reminds him she belongs to no one. In true Frankenstein monster style, she then lifts her creator over her head and tosses him out the glass window.

Lily goes to wake up Ben and tells him that she's going to destroy the lab so that no one else can take up Victor's experiments. He refuses to leave her and offers to die there with her, but she argues that he must live to make sure that the same mistakes aren't repeated again. Lily sees Ben off on a skylift as he drifts away from the Enclave. Lily takes some grenades from the belt of one of the dead sentries and heads for a nuclear reactor room within Tor Pretorius. Looking peaceful and content in her last moments, she tosses the grenades into the reactor, and everything explodes.

The next morning the sun rises over the ruins of Tor Frankenstein and Tor Pretorius. The way the tower has toppled downward makes it look like a bridge leading down to the Lower Realm. Ben stands with Elizabeth Pretorius, who remarks that it looks like a bridge, and Ben agrees. (The idea perhaps being that Ben will bridge the Enclave and the Lower Realm together finally.) The final shot would be of the two looking at the wreckage of the tower in the dawn sunlight. (Sorry, no sequel bait where Lily shoots her hand up through the wreckage.)

Though quite different from the *Bride of Frankenstein* that we all know and love, the script does present an entertaining story, even if it is more *Blade Runner* than *Bride*. Considering how different it is from Universal's recent hit *Mummy* film, one has to wonder if it was created before *The Mummy's* success. (Yes, the script is dated October of 2000, but before scripts come treatments, and it's possible the treatment was created pre-*Mummy*.) *The Mummy's* success as a light-hearted PG-13 film with higher appeal may have also been why Universal eventually passed on this high-budget R-Rated script, which would have been guaranteed lower grosses due to the rating which is simple economics. All we know about its further development was that Alex Proyas, director of 1994's *The Crow*, was attached before the *Bride* got the ax.

Though this makes for a unique twist on the Frankenstein saga, if one were to change the names and take out a few of the more overt references, one could watch the potential film and never know it was a remake of *Bride of Frankenstein*. That said, a futuristic version of *Bride of Frankenstein* is still a fascinating, fun idea, and perhaps a fitting way to end our journey into the realm of unmade monster movies.

Chapter Notes

---

[1] It is said that her work on the film amounted to a draft which may have went unused. In any case, she's probably glad that she wasn't credited on the film, and perhaps her draft was better than what was produced.

APPENDIX I
COMPLETE PROJECT LISTING

PROJECT TITLE: FRANKENSTEIN AND THE MONSTER
DEVELOPED: 1956 PRODUCER: Hammer STATUS: Screenplay by
Max J. Rosenberg & Milton Subotsky. OVERVIEW: The young
Baron Frankenstein creates a monster while he's away at school.
See main entry "*Frankenstein and the Monster*" on page 11.

PROJECT TITLE: CURSE OF FRANKENSTEIN
DEVELOPED: 1956-1957 PRODUCER: Hammer STATUS:
Synopsis by Jimmy Sangster. OVERVIEW: According to the book
Hammer Complete, this film's title was originally meant to allude
to the fact that the Baron was carrying on the experiments of his
father, hence the "Curse of Frankenstein". According to that book,
that was the original idea in Jimmy Sangster's synopsis, but it was
removed from the final screenplay.

PROJECT TITLE: CURSE OF FRANKENSTEIN
DEVELOPED: 1956-1957 PRODUCER: Hammer STATUS:
Screenplay by Jimmy Sangster. OVERVIEW: Among the *Curse of
Frankenstein's* discarded ideas was a scene where young Victor
argues with his headmaster and bests him in an argument, but
young Victor actor Melvyn Hayes recalled they decided not to shoot
the scene to save money late in the game. Also, according to
Hammer Complete, Elizabeth dies in this version, and there was to
be a scene where the creature is captured by the villagers and tied
upside down to a pole. (This conflicts with Sangster saying he
never wrote in any villagers because it was forbidden for budgetary
reasons, so perhaps the villager scene was confused for a similar
sequence from *Frankenstein and the Monster*?) Supposedly there
was also some sort of reference to Frankenstein working on a
second creature, though how he would do so from his cell is
unclear.

As for other minutia, to play the monster, initially six-foot, five-
inch comedic actor Bernard Bresslaw was considered in addition
to Christopher Lee. However, Lee was two pounds cheaper and
that's how he won the part! As for other casting changes, Hugh
Dempster was the original choice for the Burgomaster but was

replaced by Andrew Leigh. Similarly, John Trevor-Davis was originally the uncle character until he was re-cast with Raymond Ray. Additional listings in the cast for characters that don't appear in the film have surfaced in some of the production papers. Presumably the characters were done away with so as to avoid paying the actors, which included Raymond Rollett (Father Felix), Eugene Leahy (second priest), Joseph Behrman (Fritz), Henry Caine (Victor's Schoolmaster), Marjorie Hume (Mother), Bartlett Mullins (tramp) and Patrick Troughton (Kurt). As for one last aside, the movie was announced as being filmed in CinemaScope on the TV program *Film Fanfare* even though it wasn't filmed in that format.

PROJECT TITLE: UNMADE DRACULA SERIAL
DEVELOPED: 1956 PRODUCER: Associated Rediffusion Ltd. VALIDITY: Rumor [multiple sources] STATUS: Idea. OVERVIEW: In late 1956, television producer Associated Rediffusion Ltd. was planning a seven-part serial based on Bram Stoker's novel. However, Universal squashed the project as they still retained screen rights to Dracula.

PROJECT TITLE: DRACULA
DEVELOPED: 1957 PRODUCER: Hammer STATUS: Screenplay by Jimmy Sangster. OVERVIEW: Version of *Horror of Dracula* with extra scenes. See main entry *"Horror of Dracula* Uncut" on page 21.

PROJECT TITLE: AND THEN FRANKENSTEIN CREATED WOMAN
DEVELOPED: 1958 PRODUCER: Hammer STATUS: Idea. OVERVIEW: There weren't too many aborted Frankenstein sequels from Hammer compared to their Dracula series, probably because Peter Cushing was always easier to get to return to the role than Christopher Lee was with Dracula. Even the only known "aborted" Frankenstein movie was eventually produced itself. The first sequel to *Curse of Frankenstein* was to be *And Then Frankenstein Created Woman*. This was shelved in favor of *Revenge of Frankenstein*, and then in 1966 came *Frankenstein Created Woman*. Supposedly, the initial idea for *And Then Frankenstein Created Woman* was to more or less be a Hammer version of *Bride of Frankenstein*. Both the Baron and the monster would return, with the monster demanding that Frankenstein make him a mate. Or, at least, this is according to an article in *House of Hammer* (which was a Hammer endorsed magazine) entitled "The History of

Hammer" by Bob Sheldon. As it was, Lee made it very clear he would never endure the make-up process as that monster ever again. But if he did, and had also learned how to speak, it would be interesting to see how Lee's second go around as "the creature" went compared to Karloff's talking monster in *Bride*.

PROJECT TITLE: DRACULA'S REVENGE
DEVELOPED: 1958 PRODUCER: Richard Gordon VALIDITY: Rumor [multiple sources] STATUS: Idea. OVERVIEW: Supposedly in 1958, low-budget producer Richard Gordon wanted to make a Dracula movie with Boris Karloff playing the Count. It was to be titled *Dracula's Revenge*.

PROJECT TITLE: THE BLOOD OF FRANKENSTEIN
ANNOUNCED: 1958 PRODUCER: Hammer OVERVIEW: Another *Curse of Frankenstein* sequel in competition with *And Then Frankenstein Created Woman*, *The Blood of Frankenstein* was more of a title than a concept. A poster was drawn up with that title in mind and Jimmy Sangster recollects that it featured a one-eyed monster holding the severed head of a beautiful woman! Eventually, this one morphed into *Revenge of Frankenstein*.

PROJECT TITLE: DRACULA, THE DAMNED/THE REVENGE OF DRACULA DEVELOPED: 1958 PRODUCER: Hammer VALIDITY: Rumor [multiple sources] STATUS: Story pitch or treatment by Jimmy Sangster. Developed into *Dracula – Prince of Darkness* (1966) OVERVIEW: Supposedly, Jimmy Sangster's first crack at writing a Dracula sequel had the Count revived by a band of gypsies (probably a nod to the Count's gypsy servants from the Bram Stoker novel) from the blood of virgins. The central characters would be a pair of sympathetic gypsies in love. The female lead's sister would have been used as the life force to revive Dracula, hence her wanting revenge on the Count. Unverified chatter from the wilds of the internet says that the Count's gypsy servants would be used as "shock troopers," so to speak, that would wipe out entire villages that Dracula believed had betrayed him in some way or another. Dracula's end would come when a church steeple falls on him (which sounds a bit like a reverse of the ending for *Dracula Has Risen from the Grave*). However, casting a little doubt on the whole "blood of virgins" thing is that other sources indicate the method to revive Dracula wasn't thought up until 1963, because the blood on the ashes idea came about not from any Hammer writer, but the public. In 1963, *The Bernard*

Braden Show invited viewers to send Hammer ideas for their new Dracula movie. Several viewers suggested the same idea that blood be dribbled on Dracula's ashes to revive him. As for other scenes allegedly in this script was the opening scene of 1966's *Dracula - Prince of Darkness*, where an innocent corpse is about to be staked despite not being a vampire (although more reliable sources point to this scene actually being in *Disciple of Dracula*). Internet scuttlebutt, taken with the proverbial grain of salt, also says that the corporate heads at Hammer decided not to bring back Van Helsing to keep the emphasis on Dracula, which seems untrue as at the time Peter Cushing was a much bigger star than Christopher Lee.

PROJECT TITLE: KING KONG VS. THE GINGKO
DEVELOPED: 1958 PRODUCER: Willis O'Brien STATUS: Treatment by Willis O'Brien. OVERVIEW: Carl Denham arranges for King Kong to fight a giant Frankenstein monster, the Gingko, in San Francisco. See main entry "King Kong vs. Frankenstein" on page 53.

PROJECT TITLE: KING KONG VS. PROMETHEUS
DEVELOPED: 1958-1961 PRODUCER: John Beck STATUS: Treatment by George Worthington Yates. OVERVIEW: Second draft which retained Frankenstein's grandson but removed Denham. Still ends with a big fight in San Francisco. See main entry "King Kong vs. Frankenstein" on page 53.

PROJECT TITLE: UNTITLED THIRD FRANKENSTEIN FILM
ANNOUNCED: June 5, 1958 PRODUCER: Hammer VALIDITY: Verified [*Kinney Weekly*] STATUS: Idea. OVERVIEW: Before *Revenge of Frankenstein* was even released, Hammer announced that there would be a third film in *Kinney Weekly*. It was to be part of their package deal with Columbia, though they aborted it in favor of the *Tales of Frankenstein* TV series. Another reason why it went unproduced was because Peter Cushing backed away from Hammer horror in 1960 after *Brides of Dracula*.

PROJECT TITLE: THE INVISIBLE MAN
DEVELOPED: 1959 PRODUCER: Hammer VALIDITY: Verified [multiple sources] STATUS: Idea. OVERVIEW: After the success of *Horror of Dracula*, Hammer was granted remake rights to nearly all horror films within Universal's catalogue. This resulted in 1959's *The Mummy* and 1963's *Phantom of the Opera*. In 1959,

329

Hammer pondered producing a remake of *The Invisible Man*. Either that, or Universal may have themselves asked Hammer to produce one. As it turned out, the Invisible Man was the only Universal horror that Hammer never touched (well, that and the Gilman). Nothing was ever written for a Hammer *Invisible Man*, but had it gone forward their version would have likely embraced the 1897 Victorian setting from the H.G. Wells novel.

PROJECT TITLE: THE THREE FACES OF DR. JEKYLL
DEVELOPED: 1960 PRODUCER: Hammer STATUS: Screenplay by Wolf Mankowitz. OVERVIEW: More depraved version of *Two Faces of Dr. Jekyll*. See main entry *"The Three Faces of Dr. Jekyll"* on page 61.

PROJECT TITLE: DISCIPLE OF DRACULA
DEVELOPED: 1960 PRODUCER: Hammer STATUS: Screenplay by Jimmy Sangster. OVERVIEW: A vampire hunter named Latour destroys the Baron Meinster via the ghost of Dracula. See main entry *"Disciple of Dracula*: Before *Brides of Dracula"* on page 65.

PROJECT TITLE: BRIDES OF DRACULA
DEVELOPED: 1960 PRODUCER: Hammer STATUS: Second-draft screenplay by Peter Bryan. OVERVIEW: Similar to final film, except Van Helsing defeats Baron Meinster via swarm of bats. See main entry *"Disciple of Dracula*: Before *Brides of Dracula"* on page 65.

PROJECT TITLE: BRIDES OF DRACULA
DEVELOPED: 1960 PRODUCER: Hammer STATUS: Third-draft screenplay by Edward Percy. OVERVIEW: Same screenplay with revised dialogue for the benefit of Peter Cushing. See main entry *"Disciple of Dracula*: Before *Brides of Dracula"* on page 65.

PROJECT TITLE: DRACULA II
DEVELOPED: 1960 PRODUCER: Hammer STATUS: Fourth-draft screenplay by Anthony Hinds. Released as *Brides of Dracula*. OVERVIEW: Final shooting script, but under the title of *Dracula II*. See main entry *"Disciple of Dracula*: Before *Brides of Dracula"* on page 65.

PROJECT TITLE: BILLY THE KID VERSUS DRACULA
ANNOUNCED: May 1961 PRODUCER: Circle Productions, Inc. STATUS: Completed as *Billy the Kid Versus Dracula* (1966).

OVERVIEW: It's unknown why this production where the famed outlaw faced the arch-vampire stalled for five years. What is known is that Joe Breen was slated to direct, but William Beaudine directed the final film in 1966.

PROJECT TITLE:
JESSE JAMES MEETS FRANKENSTEIN'S DAUGHTER
ANNOUNCED: May 1961 PRODUCER: Circle Productions, Inc. STATUS: Completed as *Jesse James Meets Frankenstein's Daughter* (1966). OVERVIEW: Like *Billy the Kid Versus Dracula*, from the same producers, this one was eventually completed in 1966. It started out with Erle C. Kenton as director, though William Beaudine eventually did the job. Originally cast as the Frankenstein monster was the towering future Bond villain, Richard Kiel (Jaws in *The Spy Who Loved Me*). Jesse James would have also been portrayed by a different actor, Jack Buttel. In the finished film, the monster is played by Cal Bolder and Jesse James by John Lupton.

PROJECT TITLE: SCOURGE OF THE VAMPIRES
DEVELOPED: 1961 PRODUCER: Hammer VALIDITY: Hoax [multiple sources] OVERVIEW: Who concocted this hoax is unknown, but it's interesting enough to bear repeating. The faux story claimed that Hammer began filming a team-up movie for Baron Meinster from *Brides of Dracula* and Dracula himself! The fake story goes that during filming Christopher Lee walked out because he was mad about sharing screen time with David Peel, who likewise asked for more money. Hammer then put the footage in the vault. Again, absolutely none of this is true, but it is interesting!

PROJECT TITLE: THE WEREWOLF
DEVELOPED: 1961 PRODUCER: Hammer VALIDITY: Verified [multiple sources] STATUS: Screenplay by Anthony Hinds. Released as *Curse of the Werewolf*. OVERVIEW: The first draft of *Curse of the Werewolf* was simply titled *The Werewolf*. Among notable differences was that the beggar in the cellar would be a werewolf, which meant that the already touchy rape scene would be considered bestiality, or so they say.

PROJECT TITLE: THE EVIL OF FRANKENSTEIN
DEVELOPED: 1962/63 PRODUCER: Hammer STATUS: Screenplay by Anthony Hinds. OVERVIEW: This film was born out

of discarded "Story No.5" from *Tales of Frankenstein* by Peter Bryan, though a treatment from Cyril Kersh also figured into the development, and was said to feature a hypnotist named Zoltan. Jimmy Sangster was listed as a producer for a time, but he eventually backed out. Terence Fisher was also supposed to direct at one point, but was replaced by Freddie Francis. One of Francis's caveats was that this film feature a more grandiose lab, similar to the Universal films. Originally, the lab was more low-key, and a kite was used to draw electricity to power the monster. As for other changes, the beginning scenes set in the Baron's windmill-powered lab were meant to end with the lab catching on fire. However, it was decided that the script already had too many fire scenes. Also, the priest from that scene may have returned later as a priest in Karlstaad who tells the villagers that there's "a demon in their midst." It was said that sometimes during shooting, pages would literally be ripped from the script to save time and money. This may have happened during the ending of *Evil of Frankenstein*, as three scenes in a row were either deleted after being shot or weren't shot at all. The first had the town drunk sighting the monster for a second time as it came down the mountain. The monster would then enter the mountain cave of the mute girl, who welcomes him inside. The scene of the Baron being held in the police station had some interesting dialogue. After the Baron is hauled in kicking and screaming, he would beseech the Chief of Police to listen to him in "the name of Heaven." The chief mocks the Baron, telling him that he'll be hanged in the morning and that he certainly won't be going to Heaven, but to the "other place." The chief says the "other place" will be fitting for the baron since he's "used to living with monsters." When Frankenstein makes his escape in the horse and carriage, the landlord was supposed to jump down from a balcony and try to block his way, but this was never shot. The script had more to do for the creature in terms of an emotional arc as well. A few scenes were cut that would have shown its connection to the mute girl. The creature was also supposed to be shown dying in a sad scene at the very end. For that matter, as written, it was clearer that the Baron was trapped within the castle as it burned with no way out.

PROJECT TITLE: THE CREATURE FROM THE BRONX
ANNOUNCED: 1962 PRODUCER: Mike Todd, Jr. VALIDITY: Rumor [*Castle of Frankenstein* #2] OVERVIEW: All we know about this one is what *Castle of Frankenstein* #2 had to say about it, which was, "On the lighter side there are two spoofs of THE BLACK

LAGOON. Mike Todd, Jr. has commissioned Larry Gore to script THE CREATURE FROM THE BRONX, while John Halas and Joy Batchelor have contributed THE CREATURE FROM HIGHGATE POND."

PROJECT TITLE: THE ZOMBIE
DEVELOPED: 1962 PRODUCER: Hammer STATUS: Synopsis by Peter Bryan. Completed as *Plague of the Zombies* (1966). OVERVIEW: It's unknown how this proto-version of *Plague of the Zombies* differed from the final version, but the concept poster copied Hammer's *The Mummy* by having a light shining through the zombie.

PROJECT TITLE: PHANTOM OF THE OPERA
DEVELOPED: 1962 PRODUCER: Hammer STATUS: Screenplay by Anthony Hinds. OVERVIEW: As odd as this sounds, Cary Grant was envisioned for the part of the Phantom, and the role was written specifically for him. Eventually Grant dropped out, and after that Christopher Lee expressed interest in the part. "I put myself forward for the Phantom - and got turned down flat! I don't really know why...what really upset me was that I thought I'd get the opportunity to sing. Please don't interpret that as a put down for Herbert Lom - he was terrific." [Johnson, "Christopher Lee: He May Not Have Been Who You Might Have Thought He Was," *Little Shoppe of Horrors* #35 p.170]

PROJECT TITLE: FRANKENSTEIN VS. THE HUMAN VAPOR
DEVELOPED: 1963 PRODUCER: Toho STATUS: Screenplay by Shinichi Sekizawa based on a story by John Meredith Lucas. OVERVIEW: Mizuno the Human Vapor fights the Frankenstein monster. See main entry "Frankenstein vs. the Human Vapor" on page 83.

PROJECT TITLE: THE REPTILES/CURSE OF THE REPTILES
DEVELOPED: 1963-1964 PRODUCER: Hammer STATUS: Idea. Completed as *The Reptile* (1966). OVERVIEW: In 1963, Hammer announced a project called *The Reptiles*, then in 1964 it was announced again as *Curse of the Reptiles*. There aren't any records of just what the *Curse of the Reptiles* script entailed, but, judging by the poster which featured male and female reptile people, it might be a safe bet to assume that, perhaps, Anna had a brother who was also a reptile. The tagline went "From Hammer—The Kings of Horror—the story of a hideous evil...!" This was supposed to be one of Hammer's co-productions with Universal but the

studio turned it down. Instead the film was produced as *The Reptile* under Hammer's eleven-picture deal with Seven Arts two years later.

PROJECT TITLE: CURSE OF THE MUMMY'S TOMB
DEVELOPED: 1963 PRODUCER: Hammer STATUS: Treatment by Michael Carreras. OVERVIEW: A giant mummy attacks Cairo. See main entry *"Curse of the* (Monster) *Mummy's Tomb"* on page 90.

PROJECT TITLE: GODZILLA VS. FRANKENSTEIN
DEVELOPED: 1963 PRODUCER: Toho STATUS: Treatment by Jerry Sohl. OVERVIEW: The heart of the Frankenstein monster regenerates into a giant monster and fights Godzilla. See main entry *"Godzilla vs. Frankenstein"* on page 94.

PROJECT TITLE: FRANKENSTEIN VS. GODZILLA
DEVELOPED: 1964 PRODUCER: Toho STATUS: Screenplay by Kaoru Mabuchi. Completed as *Frankenstein Conquers the World* (1965). OVERVIEW: Similar to previous draft except Godzilla is found in an iceberg. See main entry *"Godzilla vs. Frankenstein"* on page 94.

PROJECT TITLE: THE REVENGE OF DRACULA
DEVELOPED: 1964 PRODUCER: Hammer STATUS: Screenplay by Jimmy Sangster OVERVIEW: This story was a resuscitated version of *Dracula the Damned* from 1959. Structurally, the story was the same as *Dracula–Prince of Darkness* only it featured Van Helsing in place of Father Shandor. What happened was, the production became delayed upon the building of new soundstages and Peter Cushing became unavailable. Therefore his part was retooled into the new character of Shandor. Alternating reports state the original script had dialogue for Dracula, which Lee loathed, and so it was removed. Other reports say there was never any dialogue for the character at all. It's relevant to note that when Lee was asked about this dialogue, he recalled one of the lines being "I am the apocalypse." That line for certain was one he removed from *Dracula A.D. 1972*, so it's possible that Lee, in later years, was mixing up *Prince* with *A.D.* As for other differences, instead of getting his throat cut, Alan's head got lopped off. Also, Ludwig may have been named Henrich in the original script, because in the final film two of the monks refer to him as Henrich as they lead him away.

PROJECT TITLE: CURSE OF THE MUMMY'S TOMB
DEVELOPED: 1964 PRODUCER: Hammer STATUS: Screenplay by Michael Carreras. OVERVIEW: There didn't seem to be too many last-minute changes this time since the censors objected to but ultimately approved of the film's more violent scenes. Some seem to think that the character of Adam Beauchamp might have been considered for Christopher Lee. However, Michael Carreras decided to cast Terrence Morgan, who was, of course, much more inexpensive than Lee. Carreras said, "I liked him. I had never worked with him. He seemed right. Also, he had a sort of name and wasn't going to cost a lot." [Hallenbeck, "The Making of the Hammer Classic *The Curse of the Mummy's Tomb*," *Little Shoppe of Horrors* #24 p.54.] *Monster World* #1 reported on Lee's near miss with the film, but misinterpreted it to mean he would have played the mummy with bandages rather than the one without: "We had understood that Lee was to appear in CURSE OF THE MUMMY'S TOMB but apparently he's been too busy with minute-made mummies, Living Skulls, the Undead, etc., elsewhere, to tend to his tana leaves so an actor named Dickie Owen inherits the icky role. Owen to Mr. Lee's absence, as it were." Furthermore, on the note of Lee, his star had risen high enough that he would by now be far too expensive to waste on a roll where no one would even see his face. On top of that, Lee had also stated he would never undergo that kind of makeup a procedure again. Not to mention, he received several injuries while working on *The Mummy* in 1959.

PROJECT TITLE: THE WEREWOLF OF MORAVIA
DEVELOPED: 1964 PRODUCER: Hammer VALIDITY: Verified [*Hammer Vault*] STATUS: Idea by Michael Carreras. OVERVIEW: During shooting of *Curse of the Mummy's Tomb,* Michael Carreras wrote a letter to Peter Cushing about a future film the duo wanted to shoot together in Czechoslovakia. According to Marcus Hearn in *The Hammer Vault,* this was to be a werewolf film (though it started out as a proto-version of *Countess Dracula* according to *Last Bus to Bray*). Carreras wrote to Cushing that, "Being unable to find a suitable legend as we discussed, I sat down and wrote one and enclose a copy herewith for your perusal." What this legend was, apart from concerning a werewolf, we do not know. The idea was revived again in 1978, with Peter Cushing still attached. Carreras wanted to film in Spain but Cushing did not.

PROJECT TITLE: FRANKENSTEIN CREATED WOMAN
DEVELOPED: 1966 PRODUCER: Hammer STATUS: Screenplay by Anthony Hinds. OVERVIEW: *Frankenstein Created Woman* was created out of several discarded story treatments for the *Tales of Frankenstein* TV series. The final script doesn't have a great deal of differences from the final film. For instance, the early scenes of the adult Hans looking at the guillotine were supposed to take place in the rain but were shot without it. Christina was supposed to witness Hans's execution more closely and would have gotten a good look at his severed head before she ran away screaming. There were also scenes shot and later deleted of villagers following Christina's body as it floats down river right after she jumps. There was supposed to be a double funeral for Christina and Hans following this. Also, the grave diggers burying Christina's coffin remark on how light it is. We would have then cut to Christina, wrapped in bandages. The Baron would then remark that she should be at a full recovery by six months. There was originally a much longer examination montage between the Baron, Hertz, and Christina, who would look at herself in the mirror and ask, "Am I beautiful? You see, I don't know." They reassure her that she is, and then Christina becomes bashful when the Baron asks her to disrobe. Dr. Hertz convinces the Baron to leave, and as he examines her, Christina asks him who she is, what her history was, etc. The ending was a bit more gruesome. The minute that the Baron calls to Christina in the woods, she was supposed to look at him and then commit suicide by stabbing herself to death! The Baron would stand over another dead creation as he hears the villagers coming nearer and nearer, calling his name. He would run away, and the credits would roll.

PROJECT TITLE: FRANKENSTEIN ON MARS
DEVELOPED: mid to late-1960s PRODUCER: unknown VALIDITY: Rumor [multiple sources] OVERVIEW: The title *Frankenstein on Mars* was floated around in several different monster magazines of the 1960s. No details on what it was have ever surfaced, but it could have been an alternate title for *Frankenstein Meets the Space Monster* (1965).

PROJECT TITLE: SHROUD OF THE MUMMY
DEVELOPED: 1966 PRODUCER: Hammer STATUS: Treatment by Anthony Hinds. Screenplay by John Gilling. Completed as *The Mummy's Shroud* (1967). OVERVIEW: Due to its rushed nature, this film went through few revisions or changes. Of the minute

changes, the character of Inspector Berani was originally named Azi. The opening narration was made to be a bit longer, but a scene where a guard was beheaded was cut. Sir Basil was originally supposed to stick his hand into a whole nest of vipers (as opposed to only one) and draw back his hand oozing with black blood. John Richardson was initially cast as Paul Preston until he became unavailable.

PROJECT TITLE: WEREWOLF WEDDING
PITCHED: 1966 PRODUCER: Hammer VALIDITY: Verified [multiple sources] STATUS: Treatment by Bob Baker OVERVIEW: Rejected werewolf story for Hammer by Bob Baker. No other known details.

PROJECT TITLE: FRANKENSTEIN TRAPPED
PITCHED: mid to late-1960s PRODUCER: Hammer VALIDITY: Verified [multiple sources] STATUS: Treatment by Bob Baker OVERVIEW: Rejected Frankenstein story for Hammer by Bob Baker. No other known details.

PROJECT TITLE: THE REPTILE
DEVELOPED: 1966 PRODUCER: Hammer STATUS: Screenplay by Anthony Hinds. OVERVIEW: As far as first draft scripts of *The Reptile* went, Dr. Franklyn was initially much more unlikeable. The script called for him to whip Anna as punishment at one point. The ending was only slightly different in that it is Harry Spalding, rather than Franklyn, who tosses Malay into the sulfur pit. Franklyn then locks Valerie and Franklyn both in the house as it burns down, though they do of course escape as in the film.

PROJECT TITLE: THE STRANGE CASE OF DR. JEKYLL AND MR. HYDE DEVELOPED: 1967 PRODUCER: Dan Curtis STATUS: Screenplay by Rod Serling. OVERVIEW: In 1967, TV producer Dan Curtis was readying his own version of the Robert Louis Stevenson classic. Though it was eventually produced starring Jack Palance, Curtis initially cast Jason Robards in the role. The script was originally written by Rod Serling and it was to be filmed in London, but had to relocate to New York, and finally Canada. The makeup was said to be heavily influenced by John Barrymore in the 1920 silent version.

PROJECT TITLE: THE HORRORS OF FRANKENSTEIN
ANNOUNCED: 1967 PRODUCER: Tigon British Film Productions
VALIDITY: Verified [multiple sources] OVERVIEW: In 1967, Tigon
films announced a film called *The Horrors of Frankenstein*, which
Hammer was somehow able to veto even though they didn't have
exclusive rights to the character. (That, or perhaps Tigon later saw
that *Frankenstein Must Be Destroyed* didn't make a dent in the
box office and dropped it.) Ironically, Hammer later adopted a
similar title for their 1970 Frankenstein feature with Ralph Bates.

PROJECT TITLE: DRACULA'S REVENGE
DEVELOPED: 1967-1968 PRODUCER: Hammer STATUS:
Screenplay by Anthony Hinds. Completed as *Dracula Has Risen
from the Grave* (1968). OVERVIEW: Before it garnered the lengthy
title of *Dracula Has Risen from the Grave*, the old *Dracula's
Revenge* title was dusted off again. Before that the film was simply
called "Dracula Subject" in 1967 meetings, which had greenlit the
film before any type of story had even been conceived. (According
to Roy Skeggs, Warner Bros requested a Dracula film.) It was also
uncertain whether or not Christopher Lee would return, and
Hammer did look at other actors as a contingency plan (though
it's never been said who). Compared to the other Draculas, this
one went through few revisions (that I know of, at least). It's
possible the first draft that Lee read was quite different from the
finished one. Before shooting started he said that he'd liked the
script in a letter to his fan club. But, a letter written during
shooting called the script "just alright." The main differences had
the priest character chopping up Xenia's dead body to dispose of
her! The censors objected, and so he stuffs her into a furnace in
the final film. Terrence Fisher was supposed to direct the film but
suffered a broken leg when hit by a motor bike and so was replaced
by Freddie Francis.

PROJECT TITLE: DRACULA'S FEAST OF BLOOD
DEVELOPED: 1969 PRODUCER: Kevin Francis/Hammer
STATUS: Treatment by Kevin Francis OVERVIEW: Van Helsing
and Dr. Seward are menaced by Dracula in London. See main
entry "*Dracula's Feast of Blood*" on page 115.

PROJECT TITLE: TASTE THE BLOOD OF DRACULA
DEVELOPED: 1969 PRODUCER: Hammer STATUS: Screenplay by
Anthony Hinds. OVERVIEW: Lord Courtley drinks Dracula's blood

338

and becomes a vampire. See main entry *"Taste the Blood of Dracula* Without the Count"* on page 118.

PROJECT TITLE: TASTE THE BLOOD OF DRACULA
DEVELOPED: 1969 PRODUCER: Hammer STATUS: Revised Screenplay by Anthony Hinds. OVERVIEW: Revised version with Dracula, but with minor differences. See main entry *"Taste the Blood of Dracula* Without the Count"* on page 118.

PROJECT TITLE: EDGE OF MIDNIGHT
DEVELOPED: Late 1960s PRODUCER: Hammer VALIDITY: Hoax [multiple sources] OVERVIEW: Probably the most legendary of all the Hammer hoaxes—or that is to say a non-existent lost film created in the rumor mill—is *Edge of Midnight*. The faux film was said to be Hammer's equivalent of *House of Frankenstein*. According to the bogus story, Jimmy Sangster was lured back to Hammer on the condition that he could both write and direct the picture, which starred Peter Cushing, Christopher Lee, and Oliver Reed. The story saw Baron Frankenstein acquiring the ashes of Dracula, so that he may revive and experiment on the Count. The Baron must flee to Spain for some reason or another, and there he hears tales of a long dead werewolf, which he also resurrects. The movie was to end with Frankenstein's monster, the werewolf, and Dracula fighting it out. The film was never finished because Lee, Cushing, and Reed couldn't keep a straight face during filming. Nor can many of you probably keep a straight face while reading this ludicrous story. Not to say that the story doesn't sound fun, but it simply isn't characteristic of Hammer and reeks of fantasy. That said, just in case, Bill Kelley asked Christopher Lee if Hammer ever contemplated conjoining the Dracula and Frankenstein series in *Little Shoppe of Horrors* #13:

LSOH: Did Hammer ever consider putting Dracula and Frankenstein together in one film?

Lee: You mean the way Universal Pictures did in the 1940s, with their monsters? No, never, I'm sure they didn't. Hammer contemplated any number of outlandish sequels and combinations that never got past the discussion stage. This would fall into that category, if it even got as far as that.

PROJECT TITLE: DRACULA'S COFFIN
DEVELOPED: 1969 PRODUCER: Al Adamson STATUS: Idea by Al Adamson. OVERVIEW: Unproduced sequel to *Blood of Dracula's Castle* (1969), which had starred John Carradine not as the Count, but as Dracula's butler. Carradine was expected to return and that's all that is known outside of the title.

PROJECT TITLE: FRANKENSTEIN: THE UNTOLD STORY
DEVELOPED: Unknown PRODUCER: Bert I. Gordon STATUS: Adaptation of the book of the same name. OVERVIEW: Nothing much is known other than Bert I. Gordon Gordon wanted Charlene (Brinke) Stevens to star. Might be related to 1973's *Frankenstein: The True Story* in some way.

PROJECT TITLE: SCARS OF DRACULA
DEVELOPED: 1970 PRODUCER: Hammer STATUS: Screenplay by Anthony Hinds. OVERVIEW: Basically same as finished film only intended for a new actor as Dracula. See main entry *"Scars of Dracula* Starring John Forbes Robertson" on page 123.

PROJECT TITLE: FRANKENSTEIN
DEVELOPED: 1970 PRODUCER: Hammer STATUS: Script by Jeremy Burnham. Completed as *Horror of Frankenstein.* OVERVIEW: This script, simply titled *Frankenstein*, was written by Jeremy Burnham and given to Hammer. It was essentially a remake of *Curse of Frankenstein* to focus on a young Baron Frankenstein. The ending was completely different from either *Curse* or *Horror* though. The story climaxed with the monster escaping the castle, terrorizing a whole village, and then returning to the castle where it confronts Elizabeth. She lights the monster on fire, and it burns to death. The script then ends with the Baron getting down on his knees and pathetically fawning over the remains of his monster. Hammer accepted Burnham's script but gave it to Jimmy Sangster to rewrite, which he agreed to do so long as he could also direct. Sangster then went on without permission to change it into a comedy. He's been quoted as saying he was surprised that no one at Hammer balked about it, but then pondered perhaps no one actually read it! This relaunch with Ralph Bates as the new Frankenstein was meant to be followed by five sequels, making a six-film series! Though it was said the double bill of this film and *Scars of Dracula* did respectable business in Britain, Hammer was apparently wise to the fact that

Scars had done the heavy lifting and audiences didn't take to Frankenstein this time around.

PROJECT TITLE: UNTITLED FOURTH MUMMY FILM
DEVELOPED: 1970 PRODUCER: Hammer VALIDITY: Verified [multiple sources] STATUS: Idea. OVERVIEW: Nothing is known about this prospective fourth Mummy film other than it had nothing to do with *Blood from the Mummy's Tomb* and would have been similar to the previous three films. All that the project amounted to was a request for a fourth Mummy movie from EMI to James Carreras. When Anthony Hinds couldn't come up with any ideas, Jimmy Sangster was approached. He couldn't come up with any ideas either and EMI lost interest.

PROJECT TITLE: DRACULA – HIGH PRIEST OF THE VAMPIRES/DRACULA IN INDIA DEVELOPED: 1970 PRODUCER: Hammer STATUS: Treatment by Anthony Hinds. OVERVIEW: Proto-version of the better-known *Unquenchable Thirst of Dracula* which may have had a contemporary setting. See main entry *"The Unquenchable Thirst of Dracula"* on page 143.

PROJECT TITLE: VAMPIRE LOVERS
DEVELOPED: 1970 PRODUCER: Hammer STATUS: Screenplay by Tudor Gates. OVERVIEW: Bond girl Shirley Eaton was originally suggested for the role of Carmilla, but James Carreras argued she was too old (Ingrid Pitt was only 10 months younger). IMDB Trivia claims Christopher Lee was offered the role of the Man in Black, which is odd considering the character did next to nothing in the film. Furthermore, some sources claim Terence Fisher was to direct the film until he broke his leg yet again. The original ending was more physical, with General Spielsdorf confronting Carmilla in the crypt. He raises his sword to strike her, but she grabs his hand and stops him effortlessly. After a moment, she dematerializes and reappears in her crypt. The film bypasses the brief confrontation to have the men simply find her in the crypt and destroy her.

PROJECT TITLE: TO LOVE A VAMPIRE
DEVELOPED: 1970 PRODUCER: Hammer STATUS: Screenplay by Tudor Gates. Completed as *Lust for a Vampire* (1971). OVERVIEW: Before bearing the more provocative moniker of *Lust for a Vampire*, *To Love a Vampire* was the title, and it would've starred Peter Cushing and been directed by Terence Fisher. Ultimately, both

dropped out. Supposedly, Ingrid Pitt was offered to return but she chose to do *Countess Dracula* instead.

PROJECT TITLE: VAMPIRE VIRGINS
DEVELOPED: 1971 PRODUCER: Hammer STATUS: Screenplay by Tudor Gates. OVERVIEW: Two vampire hunters battle Count Karnstein and his vampire virgins. See main entry "*Vampire Virgins*" on page 129.

PROJECT TITLE: UNTITLED TWIN VAMPIRE PROJECT
DEVELOPED: early 1970s PRODUCER: Hammer VALIDITY: Verified [multiple sources] STATUS: Idea by Wilbur Stark and John Peacock. OVERVIEW: Unrelated to *Twins of Evil*, this twin vampire concept had both siblings as vampires. What it entailed other than that, exactly, is unknown, but the idea was integrated into *Vampire Circus*. Outside of that, all we know is that the story concept was the idea of producer Wilbur Stark and writer John Peacock.

PROJECT TITLE: BLOOD FROM THE MUMMY'S TOMB
DEVELOPED: 1971 PRODUCER: Hammer STATUS: Screenplay by Christopher Wicking. OVERVIEW: Original version was scripted to have more nudity and elaborate Egyptian ritual scenes. Began shooting with Peter Cushing in the role of Professor Fuchs. See main entry "*Blood from the Mummy's Tomb* Starring Peter Cushing" on page 135.

PROJECT TITLE: TWINS OF DRACULA/TWINS OF EVIL
DEVELOPED: 1971 PRODUCER: Hammer STATUS: Screenplay by Tudor Gates. OVERVIEW: This wasn't an alternate story idea so much as it was an alternate title. On September 17, 1971, James Carreras (as "Jim, Baby") received a letter from the American distributor, who requested that *Twins of Evil* be retitled *Twins of Dracula!* Ingrid Pitt was supposedly offered the chance to cameo as Carmilla but declined.

PROJECT TITLE: DR. JEKYLL AND SISTER HYDE
DEVELOPED: 1971 PRODUCER: Hammer STATUS: Screenplay by Brian Clemens. OVERVIEW: Caroline Munroe, Kate O'Mara and Julie Ege were among those considered for the part of Sister Hyde. But, because the resemblance between Ralph Bates and Martine Beswick was so high, Beswick was a no brainer for the part. (That, and she would agree to nudity, which the other two wouldn't.

However, Beswick would not agree to full frontal nudity, which was apparently planned for at one point.)

PROJECT TITLE: UNTITLED 3-D DRACULA FILM
DEVELOPED: c.1970s PRODUCER: Pentagram Film Productions VALIDITY: Verified [*Hammer Complete*] STATUS: Idea. OVERVIEW: According to *Hammer Complete*, sometime in the 1970s Terence Fisher was being courted by Pentagram Film productions to shoot a 3-D Dracula film! As to just who/what Pentagram Film Productions was, *Hammer Complete* says that they were tied to Amicus Producer Milton Subotsky in some way.

PROJECT TITLE: THE ECSTASY OF DORIAN GRAY
DEVELOPED: 1970/1971 PRODUCER: Hammer STATUS: Idea. OVERVIEW: This was meant to be some sort of "spiced-up" variation on *The Picture of Dorian Gray*. The box office failure of Harry Alan Tower's version of the story was why Hammer ceased development on their version.

PROJECT TITLE: THE VAMPIRE HUNTERS
DEVELOPED: 1971 PRODUCER: Hammer VALIDITY: Verified [multiple sources] STATUS: Idea by Tudor Gates. OVERVIEW: *Hammer Complete*, in their entry for Tudor Gates, says that there was to be a fourth Karnstein film called *Vampire Hunters*, though presumably this is the same film as *Vampire Virgins*. Is this to mean that after the release of *Twins of Evil* that Hammer contemplated dusting off *Vampire Virgins* and renaming it *The Vampire Hunters*?

PROJECT TITLE: CAPTAIN KRONOS – VAMPIRE HUNTER
DEVELOPED: 1971 PRODUCER: Hammer STATUS: Screenplay by Brian Clemens. OVERVIEW: The original conception of Captain Kronos was a bit more elaborate in early versions (and Brian Clemens hoped he would be played by Simon Oates). Though we learn he was once bitten by a vampire in the film, one could assume the incident was remedied before it could take effect à la the Van Helsing scene in *Brides of Dracula*. However, initially this was supposed to give him special powers and he was to sleep in a golden coffin! "He was a vampire, but not a vampire," Clemens said once. And, as his name literally meant "time" in Greek, the idea was that he was a time traveler! This far out but ingenious ploy meant that Hammer could put Kronos in whatever time period they wanted without a worry for continuity... if there had ever been

sequels that is. Though meant as a series, it never came to be. Had the series progressed, Hammer could have had some fun by placing Kronos and Grost in the 1970s. In *Little Shoppe of Horrors* #10, in the article "The Un-Filmed Hammer: An A to Z Guide" by Glen Davies, Clemens is quoted as saying, "I had several story outlines standing by for sequels. I had also carefully named him Kronos — because that is ancient Greek for time. It was my intention to have him flexible in time and space, so that he could go back or forward in time to fight vampires and evil should the story demand it." According to *Last Bus to Bray*, Caroline Munro claimed that a second film was fairly far along in development before it was dropped. An issue of *Film Review* from the time even claimed that Kronos's future adventures would see him fight Count Dracula and Baron Frankenstein! The bit about Frankenstein could have come from a comment Clemens made during the film's production, which was later reprinted in *The Hammer Encyclopedia*: "The Kronos stories weren't all going to be about vampires. They'd have been about inexplicable events really, leaning towards the supernatural or legend.... He could easily have come up against Frankenstein's monster." As for one last aside, the produced film has a tedious tie to the Karnstein films in that the secret vampire is a Karnstein. To really hit home this idea, Ingrid Pitt was approached to guest star as Lady Durwood, who would really be Carmilla! But sadly, Pitt declined. For almost twenty years after the film was released Brian Clemens also tried to develop it as a TV series.

PROJECT TITLE: BLACULA
DEVELOPED: 1972 PRODUCER: AIP STATUS: Screenplay by Joan Torres, Raymond Koenig and Richard Glouner. OVERVIEW: The original draft of *Blacula* supposedly lacked the elegant backstory for the character being a prince and his name was Andrew Brown. It was actor William Marshall himself who insisted that Blacula be given a more dignified backstory. Also, the prologue originally took pace in 1815 rather than 1870.

PROJECT TITLE: RETURN OF THE WEREWOLF
ANNOUNCED: 1972 PRODUCER: Hammer VALIDITY: Rumor [Cinema TV7 Today] STATUS: Idea OVERVIEW: Announced as a Hammer film in *Cinema TV7 Today*, Michael Carreras later denounced the project when he stated in an interview that Hammer never intended to film another werewolf story after *Curse*

of the Werewolf. If this is in any way related to *Legend of the Werewolf* (1974) is unknown.

PROJECT TITLE: DRACULA VS. THE BEASTS OF ZARCON
DEVELOPED: 1972 PRODUCER: unknown VALIDITY: Rumor [multiple sources] STATUS: Title. OVERVIEW: Absolutely nothing is known about this story other than that it would have featured John Carradine (presumably as Dracula) and that it "mercifully" went unmade as most sources put it.

PROJECT TITLE: THE HOUSE OF DRACULA'S DAUGHTER
ANNOUNCED: 1972 PRODUCER: First Leisure Corp. VALIDITY: Verified [advertising materials] STATUS: Screenplay by Peter Crowcroft. OVERVIEW: An ad for this tantalizing film popped up in at least one early 70's era monster mag. It would've featured Loraine Day as Dracula's Daughter. Both John and David Carradine were listed on the ad as well, as was Peter Lorre Jr.

PROJECT TITLE: DRACULA CHELSEA 1973
DEVELOPED: 1971 PRODUCER: Hammer STATUS: Screenplay by Don Houghton. OVERVIEW: Warner Bros asked Hammer to do this film in response to *Count Yorga, Vampire,* which had a modern setting. Judging by the title, it would seem Hammer didn't think the movie would get released until 1973, or perhaps, wanted to set it one year into the future so that it might seem newer. In any case, early reports in monster magazines implied the leading lady would be African American, and though there is the character of Gaynor Keating, she is a supporting player while Stephanie Beacham plays the lead. If this was a blunder on the part of the reporters or if the script changed is unknown. Most accounts say there was very little script tweaking. Christopher Lee did refuse lines that would have implied Dracula to actually be the devil, though, and replaced them with classic dialogue from the Stoker novel. Jessica was initially to be Lorimer Van Helsing's daughter, but the death of Peter Cushing's wife had aged him so rapidly that it was decided to make Lorimer Jessica's grandfather instead (hence, there is no explanation of where her parents are or why she lives with dear old grandad). After throwing the Holy Water in Dracula's face, Dracula was to suddenly see Lorimer as his old nemesis Lawrence Van Helsing, but the idea was dropped, and it's not apparent in the scene. As for a few final asides, Paul Annett was offered the chance to direct the film, but apparently turned it down. There was also supposed to be a tie-in album with none

other than Rod Stewart's group The Faces. It was The Faces that were originally signed to appear as the rock group in September 1971, but they were replaced by Stoneground!

PROJECT TITLE: VICTIM OF HIS IMAGINATION
DEVELOPED: 1972 PRODUCER: Hammer STATUS: Treatment by Don Houghton. OVERVIEW: Biopic of Bram Stoker, which intended to have Christopher Lee in dual roles as Dracula and Henry Irving. See main entry *"Victim of His Imagination"* on page 155.

PROJECT TITLE: FRANKENSTEIN AND THE MONSTER FROM HELL DEVELOPED: 1972 PRODUCER: Hammer STATUS: Screenplay by Anthony Hinds. OVERVIEW: The only details known about this film in the realm of the unmade is that it had a few unshot scenes, but the concept itself of the Baron in an asylum was unchanged. It originally had two scenes of the Baron incapacitating the monster with ether, which Roy Skeggs rightly felt was repetitive, and so he suggested the monster be subdued with a hypodermic needle instead. Another short scene that went unfilmed had the monster waking up after having the new hands grafted on, and the Baron gives him a bone to gnaw on. At the film's end, the Baron was to be shown throwing pieces of the monster's flesh to some stray cats as he does his clean up!

PROJECT TITLE: DRACULA IS DEAD... BUT ALIVE AND WELL, AND LIVING IN LONDON DEVELOPED: 1972 PRODUCER: Hammer STATUS: Treatment by Jimmy Sangster/Screenplay by Don Houghton OVERVIEW: It's unknown how this story differs from *Count Dracula and His Vampire Bride*, but allegedly Jimmy Sangster wrote a treatment that both differed from and predated Don Houghton's script. As to Houghton's early drafts, Dracula had the ability to shapeshift. So, rather than Dracula hiding his appearance behind a bright light, he really would have taken on the form of the American businessman known as D.D. Denham. Houghton recycled the shape-shifter idea for *Legend of the 7 Golden Vampires* when Dracula was shoehorned into the story.

PROJECT TITLE: DRACULA ON ICE
PITCHED: 1973 PRODUCER: Hammer. VALIDITY: Verified [multiple sources] STATUS: Idea by Don Houghton. OVERVIEW: All we know about this one is the title, and that it was to be an ice

rink musical! It was written by Don Houghton and thankfully went unmade.

PROJECT TITLE: FRANKENSTEIN THE TRUE STORY
DEVELOPED: 1973 PRODUCER: NBC STATUS: Teleplay by Don Bachardy & Christopher Isherwood. OVERVIEW: Originally there was a prologue that was meant to open this story in a similar manner to *Bride of Frankenstein*. It would have seen Nicola Pagett as Mary Shelley, Leonard Whiting as Percy Shelley, David McCallum as Lord Byron, and James Mason as Polidori, who was the real author of *The Vampyre* (1819). Elsewhere, IMDB claims that the original broadcast featured a prologue with James Mason visiting the grave of Mary Shelley. The film's writers, Christopher Isherwood and Don Bachardy, were so disappointed in this adaptation that they made sure to publish their original version of the teleplay. Isherwood and Bachardy also pushed for Jon Voight be cast as Victor Frankenstein, and for John Boorman to direct.

PROJECT TITLE: BYRON'S EVIL
DEVELOPED: 1973 PRODUCER: Andrew Sinclair VALIDITY: Verified [multiple sources] STATUS: Idea. OVERVIEW: This project was developed around the same time as *Frankenstein: The True Story* and ran out of funding when that film went into development. *Byron's Evil* was the product of Andrew Sinclair with Oliver Reed set to play Lord Byron.

PROJECT TITLE: DRACULA
DEVELOPED: 1973 PRODUCER: Dan Curtis STATUS: Screenplay by Richard Matheson. OVERVIEW: Lengthier version of the TV movie. See main entry "Richard Matheson's *Dracula*" on page 308.

PROJECT TITLE: THE INSATIABLE THIRST OF DRACULA
DEVELOPED: 1973 PRODUCER: Hammer VALIDITY: Verified [multiple sources] STATUS: Story by Anthony Hinds and/or Don Houghton. OVERVIEW: Due to only the title being known, there's a lot of conjecture based around this aborted feature. Because it pre-dated *Legend of the 7 Golden Vampires*, some have speculated that it might be a contemporary set sequel to *Count Dracula and His Vampire Bride*. Others downright list it as just such a follow-up, but they cite no sources. In any case, the plan was to launch a high-publicity national talent contest to replace Christopher Lee. Eventually *Legend* derailed these plans.

PROJECT TITLE: LEGEND OF THE 7 GOLDEN VAMPIRES
DEVELOPED: 1973 PRODUCER: Hammer/Shaw Brothers
STATUS: Screenplay by Don Houghton. OVERVIEW: Original
version sans Dracula, but otherwise similar to the finished film.
See main entry *"The Seven Brothers* (Don't) *Meet Dracula"* on page
173.

PROJECT TITLE: DRACULA AND THE 7 GOLDEN VAMPIRES
DEVELOPED: 1973-1974 PRODUCER: Hammer/Shaw Brothers
STATUS: Screenplay by Don Houghton. OVERVIEW: Altered
version with Dracula. See main entry *"The Seven Brothers* (Don't)
Meet Dracula" on page 173.

PROJECT TITLE: DRACULA WALKS THE NIGHT
ANNOUNCED: 1974 PRODUCER: Hammer VALIDITY: Hoax
OVERVIEW: This tantalizing hoax purported that Terence Fisher
was going to direct a movie featuring Van Helsing and Sherlock
Holmes (along with Watson) teaming up to battle a vampiric Vlad
the Impaler! The non-existent script was said to come from the
dream team of Jimmy Sangster and Richard Matheson. Even
though the story is false, internet rumors stated the film was to
open with Dracula's origins as Vlad the Impaler before it jumped
ahead to the main setting: 1885. Not only were Peter Cushing and
Christopher Lee to play Van Helsing and Dracula, but Barbara
Shelley was to be the vampire bride and Jack Palance would be
Dracula's servant, Macata!

PROJECT TITLE: DRACULA AND THE CURSE OF KALI
DEVELOPED: May 1974 PRODUCER: Hammer STATUS:
Treatment by Don Houghton. OVERVIEW: Dr. Luis Van Helsing
discovers a heinous plot to wed Dracula and Kali in 1856 India.
See main entry *"Dracula and the Curse of Kali"* on page 185.

PROJECT TITLE: DEVIL BRIDE OF DRACULA
DEVELOPED: November 1974 PRODUCER: Hammer STATUS:
Revised treatment by Don Houghton. OVERVIEW: Houghton's
second major attempt removed Kali and replaced her with a
fictional snake goddess instead. See main entry *"Dracula and the
Curse of Kali"* on page 185.

PROJECT TITLE: JACK THE RIPPER GOES WEST
DEVELOPED: 1974 PRODUCER: Euan Lloyd VALIDITY: Verified
[multiple sources] STATUS: Screenplay by Scot Finch.

OVERVIEW: The exact story details of this project are unknown. Some say it simply reflected the title, and Jack the Ripper would have come to America in the late 1800s. Others think the story would have concerned Jack the Ripper's ghost in America, similar to the 1935 film *The Ghost Goes West*. In that film, when a Scottish castle is transported to America stone by stone, the ghost comes with it. In real life, an old London Bridge built in the 1830s was transported to Lake Havasu in Arizona in the 1960s. A TV movie, *Terror at London Bridge*, was made in 1985 which had Jack the Ripper's ghost attached to the bridge! Some think it's possible that *Jack the Ripper Goes West* was tied to this TV film. In any case, back in 1974, Euan Lloyd wanted to produce the film under his production company, and had hoped Peter Collinson would direct and that Christopher Lee could star. It was announced again in 1978 and 1979.

PROJECT TITLE: FRANKENSTEIN
DEVELOPED: 1974 PRODUCER: Ray Harryhausen VALIDITY: Verified [*Masters of the Majicks Volume 3*] STATUS: Idea OVERVIEW: As Ray Harryhausen was a student of Willis O'Brien, he tried several times to get some of his old mentor's unmade films completed. One of those, allegedly, was O'Brien's unmade *Frankenstein*. Internet chatter claims Harryhausen considered the project after completing *The Golden Voyage of Sinbad* (1973). A man in suit would have brought the monster to life in most scenes, but some would have used stopmotion for the monster's greater feats of strength and action.

PROJECT TITLE: DRACULA: THE BEGINNING
DEVELOPED: 1974 PRODUCER: Hammer STATUS: Treatment by Brian Hayles. OVERVIEW: Origin story detailing Vlad the Impaler's transformation into Dracula. See main entry "*Dracula: The Beginning*" on page 209.

PROJECT TITLE: UNHOLY DRACULA
DEVELOPED: 1975 PRODUCER: Hammer STATUS: Treatment by George Trow. OVERVIEW: Replaces the snake goddess with Durga and a subplot revolving around hidden jewels. See main entry "*Dracula and the Curse of Kali*" on page 185.

PROJECT TITLE: DEVIL BRIDE
DEVELOPED: 1975-1977 PRODUCER: Hammer STATUS: Incomplete screenplay by Christopher Wicking. OVERVIEW: Final

version of the India set follow-up to *Legend of the 7 Golden Vampires* which combined elements from *Unholy Dracula* and *Dracula and the Curse of Kali* but went unfinished. See main entry "*Dracula and the Curse of Kali*" on page 185.

PROJECT TITLE: INVISIBLE MAN VS. THE HUMAN TORCH DEVELOPED: 1975-1977 PRODUCER: Toho STATUS: Screenplay by Jun Fukuda and Masahiro Kakefuda. OVERVIEW: A detective gains the ability to turn invisible and battles a man who can envelop his body in flames. See main entry "*Invisible Man vs. the Human Torch*" on page 200.

PROJECT TITLE: SHERLOCK HOMES IN THE ADVENTURES OF THE WEREWOLF OF THE BASKERVILLES DEVELOPED: unknown, presumably mid-1970s PRODUCER: Frank R. Saletri VALIDITY: Rumor [multiple sources] STATUS: Idea by Frank R. Saletri. OVERVIEW: One of two rumored Sherlock Holmes adventures from Frank R. Saletri.

PROJECT TITLE: SHERLOCK HOMES IN THE ADVENTURES OF THE GOLDEN VAMPIRE DEVELOPED: unknown, presumably mid-1970s PRODUCER: Frank R. Saletri VALIDITY: Rumor [multiple sources] STATUS: Idea by Frank R. Saletri. OVERVIEW: The other rumored Sherlock Holmes idea from Frank R. Saletri. In this case, he wanted Alice Cooper to play Dracula!

PROJECT TITLE: THE DRACULA ODYSSEY DEVELOPED: 1976 PRODUCER: Hammer STATUS: Stories by multiple writers. OVERVIEW: In 1976, Michael Carreras and Tom Sachs envisioned a new way to reboot Dracula via an anthology film comprised of four different stories. Each would be told from the perspective of Dracula's female victim, and one, "The Lady Was a Vampire," was written by Don Houghton. Dracula might also have been played by a different actor in each segment, and the most popular could then presumably star in sequels.

PROJECT TITLE: THE DAY THE MUMMIES DANCED DEVELOPED: 1976 PRODUCER: Ed Wood STATUS: Screenplay by Ed Wood. OVERVIEW: Nothing much is known of this story, which was to be Ed Wood's return to the director's chair. It was to be set and shot in Guanajuato, Mexico, where the famous Mexican mummies exhibit was located. John Agar and Aldo Ray were to star with Dudley Manlove producing and acting.

PROJECT TITLE: UNTITLED FATHER SHANDOR FILM
DEVELOPED: 1977 PRODUCER: Hammer STATUS: Idea by Michael Carreras based upon the comic strip by Dez Skinn. OVERVIEW: In the late 1970s, a "Father Shandor" comic was serialized in the *House of Hammer* magazine. Based upon Father Sandor from *Dracula—Prince of Darkness* (but with a different spelling), the comics version of the character first appeared in issue #8 in 1977. Michael Carreras caught wind of the idea and thought he'd pitching it as a film to American investors. The editor of the magazine, Dez Skinn, is quoted as saying, "Michael Carreras actually took copies of our first Shandor story to the States as a potential film. I told him the story and he took the penciled drawings which hadn't even been inked, let alone lettered, to potential backers in America. Unfortunately, he couldn't remember the original story, so he made up a totally different one. When he got back he said can you change the story because that's not the one he'd told the Americans." It's anyone's guess what story Carreras made up, but in the comics, Father Shandor didn't just fight vampires, he also fought werewolves and demons. (I would imagine Carreras probably stuck to vampires in his pitch, but who knows?) Like Professor Zimmer in *Kiss of the Vampire*, this iteration of Father Shandor wasn't above using occult methods to confront the monsters.

PROJECT TITLE: THE UNQUENCHABLE THIRST OF DRACULA
DEVELOPED: 1977 PRODUCER: Hammer STATUS: Screenplay by Anthony Hinds. OVERVIEW: Updated version of *Dracula—High Priest of the Vampires* set in the 1930s. See main entry "*The Unquenchable Thirst of Dracula*" on page 143.

PROJECT TITLE: THE PLAGUE OF DRACULA
DEVELOPED: unknown PRODUCER: Hammer (rumored) VALIDITY: Rumor [source unknown] OVERVIEW: This story would have been set during the great plague of London in 1665, which Dracula somehow had a hand in. It might've been inspired by *Nosferatu* (1922), which featured plague-carrying rats. In any case, most sources say this project was a hoax.

FILMPLAN INTERNATIONAL

David Cronenberg's

Frankenstein

A contemporary vision of a timeless, chilling tale.

written and directed by DAVID CRONENBERG
adapted from MARY SHELLEY's classic novel

PIERRE DAVID
VICTOR SOLNICKI
CLAUDE HEROUX
Executive Producers

A MAJOR
CINEMATIC EVENT

THE INVISIBLE MAN

written by GEORGE R.R. MARTIN

A futuristic thriller of man and technology clashing...at vanishing point.

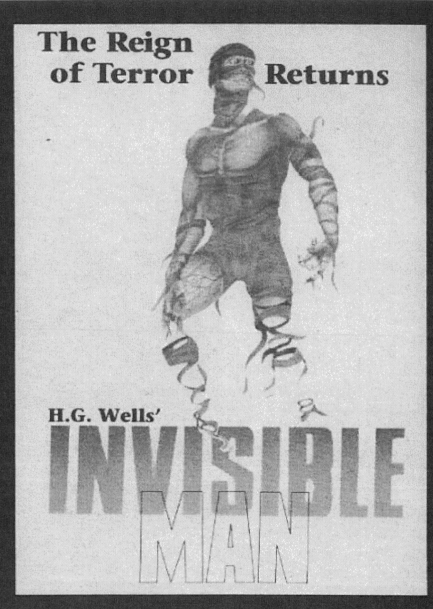

THE HOUSE OF DRACULA'S DAUGHTER

Starring: PETER LORRE JR., JOHN CARRADINE, DAVID CARRADINE, LORRAINE DAY, BRODERICK CRAWFORD. Written by: PETER CROWCROFT. Executive Producer: HARRY HOPE. Producer: PETER CROWCROFT. Director: GORDON HESSLER. A FIRST LEISURE CORPORATION PRESENTATION. RELEASED BY ELLMAN ENTERPRISES.

PROJECT TITLE: INTERVIEW WITH THE VAMPIRE
ANNOUNCED: 1977 PRODUCER: Unknown. VALIDITY: Verified
[*Famous Monsters* #136] STATUS: Idea. OVERVIEW: This
adaptation of the Anne Rice novel was to star Peter O'Toole.

PROJECT TITLE: THE INSATIABLE THIRST OF DRACULA
DEVELOPED: 1978 PRODUCER: Hammer VALIDITY: Verified
[multiple sources] STATUS: Story by Anthony Hinds and/or Don
Houghton OVERVIEW: Supposedly this project had been
considered in 1974 prior to *Legend of the 7 Golden Vampires*.
Michael Carreras either thought enough of the script (or maybe
just the title) that he considered it as part of a series of 13 feature
length movies. In England, these would be released theatrically,
but in America they would be TV movies as part of the *Hammer
House of Horror* package. The series was intended as a co-
production with Terra Filmkunst to be filmed in Germany.
American networks expressed no interest, though, and Terra
Filmkunst couldn't raise the funds. A quote from *House of
Hammer* #18 from Carreras himself implies that *Insatiable Thirst*
wouldn't be any type of sequel but rather a remake:

> Every TV show in America had to start with something
> totally familiar and with heavy American accents but this
> has changed now and after two years of planning, and
> endless trips to America to break down these barriers, we
> are at last sitting on a deal with a major American TV
> network to produce a series of TV films called *The Hammer
> House of Horror* which, in essence, will remake all the
> Hammer horror films in a new format. It will be the start of
> a whole new Hammer cycle.

Ultimately, the project never came to fruition in any form. (An
alternate report states that Carreras had ideas of 26 one-hour
films made for TV which would subsequently see release on video
cassette. This alleged iteration dated back to 1972 according to
some, which seems unlikely due to there being no such thing as
VHS in 1972! In any case, it was to be called *Hammer Horrors* and
would have been made up of remakes of all the Hammer greats
including Dracula, Frankenstein, the Werewolf, the Mummy,
Zombies, the Reptile, the Stranglers of Bombay, the Phantom of
the Opera, and more.)

PROJECT TITLE: DRACULA
ANNOUNCED: 1978 PRODUCER: Hammer/EMI VALIDITY: Verified [multiple sources] STATUS: Idea. OVERVIEW: Nothing is known of this concept other than the title and that it would be a co-production with EMI.

PROJECT TITLE:
SHERLOCK HOLMES AND THE PRINCE OF DARKNESS
DEVELOPED: Late 1970's PRODUCER: Unknown VALIDITY: Rumor [*Famous Monsters*] STATUS: Idea. OVERVIEW: This Sherlock Holmes vs. Dracula movie was to have starred Patrick McGoohan as Holmes, Nigel Davenport as Watson, and Jack Palance as Dracula (plus a cameo by Forry Ackerman). Special effects would've been done by Kenneth Strickfaden.

PROJECT TITLE: DRACULA, THE TRUE STORY
DEVELOPED: 1978 PRODUCER: unknown. STATUS: Teleplay by Dale Wasserman. OVERVIEW: Written by Dale Wasserman (*One Flew Over the Cuckoo's Nest*), this proposed TV movie may have been a spiritual sequel to *Frankenstein, The True Story* (1973). The film was never made due to the network proclaiming the script to be "too gruesome" for television.

PROJECT TITLE: THE REVENGE OF KING TUTANKHAMUN
DEVELOPED: 1978 PRODUCER: Hammer STATUS: Idea by Michael Carreras. OVERVIEW: One of Michael Carreras's last projects to dissolve before he left Hammer was *The Revenge of King Tutankhamun*. It would have been one of the Hammer TV movies proposed by Carreras that would be shown theatrically in England but on television in the U.S. This one would have dramatized the real-life discovery of King Tutankhamen by Howard Carter and Lord Carnavon in the Valley of the Kings in 1922. It was to be based upon the 1977 book *Behind the Mask of Tutankhamen* by Barry Wynne. The film was eventually realized by HTV in 1980 as *The Curse of King Tut's Tomb*.

PROJECT TITLE: HALLOWEEN HOUSE OF HORROR
DEVELOPED: 1978 PRODUCER: Hammer STATUS: Idea by Michael Carreras. OVERVIEW: Hammer pitched this rather self-indulgent TV movie to ABC in America. Their idea was that an unspecified TV personality seeks refuge in the perennial "old dark house", where he would find a "mausoleum" of old Hammer memorabilia. This would lead into a clip-show of classic Hammer

horror. Allegedly this was either written by Jimmy Sangster and Al Taylor, or would be written by them once the project got the green light. This was to be one of three TV specials to be broadcast across three consecutive nights during or leading up to Halloween night of 1978. The second was to be called *Behind the Scenes of the Halloween House of Horror*. The TV personality who had hosted the previous night's show would "return" to the old dark house during the day where he would meet the behind-the-scenes technicians of Hammer. There the process of makeup and special effects would be explained to him. Viewers would also get a behind-the-scenes look at the making of "The Werewolf of Moravia" which was itself never made. (It was to be an episode of the *Hammer House of Horror* TV series.) The third and final show was to be called *The Other Rooms in the Halloween House of Horror*, which would showcase more classic clips and provide a look into yet another unmade project: *The Revenge of King Tutankhamun!*

PROJECT TITLE: DRACULA
DEVELOPED: 1978-1979 PRODUCER: John Hawn and Michael Nolin. STATUS: Screenplay by Ken Rusell. OVERVIEW: Dracula reimagined as a tortured, immortal artist. See main entry "Ken Russell's *Dracula*" on page 214.

PROJECT TITLE: DRACULA
DEVELOPED: 1978-1979 PRODUCER: The Mirisch Company. STATUS: First draft screenplay by W. D. Richter. OVERVIEW: The first draft began on the seashore with Seward, Lucy, Mina and several of the asylum inmates walking along the pier. And, when Dracula is found, Mina and Lucy do so together, while in the film it is only Lucy. The only survivor of the crash is committed to the asylum as everyone thinks he's crazy. Renfield had more of a backstory, as he has been the caretaker of Carfax for the past twenty years. After the scene where Mina attacks the baby in the asylum, she was to be chased out into the graveyard. Later, when Mina attacks Van Helsing in the mines, Harker arrives for a last second save. In one of the bigger changes, Renfield leads Van Helsing and Harker into the depths of Carfax to kill the Count. They eventually find Dracula playing somber music on an old organ before attacking him. When Renfield's corpse is found in his cell, he's left the heroes a message: "He wants a bride. He's coming for Lucy." And the biggest change of all: Dracula turns to dust at the end.

PROJECT TITLE: DRACULA
DEVELOPED: 1978-1979 PRODUCER: The Mirisch Company.
STATUS: Second draft screenplay by W. D. Richter. OVERVIEW:
This version notes that the story is set in 1906, though the final
film would be set in 1913. As for other differences, Harker and
Lucy both meet Renfield at Carfax, and they ask him to pass along
a dinner invitation to the Count. Later, when Dracula attacks
Mina, Lucy and Harker are off together making love (in the final
film they're just talking). Dracula manipulates events more so to
get Lucy alone, sending a telegram to Dr. Seward to pick up Van
Helsing while also sending Harker away. The character of Swales,
one of Seward's workers, is more proactive in this draft and it is
he, not Van Helsing, who suggests Dracula is a vampire. When
Lucy runs away with Dracula, Renfield warns the heroes of
Dracula's intentions to vampirize her. When Dracula dies, he cries
out Lucy's name. Also, director John Badham wanted to shoot the
movie in black and white, which Universal wouldn't allow. As a
compromise, years later for the film's Laserdisc release, he
watered down and muted the colors, giving the film a greyish look.
The full color version was lost until recent years when it was
restored by Scream Factory for a Blu-Ray release.

PROJECT TITLE: UNTITLED DRACULA SEQUEL
DEVELOPED: 1979 PRODUCER: Universal. STATUS: Idea.
OVERVIEW: As odd as this may sound, Universal had hopes for a
sequel to *Dracula*. The reason we know this boils down to two
scenes in the climax. For starters, it is said that Van Helsing was
killed so that Laurence Olivier would not have to return as Van
Helsing in a sequel. (He didn't want to, and apparently nobody else
wanted him to either. Not only was he expensive at $750,000, his
performance wasn't exactly dynamic.) Second, the reason
Dracula's cape flutters around in the wind with a mind of its own
was to hint to the audience that the Count wasn't really dead. (To
hit home this idea, notice Lucy's smile as she sees the cape
fluttering in the wind.) Unfortunately, the film's mediocre grosses
crushed any hopes of a sequel.

PROJECT TITLE: DRACULA FEVER
DEVELOPED: 1979 PRODUCER: unknown. VALIDITY: Verified
[ad material] STATUS: Idea. OVERVIEW: An ad exists for this
musical but no other information is available.

PROJECT TITLE: VLAD THE IMPALER
DEVELOPED: 1983 PRODUCER: Hammer STATUS: Screenplay by Arthur Ellis & John Peacock. OVERVIEW: Updated version of *Dracula: The Beginning* with modern-set prologue and epilogue. See main entry "*Vlad the Impaler*" on page 248.

PROJECT TITLE: DRACULA
ANNOUNCED: 1980 PRODUCER: Hammer/Cinema Arts International VALIDITY: Verified [multiple sources] STATUS: Idea. OVERVIEW: All we know about this Dracula movie is that it would have been produced by Roy Skeggs and Brian Lawrence. Skeggs was quoted as saying that they planned a new Dracula because nobody had ever done it better than Hammer. He also added that there would be an intense search for a new actor to play Dracula.

PROJECT TITLE: DOREEN GRAY
DEVELOPED: 1980 PRODUCER: Hammer VALIDITY: Verified [multiple sources] STATUS: Idea. OVERVIEW: Under the leadership of Roy Skeggs and Brian Lawrence, Hammer wanted to produce a female spin on *The Picture of Dorian Gray* in the same vein as Hammer's other female horror films like *Dr. Jekyll and Sister Hyde*. Mia Farrow was eyed to play the title character.

PROJECT TITLE: DAVID CRONENBERG'S FRANKENSTEIN
ANNOUNCED: May 1980 PRODUCER: Pierre David STATUS: Idea. OVERVIEW: Sometime in 1980, Canadian film producer Pierre David pitched to David Cronenberg (recent director of 1979's *The Brood*) a version of Frankenstein. Pierre David's specific wording was, "Listen, tell me what you think... 'David Cronenberg's Frankenstein'?" Cronenberg responded that he was interested, and before he knew it a full-page ad ran in *Variety* in May of 1980 touting, "David Cronenberg's Frankenstein." Though the project never came to fruition, Cronenberg said that his version would "be a more rethinking than a remake. For one thing I'd try to retain Shelley's original concept of the creature being an intelligent, sensitive man. Not just a beast." The project *Untold Horrors* asked Pierre David about it, and he told them that the *Variety* ad failed to generate any investors as they had hoped. He also told *Untold Horrors* that, "David [Cronenberg] had other projects. And he wanted to do something. So, while we were trying to get Frankenstein done, he went to do something else. And then Frankenstein went nowhere, and the something else became much more stuff."

360

PROJECT TITLE: THE MUMMY LIVES
DEVELOPED: unknown, possibly c.1980s PRODUCER: unknown
VALIDITY: rumor [source unknown] STATUS: Idea. OVERVIEW:
All we know about this film, which may not even be real, was that
it was to star Anthony Perkins, Amanda Donohoe and Oliver Reed
with Ken Russell directing!

PROJECT TITLE: SUM VII
ANNOUNCED: 1980s PRODUCER: unknown VALIDITY: Verified
[advertising materials] STATUS: Adaptation of the 1979 novel *Sum
VII* by T.W. Hard. OVERVIEW: A modern take on the Mummy myth
that would have had an ancient Egyptian sorcerer's body
recovered and brought to the U.S. There scientists study it and are
shocked when its cells revive. The being awakens and is called
Sum VII. It then escapes to explore the modern world and shock
it with its supernatural powers. (This sounds quite similar to
Universal's aborted *Mummy* remakes of the late 1980s and early
1990s.)

PROJECT TITLE: LOVE AT SECOND BITE
DEVELOPED: 1980s PRODUCER: Melvin Simon Productions
VALIDITY: Rumor [internet] STATUS: Idea. OVERVIEW: *Love at
First Bite* star George Hamilton and director Stan Dragoti allegedly
wanted to make a sequel called *Love at Second Bite*. It would have
featured Christopher Lee as Hamilton's father, the elder Dracula!
Other titles included *Divorce, Vampire Style* and *Love at Second
Bite: Dracula Goes Hollywood*.

PROJECT TITLE: CREATURE FROM THE BLACK LAGOON
DEVELOPED: 1981-1983 PRODUCER: Universal STATUS:
Screenplay by Nigel Kneale (first draft) and Evan Kim (second
draft) OVERVIEW: See main entry Remake from the Black Lagoon
Part I on page 235.

PROJECT TITLE: UNTITLED CREATURE SEQUEL
DEVELOPED: Early 1980s PRODUCER: William Alland STATUS:
Treatment by William Alland. OVERVIEW: When William Alland
heard about the proposed *Creature* remake in the 1980s under
Jack Arnold he was incensed, and so he wrote his own sequel idea
to counter the remake. Possibly inspired by kid-friendly fare like
E.T., he envisioned the Creature as having a family. Specifically,
there would be a female creature to join the original (no, we don't

know how he survived *Walks Among Us*) plus one or two "little ones". In *Creature Chronicles*, Alland is quoted as saying,

> Since the Creature that I had originally envisioned was so romantic, I thought he should have a family—a mate, and one or two little ones. In my story, they're all removed from the Black Lagoon and secretly transported to a lake on the big estate of a very wealthy family in the United States. They can communicate with the family, and a whole relationship develops. Unfortunately, some baddies do find out about 'em and try to catch 'em—they capture one or both of the children, and the mother and the father go after them and kill the baddies. Now they're wanted. [Weaver, Schecter and Kronenberg, *The Creature Chronicles* (Kindle Edition).]

He then revealed that he never got as far as pitching it to a studio though, and that Creature Chronicles was the first time he ever revealed it to anyone.

PROJECT TITLE: DRACULA WHO?
DEVELOPED: 1983 PRODUCER: Hammer STATUS: Treatment by Ingrid Pitt. OVERVIEW: This spoof was thought up by Ingrid Pitt while filming *The Wicker Man* with Christopher Lee. Apparently, Peter Snell made a joke about how Pitt and Lee had both played vampires in the past. Pitt then envisioned a funny story where Dracula decides to become a vegetarian, much to the chagrin of his wife. Dracula and wife would have been played by Pitt and Lee, which certainly would have been fun. Pitt wrote the story into a book, but the film was never produced. Robert Young (director of 1972's *Vampire Circus*) was eyed to direct when Hammer briefly considered the project. Supposedly, the idea was considered all the way up until 1996, with producer Gary Kurtz (a Lucasfilm producer) working on it.

PROJECT TITLE: THE INVISIBLE MAN
DEVELOPED: Late 1980s-early 1990s PRODUCER: Brian Yunza VALIDITY: Verified [advertising materials] STATUS: Screenplay by George R.R. Martin OVERVIEW: In the late 1980s, Brian Yunza began developing a remake of *The Invisible Man* which was written by George R.R. Martin (*Game of Thrones*)! Several ads for the film exist, but we know nothing of the story.

PROJECT TITLE: VLAD THE IMPALER
DEVELOPED: 1988 PRODUCER: Hammer STATUS: Screenplay by Arthur Ellis & John Peacock (revised). OVERVIEW: New version that removed some of the more supernatural elements but retained the prologue and epilogue. See main entry *"Vlad the Impaler"* on page 248.

PROJECT TITLE: THE MUMMY
DEVELOPED: Late 1980s PRODUCER: Universal STATUS: Treatment by Abbie Bernstein. OVERVIEW: Scientists have to keep a Mummy from causing the apocalypse. See main entry "Clive Barker's *Mummy*" on page 251.

PROJECT TITLE: BRIDE OF FRANKENSTEIN
DEVELOPED: 1991 PRODUCER: unknown VALIDITY: Rumor [source unknown] STATUS: Idea. OVERVIEW: According to online rumors, Martin Scorsese was supposed to do a remake of *Bride of Frankenstein* for cable TV!

PROJECT TITLE: DRACULA
DEVELOPED: 1991 PRODUCER: unknown STATUS: Screenplay by James V. Hart. OVERVIEW: Believe it or not, Francis Ford Coppola's 1992 *Dracula* was originally to be a TV movie directed by Michael Apted. Winona Ryder had been given the script and showed it to Coppola, who decided he'd like to direct. Apted stayed on as a producer, and the project switched from television to film.

PROJECT TITLE: KEVIN JARE'S DRACULA
DEVELOPED: 1991 PRODUCER: unknown STATUS: Screenplay by Kevin Jarre. OVERVIEW: Similar to the case of Ken Russell's *Dracula* vs. the Mirisch Company's *Dracula*, in the early 1990s there was again two competing *Dracula* remakes in the works. The one that got made was Francis Ford Coppola's version. The one that didn't was Kevin Jarre's. A 113-page first draft of his *Dracula* was completed on March 5, 1991.

PROJECT TITLE: DRACULA
DEVELOPED: 1991-1992 PRODUCER: Francis Ford Coppola STATUS: Screenplay by James V. Hart. OVERVIEW: Originally, the ambitious opening battle was supposed to be brough to life by puppets as a historical recreation. A hallucination scene was also scrapped where Seward and Holmwood find the bodies of Harker, Morris, and Van Helsing impaled on posts at Dracula's castle.

PROJECT TITLE: THE MUMMY
DEVELOPED: 1992 PRODUCER: Universal STATUS: Screenplay by Mick Garris. OVERVIEW: Creatures not of this earth attack an Egyptian exhibit in Los Angeles. See main entry "Clive Barker's *Mummy*" on page 251.

PROJECT TITLE: CREATURE FROM THE BLACK LAGOON
DEVELOPED: 1992 PRODUCER: Universal STATUS: Idea. OVERVIEW: Before Ivan Rietman came on board, there was a brief flirtation with *The Beast* director Jeff Bleckner. (*The Beast* was an NBC mini-series adaptation of Peter Benchley's novel about a giant squid.)

PROJECT TITLE: CREATURE FROM THE BLACK LAGOON
DEVELOPED: 1992-1993 PRODUCER: Universal STATUS: Screenplay by Bill Phillips (first draft) and John Carpenter (second draft) OVERVIEW: A giant underwater temple in the Amazon is the lair of a half man, half fish monster. See main entry "Remake from the Black Lagoon Part II" on page 255.

PROJECT TITLE: THE MUMMY
DEVELOPED: 1993-1994 PRODUCER: Universal STATUS: Screenplay by Alan Ormsby and John Sayles. OVERVIEW: A reanimated Mummy stalks modern day L.A. See main entry "Joe Dante's *Mummy*" on page 268.

PROJECT TITLE: THE MUMMY
DEVELOPED: 1994 PRODUCER: Universal STATUS: Screenplay by Mick Garris and George Romero. OVERVIEW: A revived Imhotep and Kharis cause chaos in the modern day. See main entry "George Romero's *Mummy*" on page 274.

PROJECT TITLE: THE MUMMY
DEVELOPED: Mid-1990s PRODUCER: Universal STATUS: Idea. OVERVIEW: It's unknown where this idea came from, but Universal also contemplated making a heroic Mummy movie similar to *Star Man* which would tie in with the Millennium somehow.

PROJECT TITLE: VLAD THE IMPALER
DEVELOPED: 1993-1997 PRODUCER: Hammer STATUS: Screenplay by Arthur Ellis & John Peacock (revised). OVERVIEW:

Final attempt at Hammer's Dracula prequel. See main entry *"Vlad the Impaler"* on page 248.

PROJECT TITLE: THE CREATURE FROM THE BLACK LAGOON
DEVELOPED: 1994-1997 PRODUCER: Universal STATUS: Screenplay by Timothy Harris and Herschel Weingrod OVERVIEW: A Florida resort is plagued by an amphibious man-like sea monster. See main entry "Remake from the Black Lagoon Part III" on page 279.

PROJECT TITLE: CREATURE IN THE HOOD
DEVELOPED: mid-1990s PRODUCER: John Landis VALIDITY: Rumor [internet] STATUS: Idea by John Landis. OVERVIEW: Allegedly John Landis pitched this spoof of *Creature from the Black Lagoon* after all the failed remake attempts, but no proof of this concept can be found.

PROJECT TITLE: FRANCIS FORD COPPOLA'S FRANKENSTEIN
DEVELOPED: 1993 PRODUCER: Francis Ford Coppola STATUS: Screenplay by Steph Lady and Frank Darabont. OVERVIEW: Inspired by the success of *Bram Stoker's Dracula*, this film was meant to be a companion piece also by Francis Ford Coppola. Instead, he stepped back to let Kenneth Branaugh direct, a decision he supposedly regretted as he didn't agree with many of his changes. As for other decisions, at another point, Tim Burton was considered to direct with Arnold Schwarzenegger as the monster!

PROJECT TITLE: THE VAN HELSING CHRONICLES
DEVELOPED: 1993-late 1990s PRODUCER: Francis Ford Coppola STATUS: Idea. OVERVIEW: This unmade spinoff/sequel to *Bram Stoker's Dracula* was first reported on in *Variety* in 1993. In an interview, Francis Ford Coppola stated that film would see Anthony Hopkin's Van Helsing "go against new malevolent forces" and "combat satanic forces from Hong Kong to San Francisco." Though the film was never made, it's possible that in a strange way it helped pave the way for *Van Helsing* (2004).

PROJECT TITLE: THE MUMMY
DEVELOPED: 1997 PRODUCER: Universal STATUS: Screenplay by Kevin Jare. OVERVIEW: This version of *The Mummy* is closer to the 1999 film and even includes an ex-foreign legion soldier with a troubled past named Brian O'Connell (changed to Rick in the

film). The female lead is an archeologist named Connie, and in this version she is the reincarnation of Anck-su-namun, while O'Connell turns out to be the reincarnation of her secret Greek lover from Egypt. Over the course of the story they learn this as they battle the seven-foot-tall mummy Kharis. The mummy was resurrected by natives to drive away Brian and Connie from the Valley of the Seven Jackals. Like the Stephen Sommer's *Mummy*, it absorbs people's life-forces and takes the eyes of one character, causing him to go blind. Kharis can also create Frankenstein-monster-like zombies out of his dead victims. And, ridiculously, Kharis can't move in sunlight or moonlight! The first half of the script takes place in Egypt, and the latter half takes place in New York where the final confrontation with Kharis occurs. Due to a complicated backstory involving reincarnation, Connie must stab Brian in the heart to undue a curse. This kills Kharis, and Brian is later resurrected so that he and Connie can have a happy ending.

PROJECT TITLE: THE MUMMY
DEVELOPED: 1997-1999 PRODUCER: Universal STATUS: Screenplay by Stephen Sommers. OVERVIEW: This next to last version of the finished *Mummy* has only minor differences, the first of which was that the film was originally going to open with the old black and white Universal logo which would then dissolve into the desert sun. The opening narration that follows was supposed to have been done by Imhotep. However, Stephen Sommers realized that Imhotep couldn't speak English, and so changed it to Ardeth Bay. Also, the Medjai were originally supposed to be covered in tattoos until Sommers decided that Ardeth Bay actor Oded Fehr was "too good-looking" to be covered up. Furthermore, Ardeth Bay was originally supposed to die at the end (perhaps they could smell a sequel?). One of the bigger deleted elements had a statue of Anubis coming to life when Jonathan reads the Book of the Living. In the revised version the book awakens the pharaoh's guards instead.

PROJECT TITLE:
SHERLOCK HOLMES AND THE VENGEANCE OF DRACULA
DEVELOPED: unknown-1999 PRODUCER: 1492 Pictures STATUS: Screenplay by Michael B. Valle OVERVIEW: Dracula returns to London to kill those who thwarted him the last time but is opposed by Sherlock Holmes. See main entry *"Sherlock Holmes and the Vengeance of Dracula"* on page 286.

PROJECT TITLE: THE BRIDE OF FRANKENSTEIN
DEVELOPED: unknown-2000 PRODUCER: Universal STATUS:
Screenplay by Laeta Kalogridis. OVERVIEW: Futuristic
reimagining of *Bride of Frankenstein*. See main entry *"Bride of
Frankenstein"* on page 312.

APPENDIX II
ALTERNATE CUTS AND
DELETED SCENES

DELETED SCENE: CURSE OF FRANKENSTEIN (1957)
Supposedly Patrick Troughton had a small role as a mortuary
attendant (his name is credited in some early publicity material as
such) but his scenes were cut from the finished film.

ALTERNATE CUT: DRACULA HAS RISEN FROM THE GRAVE
(1968) In the documentary *Flesh and Blood* Freddie Francis stated
that he had emphasized the romance between Paul and Maria
more so than the final cut did. Francis implies the two had more
footage shot that didn't make it into the final cut, which was put
together while he was away. In *Little Shoppe of Horrors* #13,
Francis was asked about this:

> **LSOH:** Is there truth to the rumor that you were displeased
> with the finished film?
> **Francis:** I shot the film and then went on holiday. By the
> time I got back, the film had been edited, and I was a bit
> angry because Hammer hadn't understood the romance
> between Paul and Maria and had taken much of it out. But
> that was Tony and Jim Needs, the editor, I'm sure.

James Bernard mirrored these sentiments, and said he would
have liked to have composed a score more akin to *Taste the Blood
of Dracula's* more romantic compositions. In fact, part of the
reason that Taste had a different score was because Bernard had
heard it through the grapevine, so to speak, that Aida Young had
wished his *Grave* score was more melodious. The ending sequence
of Dracula's death was also originally longer, and was created via
the use of several dummies. Effects technician Bert Luxford,
recalled that time-lapse photography and dissolves were used to
show Dracula disintegrating into ash. All of this footage was cut
from the release print, so that we simply see Dracula's blood
dripping down the cross.

DELETED SCENE: FRANKENSTEIN AND THE MONSTER FROM HELL (1974) One short scene that was shot and later deleted had Simon and Sara finding Frankenstein crumpled on the floor after his fight with the monster.

DELETED SCENE: DRACULA A.D. 1972 (1972) In the final cut we don't see Bob die, but a scene of his death was shot. (Did he get exposed to sunlight? Did Dracula kill him? We're not sure, but Bob's death scene was filmed.)

PREVIEW CUT: BRAM STOKER'S DRACULA (1992) The original cut of this film was far too gory for test audiences, and twenty-five minutes of footage was removed. At a private screening, George Lucas suggested that Mina should decapitate Dracula in accordance to vampire mythology. Coppola shot the scene three weeks before the movie's release.

DELETED SCENES: THE MUMMY (1999)
A deleted scene showed Rick, Evelyn, and Jonathan crossing a field of skeletons that belonged to the foreign legion that Rick had been part of on their way to Hamunaptra. Later, when Rick and Jonathan pry the Book of Amun-Ra from the statue of Horus several mummies burst through the floor and attack them. The mummies are doused by pressurized acid which also burns a hole in the floor (which can be seen in the final cut).

BIBLIOGRAPHY

Articles

Blaine, Richard. "Terence Fisher—A Few Bytes from *The Brides of Dracula.*" *Little Shoppe of Horrors* #14.

Cairns, David. "I want to give you a piece of my mind: Interview with Joe Dante (Part 1)." (July 6, 2009). https://mubi.com/notebook/posts/i-want-to-give-you-a-piece-of-my-mind-interview-with-joe-dante-part-1

Davies, Glen. "The Un-Filmed Hammer: An A to Z Guide." *Little Shoppe of Horrors* #10 (Kindle Edition).

Hallenbeck, Bruce G. "The Making of the Hammer Classic *Blood from the Mummy's Tomb.*" *Little Shoppe of Horrors* #24.

-------------------------- "*Scars of Dracula.*" *Little Shoppe of Horrors* #13 (Kindle Edition).

Johnson, Tom. "Christopher Lee: He May Not Have Been Who You Might Have Thought He Was." *Little Shoppe of Horrors* #35 (Kindle Edition).

Kelley, Bill. "Peter Cushing on *The Brides of Dracula.*" *Little Shoppe of Horrors* #14.

Kinsey, Wayne. "Interview with John Forbes Robertson." *Little Shoppe of Horrors* #32 (Kindle Edition).

Klemensen, Richard. "Roy's Nightmares: The Life of Hammer's Makeup Master Roy Ashton (1909-1995)." *Little Shoppe of Horrors* #14.

Koetting, Christopher. "John Elder, Christopher Lee and TASTE THE BLOOD OF DRACULA." *Little Shoppe of Horrors* #13.

Martinez, Oscar. "Andree Melly Interview." *Little Shoppe of Horrors* #14.

Meikle, Dennis. "Anthony Hinds: The Man Who Made the Monsters." *Little Shoppe of Horrors* #32.

----------------------"Remembering 1959: Michael Carreras in Conversation with Dennis Meikle." *Little Shoppe of Horrors* #24.

Meikle, Dennis and Dennis Lynch. "Len Harris: A Tribute..." *Little Shoppe of Horrors* #14.

Murphy, Mike. "Anthony Hinds." *Dark Terrors* #16 (September 2008).

Newsom, Ted. "The Series That Never Was: *Tales of Frankenstein*." *Little Shoppe of Horrors* #21.

Swires, Steve. "John Carpenter: Creature Features." *Starlog* #177 (April 1992)

Books

Archer, Steve. *Willis O'Brien: Special Effects Genius.* Jefferson, NC: McFarland & Company, Inc., 1993.

Fellner, Chris. *The Encyclopedia of Hammer Films.* Rowman & Littlefield Publishers, 2019.

Hearn, Marcus. *The Hammer Vault: Treasures From the Archive of Hammer Films.* Titan Books, 2016.

Kinsey, Wayne & Tom Johnson and Joyce Broughton. *The Peter Cushing Scrapbook.* Peveril Publishing, 2013.

Kinsey, Wayne. *The Legend of the 7 Golden Vampires Scrapbook.* Peveril Publishing, 2020.

Maxford, Howard. *Hammer Complete: The Films, the Personnel, the Company.* McFarland & Company, 2018.

Pierson, Jim. *Produced and Directed by Dan Curtis.* Pomegranate Press, 2004.

Riley, Philip J. (Ed.). *Horror of Dracula*. BearManor Media, 2013.

Sangster, Jimmy. *Inside Hammer: Behind the Scenes at the Legendary Film Studio*. Reynolds & Hearn, 2001.

Sutton, Paul and Ken Russell. *Ken Russell's Dracula*. Bear Claw Publishing, 2012.

Weaver, Tom & David Schecter and Steve Kronenberg. *The Creature Chronicles: Exploring the Black Lagoon Trilogy*. McFarland & Company, 2018.

Other Sources

Screenplay Archaeology Podcast. Episode 27: The Mummy. (June 11, 2017).

------------------------------------- Episode 88: Creature from the Black Lagoon (1981-2018). (May 18, 2021).

Scars of Dracula audio commentary by Constantine Nasr and Ted Newsom, SCREAM FACTORY.

Foster, Kieran. "Unseen Horrors: The Unmade Films of Hammer." March 2019.

Index

Abbott and Costello Meet Frankenstein, 11
Alland, William, 258, 361
Alperson, Edward, 84
Arnold, Jack, 235, 361
Baker, Rick, 237, 255, 285
Barker, Clive, 251-254, 268
Bates, Ralph, 120, 124, 134, 338, 342
Batman Fights Dracula, 103-105
Beck, John, 53, 57, 59
Bernstein, Abbie, 252-254, 363
Billy the Kid Versus Dracula, 330-331
Black the Ripper, 181-184
Blackenstein, 181-183
Blacula, 181, 183
Blood from the Mummy's Tomb, 8, 41, 135-142, 341-342
Blood of Frankenstein, The, 328
Bram Stoker's Dracula, 172, 249, 252, 363, 365, 369
Branaugh, Kenneth, 365
Briant, Shane, 155
Bride of Frankenstein (1935), 13, 312, 327, 347
Bride of Frankenstein (2000), 312-325, 367
Brides of Dracula, 65-82, 127, 147, 306, 329-331, 343
Bryan, Peter, 51, 76, 330, 332
Burton, Tim, 365
Byron's Evil, 347
Cagliostro, King of the Dead, 271
Captain Kronos Vampire Hunter, 343
Carpenter, John, 255, 266-267, 279, 364, 371
Carradine, John, 340, 345
Carreras, James, 11, 43, 45, 91, 135, 137, 341-342
Carreras, Michael, 36-39, 41, 43, 45, 91, 138-139, 146, 155, 175, 177, 189, 195, 197, 209, 248, 334-335, 344, 350-351, 356-357
Chantrell, Tom, 124, 129, 187-189
Clemens, Brian, 342-344
Columbus, Christopher, 310
Cooper, Merian C., 59
Coppola, Francis Ford, 168, 172, 253, 363, 365, 369

Corman, Roger, 113
Count Dracula and his Vampire Bride, 149, 346-347
Count Yorga, Vampire, 146, 181, 345
Countess Dracula, 342
Creature from the Black Lagoon, 11, 235, 255, 267, 279
Creature from the Black Lagoon (remakes), 235-243, 255-267, 279-285, 361, 364
Creature from the Bronx, 333
Creature in the Hood, 365
Creature Walks Among Us, 239, 242, 262, 362
Curse of Frankenstein, The, 10-19, 21, 37-38, 43-47, 124, 326-328, 340
Curse of the Mummy's Tomb, The, 40, 90-93, 334-335
Curse of the Werewolf, 245, 331, 345
Curtis, Dan, 169, 172, 337, 347
Cushing, Helen, 138
Cushing, Peter, 8, 17, 35, 43, 47-48, 61, 66-68, 78-82, 124-125, 127, 129-131, 134, 138, 141-142, 161, 175, 187, 199, 327, 329-330, 334-335, 339, 341-342, 345, 348
Dan Curtis's Dracula, 169-172
Dante, Joe, 243, 249, 268, 272-273, 364, 370
Dark Shadows, 169
David Cronenberg's Frankenstein, 360
Day-Lewis, Daniel, 268
Diffring, Anton, 42-43, 48
Disciple of Dracula, 65-82, 329-330
Doreen Gray, 360
Dr. Jekyll and Sister Hyde, 343, 360
Dracula: The Beginning, 209-212, 248, 349
Dracula – High Priest of the Vampires, 145-146, 186
Dracula – Prince of Darkness, 37, 66, 71, 117, 142, 328, 334
Dracula (1931), 24, 47, 66
Dracula (1973), 347
Dracula (1979), 214, 227, 358-359

Dracula (Ken Russell version), 214-234
Dracula A.D. 1972, 72, 146-148, 181, 196, 209, 249, 308, 334, 345, 369
Dracula and the Curse of Kali, 185-189, 348-350
Dracula Has Risen from the Grave, 37, 115, 119, 153, 328, 338, 368
Dracula in India, 8, 146
Dracula Odyssey, The, 350
Dracula on Ice, 347
Dracula the True Story, 357
Dracula vs. the Beasts of Zarcon, 345
Dracula Walks the Night, 348
Dracula Who?, 362
Dracula's Coffin, 340
Dracula's Feast of Blood, 115-117, 338
Dracula's Guest, 216-217
Dracula's Revenge, 328, 338
Ecstasy of Dorian Gray, The, 343
Edge of Midnight, 339
Ege, Julie, 147, 342
EMI, 124, 137, 341, 357
Evil of Frankenstein, 51-52, 107, 109, 110, 332
Father Shandor film, 351
Fisher, Terence, 23-30, 35, 38-39, 63, 77-78, 91, 332, 338, 341, 343, 348
Fleetwood, Mick, 214-216
Forbes-Robertson, John, 127, 175, 177, 180, 197-199, 340
Francis, Freddie, 115, 332, 338, 368
Francis, Kevin, 115-117, 338
Frankenstein 1970, 12, 14
Frankenstein and the Monster, 11-19, 326
Frankenstein and the Monster from Hell, 155, 346, 369
Frankenstein Conquers the World, 60, 89, 94-96, 99, 102, 334
Frankenstein Created Woman, 48, 51-52, 327-328, 336
Frankenstein Meets the Space Monster, 336
Frankenstein Meets the Wolf Man, 84
Frankenstein Must Be Destroyed, 134, 338
Frankenstein on Mars, 336

Frankenstein Trapped, 337
Frankenstein vs. Godzilla, 94-102
Frankenstein vs. the Human Vapor, 83-89, 333
Frankenstein: The True Story, 340, 347, 357
Fury of the Wolfman, The, 114
Garris, Mick, 253, 274, 277-278, 364
Gates, Tudor, 342
Ghost of Frankenstein, The, 88
Godzilla, 6, 8, 37, 60, 84, 94-102, 201, 207, 245-246, 334
Godzilla vs. Frankenstein, 94-102, 334
Gordon, Bert I., 340
Gorgon, The, 91, 193
Hamilton, George, 361
Hammer House of Horror, 38, 356, 358
Hammer House of Mystery and Suspense, 249
Hayles, Brian, 209-210, 349
Hinds, Anthony, 17, 45, 49, 52, 68, 79, 82, 91, 117, 119-121, 125, 135, 142, 146-147, 330-331, 336-341, 346-347, 351, 356
Holt, Seth, 135, 137-138
Horror of Dracula, 21-38, 66-67, 77-78, 124, 126-127, 165, 172, 186-187, 327, 329
Horror of Frankenstein, 124, 127, 136, 340
Houghton, Don, 155, 158-167, 175-176, 180, 186-187, 189, 192-196, 345-350, 356
House of Dracula's Daughter, 345, 355
House of Frankenstein, 339
Hughes, Donald E., 59
Hyman, Elliot, 11
Insatiable Thirst of Dracula, The, 153, 347, 356
Interview with a Vampire (unmade version), 356
Invisible Man vs. the Human Torch, 6, 200-207, 350
Invisible Man, The (unmade Hammer remake), 330
Jack the Ripper Goes West, 349
Jackson, Peter, 285
Jaws 3-D, 237, 255, 279
Jesse James Meets Frankenstein's Daughter, 331

Jewel of the Seven Stars, 137
Journey to the Unknown, 117
Kali – Devil Bride of Dracula, see
  Dracula and the Curse of Kali
Kalogridis, Laeta, 312, 367
Karloff, Boris, 12, 14, 45
Keir, Andrew, 138-139, 141
Kenton, Erle, 331
King Kong, 8, 53-60, 92, 94, 98,
  245-246, 265, 285, 329
King Kong vs. Frankenstein (Toho
  version), 60
King Kong vs. Godzilla, 59, 60, 101,
  245
King Kong vs. Prometheus, 53-60
King Kong vs. the Gingko, 53-60
Kiss of Evil, 109, 110
Kiss of the Vampire, 81, 109, 139,
  148-149, 151, 217, 351
Kneale, Nigel, 235, 255, 361
Lair of the White Worm, 156, 160-
  162
Landis, John, 235, 237, 255, 365
Langella, Frank, 214-215, 234
Lawrence, Brian, 68, 119, 195, 248,
  360
Lee, Christopher, 36, 39, 61, 63-64,
  67-68, 115-117, 119-121, 123-
  124, 127, 145-146, 148, 155,
  160, 167, 175, 177, 186, 197,
  269, 276, 293, 326, 331, 333,
  335, 339, 341, 345, 347-349,
  361, 362
Legend of the 7 Golden Vampires,
  127, 145, 146, 147, 156, 175,
  186, 209, 346, 347, 348, 350,
  356
Legend of the Werewolf, 345
*Legendary Beast Wolfman vs.
  Godzilla*, 245-247
Leon, Valerie, 135-136, 138-141
Lloyd, Euan, 349
Love at First Bite, 214, 361
Love at Second Bite, 361
Lucas, John Meredith, 84
Lugosi, Bela, 66
Lust for a Vampire, 129, 341
Mankowitz, Wolf, 61, 63, 330
Mark of the Wolfman, The, 113
Martin, George R.R., 362
Mary Shelley's Frankenstein, 365
Matheson, Richard, 171-172, 242,
  347-348
Melly, Andree, 77, 82

Mummy Lives, The, 361
Mummy, The (1932), 90
Mummy, The (1959), 24, 38, 40, 67,
  187, 335
Mummy, The (1999), 252, 270-271,
  285, 312, 366, 369
Mummy's Hand, The, 276
Mummy's Shroud, The, 135, 337
Mummy's Tomb, The, 90
Munro, Caroline, 344
Nakajima, Shizuo, 245, 247
Naschy, Paul, 112-114
Nessie, 207, 211
Nights of the Werewolf, 112-114
O'Brien, Darlyne, 58-59
O'Brien, Willis, 53-60, 329, 349
O'Shea, Daniel, 57
O'Toole, Peter, 356
Olivier, Laurence, 214, 359
Perkins, Anthony, 361
Phantom of the Opera (1963), 110-
  111, 329
Pierce, Jack P., 13, 45
Pitt, Ingrid, 341-342, 344, 362
Plague of Dracula, The, 351
Proyas, Alex, 325
Quatermass Experiment, The, 11
Reed, Oliver, 215, 225, 339, 347,
  361
Reptile, The (1966), 333, 337
Revenge of Dracula, The, 66-67,
  125, 334
Revenge of Frankenstein, 43, 49,
  66, 327-329
Revenge of King Tutankhamun, The,
  357
Revenge of the Creature, 237, 240,
  242
Rietman, Ivan, 279, 364
Romero, George A., 274, 277, 364
Rosenberg, Max J., 11, 17, 19, 326
Russell, Ken, 214-215, 234, 358,
  361, 363
Ryder, Winona, 363
Sangster, Jimmy, 13, 18, 21-41,
  44-45, 66, 68, 70-72, 75-78, 82,
  115, 135, 137, 326-328, 330,
  332, 334, 339-341, 346, 348,
  358
Sasdy, Peter, 120
Sayles, John, 268, 364
Scars of Dracula, 123-127, 145,
  149, 151, 177, 340
Scorsese, Martin, 363

Scourge of the Vampires, 331
Screen Gems, 45-46, 51
Sekizawa, Shinichi, 83-84
Shaw Brothers, 175, 180, 348
Sheinberg, Sid, 237, 272
Sherlock Holmes and the Prince of
    Darkness, 357
Sherlock Holmes and the Vengeance
    of Dracula, 286-311, 366
Siodmak, Curt, 45
Skeggs, Roy, 248-250, 338, 346,
    360
Sohl, Jerry, 95-98, 101-102
Sommers, Stephen, 252, 268, 270,
    273-274, 277, 285, 366
Son of Dracula, 290
Stevenson, Robert Louis, 61
Stoker, Bram, 21, 24, 29, 115, 125,
    137, 155-156, 159, 162, 165,
    167, 209, 212, 214, 249, 252,
    327-328, 345, 365
Strange Case of Dr. Jekyll and Mr.
    Hyde, The (1967), 337
Subotsky, Milton, 11-13, 17, 19,
    326, 343
Sum VII, 361
Tales of Frankenstein, 42-52, 329,
    332, 336
Taste the Blood of Dracula, 37, 115,
    118-121, 124, 127, 134, 145,
    149, 153, 339, 368
Three Faces of Dr. Jekyll, The, 61-
    64, 330

Toho Studios, 6-7, 37, 59, 84, 89,
    94-95, 102, 200, 207, 211, 245-
    247, 333-334, 350
Twins of Dracula, 342
Twins of Evil, 129, 133-134, 342-
    343
Two Faces of Dr. Jekyll, The, 68
Tyburn, 117
Unquenchable Thirst of Dracula,
    The, 143-154, 186, 341, 351
Valle, Michael B., 286-287, 290,
    305-306, 308-311, 366
Vampire Circus, 133-134, 342, 362
Vampire Lovers, The, 125, 130, 134,
    137, 341
Vampire Virgins, 8, 129-134, 342-
    343
Van Eyssen, John, 24, 28
Van Helsing (2004), 365
Van Helsing Chronicles, The, 365
Victim of His Imagination, 155-168,
    346
Vlad the Impaler, 248-250, 360,
    363, 365
Ward Baker, Roy, 125, 177
Werewolf of Moravia, The, 335
Werewolf Wedding, 337
Wicking, Christopher, 137-138,
    142, 196-197, 342, 349
Wood, Ed, 350
X the Unknown, 18
Yates, George Worthington, 53, 57

About the Author

John LeMay is the author of over 25 books that include *Kong Unmade: The Lost Films of Skull Island*; *The Big Book of Japanese Giant Monster Movies: The Lost Films* and *Jaws Unmade: The Lost Sequels, Prequels, Remakes, and Rip-Offs*. He is also the editor and publisher of *The Lost Films Fanzine*, published quarterly. LeMay also writes on the history of the Old West, with a focus on folklore. Some of these titles include *The Real Cowboys and Aliens* series with Noe Torres, *Tall Tales and Half Truths of Billy the Kid*, and *Cowboys & Saurians: Dinosaurs and Prehistoric Beasts as Seen by the Pioneers*. He is a contributor to magazines such as *G-Fan*, *Mad Scientist*, *Xenorama*, and *Cinema Retro*.

THE BICEP BOOKS CATALOGUE

The following titles are available for purchase on Amazon.com, and are available to bookstores at a wholesale discount via Ingram Content Group (ISBNs of available editions listed for this purpose)

THE BIG BOOK OF JAPANESE GIANT MONSTER MOVIES SERIES

The third edition of the book that started it all! Reviews over 100 tokusatsu films between 1954 and 1988. All the Godzilla, Gamera, and Daimajin movies made during the Showa era are covered plus lesser known fare like *Invisible Man vs. The Human Fly* (1957) and *Conflagration* (1975). Softcover (380 pp/5.83" X 8.27") Suggested Retail: $19.99 SBN:978-1-7341546-4-1

This third edition reviews over 75 tokusatsu films between 1989 and 2019. All the Godzilla, Gamera, and Ultraman movies made during the Heisei era are covered plus independent films like *Reigo, King of the Sea Monsters* (2005), *Demeking, the Sea Monster* (2009) and *Attack of the Giant Teacher* (2019)! Softcover (260 pp/5.83" X 8.27") Suggested Retail: $19.99 ISBN: 978-1- 7347816-4-9

This second edition of the Rondo Award nominated book covers un-produced scripts like *Bride of Godzilla* (1955), partially shot movies like *Giant Horde Beast Nezura* (1963), and banned films like *Prophecies of Nostradamus* (1974), plus hundreds of other lost productions. Softcover/Hard-cover (470pp. /7" X 10") Suggested Retail: X 10") Suggested Retail: $24.99 (sc)/$39.95(hc)ISBN: 978-1-73 41546-0-3 (hc)

This sequel to *The Lost Films* covers the non-giant monster unmade movie scripts from Japan such as *Frankenstein vs. the Human Vapor* (1963), *After Japan Sinks* (1974-76), plus lost movies like *Fearful Attack of the Flying Saucers* (1956) and *Venus Flytrap* (1968). Hardcover (200 pp/5.83" X 8.27")/Softcover (216 pp/ 5.5" X 8.5") Suggested Retail: $9.99 (sc)/$24.99(hc) ISBN:978-1-7341546 -3-4 (hc)

HUMOR

This companion book to *The Lost Films* charts the development of all the prominent Japanese monster movies including discarded screenplays, story ideas, and deleted scenes. Also includes bios for writers like Shinichi Sekizawa, Niisan Takahashi and many others. Comprehensive script listing and appendices as well. Hardcover/Softcover (370 pp./ 6"X9") Suggested Retail: $16.95(sc)/$34.99(hc)ISBN: 978-1-7341546-5-8 (hc)

Examines the differences between the U.S. and Japanese versions of over 50 different tokusatsu films like *Gojira* (1954)/*Godzilla, King of the Monsters!* (1956), *Gamera* (1965)/ *Gammera, the Invincible* (1966), *Submersion of Japan* (1973)/*Tidal Wave* (1975), and many, many more! Softcover (540 pp./ 6"X9") Suggested Retail: $22.99(sc) ISBN: 978-1- 953221-77-3

This second volume examines the differences between the European and Japanese versions of tokusatsu films including the infamous "Cozzilla" colorized version of *Godzilla, King of the Monsters!* from 1977, plus rarities like *Terremoto 10 Grado*, the Italian cut of *Legend of Dinosaurs*. The book also examines the condensed Champion Matsuri edits of Toho's effects films. Coming 2022.

Throughout the 1960s and 1970s the Italian film industry cranked out over 600 "Spaghetti Westerns" and for every *Fistful of Dollars* were a dozen pale imitations, some of them hilarious. Many of these lesser known Spaghettis are available in bargain bin DVD packs and stream for free online. If ever you've wondered which are worth your time and which aren't, this is the book for you. Softcover (160pp./5.06" X 7.8") Suggested Retail: $9.99

THE BICEP BOOKS CATALOGUE

CLASSIC MONSTERS SERIES

Kong Unmade explores unproduced scripts like *King Kong vs. Frankenstein* (1958), unfinished films like *The Lost Island* (1934), and lost movies like *King Kong Appears in Edo* (1938). As a bonus, all the Kong rip-offs like *Konga* (1961) and *Queen Kong* (1976) are reviewed. Hardcover (350 pp/5.83" X 8.27")/Softcover (376 pp/ 5.5" X 8.5") Suggested Retail: $24.99 (hc)/$19.99(sc) ISBN: 978-1-7341546-2-7(hc)

Jaws Unmade explores unproduced scripts like *Jaws 3, People 0* (1979), abandoned ideas like a Quint prequel, and even aborted sequels to Jaws inspired movies like *Orca Part II*. As a bonus, all the Jaws rip-offs like *Grizzly* (1976) and *Tentacles* (1977) are reviewed. Hardcover (316 pp/5.83" X 8.27")/Softcover (340 pp/5.5" X 8.5") Suggested Retail: $29.99 (hc)/$17.95(sc) ISBN: 978-1-7344730-1-8

Classic Monsters Unmade covers lost and unmade films starring Dracula, Frankenstein, the Mummy and more monsters. Reviews unmade scripts like *The Return of Frankenstein* (1934) and *Wolf Man vs. Dracula* (1944). It also examines lost films of the silent era such as *The Werewolf* (1913) and *Drakula's Death* (1923). Softcover/Hardcover(428pp/5.83"X8.27") Suggested Retail: $22.99(hc)/ $27.99(hc)ISBN:978-1-953221-85-8(hc)

Volume 2 explores the Hammer era and beyond, from unmade versions of *Brides of Dracula* (called *Disciple of Dracula*) to remakes of *Creature from the Black Lagoon*. Completely unmade films like *Kali: Devil Bride of Dracula* (1975) and *Godzilla vs. Frankenstein* (1964) are covered along with lost completed films like *Batman Fights Dracula* (1967) and *Black the Ripper* (1974). Coming Fall 2021.

NOSTALGIA

Written in the same spirit as *The Big Book of Japanese Giant Monster Movies*, this tome reviews all the classic Universal and Hammer horrors to star Dracula, Frankenstein, the Gillman and the rest along with obscure flicks like *The New Invisible Man* (1958), *Billy the Kid versus Dracula* (1966), *Blackenstein* (1973) and *Legend of the Werewolf* (1974). Coming 2021.

Written at an intermediate reading level for the kid in all of us, these picture books will take you back to your youth. In the spirit of the old Ian Thorne books covered *Nabonga* (1944), *White Pongo* (1945) and more! Hardcover/Softcover (44 pp/7.5" X 9.25") Suggested Retail: $17.95(hc)/$9.99(sc) ISBN: 978- 1-7341546-9-6 (hc) 978- 1-7344730-5-6 (sc)

Written at an intermediate reading level for the kid in all of us, these picture books take you back to your youth. In the spirit of the old Ian Thorne books are covered *The Lost World* (1925), *The Land That Time Forgot* (1975) and more! Hardcover/Softcover (44 pp/7.5" X 9.25") Suggested Retail: $17.95 (hc)/$9.99(sc) ISBN: 978-1-7344730 -6-3 (hc) 978- 1-7344730-7-0 (sc)

Written at an intermediate reading level for the kid in all of us, these picture books will take you back to your youth. In the spirit of the old Ian Thorne books are covered *Them!* (1954), *Empire of the Ants* (1977) and more! Hardcover/Softcover (44 pp/7.5" X 9.25") Suggested Retail: $17.95(hc)/ $9.99(sc) ISBN: 978-1-7347816 -3-2 (hc) 978 -1-7347816-2-5 (sc)

THE BICEP BOOKS CATALOGUE

CRYPTOZOOLOGY/COWBOYS & SAURIANS

Cowboys & Saurians: Prehistoric Beasts as Seen by the Pioneers explores dinosaur sightings from the pioneer period via real newspaper reports from the time. Well-known cases like the Tombstone Thunderbird are covered along with more obscure cases like the Crosswicks Monster and more. Softcover (357 pp/5.06" X 7.8") Suggested Retail: $19.95 ISBN: 978-1-7341546-1-0

Cowboys & Saurians: Ice Age zeroes in on snowbound saurians like the Cerato-saurus of the Arctic Circle and a Tyrannosaurus of the Tundra, as well as sightings of Ice Age megafauna like mammoths, glyptodonts, Sarkastodons and Saber-toothed tigers. Tales of a land that time forgot in the Arctic are also covered. Softcover (264 pp/5.06" X 7.8") Suggested Retail: $14.99 ISBN: 978-1-7341546-7-2

Southerners & Saurians takes the series formula of exploring newspaper accounts of monsters in the pioneer period with an eye to the Old South. In addition to dinosaurs are covered Lizardmen, Frogmen, giant leeches and mosquitoes, and the Dingocroc, which might be an alien rather than a prehistoric survivor. Softcover (202 pp/5.06" X 7.8") Suggested Retail: $13.99 ISBN: 978-1-7344730-4-9

Cowboys & Saurians South of the Border explores the saurians of Central and South America, like the Patagonian Plesiosaurus that was really an Iemisch, plus tales of the Neo-Mylodon, a menacing monster from underground called the Minhocao, Glyptodonts, and even Bolivia's three-headed dinosaur! Softcover (412 pp/5.06"X7.8") Suggested Retail: $17.95 ISBN: 978-1-953221-73-5

UFOLOGY/THE REAL COWBOYS & ALIENS IN CONJUNCTION WITH ROSWELL BOOKS

The Real Cowboys and Aliens: Early American UFOs explores UFO sightings in the USA between the years 1800-1864. Stories of encounters sometimes involved famous figures in U.S. history such as Lewis and Clark, and Thomas Jefferson.Hardcover (242pp/6" X 9") Softcover (262 pp/5.06" X 7.8") Suggested Retail: $24.99 (hc)/$15.95(sc) ISBN: 978-1-7341546-8-9\(hc)/978-1-7344730-8-7(sc)

The second entry in the series, *Old West UFOs*, covers reports spanning the years 1865-1895. Includes tales of Men in Black, Reptilians, Spring-Heeled Jack, Sasquatch from space, and other alien beings, in addition to the UFOs and airships. Hardcover (276 pp/6" X 9") Softcover (308 pp/5.06" X 7.8") Suggested Retail: $29.95 (hc)/$17.95(sc) ISBN: 978-1-7344730-0-1 (hc)/ 978-1-7344730-2-5 (sc)

The third entry in the series, *The Coming of the Airships*, encompasses a short time frame with an incredibly high concentration of airship sightings between 1896-1899. The famous Aurora, Texas, UFO crash of 1897 is covered in depth along with many others. Hardcover (196 pp/6" X 9") Softcover (222 pp/5.06" X 7.8") Suggested Retail: $24.99 (hc)/$15.95(sc) ISBN: 978-1-7347816 -1-8 (hc)/978-1-7347816-0-1(sc)

Early 20th Century UFOs kicks off a new series that investigates UFO sightings of the early 1900s. Includes tales of UFOs sighted over the *Titanic* as it sank, Nikola Tesla receiving messages from the stars, an alien being found encased in ice, and a possible virus from outer space!Hardcover (196 pp/6" X 9") Softcover (222 pp/5.06" X 7.8") Suggested Retail: $27.99 (hc)/$16.95(sc) ISBN: 978-1-7347816-1-8 (hc)/978-1-73478 16-0-1(sc)

BACK ISSUES

ISSUE #1 SPRING 2020 The lost Italian cut of *Legend of Dinosaurs and Monster Birds* called *Terremoto 10 Grado*, plus *Bride of Dr. Phibes* script, *Good Luck! Godzilla*, the King Kong remake that became a car comm ercial, Bollywood's lost *Jaws* rip-off, Top Ten Best Fan Made Godzilla trailers plus an interview with Scott David Lister. 60 pages. Three variant covers/editions (premium color/basic color/b&w)

ISSUE #2 SUMMER 2020 How 1935's *The Capture of Tarzan* became 1936's *Tarzan Escapes*, the Orca sequels that weren't, Baragon in Bollywood's *One Million B.C.*, unmade *Kolchak: The Night Stalker* movies, *The Norliss Tapes*, *Superman V: The New Movie*, why there were no *Curse of the Pink Panther* sequels, *Moonlight Mask: The Movie*. 64 pages. Two covers/ editions (basic color/b&w)

ISSUE #3 FALL 2020 *Blob* sequels both forgotten and unproduced, *Horror of Dracula* uncut, *Frankenstein Meets the Wolfman* and talks, myths of the lost *King Kong* Spider-Pit sequence debunked, the *Carnosaur* novel vs. the movies, *Terror in the Streets* 50th anniversary, *Bride of Godzilla* 55th Unniversary, Lee Powers sketchbook. 100 pages. Two covers/editions (basic color/b&w)

ISSUE #4 WINTER 2020/21 *Diamonds Are Forever's* first draft with Goldfinger, *Disciple of Dracula* into *Brides of Dracula*, *War of the Worlds That Weren't Still II* by Ray Bradbury, *Deathwish 6, Atomic War Bride*, *What Am I Doing in the Middle of a Revolution?*, *Spring Dream in the Old Capital* and more. 70 pages. Two covers/editions (basic color/b&w)

ISSUE #1 AUGUST 2020 Debut issue celebrating 80 years of *One Million B.C.* (1940), and an early 55th Anniversary for *One Million Years B.C.* (1966). Abandoned ideas, casting changes, and deleted scenes are covered, plus a mini-B.C. stock-footage filmography and much more! 54 pages. Three collectible covers/ editions (premium color/ basic color/b&w)

ISSUE #2 OCTOBER 2020 Celebrates the joint 50th Anniversaries of *When Dinosaurs Ruled the Earth* (1970) and *Creatures the World Forgot* (1971). Also includes looks at *Prehistoric Women* (1967), *When Women Had Tails* (1970), and *Caveman* (1981), plus unmade films like *When the World Cracked Open*. 72 pages. Three collectible covers/editions (premium color/basic color/b&w)

ISSUE #3 WINTER 2021 Japanese 'Panic Movies' like *The Last War* (1961), *Submersion of Japan* (1973), and *Bullet Train* (1975) are covered on celebrated author Sakyo Komatsu's 90th birthday. The famous banned Toho film *Prophecies of Nostradamus* (1974) also covered. 124 pages. Three collectible editions (premium color/ basic color/ b&w)

ISSUE #4 SPRING 2021 This issue celebrates the joint 60th Anniversaries of *Gorgo*, *Reptilicus* and *Konga* examining unmade sequels like *Reptilicus 2*, and other related lost projects like *Kuru Island* and *The Volcano Monsters*. Also explores the Gorgo, Konga and Reptilicus comic books from Charlton. 72 pages. Three collectible covers/editions (premium color/basic color/b&w)

Made in the USA
Columbia, SC
19 September 2021